MODERNISMS

Also by Peter Nicholls

EZRA POUND: POLITICS, ECONOMICS AND WRITING

Modernisms

A Literary Guide

Peter Nicholls

University of California Press
Berkeley   Los Angeles

University of California Press
Berkeley and Los Angeles, California

Library of Congress Cataloging-in-Publication Data

Nicholls, Peter, 1950–
    Modernisms : a literary guide / Peter Nicholls.
      p. cm.
    Includes bibliographical references and index.
    ISBN 0–520–20102–7 — ISBN 0–520–20103–5 (pbk.)
    1. Modernism (Literature) I. Title.
PN56.M54N53   1995
809′.91—dc20   94–32407
                                                    CIP

Printed in Malaysia

9   8   7   6   5   4   3   2

Contents

For Nick and Bet

Preface

When I began work on this book, postmodernism was in its heyday. The plural form of my title – Modernism*s* – thus had something of a polemical intent, since so much of the debate about the 'post' hinged upon what Marjorie Perloff has called a 'straw-man modernism', one characterised primarily by its commitment to reactionary 'grand narratives' of social and psychic order.[1] My aim in the book was mainly to show that such a modernism, caricatured as it now frequently was, could be seen to constitute only one strand of a highly complex set of cultural developments at the beginning of the twentieth century. Furthermore, as 'modernism' came to be presented as a sort of monolithic ideological formation, it seemed increasingly necessary to explore the interactions between politics and literary *style* during this intensive period of experimentation.

The issue of postmodernism may now appear less pressing, but the one-dimensional view of modernism which it has frequently proposed is with us still. A case in point is John Carey's recent *The Intellectuals and the Masses*, a tirade against the reactionary politics of canonical modernists such as Ezra Pound, T. S. Eliot, Wyndham Lewis, and D. H. Lawrence. The problems Carey raises are undoubtedly central ones, though he abridges their real difficulty by construing 'politics' simply at the level of rhetorical expression, overlooking the more complex inscription of ideologies in the modernist styles which frequently became their most powerful and ambiguous vehicle. It is this translation of politics into style, and the tensions it reflects between the social and the aesthetic, which are the main subject of the following pages.

That focus has determined the shape of the book in several important ways. First, it has required close attention to the formation and evolution of early modernism, tracing its origins in the aesthetics of Baudelaire and the Symbolists. Secondly, my concentration on the various avant-gardes, from Futurism to Surrealism, has placed the burden of emphasis on modernist developments prior to those of the thirties. That has meant, in turn, that the discussion of modernist politics has not dealt in detail with the well-known history of certain writers' move towards fascism and the Right. At the same time, though, the basis on which such decisions were made is explored in depth, through the connections between style, authority and gender which underpinned the various constructions of modernism. That particular history now seems, if anything, more complex and tangled, and one which it is all too easy to misread from our present vantage-point.

As to method, *Modernisms* is not a documentary survey and makes no real claims to completeness. Rather than simply to bombard the reader with great names, I have tried to provide a conceptual map of the different modernist tendencies. This has meant omissions, of course, some serious, others less so; but in each case I have valued the possibilities of analytic reading above mere comprehensiveness. The reader must be the ultimate judge as to whether that decision was the right one.

List of Abbreviations

AA   Antonin Artaud, *Selected Writings*, ed. Susan Sontag (Berkeley and Los Angeles: University of California Press, 1988).

AOA   *Apollinaire on Art: Essays and Reviews, 1902–1918*, ed. Leroy C. Breunig (New York: Viking Press, 1972).

BSW   *Baudelaire: Selected Writings on Art and Artists*, trans. P. E. Charvet (Harmondsworth: Penguin Books, 1972).

F   *Marinetti: Selected Writings*, trans. R. W. Flint (London: Secker & Warburg, 1972).

FM   *Futurist Manifestos*, ed. Umbro Apollonio (London: Thames and Hudson, 1973).

I   William Carlos Williams, *Imaginations*, ed. Webster Schott (New York: New Directions, 1971).

LMN   Gertrude Stein, *Look at Me Now and Here I Am: Writings and Lectures 1909–45*, ed. Patricia Meyerowitz (Harmondsworth: Penguin Books, 1971).

MFT   *Modern French Theater: The Avant-Garde, Dada and Surrealism*, trans. George Wellwarth and Michael Benedikt (New York: Dutton, 1966).

MS   André Breton, *Manifestos of Surrealism*, trans. Richard Seaver and Helen R. Lane (Ann Arbor: University of Michigan Press, 1972).

MSP   *Mallarmé: Selected Prose Poems, Essays, and Letters*, trans. Bradford Cook (Baltimore: Johns Hopkins University Press, 1956).

NS   Pierre Reverdy, *Nord-Sud, Self-Defence et autres écrits sur l'art et la poésie (1917–1926)* (Paris: Flammarion, 1975).

NT   Ezra Pound and Ernest Fenollosa, *The Classic Noh Theatre of Japan* (New York: New Directions, 1959).

PL   *Poems of Jules Laforgue*, trans. Peter Dale (London: Anvil Press, 1986).

RFM   *Russian Futurism through its Manifestos, 1912–1928*, trans. Anna Lawton and Herbert Eagle (Ithaca and London: Cornell University Press, 1988).

RP   *Arthur Rimbaud: Collected Poems*, trans. Oliver Bernard (Harmondsworth: Penguin Books, 1987).

SML   Tristan Tzara, *Seven Dada Manifestos and Lampisteries*, trans. Barbara Wright (London: John Calder, 1977).
TIF   *Opere di F. T. Marinetti*, vol. 2: *Teoria e invenzione futurista*, ed. Luciano De Maria (Milan: Mondadori, 1968).
VK   *Collected Works of Velimir Khlebnikov*, vol. I: *Letters and Theoretical Writings*, trans. Paul Schmidt and Charlotte Douglas (Cambridge, MA and London: Harvard University Press, 1987).

Acknowledgements

I owe a special debt of thanks to Jane Lane, not only for putting up with Modernism but also for her keen critical sense of how it should be thought about. I am grateful, too, to Richard Godden, whose generous reading of the whole manuscript finally helped me to see the wood for the trees. Thanks also to Rachel Bowlby for many illuminating comments and for convincing me that the book could be finished. Other friends brought their expertise to bear on parts of the manuscript, and it is a pleasure to be able to thank Ian Bell, Nat Chase, Paul Edwards, Alan Munton, and Lisa Robertson for their help with particular sections. I am also grateful to the University of Sussex for granting me two terms of study leave in which to work on the book, and to the British Academy for funding a period of research in the United States. Lastly, my thanks to the staff of the University of Sussex Library for many kinds of help, and to Public House Bookshop (Brighton) and Compendium Books (London), for being there.

Parts of this book have appeared in other publications. I should like to thank the following publishers for granting me permission to quote from my earlier published articles:

Blackwell Publishers, for the extracts from 'Divergences: Modernism, Postmodernism, Jameson and Lyotard', *Critical Quarterly* (Autumn 1991);

Cambridge University Press, for the extracts from ' "A consciousness disjunct": Sex and the Writer in Ezra Pound's *Hugh Selwyn Mauberley*', *Journal of American Studies* (April 1994);

Editions Rodopi B. V., Amsterdam, for the extracts from 'Lost Object(s): Ezra Pound and the Idea of Italy', in *Ezra Pound and Europe*, ed. Richard Taylor and Claus Melchior (1993);

Harvester-Wheatsheaf and the University of Toronto Press, for the extracts from 'Difference Spreading: from Gertrude Stein to L=A=N=G=U=A=G=E Poetry', in *Contemporary Poetry Meets Modern Theory*, ed. Antony Easthope and John Thompson (1991);

Lawrence and Wishart Ltd, for the extracts from 'Consumer Poetics: A French Episode', *New Formations* (Spring 1991);

Modern Language Review, for the extracts from 'An Experiment with Time: Ezra Pound and the Example of Japanese Noh' (January 1995);

New Theatre Quarterly, for the extracts from 'Sexuality and Structure: Tensions in Early Expressionism' (May 1991) and 'Anti-Oedipus? Dada and Surrealist Theatre, 1916–1935' (November 1991);

Oxford University Press, for the extracts from 'From Fantasy to Structure: Two Moments of Literary Cubism', *Forum for Modern Language Studies* (Summer 1992);

Parataxis, for the extracts from 'Violence, Recognition, and Some Versions of Modernism' (Summer 1993);

Routledge, for the extracts from 'Futurism, Gender, and Theories of Postmodernity', *Textual Practice* (Summer 1989), and 'Apes and Familiars: Modernism, Mimesis, and the Work of Wyndham Lewis', *Textual Practice* (Winter 1992).

The author and publishers wish to thank the following for permission to use copyright material by other authors:

Agenda Magazine for material from Giuseppe Ungaretti, 'Watch' and 'Vanity', trans. Andrew Wylie, *Agenda*, 8:2 (Ungaretti Special Issue, Spring 1970);

Carcanet Press Ltd, with New Directions Publishing Corp., for the extracts from William Carlos Williams, 'Good Night' from *The Collected Poems of William Carlos Williams, 1909–1939*, vol. I, copyright © 1938 by New Directions Publishing Corp.; and William Carlos Williams, 'Poem VIII' from *Imaginations*, copyright © 1971 by New Directions Publishing Corp.; for the extracts from 'H.D.', *Collected Poems 1912–1944*, ed. Louis Martz; for the extracts from 'Western Song' from *Georg Trakl: A Profile*;

Acknowledgements xiii

Roger L. Conover, literary executor to the estate of Mina Loy, for the extracts from Mina Loy, 'Love Songs' from *The Last Lunar Baedeker*, ed. Robert L. Conover (Jargon Society, 1982).

Faber & Faber Ltd, with Simon & Schuster, for the extracts from Marianne Moore, 'The Buffalo' from *The Complete Poems of Marianne Moore*, copyright © 1935 by Marianne Moore, renewed 1963 by Marianne Moore and T. S. Eliot; and with New Directions Publishing Corp., for the extracts from Ezra Pound, 'Canto XX' and 'Canto XVI' from *'The Cantos of Ezra Pound*, copyright © 1934 by Ezra Pound, and Ezra Pound, 'Liu Ch'e' from *Personae*, copyright © 1926 by Ezra Pound;

Michael Hamburger, for the extracts from August Stramm, 'Melancholy' and extracts from van Hoddis, 'End of the World', both translated by Michael Hamburger;

Mosaic Press, for the extracts from *The Bones of Cuttlefish: Eugenio Montale*, trans. Antonino Mazza (1983);

New Directions Publishing Corp., for the extracts from Pierre Reverdy, 'False Door or Portrait' from *Selected Writings*, copyright © 1969 by New Directions Publishing Corp.; and the extracts from Guillaume Apollinaire, 'Zone' from *Selected Writings*, copyright © 1971 by New Directions Publishing Corp.;

Felix Stefanile, for the extracts from *The Blue Moustache: Some Italian Futurist Poets*, trans. Felix Stefanile, Elizabeth Press, 1980; Carcanet Press, 1981.

University of Iowa Press, for the extracts from Vladimir Mayakovsky, 'A Cloud in Trousers', trans. Bob Perelman and Kathy Lewis, in *Russian Poetry: The Modern Poetry*, ed. John Glad and Daniel Weissbort, copyright © 1978 by University of Iowa Press.

Every effort has been made to trace all the copyright-holders, but if any have been inadvertently overlooked the publishers will be pleased to make the necessary arrangement at the first opportunity.

Introduction:
Of a Certain Tone

The beginnings of modernism, like its endings, are largely indeterminate, a matter of traces rather than of clearly defined historical moments. To make those traces visible, as I shall try to do in my opening chapters, is to reconstitute a pre-history of the various modernisms without which their own exemplary works can hardly be understood. Indeed, much that has proved controversial about the literary forms of modernism has its origins in the writing of the nineteenth century, and especially in the work of French poets such as Charles Baudelaire, Arthur Rimbaud, and Stéphane Mallarmé.

In pursuit of those traces of modernism, then, we might return to Paris in the early 1840s, and specifically to a moment when visitors to the Champs-Elysées were entertained by the music of two young girls who begged their way between cafés, singing and playing the guitar. The striking beauty of one of them fascinated the writers and artists who frequented this part of the city. Théodore de Banville wrote a poem about her, and Emile Deroy, a friend of Charles Baudelaire, painted her portrait. Baudelaire himself devised his own poetic tribute, 'To a Red-haired Beggar Girl' (probably composed around 1845/6) in which he praises her beauty and imagines her in courtly dress. There was already something of a vogue for poems on this topic, and Baudelaire plays quite deliberately with established convention.[1] At the same time, though, this early work already shows traces of what we might think of as a distinctively 'modern' style. This is partly an effect of the glimpses the poem gives of the new urban scene and of the poet as one of its *déclassé* inhabitants; but mostly, I think, it has to do with a certain complexity of *tone*.

For some critics, the poet's way of identifying with the beggar-girl – they both share in a 'reduced' state which is characteristic of the fate of beauty in the modern world – testifies to an 'humanitarian' impulse beneath the deliberate playfulness of the poem's pastiche.[2]

1

Pale girl with ginger hair whose dress through
its tatters reveals poverty and beauty;

for me, wretched poet that I am, your frail,
freckled body has an appeal.

You wear your heavy clogs more regally than a
queen from a romance her velvet buskins.[3]

The poet cannot afford to give the girl the finery she craves, and
his own poverty is set against the 'courtly' culture associated with
the baroque writers Ronsard and Belleau. The closing lines of the
poem then seem to reassure us that finery and artifice are actually
superfluous given the girl's natural beauty (much of which is on
show through her ragged garments):

Meanwhile you go about begging for scraps at
the door of some cross-roads restaurant;

slyly coveting cheap trinkets which (pardon
me!) I cannot afford to give you.

Go then, my beauty, with no ornament, no
perfume, diamonds, pearls, but your own frail nakedness!

This praise of nature is, however, more ambiguous than it seems,
as is the sense of a shared social fate that the poem proposes. For
while the poet claims to abolish the social distance between himself
and the girl, he actually replaces it with another which is primarily
aesthetic. The element of voyeurism here, as the poet clothes and
unclothes the girl, is closely bound up with what Baudelaire celebrates elsewhere as the 'cold detachment' of the poet-as-dandy
(*BSW*, 399). It is as if there are two voices at work in the poem: one
which sympathises with the girl and expresses admiration for her
'natural' charms, and another which simply takes her as an occasion for a poem. This second, more devious voice will force upon
the reader the unsentimental and cruelly ironic recognition that in
fact she is nothing without the artifice of his poem to commemorate
her. They may both be poor, but the gap between them is not one
which the poet wishes to cross. Her paradoxical beauty, both allur-
ing and somehow inadequate, is, we are meant to realise, finally

too compromised by the feminine 'naturalness' which prevents her from conceiving of herself as something other than she is or from· commanding two voices, like the poet. The girl may be sexy, but she is self-presence incarnate; and while her body certainly exerts an 'appeal' for Baudelaire's poet, that is primarily because it prompts him to create the ironic distance which is the foundation of this particular aesthetic. In submitting his desire to the discipline of irony, the poet thus achieves a contrasting *dis*embodiment (he is absent from his words and the text says the opposite of what it seems to say).

This may seem excessive commentary on a relatively frivolous poem, but Baudelaire's way of making a representation of the feminine the means by which to construct an ironically anti-social position for the writer contains in germ many of the problems of the later modernisms. It is as if the poem's success must be measured by the degree to which the beggar-girl is finally objectified, for it is this which ensures the poet's *separateness* from the social world of which he writes. To gauge the extent of Baudelaire's departure from the 'social romanticism' of his time, one has only to compare Victor Hugo's representation of the exploited factory-girls of Lille in his poem 'Joyful Life' (in *The Castigations* [1853]). Hugo speaks forcefully on behalf of the oppressed, and his angry allusions to Dante's *Inferno* contrast vividly with the tricky irony of Baudelaire's tone which is tacitly premised on the writer's assumption of some sort of superiority.

But what is the ground of that superiority, since it is not, as the 'wretched poet' makes clear at the beginning, simply a matter of social class? In part Baudelaire invokes the privileged duplicity of the romantic ironist, his capacity to cast himself as observer and observed, and to make that division the ground of a judgmental authority located somewhere outside the action of the poem. The act of dissociation is vital, of course, since if irony is in some sense 'cruel' it is because it offends against an apparently 'sentimental' view of (human) nature. This is the spirit in which Baudelaire speaks of ways 'to instil in the spectator, or rather in the reader, the feeling of joy at his own superiority and the joy of man's superiority over nature' (*BSW*, 161). The relation of irony to this kind of 'superiority' is governed, it turns out, by an assumption not simply that the masterful style is one which is chosen by the poet but that it is somehow forced upon him by the 'challenge' of the feminine or natural.

This is rather more complicated than the commonplace claim that 'she made me do it', for the cruelty of seduction collapses ethical values into aesthetic ones, making the 'elimination' of the feminine the very mark of that triumph of form over 'bodily' content on which one major strand of modernism will depend.[4] It is here that the various conventional fantasies of Woman as 'dangerous' and overpowering come into play, suggesting that aesthetic form and ironic tone are necessary *defences* against the other.[5] If the feminine seems a suitable surrogate for social relations in general it is because the illusion of some absolute otherness is required to protect the poet's self from the full recognition of identity with other people. Ironic tonal play and the related interest, later in the period, in elaborate masks of the self thus serve a kind of double function, obscuring the social location of the writer's voice at the same time as they cultivate an essentially closed model of the self. Is it too much to say that this grounding of the aesthetic in an objectification of the other would constitute *the* recurring problem of the later modernisms? In the next chapter we shall see, at any rate, how writers began to conceive of modernity as a condition which seemed to *require* such an aesthetic.

1
Ironies of the Modern

Perhaps the real paradox of Baudelaire's 'To a Red-haired Beggar Girl' is that it suggests that irony is a necessary defence against modernity even as it seems to assume that to be distinctively modern the poet must be ironic. In this chapter I shall try to unpick this complicated response to 'modernity' and to trace its ambiguous relation to ideas of the social in the work of Baudelaire and some of his contemporaries, writers such as Gustave Flaubert, Herman Melville and Fyodor Dostoyevsky.

We can begin with an essay by Baudelaire which opened the debate about modernity in a highly suggestive way. Called 'The Painter of Modern Life' (1859–60), the essay is nominally about the painter Constantin Guys, but Baudelaire uses Guys's work as an occasion for a series of connected meditations on the theme of modernity. Part of his purpose here is to overcome the neo-classical fetish of the antique and to argue the case for the modern as legitimate artistic subject-matter. 'The pleasure we derive from the representation of the present', he claims, 'is due, not only to the beauty it can be clothed in, but also to its essential quality of being the present' (*BSW*, 391). The neo-classical ideal of unchanging beauty is complicated here by a vivid sense of the flux and movement of life in the present. Bringing together the metaphysical and the temporal, Baudelaire invents a poetics of sudden 'correspondences', of moments when the rapid passage of forms which characterises contemporary experience is suddenly illuminated by an intuition of the atemporal or spiritual. 'Modernity', he concludes, 'is the transient, the fleeting, the contingent; it is one half of art, the other being the eternal and immutable' (*BSW*, 403). The element of idealism here is, however, to be dissociated from the neo-classical 'theory of a unique and absolute beauty' (*BSW*, 392), since it derives from the process of 'deliberate idealization' which is art (*BSW*, 402):

> the ideal is not that vague thing, that boring and intangible dream floating on the ceilings of academies; an ideal is the

individual modified by the individual, rebuilt and restored by brush or chisel to the dazzling truth of its own essential harmony. (*BSW*, 78)

The sense of the 'fleeting' and 'contingent' is perhaps the definitive mark of the early grasp of the modern. In America, for example, Ralph Waldo Emerson had already commented enthusiastically on the momentum of social change in the new era:

> The new continents are built out of the ruins of an old planet; the new races fed out of the decomposition of the foregoing. New arts destroy the old. See the investment of capital in aqueducts, made useless by hydraulics; fortifications, by gunpowder; roads and canals, by railways; sails, by steam; steam, by electricity.[1]

Celebrating the rapid expansion of Jacksonian capitalism, Emerson could find in technological progress an affirmation of the evolutionary principle of nature ('There are no fixtures in nature'[2]).

Several years after Emerson, Marx and Engels also wrote of the 'constant revolutionising of production' as the definitive action of an emergent bourgeoisie. Like Emerson and Baudelaire, the writers of *The Communist Manifesto* (1848) stressed the impulse towards innovation and diversification which marked the age, but at the same time they revealed a darker paradox at the heart of modernity: for while change was everywhere apparent and seemed to herald the appearance of a new and more humane world, the process of modernisation actually entailed the continuous reproduction of the same relations, the relations which govern capitalist production.[3]

For Marx, as, in a different way, for Baudelaire, this paradox had become painfully clear with the failure of revolutionary hopes after 1848. Indeed, the period that began with Louis Napoléon's *coup d'état* in December 1851 and the inauguration of his intolerant, commercialist regime did much to define the shape of the later avant-garde. It was not simply that the promise of radical change had suddenly evaporated, but that state institutions and the political life circulating around them now seemed degraded and farcical. Marx caught the tone of this perfectly in *The Eighteenth Brumaire* (1852), where he depicted Louis Napoléon's imperial regime as a grotesquely theatrical simulation of the original Napoleonic state. Grandiose repetition could not conceal the one-dimensional character of a new bourgeois society marked by passions without truth, truth without passions; heroes without deeds of heroism, history without events; a course of development only driven forward by the calendar, and made wearisome by the constant repetition of the same tension and relaxations.... If any section of history has been painted grey on grey, it is this.[4]

Modernity, it seemed, was the time of the copy, an insight expressed with equal pungency in Victor Hugo's *Little Napoleon* (1852) and Gustave Flaubert's *Sentimental Education* (1869).

This 'grey' period, which would last until 1870, combined rapid material progress with political intolerance; writers could hardly help seeing a connection between capitalistic values and a government hostility to creative work at a time when tough new censorship laws brought well-known figures like Baudelaire, Flaubert and the Goncourt brothers into the dock. Not surprisingly, the surge of economic growth and the popular gospel of progress were often equated with philistinism and cultural stagnation. Baudelaire, for example, described society after 1848 as 'wholly worn-out – worse than worn-out – brutalised and greedy, wholly repelled by fiction, adoring only material possession' (*BSW*, 248). What, then, of his equally forceful arguments for modernity as subject-matter of the new arts? Here a cleavage begins to open between bourgeois modernity, on the one hand, and aesthetic modernity, on the other.[5] The later claims of the various modernisms to create the authentically new can be traced back to this early sense of a 'false' modernity whose surface momentum conceals its inner sameness, its unceasing reproduction of the safe limits of the bourgeois world. Here too the particular modernist preoccupation with *time* begins, for as Baudelaire's comment suggests, the conjunction of greed and inertia implies that the market has somehow frozen the movement of history, installing in its place a procession of ever 'new' commodities (as Walter Benjamin neatly remarks, 'Fashion is the eternal recurrence of the new'[6]).

If everyday life is now felt to be oppressive it is partly because time is experienced as endless repetition. This is the condition of Baudelaire's *ennui*, when subjective time becomes mechanical, the passing moments palpable, like 'snow flakes'.[7] We might define that 'great modern monster', *ennui*,[8] as a kind of primal melancholy, a combination of apathy and boredom which, in rendering the subject claustrophobically inactive, also brings painful hypersensitivity and nervousness (the poet Paul Verlaine, for example, would later write of 'modern man with his sharpened and vibrating senses, his painfully subtle sensibility'[9]). Modern man is 'nerve-ridden', in Baudelaire's phrase (*BSW*, 186), dominated by a 'psychology of nerves' and increasingly unpredictable, caught between a cult of 'multiplied sensation', on the one hand, and an impasse of inaction and impotence, on the other. Afflicted by this typically 'modern' vacillation, the axis of the self seems precarious, barely sustainable, as it is buffetted by dizzying excesses of emotion which veer from disgust to inexplicable exaltation. Modern life is thus an experience of extremes, as the narrator of Dostoyevsky's *Notes from Underground* (1864) observes:

> And what softening effect has civilization had on us? Civilization develops in man only a many-sided sensitivity to sensations, and ... definitely nothing more. And through the development of that many-sidedness man may perhaps progress to the point where he finds pleasure in blood.[10]

At once vulnerable because of hypersensitivity and dangerous because of his desire for ever greater intensity of sensation, the authentically modern subject thus seems to slip the social moorings of the rational bourgeois self and its 'counting-house morality' (*BSW*, 197).

This new form of subjectivity is accompanied by a rejection of art's traditional role as an arbiter of moral truths. Following the argument of Poe's 'The Poetic Principle', Baudelaire declares that 'Poetry cannot, except at the price of death or decay, assume the mantle of science or morality; the pursuit of truth is not its aim, it has nothing outside itself' (*BSW*, 204). Yet here another paradox looms into view, for this emancipation of art from the sphere of science and morality has been brought about by art's absorption into that very world of commodities and commercial values which the modern artist so contemptuously rejects. Emancipation is thus something of a mixed blessing, especially as the new autonomy of the art-work can lead, on the one hand, to its being manoeuvred into irrelevance, and, on the other, to its being made to function as the ideological legitimation of capitalist society, the values exiled in the aesthetic now seeming to enshrine the truths to which the social order is committed at the level of ideology.[11]

For the writer who, like Baudelaire, had only contempt for the culture of his day, it was thus crucial that art be in no sense 'useful'.

Théophile Gautier, one of his mentors and an early proponent of the 'art for art's sake' doctrine, had already provided the essential formulation in the preface to his novel *Mademoiselle de Maupin* (1835):

> Nothing beautiful is indispensable to life. ... Nothing is really beautiful unless it is useless; everything useful is ugly, for it expresses a need, and the needs of man are ignoble and disgusting, like his poor weak nature. The most useful place in a house is the lavatory.[12]

Developing Gautier's aversion to utility into an attack on both French intellectual tradition and contemporary bourgeois ideology, Baudelaire now characterises France as 'the home of clear thought and demonstration, where art aims naturally and directly at utility' (*BSW*, 154). 'Utility' here denotes forms of ideological usefulness: bourgeois art is expected to conceal and in that way naturalise the damaging effects of 'progress', rationalising change by making it somehow continuous with a familiar, academic culture. The neo-classical revival in the French theatre of the 1840s is one example of the official culture's appeal to tradition and imitation. On a larger scale, recourse to cultural pastiche and repetition to conceal the disruptive effects of the new might be seen in the architecture of nineteenth-century railway stations in European cities such as Milan, Cologne and London.[13]

For Baudelaire, cultural manifestations of this sort simply illuminate the principal affectation of bourgeois culture – its 'naturalness'. The Romantic aura attaching to 'nature' here disappears as Baudelaire redefines it as 'nothing but the inner voice of self-interest' (*BSW*, 425). He now goes on to appropriate the bourgeois legitimation of egoism in order to turn it inside out. 'Modern art', he declares, 'has an essentially demonic tendency', a statement which scandalously inverts Christian values at the same time as it claims as the fundamental subject-matter of art the very negativity which is repressed in the bourgeois doctrine of 'universal progress' (or 'universal ruin' – 'it matters little what name it is given'[14]). The egoism and self-seeking which underpin the ideal of the free market are testimony to 'the infernal part of man'. So, in Baudelaire's poems, the everyday life of commercial society is forced to reveal its darker, nocturnal side, as the self is unravelled through tropes of intoxication, violence and perversity.

Baudelaire was not alone in his way of construing modernity, and we find the same fascination with the 'evil' underside of bourgeois human nature in the work of writers such as Hawthorne, Melville and Dostoyevsky. Each in his own way twisted the doctrine of nature against itself, so that evil became the very principle of the natural. As Baudelaire put it, 'Evil is done without effort, *naturally*, it is the working of fate; good is always the product of an art' (*BSW*, 425). In that formulation we see how a moral principle (rooted, in Baudelaire's case, in the doctrine of original sin) is smoothly transposed into the aesthetic domain; and we can also begin to see how devious and perverse the artistic principle might become, since it must now always articulate what does *not* come naturally.

*   *   *

In rejecting 'nature', Baudelaire and his avant-garde contemporaries were not simply rejecting a poetic taste for trees and rivers; more fundamentally, they were denying the connection between poetic vision and social transformation which had underpinned the political optimism of an earlier Romanticism. As Baudelaire put it:

> Most wrong ideas about beauty derive from the false notion the eighteenth century had about ethics. In those days, Nature was taken as a basis, source and prototype of all possible forms of good and beauty. The rejection of original sin is in no small measure responsible for the general blindness of those days. (*BSW*, 425)

In the wake of 1848, a disillusioned avant-garde tended to conceive of humanity as neither perfectible nor evolutionary, but as flawed and corrupt, a shift in perspective which was bound up with a thoroughgoing loss of faith in any kind of political action. Again, Baudelaire's case is exemplary. It seems likely that he fought at the barricades in 1848, but by 1852 he had renounced all forms of political activity.[15] As Jean-Paul Sartre observes, 'The treason of the petty bourgeois in 1848 discredited *politics* in the eyes of the exploited – all politics was bourgeois, even when practised by politicians who claimed to be socialists.'[16]

Louis Napoléon's *coup d'état* thus produced a failure of political representation which required a fundamental redefinition of individual agency. As one critic puts it, capital began to 'break free from certain specific political – and in this sense, representational – relations and structures that were the condition of its initial autonomy and, thereby, to take on the attributes of a superordinate social agency with no fixed political or cultural subjectivity'.[17] It was Baudelaire's generation which took the first step toward a substitution of the aesthetic for 'the lost terrain of social representation'. This is not to suggest that writers suddenly ceased to be oppositional, but rather that the ground of opposition shifted from political rhetoric and polemic to literary 'style'. The redefinition of the artist's role which would accomplish this is most clearly seen in another section of Baudelaire's 'The Painter of Modern Life', where he sketches his ideal of the dandy:

> Dandyism appears especially in those periods of transition when democracy has not yet become all-powerful, and when aristocracy is only partially weakened and discredited. In the confusion of such times, a certain number of men, disenchanted and leisured 'outsiders', but all of them richly endowed with native energy, may conceive the idea of establishing a new kind of aristocracy, all the more difficult to break down because established on the most precious, the most indestructible faculties, on the divine gifts that neither work nor money can give. Dandyism is the last flicker of heroism in decadent ages. ... (*BSW*, 421)

Characteristically, Baudelaire regards the present as a time of dramatic transition; it is because the future relations of aristocracy and bourgeoisie have not yet crystallised that the intelligentsia can make its own bid for power. This particular kind of 'power' is possible because the present is also a 'decadent' age. We shall return to this complex and loaded word in Chapter 3, but in the context of Baudelaire's essay it refers primarily to the absence of a class capable of combining the exercise of political power with cultural appreciation. The dandy, disdaining politics as such, will accordingly assert his absolute authority in the cultural realm. It is, however, an authority which is not without its own particular pathos, for this 'last flicker' of taste and refinement represents an heroic, because doomed, resistance to what Baudelaire goes on to call 'the rising tide of democracy, which spreads everywhere and reduces everything to the same level'.

The implication of Baudelaire's essay is that the public sphere and 'culture' have become two separate and opposed domains, and, furthermore, that 'culture' itself has split into 'high' and 'low' forms. As an arbiter of 'style', of course, the dandy is 'leisured', and his aloofness from life's practical necessities allows him to remain uncompromised either by the ideological imperatives of academic culture or by what had become known (after the critic Sainte-Beuve) as 'industrial literature' – journalism, that is, and popular episodic fiction, that 'trade of literature' which Alexis de Tocqueville had projected as a significant feature of the new democratic societies.[18] The contempt for forms of popular culture which would determine some of the avant-garde positions of the later modernism has its roots in these nineteenth-century responses to the growth of the literary market. It is rare indeed to find a writer at this time arguing, as did Emile Zola in a piece called 'Money and Literature', that the decline of literary patronage would promote new authorial freedoms.[19] For the most part the rise of so-called literary 'factories' and the new practice of paying by the line seemed, to most serious writers, the very embodiment of modern philistinism. The figure of the leisured dandy thus aligned 'style' with the refusal to compromise (Baudelaire's ironic advice to young writers was to produce a lot and work fast[20]).

If politics was now thoroughly tainted by the commercialism of the Second Empire, the only way forward for art seemed, to some, to lie in the deliberate cultivation of an anti-social stance. So, in a slightly later essay, Baudelaire contrasts 'misanthropic republicanism' (which, he says, can be both literary and political) with 'the democratic and bourgeois passion which has lately so cruelly oppressed us'. The former, he claims, is to be preferred, since it is driven by 'a limitless aristocratic hatred, without pity or bounds, for monarchs and bourgeois, and by a broad sympathy for everything in art which is excessive in colour and form, everything which is intense, pessimistic and Byronic'.[21] We may note how an artistic intensity which 'exceeds' the limits of the bourgeois world is also cruel, inhuman even, because it comes into being as a negation of social bonds. The creative act, so Baudelaire implies, is opposed to 'slavish imitation' (*BSW*, 77), 'excessive in colour and form' and destructive of the ties of social identification which bind the artist to a particular class. As he explains in his account of the dandy, such men become disenchanted 'outsiders' – the French word is *déclassés* – whose willed estrangement exemplifies a new sense of the incompatibility between artistic vocation and social obligation. As the two pull further apart, a modern aesthetic comes to imply a sort of triumph over social origins; 'Perhaps the future will belong to men of no class [*déclassés*]', muses Baudelaire.[22]

This celebration of artistic independence had already been a notable feature of Romanticism, where it had emerged in two main forms: either the writer's genius apparently separated him from the crowd and gave a special authority to his words, or he was condemned to isolation and disregard because the new 'democratic' audience lacked the ability to understand him. In France, Victor Hugo might provide a good example of the first kind of writer, while Alfred de Vigny (in, say, the 'Preface' to his *Chatterton* [1835]) might exemplify the second. In each case, though, the Romantic writers, for all their attempts to work free of the fetters of academic convention, still operated within a horizon of recognisable rhetorical objectives. After 1848, writers began to adopt a kind of self-imposed exile as a necessary condition of creativity, and with that gesture went a new conception of poetic language as something quite distinct from a shared language of communication. This is the implication behind Gérard de Nerval's famous declaration that, in a rampantly materialistic age, 'The only refuge left to us was the poet's ivory tower, which we climbed, ever higher, to isolate ourselves from the mob.'[23] The image would be a favourite one as the century went on; Flaubert, for example, remarked in characteristically acerbic tone that 'I have always tried to live in an ivory tower, but a tide of shit is beating at its walls to undermine it.'[24]

The image of the ivory tower memorably expresses the desire to evade the pressure in a modern democratic society to conform and identify with others. Writers and artists at this time were increasingly aware of a mimetic principle at work in bourgeois modernity, in its fondness for representational art, in its parasitic dependence on 'tradition', and in the psychology of emulation underpinning a culture in which moral continuity was ensured by institutionalised habits of imitation. Bourgeois culture thus seemed to ground itself in the awkward paradox that we become truly ourselves only by copying others. The tone of sharp irony and duplicity which is variously present in the work of Baudelaire, Dostoyevsky and Melville responds to this contradiction, that our words, our actions, our most intimate desires always seem to bear the trace of an other who was first on the scene and whom we unwittingly copy.

The quarrel with mimesis which is often taken to define a pivotal moment of modernism's inception had, then, implications beyond the purely formal or stylistic. Indeed, as René Girard has shown, the practice of imitation and its attendant psychology of 'imitative desire' lay at the heart of that restructuring of social relations which would ultimately generate the aesthetics of modernism. In *Deceit, Desire and the Novel*, Girard describes what he calls the 'triangulation of desire', a relation structured around subject, model, and object. It is the great discovery of the nineteenth-century novel, he argues, that desire is thus mediated by and copied from a third party whose function as a model turns out to be more important than the actual object of desire. According to Girard, the transition to modernity can be mapped by the shift from 'external' to 'internal' mediation: where, under the *ancien régime,* the model to be copied had been transcendent to the subject ('beyond the universe of the hero'[25]), 'internal mediation triumphs in a universe where the differences between men are gradually erased' (14) and the model becomes increasingly like the subject. All desire is in this sense 'Desire according to the Other' (5), and internal mediation is fraught with hatred and rivalry, since the model functions as both the origin of the subject's desire and as the obstacle to any realisation of it. Desire thus becomes 'metaphysical', detached from pragmatic considerations and the pursuit of any 'tangible advantage' (86). This, argues Girard, is the world of Stendhal, Flaubert, Dostoyevsky and Proust, whose work exposes the romantic myth of spontaneous desire and explores the violence on which social relations are founded.

Identification with others was now something to be feared and resisted, and this perhaps accounts for Baudelaire's appeal to dandyism as a way of redefining class divisions along a cultural axis (the term 'bourgeois' was coming to signify not simply the middle class, but that sector of it which seemed wilfully lacking in cultural values). The concept of a 'new aristocracy' was actually rooted in contradiction, since the whole thrust of its artistic endeavour was to be directed against the very class to which its members themselves belonged – the class which, to twist the paradox a little more, provided the only real audience it could expect to have. As Renato Poggioli puts it in his study of the modernist avant-garde, 'the genuine art of a bourgeois society can only be anti-bourgeois'.[26] The artist-as-dandy acknowledges his potentially compromised position in the intensity of his refusal of alliances with others, a gesture which we see duplicated at the technical level of

Baudelaire's writing by his rejection of any political rhetoric of identification. Not that he is blind to class tensions in contemporary life; to the contrary, many of his most powerful works record the sufferings of a disenfranchised urban proletariat. It is rather that he distrusts the rhetorical appeal to a shared human nature – a rhetoric associated, of course, with Victor Hugo, of whom Paul Valéry would later remark that 'He flirted with the crowd, he exchanged dialogues with God.'[27] Hence, also, Baudelaire's loathing for George Sand, which was motivated not only by his characteristic misogyny but also by contempt for 'Her love of the working-class' and her 'wish to abolish Hell': 'It was the Devil who persuaded her to rely on her "good heart" and her "good sense", so that she might persuade all the other ponderous animals to rely upon *their* good heart and good sense.'[28]

This is the gospel of social identification, and Baudelaire pits against it an individualism which requires a radical, and often violent, demarcation of limits and boundaries. Perhaps the most extreme example is the prose poem 'Bash the Poor!', where the narrator responds to the entreaties of a beggar with an onslaught of violence. Much to his delight, the beggar retaliates – 'Thus, by means of the vigorous treatment I subjected him to, I had restored to him his self-esteem and zest for life.'[29] The beggar is now 'an equal' and the narrator gladly shares his purse with him. Individuality, we conclude, is won through an assertion of difference, and the violent struggle in this story is just one example of the way in which Baudelaire assumes that a sense of self has somehow to be acquired at the expense of the other.

The greatest fear is now provoked by the spectre of the Double, by the appearance of an other who somehow mirrors oneself, for in this confrontation, as we find it staged in the work of Poe, Baudelaire and Dostoyevsky, the self is drawn back into that social body from which art had seemed to offer a privileged liberation. The threat of this specular relation can be overcome only by fully *objectifying* the other, and typically (as we saw in the case of 'To a Red-haired Beggar Girl') the problem seems most pressing when Woman is involved:

> In love, as in almost all human affairs, sympathy is the result of a misunderstanding. This misunderstanding is the physical pleasure. ... the two imbeciles are convinced that they are thinking in harmony. The unbridgeable gulf which prevents communication remains unbridged.[30]

Not only does the man of genius accept this gulf, he depends upon it to create his 'personal form of originality' (*BSW*, 420). Hence his 'revengeful indifference' (*BSW*, 163), for he 'wants to be *one* – that is, *solitary*'.[31] So much for his desire, but 'Who amongst us is not a *homo duplex*? I speak of those whose mind since childhood has been *touched with pensiveness*; always double, action and intention, dream and reality; always one hindering the other, one usurping the place of the other.'[32] The solitary, then, is in fact always 'double': he reacts violently to aspects of himself glimpsed in others, only to find in the same moment that it is he himself who is the target of his own violence; he is both victim and executioner, as Baudelaire so memorably puts it,[33] a doubling of role which associates a certain desire for self-wounding and mutilation with a mechanising of the self in defiance of bodily needs and social dependencies. Viewed in this light, Baudelaire's dandy and Melville's Ahab may appear in unexpected proximity.

*   *   *

For Baudelaire, then, this tortured disunity was the tragic condition of the modern poet, but it was also, in a curious way, his strength. The very nature of metropolitan life offered the opportunity to exploit this doubleness of the self, to make duplicity a sort of defence against the modern. For while the eighteenth-century city had seemed the very model of social order, the rapidly expanding metropolis of the new era appeared increasingly unintelligible and contradictory. London epitomised the almost infernal effects of urban over-crowding during this period, as we can see from the shocked responses to its conditions by writers like Dickens, Engels, Dostoyevsky and Melville.[34] The experience was unsettling in the extreme; Engels observed, for example, that people 'crowd by one another as though they had nothing in common, nothing to do with one another, and their only agreement is the tacit one, that each keep to his own side of the pavement, so as not to delay the oppos-ing streams of the crowd'.[35] This was collective experience but without any sense of communal relationship; using an increasingly popular metaphor, the English art-critic John Ruskin noted that 'every creature is only one atom in a drift of human dust, and current of interchanging particles'.[36] And it was not always just a matter of 'drift', for the new pace of life in the city made the streets, as we have seen in 'Bash the Poor!', a setting for violent collisions and confrontations. The metropolis could become a theatre of vendettas, surveillance and bitter psychological conflict; when, for example, the narrator of *Notes from Underground* is swept aside by an impatient officer, the trivial and unthinking act seems to condense a lifetime's fears of contact with and oppression by other people. These new social relations seemed characterised by the random and accidental, and the modern sensibility was increasingly compelled to look to its own defence in a world in which even class lines no longer seemed secure ('since the invention of the public bus,' observed Flaubert, 'the bourgeoisie is dead; they sit there in the bus alongside the "lower classes", and not only think like them and look like them but even dress like them'[37]).

The city, then, was both dangerous and exhilarating. Writers could either retreat from it into pastoral fantasy, withdrawing into the safer, more remote worlds of Arthurian legend or Trecento Italy; or they could plunge into the urban chaos, moving into the crowd 'as though into an enormous reservoir of electricity' (*BSW*, 400). The second option, to be variously encoded within the later modernisms, was the one grasped by Baudelaire (the first characterised much of the work of British poets like Tennyson and Rossetti). Once again, the conditions of modernity seemed to foster a certain duplicity in the writer, allowing him to 'see the world, to be at the very centre of the world, and yet to be unseen of the world'. The crowded thoroughfares of the city now provided a setting for a private drama in which the artist as stroller (or *flâneur*) could shift at will between postures of aloofness and surrender.

A wager of a kind was involved in this exhilarating experience, for in so far as the abrupt movements of the city were incorporated into the artist's internal life, so the self began to lose its boundaries, becoming instead a flux of sensation and contradictory states of mind. Baudelaire depicts this as an almost erotic experience:

> The poet enjoys the incomparable privilege of being, at will, both himself and other people. Like a wandering soul seeking a body, he can enter, whenever he wishes, into anybody's personality.[38]

The poet's ego may thus be 'dispersed' at one moment and 'centralised' at another,[39] and this constant oscillation in the crowd saves him from the passive identification with others which is the lot of the tailor and the hairdresser in 'The Painter of Modern Life':

Neither of these two beings has a thought in his head. Can one even be sure they are looking at anything – unless, like Narcissuses of fat-headedness, they are contemplating the crowd, as though it were a river, offering them their own image. In reality they exist much more for the joy of the observer than for their own. (*BSW*, 429)

It took a special kind of sensibility to accept such a wager, a distinctively modern one, of course, whose specialness derived from its volatile disunity. Again, we have to do with a legacy of the Romantic period, with its investment in personal uniqueness. Baudelaire, for example, would write to his mother that 'I am not made like other men'; Flaubert sees himself as having 'the infirmity of being born with a special language, to which I alone have the key'; and Dostoyevsky's anti-hero in *Notes from Underground*, explains that 'There was one other circumstance that tormented me at that time, namely that nobody else was like me, and I wasn't like anybody else. "I am one person, and they are everybody," I would think.'[40]

The sense of personal difference, coupled with that of speaking 'a special language', now complicated the Romantic concept of uniqueness by locating the trauma of division and separation within subjectivity rather than in the external relation of self to other. As writers abandoned the communicative spaces of the public sphere, so they were increasingly haunted by the spectre of the double – the other, we might say, was now 'inside', as we see from Poe's 'William Wilson' (1839) and Dostoyevsky's *The Double* (1846). This inward turn set language at odds with normal discourse, pressuring it to articulate an ever more intense self-consciousness (here, in germ, was the cultivation of linguistic *difficulty* which would become a trademark of the later modernism). The writer focused a cruelly analytic eye upon himself, making alien and objective what hitherto had been inward and personal. That tactic was partly indebted to the Baudelairean distrust of 'natural' emotion and the desire for aesthetic detachment (the hero of his early novel *La Fanfarlo* [1847] goes to the mirror to watch himself weep; and Sartre describes Baudelaire himself as a man 'bending over his own reflection like Narcissus'[41]). The habit of self-analysis could easily degenerate into mannerism, but beyond the gesture lay a deeper recognition of some fissure in the self, which Freud would later formulate in terms of the conscious and unconscious. It was Baudelaire's belief in original sin that led his thought in this direction, prompting the speculation that 'Every well-ordered brain has within it two postulations, toward heaven and hell; and in any image of one of these it suddenly recognises the half of itself' (*BSW*, 342).

That sense of splitting and of contradictory impulses at war within the self underlay Baudelaire's concept of the perverse, which he developed from Poe. Why do we persist in actions which run counter to our own best interests? Partly, said Poe, because we are always drawn towards the idea of self-destruction, like the hero of his story 'The Imp of the Perverse' who, having committed the perfect murder, cannot refrain from confessing it. Dostoyevsky defines it as that mood in which a man will 'consciously and purposely desire for himself what is positively harmful and stupid',[42] while Baudelaire finds its effects in 'man's being constantly, and at one and the same time, homicidal and suicidal, murderer and executioner' (*BSW*, 192). Humanity's aspiration to metaphysical values collapses into egoistic desires and interests (a point soon to be hammered home by Nietzsche and Max Stirner[43]), with social relations and psychological stability equally torn by a 'primaeval' violence (*BSW*, 192).

Perversity thus spells the ruin of bourgeois rationalism, and if Baudelaire was in some sense the secret agent of his class's discontent with itself (the suggestion is Walter Benjamin's), it is not surprising that he should exploit Poe's principle to the full. And what, after all, could be more perverse than writing, a pursuit of the ineffable which constantly hurls the writer back into the abyss of failure? Writing, too, is the very embodiment of something monstrous, a mutilation of the 'natural' self by its transformation into style; so Baudelaire led the way in discarding the earlier Romantic view of poetry as the product of lyrical inspiration (the expression of the poet's nature) and, following Poe, replaced it with an ideal of technical skill and craftsmanship. Discredited is Alphonse de Lamartine's lofty verdict that 'To create is beautiful, but to correct, to alter, to spoil, is poor and tedious. It is the work of masons, not of artists'[44]; in its place is Baudelaire's new view that 'Inspiration is definitely the sister of journalism.'[45] Rather be a mason than a banker, then, for the true work of aesthetic modernity depends on the assiduous cultivation of style, on that 'atrocious labour' of which Flaubert was to become an exemplary practitioner ('Last week I spent 5 *days writing one page*'[46]).

This work is both 'unnatural' and self-defining; style becomes, in Flaubert's words, 'an absolute manner of seeing things',[47] and the objective might now be 'a book about nothing, a book dependent on nothing external'.[48] The artist is 'a monstrosity, something outside nature',[49] partly because of the 'fanatical' dedication to style, but also because the rejection of the purely mimetic to which this is pledged produces a 'scientific' detachment which can appear 'inhuman'. So Flaubert remarked with satisfaction of his *Madame Bovary* (1857) that 'This will be the first time, I think, that a book makes fun of its leading lady and its leading man', and Matthew Arnold, understandably missing the point, lamented that Flaubert 'is cruel, with the cruelty of petrified feeling, to his poor heroine; he pursues her without pity or pause, as with malignity; he is harder upon her himself than any reader even, I think, will be inclined to be'.[50] Flaubert's 'hardness' is recognisably modernist in its way of pitting style against debased forms of cultural imitation. Indeed, this is the principal theme of his novel, for while Emma Bovary's career is the very embodiment of a secondhand desire derived from romantic fiction, Flaubert's countervailing model of verbal precision – the novel itself – tacitly proposes a 'genuine' aesthetic as a ground of critical distance. A literary style thus steeped in self-reflexivity at once reveals the illusion of spontaneous desire *and* presents itself as an alternative model to be copied. That 'copying', however, is a process grounded in self-irony, since the fundamental presupposition of 'style' is that desire is always mediated by textuality and thus has to be grasped, as it were, from the outside, from the standpoint of 'writing' rather than by an act of imaginative identification. This move sums up most of what has been said above, for now perfection of style is intimately bound up with a certain cruelty and lack of human sympathy.

Suddenly it seems that the writer is less concerned with the problems of representing other people than with the 'atrocious' psychic drama which the act of writing itself sets in motion. Regarded as 'labour', writing is set apart from pragmatic bourgeois employments partly because it promises beauty and transcendence, but also because in doing so it presents a mirror to the corrupt and 'unnatural' self. It is as if writing gives us access to the innermost mechanisms of the psyche, revealing a violent disunity within the subject. Baudelaire offers a vivid account of this view of writing in the prose poem called 'The Double Room', where the fantasy of 'a really *spiritual* room' in which the 'pure dream' centres around a beautiful woman ('the sovereign of dreams') suddenly yields to a claustrophobic room in which 'time has reappeared'. Death and the Law invade this space, which we suddenly learn is the writer's room, strewn with 'manuscripts crossed out or not completed'. The incompleteness of this writing seems to make it the very medium of a temporality in which language can never do more than remind us of things already lost. So the 'dream' of perfection embodied in the symbolic presence of the Woman yields to the purely allegorical procession of 'Memories and Regrets, Fits, Fears, Anguishes, Nightmares, Angers and Neuroses.'[51]

To define this descent into allegory, we might say that language is of its nature inherently allegorical since each sign inevitably refers to one which precedes it, thus opening a sense of time and anteriority which parallels the gap between 'levels' in a conventional allegory. Baudelaire's great desire is, in this respect, to secure moments of plenitude which transcend the leaden seriality of time, freeing us into a world of unmediated experience. Walter Benjamin observes that Baudelaire thus summons up 'not historical data, but data of pre-history',[52] a distinction which is particularly helpful when we observe that, in *The Flowers of Evil* (1857), the liberating force of an aesthetic modernity freed from imitation can be felt only as a quasi-Platonic recollection. It is in *memory* that we may secure that moment of full presence which the actual present never seems to yield. 'History', in contrast, appears as an unrelieved temporality which frustrates any metaphysical connection between visible and invisible. And where the symbolic medium of language should reaffirm a primordial bonding of word and meaning, writers like Baudelaire are increasingly aware of the inaccessibility of truth and the consequences of that for fantasies of harmony between mind and nature. Metaphysics now comes to denote the remoteness of truth, and we find in Baudelaire's poems that the modern is constantly experienced as loss and aporia. In 'The Swan', for example, the absence of stable meaning in the contemporary world is linked to the poet's recollection of 'the Paris of old', which turns the modern scene into a complex of signs pointing to things now disappeared: 'Paris is changing, but naught in my melancholy / Has moved. These new palaces and scaffoldings, blocks of stone, / Old suburbs – everything for me is turned to allegory, / And my memories are heavier than rocks'.[53])

It is not, then, that allegory fails to recognise a realm of 'truth', but rather that in according it some sort of transcendent origin it also acknowledges its absence. In thus pointing up the distance between fiction and meaning, allegory also displays a strong hierarchical tendency, valuing meaning only to degrade its material embodiment. The social world is drained of life in order to submit difference to the rule of typicality, producing in this way a mass of signs each of which could be exchanged for another. Modern allegories lack the systematic motivation of earlier forms, and they thus function not to provide metaphysical reassurance but to reveal the metaphysical itself as willed and constructed. Allegory, we might conclude, presents a 'history' in which human purpose and intention are no longer legible; hence Baudelaire's nightmare evocations of unendingly empty Time, and the related sense of language as a body of inert and reified signs from which the human guarantee of meaning has fled along with the divine.

Faced with the barren perspectives of allegory, the writer's irony comes to seem a legitimate rejoinder to an irony buried in the very frame of things. Nature, once more, is the prime deceiver; as Ishmael learns in Melville's *Moby-Dick* (1851), 'all deified Nature absolutely paints like the harlot, whose allurements cover nothing but the charnel-house within'.[54] In Ahab's pursuit of Moby-Dick, the meaning to be uncovered is inextricably bound up with death itself, and the final wreckage embodies the collapse of Romantic vision in a world which has room only for the harsher solvents of allegory. For dreams of cosmic unity, of an identification of self and non-self, are dangerously deceptive, as Ishmael discovers when he almost falls from the mast-head during a pantheistic revery. Melville's novel constantly pits the individualism of Ahab's metaphysical quest for meaning against a social ideal of interdependency ('Nothing exists in itself' [148]), showing the two to be not only disjunct but separated by a void in which human meanings expire. For Melville, as in a different way for Nietzsche, humanity is committed in advance to a restless quest for 'truth', but because that truth is situated beyond the human, the outer limit of the quest must always be the point at which the bonds of sociality are finally destroyed. Metaphysics means the death of the world – Ahab must destroy Moby-Dick in order to prove the correctness of his own interpretation of nature – just as the ideological 'truths' of Manifest Destiny must be purchased through genocide.

This perhaps explains why the conclusion of the novel seems in some way unresolved – does it imply the salvation or wreckage of the ship of state through expansionism and slavery? – for the wealth of allegorical allusion to the politics of the time fails to yield a key to the narrative as a whole.[55] The text gestures instead to a politics which has become frozen as allegory, sealed by an inflated, often biblical rhetoric into a timeless recurrence of the typical and abstract. In his work after *Moby-Dick*, Melville would discern even fewer signs of human connection, imprisoning his characters in a world like Bartleby's, where confinement is relieved only by the sight of a blank wall. Such images of a failed sociality are intended, like the claustrophobic tableaux of Baudelaire and the stone walls of *Notes from Underground*, as ever-present reminders of the *limits* of modernity. This world is hollowed-out, devoid of any transfiguring human presence, yet even as it compels the writer to adopt violent postures of recoil and 'revengeful indifference' (*BSW*, 163), it somehow retains the inscription of the social – a sign, but one now barely legible.

2
Breaking the Rules: Symbolism in France

If the work of Baudelaire, Melville and Dostoyevsky seems indelibly marked by an experience of aporia and loss it is because they are finally unable to escape the confines of a degraded social world; their texts bear the traces of that world, even as they curse, repudiate, and try to transcend it. The failure of metaphysical values destroys the hope that a coincidence between self and world might be achieved through sociality and a shared language. As we have seen, the alternative often canvassed by these writers is some kind of intense solitariness which might make the connection between self and world realisable without the intermediary forms of the social. But, as each writer discovers in a different way, this cultivation of the solitary stance is both ambivalent and dangerous, threatening to produce precisely the narcissistic atomism which characterises a degraded social sphere.

Nor can politics any longer provide a public context in which the individual finds a place in a larger whole – as Marx put it in an early essay called 'On the Jewish Question' (1844), bourgeois society produces an irreconcilable division between civil and political worlds. Civil society comprises the world of labour, of needs and of private interests; it is, says Marx (in terms similar to Baudelaire's) the domain of 'natural man', of egoism and self-interest. Yet individuals also have a role to play as members of political society, as citizens concerned for the common good. The problem is that this second role conflicts radically with the first, since bourgeois societies equate political rights with the rights of egoistic man. The two can never properly coincide, and the result is that the political sphere seems to rigidify into a ritual 'allegory' of social process:

> man as he is a member of civil society is taken to be the *real* man, *man* as distinct from *citizen*, since he is man in his sensuous, indi-

vidual and *immediate* existence, whereas *political* man is simply abstract, artificial man, man as an *allegorical, moral* person.[1]

For writers like Baudelaire, Melville and Dostoyevsky, this reduction of political life to allegory remained an inescapable horizon, a stark backdrop to any countervailing fantasy of transcendence.

To move beyond this apparent impasse meant finding a literary language which would make stronger claims to transcendence as it seemed less compromised by the traces it carried of its failed social function. The way forward was now to exploit to the full the non-social registers of language and in that way to exceed the binary structure of an allegorical world. In short, *all* the rules of normal communication must now be broken if the relation between art and society was to be significantly transformed. This new possibility came to be known as Symbolism and was first named as a movement in the manifesto of a relatively minor poet called Jean Moréas. Published in the *Figaro* in September 1886, Moréas's manifesto offered a sort of digest of modern poetics: 'Baudelaire should be considered as the true forerunner of the present movement; M. Stéphane Mallarmé endowed it with a sense of mystery, and the ineffable M. Paul Verlaine broke in its honor the cruel bonds of verses which the prestigious fingers of M. Théodore de Banville had previously softened.'[2] Intuition, mystery, suggestiveness: these were the watchwords of the new tendency:

> Opposed to 'teaching, declamation, false sensibility, objective description,' symbolic poetry seeks to clothe the Idea in a perceptible form which, nevertheless, would not be an end in itself; rather, while serving to express the idea, it would remain subject to it.

A debt to Baudelaire was inevitable, but it was less the 'Spleen' side of his literary psychology than his visionary capacity for insights into the 'Ideal' which stimulated these younger writers. Not that they were immune to those feelings of *ennui* and depression which had coloured so much of Baudelaire's work, but their main concern was now to develop systematic ways of overcoming those moods of transience and impotence which had come to seem endemic to modernity. It is striking that Baudelaire, Dostoyevsky and Melville, while writing in very different traditions and contexts, had each had recourse to images of enclosure and blank walls as expressive of the allegorical condition. In contrast, the two writers whose work determined the forms of Symbolism, Arthur Rimbaud and Stéphane Mallarmé, took their cue from the images of expansion and transcendence which occur in Baudelaire's work; the tearing of the theatrical backdrop in Mallarmé's poem 'The Clown Punished' provides one memorable instance of this desire to step beyond the limits of the world as given.

One of the key texts for these writers was Baudelaire's 'Correspondences', a sonnet which soon came to be read as an almost programmatic expression of the Symbolist sensibility. Baudelaire imagines nature as a temple whose pillars emit confused, indistinct words, while Man passes through 'forests of symbols' where 'perfumes, sounds, and colours answer each to each'.[3] The various sense-impressions have 'the infinite expansion of infinite things', enrapturing the mind and drawing the self into a momentary union with the wealth of signs which surround it. Baudelaire thus offers a fantasy in which the alienating distances of allegory are overcome through the sheer connectedness of the impressions, one sensory register overlapping and being displaced into another: perfumes are 'mellow as oboes, green as fields', and this cross-cutting of sensations (or synaesthesia) only seems incomplete when we acknowledge the remoteness of the experience. For such moments seem to take place only in recollection, and the rich fusion of images in the poem produces 'prolonged echoes which merge far away in an opaque, deep oneness'. And while the poem conjures with its plenitude of signs, the semantic force of these is undermined by an atmospheric suggestiveness which is both a theme and a condition of the writing. Already 'Correspondences' predicts the psychological (or interior) landscape of the Symbolists, the natural setting of the poem no longer an ordinary, external one, but rather a zone of the mind where objects pulse with the same inner vibration.

*   *   *

After the tense city-scapes of some of Baudelaire's other poems, 'Correspondences' might strike us as a little too hushed and reverent in tone (being in Nature really *is* like being in a temple here). As the various sense impressions cross-connect, the reader is transported as if on waves of incense to a perception of some kind of trance-like unity of mood. This would be a recurring feature of Symbolist writing and its various attempts to approximate the condition of music – at the end of the century W. B. Yeats, for example, would define the purpose of poetic rhythm as 'to prolong that moment of contemplation, when we are neither awake nor asleep'.[4] But there is another kind of visionary writing which creates what Jean-Paul Sartre calls 'an *explosive unity*'. The great representative of this mode is Arthur Rimbaud, in whose work, says Sartre,

> We are gradually made to see in a miscellaneous collection the breaking up of a prior totality whose elements, set in motion by a centrifugal force, break away from each other and fly off into space, colonizing it and there reconstituting a new unity. To see the dawn as a 'people of doves' is to blow up the morning as if it were a powder keg.[5]

Rimbaud's poetic career was itself 'explosively' brief, compressed between his fifteenth and nineteenth years (1869–73) and yielding a body of work which seemed to disappear with equal suddenness after his spectacular renunciation of poetry. During the period of his literary life, however, Rimbaud's ostentatious contempt for all forms of convention and authority, both in his behaviour and his writing, was the stuff of which innumerable myths would eventually be made.[6] Naif, anarchist, scruffy adolescent, drug-taker, drunk, homosexual, vagrant, self-proclaimed genius – Rimbaud was all these at one time or another, pushing earlier artistic bohemianism to the very limit and seeming to break through some of the self-imposed constraints of Baudelaire's work.

For while Baudelaire had sought art's independence from the didactic functions of religion and morality, he had at the same time retained a commitment to certain literary conventions, observing, for example, that 'systems of rhetoric and prosody are not arbitrarily invented forms of tyranny, but collections of rules demanded by the very structure of a man's spiritual being' (*BSW*, 306). Baudelaire's way of speaking of spiritual being as if it comprised some ascertainable 'structure' was true to his deeply engrained sense of original sin, but it was quite at odds with the young Rimbaud's way of associating the spiritual with the 'unknown' (hence, perhaps, Jacques Rivière's observation, that 'Rimbaud is the man exempt from original sin'[7]). So, while he regarded Baudelaire as unequivocally 'the first seer, king of poets, a true God', admiration did not prevent Rimbaud from concluding in a letter to Paul Demeny that 'the form which is so much praised in him is trivial. Inventions from the unknown demand new forms' (*RP*, 16). As he later put it, in *A Season in Hell* (thus formulating one of the great principles of the avant-gardes to come), 'One must be absolutely modern' (*RP*, 346), and this absoluteness of intention is understood to absolve the poet from the obligation to observe any rules at all, be they aesthetic or moral: as he explained to Demeny, the poet 'really is the thief of fire … if what he brings back from *down there* has form, he brings forth form; if it is formless, he brings forth formlessness' (*RP*, 12).

As it happened, Rimbaud's principal innovations had less to do with prosody than with syntax and imagery: only two of his poems – 'Seascape' and 'Movement' – move unmistakably toward free verse, and 'The Drunken Boat', that epitome of intoxication and 'explosive unity', is actually written in alexandrines. But Rimbaud's comment about form has two very important implications for his own work and for much that would follow: first, the idea of an 'organic' formlessness points to a writing that exploits the fantastic and unfamiliar, freely developing that vein of the hallucinatory and bizarre which had emerged intermittently in Baudelaire's work;[8] secondly, it implies that the poem may be adequate to its occasion without having a supplementary (or allegorical) significance. An early example is 'The Green Cabaret', which begins:

> Wearing out my shoes, 8th day
> On the bad roads, I got into Charleroi.
> Bread, butter, at the Green Cabaret
> And the ham half cold.[9]

The translation is by Ezra Pound, who clearly preferred this 'anecdotal' side of Rimbaud to the more ecstatic visionary perspectives of 'The Drunken Boat'. The earlier poem simply registers a mood, anchoring it in a sequence of clear perceptions and concluding with a pleasurable image which has no significance beyond itself (the maid has just brought the poet a plate of ham):

> Pink ham, white fat and a sprig
> Of garlic, and a great chope of foamy beer
> Gilt by the sun in that atmosphere.

What Rimbaud calls his 'alchemy of the word' (*RP*, 326) has the power to transmute ordinary occasions into special events, a technique learned in part from Baudelaire's cultivation of flowers from evil and sometimes leading to a deliberately coarsened subject-matter (as, for example, in Rimbaud's 'Venus Anadyomeme').

This deliberately scandalous expansion of the poetic register is typical of the energy and confidence of Rimbaud's verse. Where, for the allegorist, the lack of coincidence between self and world had stemmed from a loss of social coherence, for Rimbaud, society is to be forged anew through the medium of poetic language. The recognition of a disjunction between words and things no longer generates feelings of loss and anxiety but provides a sort of mandate for a creative destruction of the world (another paradox which was to have a long and distinguished avant-garde career). Rimbaud therefore seeks not to represent the world but to transform it, and where the allegorist tends to think in terms of opposites and contraries, Rimbaud's whole enterprise is founded on an intoxicating idea of the modern which overleaps thesis and antithesis as if to *begin* from the synthesis. This is the experience of his best-known poem, 'The Drunken Boat', where the momentum carries us ever further from familiar landmarks as 'I made my own course down the passive rivers'.[10] There is a constant shattering of the frame of vision here as vivid images crash together, seeming as out of control as the intoxicated craft of the poem:

> Thenceforward, fused in the poem, milk of stars,
> Of the sea, I coiled through deeps of cloudless green,
> Where, dimly, they come swaying down,
> Rapt and sad, singly, the drowned. ...

The 'I' tosses about, dances 'like a cork on the billows', fuses with things outside itself, and is finally satiated, 'bloated with the stagnant fumes of acrid loving – / May I split from stem to stern and founder, ah founder!'

The extremity of the poetic gesture here frees Rimbaud from the devious ironic discipline of Baudelaire's work. The poet is no longer 'double' but caught up in the shock-waves of his own 'exploding' identity. Where Baudelaire's risk-taking in the city had involved a calculated play of aloofness and surrender (he had, after all, approved Emerson's definition of the hero as 'he who is immovably centred' [*BSW*, 372]), Rimbaud seems determined to destroy the very axis of the self. The synaesthetic weave of Baudelaire's 'Correspondences' had still offered the subject a momentary stability and habitation, but when Rimbaud develops the method it is to produce a new language which 'would be of the soul, for the soul, containing everything, smells, sounds, colours; thought latching on to thought and pulling. The poet would define the amount of the unknown awakening in the universal soul in his own time' (*RP*, 13). The 'unknown' exceeds all rule-based economies and can only be grasped through a deliberate derangement of the consciously-directed self. So he writes in a letter to his teacher Izambard, which would become a canonical text of Surrealism:

> I'm lousing myself up as much as I can these days. Why? I want to be a poet, and I am working to make myself a *seer*: you won't understand this at all, and I hardly know how to explain it to you. The point is, to arrive at the unknown by the disordering of *all the senses*. The sufferings are enormous, but one has to be strong, to be born a poet, and I have discovered I *am* a poet. It is not my fault at all. It is a mistake to say: I think. One ought to say: I am thought. … *I* is someone else. So much the worse for the wood if it finds itself a violin, and contempt to the heedless who argue about something they know nothing about!   (*RP*, 6)

The idea of 'disorganizing all the senses' carries, in the French, a significant ambiguity, suggesting also that the aim is to bring disorder to meanings (*sens*). Rimbaud's poetics thus entails a systematic assault on the French ideal of clarity in the name of multiplicity and indeterminacy. The very notion of a rational discourse is thereby called into question, since poetic language is seen to originate not from a stable centre but from the point at which the boundaries of the self begin to fray, where subject and object flow into each other. The Cartesian 'I think' dissolves into the fluid condition of 'I am thought', the 'I' now a medium or conduit for images released from the unconscious and ready to undergo systematic development according to the law of their own form.

While Baudelaire's dandy could hardly escape the resentment which, according to Girard, is the inevitable product of imitative rivalry, Rimbaud's attempt to abolish 'the false meaning of *EGO*', as he put it in the letter to Demeny, was at once to sidestep the trap of passive identification and to celebrate the transformative power of the self. His famous claim that 'I is an other' encapsulates at least two complementary ideas: that I can think myself other than I am, and that I can *make* myself other than I am.[11] Almost at a stroke, Rimbaud dissolves the Baudelairean poetics of memory, putting in its place a radically discontinuous temporality in which the subject recognises itself only in the present moment of its thought ('I witness the unfolding of my own thought', he declares to Demeny). This is very different from the half-fascinated, half-anguished self-scrutiny of the Baudelairean dandy, for this moment of recognition entails for Rimbaud 'a letting go of the power to say "I"',[12] an expansive opening of the ego which projects a writing freed from the necessity of self-defence.

Rimbaud's various appeals to the 'universal soul' and the 'universal intelligence' now disclose the possibility of a utopian politics no longer bound by bourgeois modes of identification and linking the destruction of 'EGO' to a radical break with social authority. Rimbaud's poetics is, in fact, hardly intelligible without reference to the revolutionary Paris Commune of 1871 and its bloody suppression. One of the poet's flights from home (aged seventeen) took him to the capital, where he passed through the lines of the Prussians who were preparing to enter Paris. That was in February; by 13 May, one week before the government's massacre of the workers, he was writing to his teacher Georges Izambard that 'mad rage drives me towards the battle of Paris – where so many workers are still dying as I write to you! Work now? – never, never; I'm on strike' (*RP*, 6). The hostility to work speaks for an absolute refusal to compromise, associating idleness and hedonism with a rejection of Christian social values. Like Blake, Swinburne and Nietzsche, Rimbaud sees Christ as the 'eternal thief of vigour' (*RP*, 152), and his thought is permeated with anticlericalism, communism (for which he wrote a manifesto, now lost), illuminism, and, above all, with a belief that imaginative energy is the motor of revolution (see, for example, two of the poems written in May, 'Parisian War Song' and 'The Parisian Orgy'). Rimbaud's praise of idleness is, however, quite unlike the dandy's celebration of leisure, since it involves not a withdrawal into isolation but, rather, an attempt to abolish social convention in an act of subversive identification. The revolutionary poet thus finds kinship with the displaced and the marginal, with women, thieves, the poor, and with colonised peoples (in *A Season in Hell*, for example, the poet sees himself as one of 'the children of Ham' invaded by European imperialists:

'The whites are landing. The cannon! We shall have to submit to baptism, dress, and work' [*RP*, 309]).

Such categories of 'otherness' were staples of anti-Communard invective,[13] and in appropriating them as points of identification Rimbaud made the dissolution of psychic coherence part of an attack on all 'civilised' values. It is the potential of poetry for the extreme, its capacity to explode those structures whose permanence is guaranteed by common sense, which underwrites the utopian thrust of his work. The others with whom the poet aligns himself are without a history, and the present tense of 'I is an other' secures identification by shattering the linear narrative of progress. Family, religion, government, the nation, each seems life-denying as it embodies the legacy of mediocrity (of 'reason, nationality, science' [*RP*, 303]). Yet much of the power of Rimbaud's vision comes from his sense of the difficulty of realising utopia – if 'The Drunken Boat' seems to free the self from its customary social constraints, it also registers, in Bertolt Brecht's words, 'the escape of a man who cannot bear to live any longer inside the barriers of a class which – with the Crimean War, with the Mexican adventure – was then beginning to open up even the more exotic continents to its mercantile interests'.[14] 'Progress' seems inexorable, and Rimbaud's attempt to articulate the 'universal intelligence' constantly threatens to be shipwrecked on the margins, leaving the 'Leviathan' of capital intact (hence, perhaps, the pathos of the concluding stanza: 'I can no more, bathed in your langors, O waves, sail in the wake of the carriers of cottons; nor undergo the pride of the flags and the pennants; nor pull past the horrible eyes of the hulks' [*RP*, 171]).

The tone here reminds us that while the poet must in all conscience refuse any accepted social location, the alternative forms of identification he seeks with those 'outside' are always likely to lead back to the lonely egoism of the imperial self. To avoid the Baudelairean resentment which lies down that path, Rimbaud submits himself to what he regards as the only acceptable discipline, that of conceiving both life and art as unremitting acts of violence against the tedium of common sense. Perhaps his most radical idea in this regard is that the concept of genius might actually become the means of *transcending* private egotism: as art flows into life, the acts of genius might become in some new sense collective ones. As that paradox suggests, this is a politics which defines itself against any and all forms of political logic (hence Brecht's conclusion that it is 'impossible to turn Rimbaud's attitude – the attitude of the footloose vagabond who puts himself at the mercy of chance and turns his back upon society – into a model representation of a proletarian fighter').

But can a language which deliberately exceeds all social function then become the language of genuine sociality? Brecht's conclusion suggests that if Rimbaud's position is politically unserviceable it is because the poet seeks a social language which is unmediated by difference and historical particularity (as Kristin Ross observes, Rimbaud is concerned not with 'the interests of a particular class, but a half-real, half-fantastic libidinal geography of migrants displaced at the limits of class: classes that are fractured, in flight')[15]. With the exception of *A Season in Hell*, Rimbaud's work does suggest that that is the only way of thinking about poetry. The 'infernal' perspective, however, is rather different: if the poet's great aim hitherto had been to deny his past in a fantasy of self-authoring (the self claimed as its own origin), here the burden of the family seems to return: 'I am the slave of my baptism', he laments, 'Parents, you have caused my misfortune, and you have caused your own' (*RP*, 313). Just as the final stanzas of 'The Drunken Boat' suddenly switch from the infinite reaches of the ocean to the puddle in which the child launches his boat, so in *A Season in Hell* the universal scope of Rimbaud's poetics unexpectedly contracts to the confines of the individual self: 'I accustomed myself to pure hallucination,' he says dismissively, 'I ended up by regarding my mental disorder as sacred' (*RP*, 331–2).

For Rimbaud, then, the attempt to transcend 'the false meaning of EGO' had failed; to many later readers, though, his renunciation of poetry would seem less a sign of failure than a measure of the extremity of his original ambition. Certainly, his examples of 'pure hallucination' – seeing 'a mosque instead of a factory, a drummers' school consisting of angels, coaches on the roads of the sky, a drawing room at the bottom of a lake' (*RP*, 329) – remind us that there would always be writers to continue the project of 'blow[ing] up the morning', as Sartre put it, and that the dream of a transformed, unmediated social language would remain. But we shall have to wait to see the effects of Rimbaud's influence until a later chapter. In his own time, his work quickly disappeared from view. Moréas omitted him from his roll of honour in the manifesto, and it was not until the next century that his writing became widely known. (*Illuminations* did cause something of a stir in the Symbolist circle when it appeared in *La Vogue* in 1886, but *A Season in Hell* was not published until 1895, and the two famous 'visionary letters' did not become available until 1912 and 1926.)

*   *   *

Even Stéphane Mallarmé was barely aware of Rimbaud's work,[16] though he too was pledged to an art radically at odds with accepted norms and limits. Yet while Rimbaud seemed to be seeking ways of destroying the boundary between life and art, it is with Mallarmé that we discern the outlines of that 'religion' of art which would colour end-of-the-century aestheticism and provide one main spur to modernist innovation.

The shape of Mallarmé's poetics was determined in large part by the spiritual crisis which he experienced in 1866, the so-called 'nights of Tournon', which provoked both a failure of religious faith and a new discovery: 'After I had found Nothingness,' he wrote, 'I found Beauty' (*MSP*, 89–90). The reference to Nothingness may recall those images of vacancy and 'dead' space in Baudelaire and Melville, but for Mallarmé the experience of negation was to become the fundamental impulse of aesthetics as it confronts the oppressive materiality of the world.

This paradoxical connection between creation and negation – 'Destruction was my Beatrice' (*MSP*, 95), he recalled – indicates a shift in focus between Mallarmé and Baudelaire which situates the problem of meaning within the system of language rather than within an ambivalent self. In Mallarmé's work, the Baudelairean rhetoric of irony, with its dependence on forms of authorial mastery and duplicity, is displaced into something very different. 'If the poem is to be pure,' he announces, 'the poet's voice must be stilled and the initiative taken by the words themselves, which will be set in motion as they meet unequally in collision' (*MSP*, 40), a handing over of initiative which now translates irony into an arbitrariness and multiplicity of meaning which is rooted in language itself. If a certain violence was implied in the 'cold detachment' of Baudelairean irony, here the abstractive quality of language, its power to take the place of the thing it names, implies a sort of destructiveness which is also a transcendence.[17] Ambivalence is now discovered in the materials of language itself: on the one hand, the concept of the word as a substitution makes language a register of separation, of the loss of some original plenitude; on the other, the notion that language, in denying reality, triumphs over it promotes pleasure in the transgression of rules and limits.

Mallarmé and Rimbaud are, then, alike in this respect, that they both commit poetry to the supreme task of transfiguring things through this act of verbal destruction. Mallarmé's approach is cooler than Rimbaud's, however, his verse eschewing fiery apocalyptics in favour of a rigorously 'analytic' purity of response. Protracted syntactical structures are used to create a curiously weightless language which displaces the concreteness of a particular object into the set of 'musical' relations which constitute its being-in-the-world. Mallarmé explains his approach in *Variations on a Subject* (note that his prose is equally concerned with nuance and will circle a proposition until it catches precisely the shade of meaning required):

> Why should we perform the miracle by which a natural object is almost made to disappear beneath the magic waving wand of the written word, if not to divorce that object from the direct and the palpable, and so conjure up its *essence* in all purity?

> When I say: 'a flower!' then from that forgetfulness to which my voice consigns all floral form, something different from the usual calyces arises, something all music, essence, softness: the flower which is absent from all bouquets.   (*MSP*, 42)

This famous passage crystallises much of the doctrine that after 1886 would come to be known as Symbolism. According to Mallarmé, the object of art is not reality as such but the 'pure notion' which invests it. The techniques needed to evoke the 'Ideal' are therefore those of indirection and suggestiveness which Mallarmé associates with musicality. This is not merely to create some hazily grasped view of the world, but it does involve attending to something other than 'the usual calyces' – the *idea* of the flower, in short, and not a representation of it as a particular concrete thing.

A strong vein of Platonism runs through Mallarmé's poetics and places it in deliberately stark contrast to the currently competing schools of naturalism and impressionism. But he was less concerned with elaborating a systematic philosophical doctrine than with reckoning the effects of language from within.[18] So the act of 'abolishing' the real flower (the verb *abolir* figures prominently in Mallarmé's deliberately restricted lexicon) is the means of disclosing an essence located not within some external Platonic realm, but within the interstices of language itself. This is quite different from the more schematic terms of Moréas's Symbolist manifesto, with its talk of 'cloth[ing] the Idea in a perceptible form'.[19] For all the rather pompous transcendentalism of his manifesto, Moréas's understanding of language is actually very mechanical, suggesting that, as something external, the Idea can simply be represented in discourse. Mallarmé's work, however, calls into question the possibility of such a representation, dramatising instead the 'allegorical' condition of language, which condemns it to systematic but arbitrary relations. Directness of presentation is seen to be both delusory and undesirable, since only a vulgar naturalism would try to capture in writing 'the actual and palpable wood of trees' rather than the state of mind which the forest inspires (*MSP*, 40). Mallarmé thus concludes that

> The ideal is to *suggest* the object. It is the perfect use of this mystery which constitutes the symbol. An object must be gradually evoked in order to show a state of soul; or else, choose an object and from it elicit a state of soul by means of a series of decodings.   (*MSP*, 21)

Mallarmé's poetics of the 'vague and the intuitive', qualities he praises in Wagner's music (*MSP*, 75), thus entails a work of 'elimination' (*MSP*, 95) whose aim is to free language from its referential bondage to things ('Describe not the object, but the effect it produces' [*MSP*, 83]). If we compare Mallarmé's language with Baudelaire's, the effect of this objective is clear: for, as Walter Benjamin observes, 'The *Fleurs du mal* is the first book that used in poetry not only words of ordinary provenance but words of urban origin as well.'[20] Baudelaire thus introduced into lyric poetry a vocabulary which was both distinctly modern and, by academic standards of the time, 'non-poetic'. We might say that he thus rendered the language of lyric 'impure', displacing the unified modality of the poet's voice by a clash of different social accents. Mallarmé's desire to 'hand over' to language works to a very different end and is oriented towards a writing which abolishes voice and idiom in 'pure poetry'.[21]

Once again, there is a kind of irony in his approach to language, for the allegorical quality gives it the character of a 'fallen' medium, which means in turn that the poet is somehow always doomed to failure:

Languages are imperfect because multiple; the supreme language is missing. Inasmuch as thought consists of writing without pen and paper, without the sound of the immortal Word, the diversity of languages on earth means that no one can utter words which would bear the miraculous stamp of Truth Herself Incarnate. (*MSP*, 38)

Words, then, do not offer a transparent passage to referents outside language; there is no 'immaculate language' (*MSP*, 10) unspotted by human particularity and its interests. Of course, the dream of an unmediated relation between the sign and what it signifies has never ceased to fascinate Western cultures, and Mallarmé certainly inherits that fascination, directing all his labours to the production of the unique Book ('I am convinced there is only One' [*MSP*,15]), whose language will be absolutely 'virginal' in this sense (*MSP*, 27). Yet at the same time he realises that such a project is doomed to failure, since the 'supreme' language will always be lacking. It is in this space between hope and failure that his work is situated: 'let us remember that if our dream were fulfilled, *verse would not exist* – verse which, in all its wisdom, atones for the sins of language, comes nobly to their aid' (*MSP*, 38).

Poetry, then, provides a kind of compensation for the arbitrariness of language, for the perverseness which makes the word for 'day' (*jour*) sound 'dark', while the word for night (*nuit*) sounds 'light' (*MSP*, 38). Mallarmé's poems seek to create not a new *language*, but a particular web of words which will gesture toward the Absolute while at the same time acknowledging the 'fallen' language which makes poetry's existence necessary.[22] As he puts it at the end of *Variations on a Subject*:

Out of a number of words, poetry fashions a single new word which is total in itself and foreign to the language – a kind of incantation. Thus the desired isolation of language is effected; and chance (which might still have governed these elements, despite their artful and alternating renewal through meaning and sound) is thereby instantly and thoroughly abolished. (*MSP*, 43)

The *words* of the poem thus offer some hope of transcending for a moment the accidental and unmotivated production of meaning that characterises *language* as a system; this opposition between poetic words and language runs through Mallarmé's theory.

Mallarmé's poetics thus calls for 'the discarding of the spoken word' and the cultivation of 'that part of speech which is not spoken' (*MSP*, 32, 33), for speech is imbricated with a social world which seems to him to operate according to purely economic laws. 'Speech is no more than a commercial approach to reality' (*MSP*, 40) and 'Language, in the hands of the mob, leads to the same facility and directness as does money' (*MSP*, 42–3). A social language might be marked by 'a criss-crossing of differently oriented social accents',[23] but it is precisely this *traffic* in the word which is so offensive to Mallarmé. If 'the artist must separate and remain an aristocrat' (*MSP*, 12), then entanglement in the language of others will trap him in all the old pitfalls of imitative desire (the whole thrust of Mallarmé's poetics is against the recognition later expressed by Bakhtin, that 'The word in language is half someone else's'[24]). It may be surprising to find speech, which is so damagingly mired in the specificity of idiom and dialect, being compared to the pure abstraction which is money, but what Mallarmé means is that in the pragmatic context of use and exchange, words are degraded into univocal counters which seem merely transparent vehicles for meaning.

Mallarmé's counter-move is to create in his writing a syntactic opacity which will abolish any dream of one-to-one referentiality. 'Our principal aim', he says, 'should be to make the words of a poem self-mirroring' (*MSP*, 93), a comment which implies that the texture of the poem will acknowledge the arbitrary interconnections which structure the linguistic system as a whole: 'for every sound, there is an echo' (*MSP*, 41), and when the poet hands over the initiative to words, 'in an exchange of gleams they will flame out like some glittering swath of fire sweeping over precious stones, and thus replace the audible breathing in lyric poetry of old – replace the poet's own personal and passionate control of verse' (*MSP*, 40–41). Meaning, Mallarmé implies, derives not from some authorial intention prior to the writing of the poem (that is an obvious illusion of 'speech'), but from the differences between the words themselves.

It is tempting, perhaps, to see in such a poetics a prefiguring of the momentously influential theory of the Swiss linguist Ferdinand de Saussure. In his *Course in General Linguistics* (1916) Saussure would conclude rather similarly that 'in a language there are only differences, and no positive terms'.[25] So, 'The idea or phonic substance that a sign contains is of less importance than the other signs that surround it.'[26] Saussure, however, attends almost completely to the linguistic *system* (*langue*) rather than to the act of expression (*parole*) which embodies part of the system in a particular utterance. The result of this emphasis is to cast intensive light on the arbitrary relation of signifier (or acoustic image) to signified (concept), but at the same time to ignore questions about meaning as a product of social interaction.[27] Mallarmé also wants to detach the word from its relation to particular speakers, but, as we have seen, he looks to poetry for some sort of compensation for the purely functional and abstract system of differences which Saussure later describes.

We can illustrate this by looking at one of Mallarmé's best-known sonnets, 'The virginal, living, and beautiful day'.[28] The poem evokes a symbolic winter landscape in which a swan is trapped in a frozen lake. The bird stands for the poet, conventionally enough, and its sorry plight is the occasion for feelings which range from impotence and failure, on the one hand, to stoic idealism and *hauteur*, on the other. The swan's exile, which Mallarmé describes as 'useless' (just as poetry must henceforth be 'useless'), represents the 'sterile winter' of an art which is pledged to the Absolute. The swan is condemned to the icy prison by his 'pure brilliance', a 'brilliance' for which a high price must be paid: for his exile is from a 'country to live in', which is why the unanswered question that opens the poem allows us to glimpse the possibility that a new and 'living' day might tear the surface of the frozen lake. But in contrast to Baudelaire's Swan, who is exiled in the modern city, Mallarmé's bird is caught fast in language, its feet clamped to the earth while 'its cold dream of contempt' signals its refusal to forget transcendence. On one level, the poem articulates a familiar Mallarméan theme: the poet yearns to free himself from the material world, to achieve absolute purity, but his art will be lifeless if he does so. At the same time, the poem is intensely self-reflexive and, in its *tour de force* rhyme scheme (a strangely empty ligature of 'i' sounds), seems to foreground the differential production of meaning while also giving the words a materiality which is not simply reducible to meaning: words seem to encode each other – *givre/ivre*, *agonie/nie* – forging links which seem necessary but which, like the symbol itself, are so only for the duration of this particular poem.

Mallarmé, then, like his stoic Swan, cannot extricate himself from language and its attendant difficulties; if he could, we would have pure transcendence – death, the sterile iciness of the Absolute – and not those compromised forms we call art. Art, though, comes into being as part of the struggle against language and the invariant rules by which it functions, and just as Mallarmé concerns himself with 'that part of speech which is not spoken', so the construction of a poem should yield a heightened sense of those aspects of language which cannot be reduced to arbitrary equivalences and oppositions. Something else emerges in the poem, rather as if (to take Freud's terms *avant la lettre*) Mallarmé is seeking to articulate the polymorphous play of the pleasure principle before the reality principle intervenes to bind it. But, of course, we cannot fully recover that original state and it remains a possibility to be glimpsed within the necessary ordering forms of discourse. Hence Mallarmé's interest in *relations* rather than in objects themselves, in patterns and forms which cannot be accounted for simply in terms of meaning:

> To create is to conceive an object in its fleeting moment, in its absence. … We conjure up a scene of lovely, evanescent, intersecting forms. We recognize the entire and binding arabesque thus formed as it leaps dizzily in terror or plays disquieting chords; or, through a sudden digression (by no means disconcerting), we are warned of its likeness unto itself even as it hides.   (*MSP*, 48–9)

The motifs of movement, femininity, and sexuality which permeate Mallarmé's work articulate this 'arabesque' of desire which runs through the words, giving language structure even as it strives to exceed its constraints. His favourite figure for this effect is the motion of the dancer:

> the ballerina *is not a girl dancing*; considering the juxtaposition of those group motifs, *she is not a girl*, but rather a metaphor which symbolizes some elemental aspect of earthly form: sword, cup, flower, etc., and *she does not dance* but rather, with miraculous lunges and abbreviations, with a bodily writing [*une écriture corporelle*], she suggests things which the written work could express only in several paragraphs of dialogue or descriptive prose. Her poem is written without the writer's tools.   (*MSP*, 62; translation modified)

While Baudelaire's beggar girl was an object to be gazed at from a distance, Mallarmé's dancer seems to trace a figure which is somehow within language but not completely assimilable to it (it is 'bodily writing'). There is a kind of double articulation at work: first, the dancer is disembodied as metaphor, with her gestures coded as signs; then we find that the 'bodily writing' is partly external to language. On one level, this dance is emblematic of the power of Mallarméan syntax (its 'musicality'), but the real force of the example derives from the insistence that the 'figure' of the dance creates a space which is within but not reducible to the regulated spacing of language.

Mallarmé's late poem *A Throw of the Dice* (1897), a fragment of his never-completed *magnum opus*, the Book, pursued these implications in a more extreme way, experimenting with typographical space and layout. The poem opens once again Mallarmé's protracted meditation on language and chance: here a shipmaster has to decide whether to throw the dice which, in yielding a definite number, will overcome chance and the chaos of the raging sea. But the act of throwing the dice depends upon chance ('Any Thought utters a Dice Throw'[29]) and the knowledge that the ship must perish is mitigated only by the appearance of a constellation whose stars seem to be imaged in the lapidary words strung out across the white space of Mallarmé's pages. *A Throw of the Dice* would predict many of the discoveries of later avant-garde writing, with its 'simultaneous vision of the Page' and its 'scoring' of 'prismatic subdivisions of the Idea'.[30] Yet while the poem already implied a modernist aesthetic of fragmentation and discontinuity, its principal achievement was to crystallise a negative poetics which would continue to reverberate in the work of writers as diverse as Valéry, Ungaretti, Reverdy, Kafka and Beckett. Here Baudelairean irony, with its dependence on forms of authorial mastery and duplicity, was dissolved in a particular conception of a writing without purpose, in a poetry whose power, as Maurice Blanchot puts it, 'lies in its not being, whose very glory is to evoke, in its own absence, the absence of everything. The language of the unreal, this fictive language which delivers us to fiction, comes from silence and returns to silence.'[31] Mallarmé's negative poetics already contained a challenge to some of the more metaphysical and celebratory forms of modernism to come, but it would take time for that to become clear, partly because, as we shall see in the next chapter, Mallarmé's contemporaries were intent on reading his work as the very epitome of literary 'decadence'.

3

Decadence and the Art of Death

Mallarmé's importance to writers in the last two decades of the nineteenth century can hardly be overestimated – in fact the literary history of that period might be written in terms of the various twists and distortions given to his poetic theory. One reason for his centrality was precisely that his work made itself available to such a range of appropriations. There was, for example, the Symbolist Mallarmé, whose opposition to 'teaching, declamation, false sensibility, [and] objective description' Moréas had invoked in his manifesto; but there was also the more hermetic, not to say precious Mallarmé, the Master presiding over those exclusive Tuesday salons where disciples debated his hyper-refined aesthetic in hushed and reverent tones. As the *fin de siècle* approached, French culture became obsessed with this second image of the writer as epitomising the *decadence* of the modern period. Concepts of Symbolism and decadence now began to flow together, becoming inextricably confused by the beginning of the new century. Fundamental to each was a complex idea of 'refinement' which brought to one focus the social and aesthetic entailments of 'style'.

The work of another poet, so far mentioned only in passing, was to play a special role in the invention of literary decadence. Paul Verlaine, widely known because of his scandalous liaison with Rimbaud, was in all respects a less hermetic figure than Mallarmé, developing a verse which was to be much celebrated for its limpidity and musicality. His early work was loosely associated with that of the 'Parnassian' group, whose members included Leconte de Lisle and José-Maria de Heredia and whose main commitment was to an anti-Romantic objectivity and impersonality. Gautier's collection *Enamels and Cameos* (1852), with its sculptural ideal of poetic expression, was a principal influence for these writers, and a poem like Leconte de Lisle's famous 'Noon' is representative of the Parnassian preoccupation with hard-edged pictorial presentation.[1]

Verlaine shared the group's interest in questions of rhythm, but his own work quickly moved toward a form of poetic impressionism, with early collections like *Saturnian Poems* (1866) and *Gallant Festivals* (1869) using pastoral convention to capture the intricacies of shifting moods.

In these early poems, the world of stylised play, of Pierrot and Harlequin, is also a world of artifice and pretence where all is 'fleeting and contingent', to borrow Baudelaire's phrase. In 'Moonlight', for example, the soul of the beloved is said to be like a 'painter's landscape' in which 'charming masks in shepherd's mummeries / are playing lutes'.[2] But the players are also 'Sad in their fantastic guise' and the instability of the mood is reflected in the impressionistic play of light and colour which invests the landscape. We are left with a characteristically ornamental image which recalls the stylised pastorals of Watteau: 'among the statues...the jets of slender fountains sob with ecstasy'. Most striking, perhaps, is the sense of slightness and frailty which attaches to the human presence in such poems – in 'Moonlight', for example, the wraithlike *Commedia dell'Arte* figures who take part in the masque 'do not seem to believe in their good fortune', with the implication that they can never be more than the pawns of fate. The lightness of the form and its connections with popular song almost conceal the doubt that lies beneath the formal patterning – for Verlaine's haunting musicality seems to imply that the act of singing, or writing, is always a repression of a deeper sadness and anxiety. The characteristic edginess beneath the languorous swoon reminds us, however, that such repression can only ever be partial, that art cannot abolish this melancholy but only defer it through a calculated play and indeterminacy of tone.

The mood of such poems is close to Baudelairean *ennui*, but along with melancholy and hypersensitivity Verlaine also places a particular emphasis on the passivity of the poetic sensibility. In 'Muted', for example, the tone is initially one of celebration ('Let us join our souls, our senses, / and our hearts in ecstasies'), but a warning note sounds in the next stanza with the reference to 'the uncertain languishments / of the pines and strawberry-trees'. The languorous attitude is, we now realise, a consciously adopted one, and what at first sight seems like mere self-indulgence turns out to be a means of keeping something ominous at bay. 'Let's convince ourselves', begins the fourth stanza, and the reader quickly concludes that it is the reality of the poem's world which is at issue. In the final lines we are left with the song of the nightingale, 'the voice

of our despair' and the epitome of a tremulousness of tone which is
so characteristic of Verlaine's early work. For it is ultimately not so
much a matter of pessimism here as of the self's constant *vulnerability* to change, to the future and to mortality. The shimmering sterility of these landscapes is thus a sort of fragile defence against
experience, offering (as one critic puts it) 'safeness and protection
from catastrophes of desire'.[3] As the fountains 'sob' we know that
such defences will finally prove inadequate, but Verlaine's fatalism
is leavened by a conviction that an ever greater refinement and
artifice might postpone that awful moment.

* * *

It was the paradoxical nature of that 'refinement' which defined the
decadent mood, for art now toyed self-consciously with the possibility of its own extinction, as the desire for an ever more intensive
artificiality compelled expression away from the organic towards
the sterile and inanimate. In his later poems, Verlaine reached out
for religious faith, but as he did so he also produced a highly
influential weaving together of Symbolist and decadent styles. Two
of the poems from *Of Old and Late* (1884) assumed a sort of programmatic significance in this respect. Although the first of these,
'The Art of Poetry', had actually been written as early as 1874, and
while Verlaine urged his contemporaries not to read it as a statement of 'theory',[4] the poem had an almost aphoristic quality which
made it hard not to construe it as a manifesto:

> You must have music first of all,
> and for that a rhythm uneven is best,
> vague in the air and soluble,
> with nothing heavy and nothing at rest.

Suggestiveness, nuance, an 'uneven', partly accentual rhythm –
Verlaine's poem presented these qualities as the antitheses of metrical conformity and rhetoric ('Take eloquence and wring its neck!').
It was 'music' or nothing; for 'all the rest is literature', as Verlaine
put it in his final line. The contemptuous rejection of 'official' litera-

ture was a recognisable anti-bourgeois gesture, but, as we see from the second poem in the collection, 'Apathy', the avant-garde alternative was now hailed for its decadent quality:

I am the Empire in its *décadence*
watching the tall blond Norsemen march, meanwhile
writing indolently, with a golden style,
acrostics where the sunlight's languours dance.

The main elements in these lines – the association of contemporary culture with that of the declining Roman Empire, the disengaged indolence of the writer's pose and the refined formalism of his style (the poem now imagined as a set of acrostics) – also featured in Gautier's 'Notice' to the 1868 edition of Baudelaire's poems. That edition would remain the only popular one in circulation until 1917, so Gautier's essay quickly took on the status of a manifesto of decadent writing.[5] It is, of course, a particular Baudelaire who is presented here, a decadent one whose 'art ... has reached the extreme point of maturity which marks the setting of ancient civilisations'.[6] The result is 'an ingenious, complex, learned style, full of shades and refinements of meaning, ever extending the language, borrowing from every technical vocabulary, taking colours from every palette and notes from every keyboard' (39–40).

Decadence, Gautier suggests, expresses the inner logic of a modernity which has reached the terminal point in a cultural parabola already traced by the ancient civilisations. Like them, the modern period has exhausted itself in the search for ever greater sophistication and intensity of experience. The new artistic styles which have appeared therefore aim, like their decadent precursors, at impossible horizons and are condemned to endless disappointment:

This decadent style is the final expression of the Word which is called upon to express everything, and which is worked for all it is worth. In connection with this style may be recalled the speech of the Lower Empire, that was already veined with the greenish streaking of decomposition, and the complex refinement of the Byzantine school, the ultimate form of decadent Greek art. Such, however, is the necessary, the inevitable speech [*idiome*] of nations and civilisations when fictitious life has taken the place of natural life and developed in man wants till then unknown. (40)

'Refinement' is not only complex but excessive, and speech itself starts to become strained and corrupt as man's desires exceed the norms of nature. Gautier understands the decadent style not as just one style among many, but as the expression of a deeper logic in all cultural production: for in so far as the arts seem to develop towards ever greater formal complexity, so style is at once supplementary – it adds nuance and detail to its object – and destructive – it 'decomposes' the matter upon which it 'works'. Not fortuitously, such a style thus proves to inhabit the same contradictory space as the feminine, twinning ornament with mortality.[7] In a decadent period, Gautier suggests, death and corruption will find their true home in the domain of such an aesthetic.

*   *   *

By 1884, when Verlaine's collection of poems appeared, this set of ideas had acquired a sharper edge. Allusions to the fall of the Roman Empire and the rise of the barbarian races took on a special resonance in the wake of France's humiliation at Sedan in 1870; the Prussians, it seemed, had put an end to France's vision of itself as the Great Nation.[8] That failure of national muscle was reflected in the private sphere by a growing sense of individual frailty and illness. Gautier, for example, said of himself and the Goncourt brothers that 'we are sick men, decadents', and Zola spoke in similar tones, for his generation, when he claimed that 'We are sick, that is for certain, made sick by progress.'[9] Modernity was now imagined as a kind of disease whose ravages, felt equally in aesthetic, moral, and psychological realms, were attributable to a general malady often called 'Americanisation'. Baudelaire had already used that word in his account of America as a 'vast prison house' for Poe (*BSW*, 163), and elsewhere he spoke of 'the period we shall next be entering, of which the beginning is marked by the supremacy of America and industry'.[10] If London had previously supplied the admonitory symbol of capitalist progress, now the rapidly industrialising United States seemed the epitome of vulgar modern commercialism. In the notes for his last, unfinished novel, *Bouvard and Pécuchet* (1881), Flaubert had the pessimist Pécuchet envision the future: 'Barbarity caused by excessive individualism and ravings of science. ...There will be no more ideal, religion, morality. America will have conquered the world.'[11]

Pécuchet's words catch perfectly the pessimistic tone which came to permeate *fin de siècle* writing. Once decadence had been named as a leading artistic tendency – first by Maurice Barrès in 1883[12] – the fashionable pose quickly became one of melancholy disengagement. By April 1886, just months before the publication of Moréas's Symbolist manifesto, one Anatole Baju launched a new magazine called *Le Décadent*, whose front page declared unequivocally that:

Society is disintegrating under the corrosive action of a decaying civilization.

Modern man is *blasé* about it.

Refinement of appetites, sensations, taste, luxury; pleasures; neurosis, hysteria, hypnotism, morphine addiction, scientific quackery, excessive Schopenhauerism, these are the symptoms of social evolution.[13]

Baju's 'movement' would have a predictably short life (by 1889 it had disappeared), but it did show how easy it was to vulgarise the more sensational aspects of Baudelaire's aesthetic philosophy. For example, Baju now saw the dandification of modern writing not as a necessary response to particular social conditions but as simply a way of enforcing a snobbish dislike of the popular: 'To escape from democratic pollution', he declared, 'art will increasingly refine itself, will become daily more subtle, impalpable, and will end by being the exclusive prerogative of the aristocracy and the literati.'[14]

As Baju indicated in his manifesto statement, the 'exotic virus of the melancholico-pessimo-naturalism' which defined decadentism had a strong debt to the work of Arthur Schopenhauer. The author of the monumental *The World as Will and Idea* (1819), Schopenhauer had in fact become known in Germany only after the publication of a series of essays, *Parerga and Parilopomena* (1851). His writings offered a strong repudiation of Hegelian idealism, putting in its place a bleak vision of a universe lacking sense and logic, motivated by a blind force – the Will – which parallels the human appetites: 'what boundless egotism is to be found in almost every human breast, associated in most cases with an accumulated store of hatred and malice'.[15] Schopenhauer proposed only two ways of overcoming the negative thrust of the Will: by a kind of Buddhist renunciation of the world which would extinguish the Will, and by artistic creation, which had the power to transform Will to Idea.

Schopenhauer's philosophy became common intellectual currency in France during the 1870s, though in predictably simplified form. Both decadents and Symbolists could draw on this set of ideas, the first for its mordant pessimism, the second for its promise of a resurgent idealism. The opening sentence of *The World as Will and Idea* offered, in fact, a definitive statement of the Symbolist creed: 'The world is my representation [*Vorstellung*]', wrote Schopenhauer, thus providing a simple and talismanic expression of his view that 'everything that exists for knowledge, and hence the whole of this world, is only object in relation to the subject, perception of the perceiver, in a word, representation'.[16] Here was powerful confirmation of the Symbolist concept of art as the disinterested contemplation of pure forms (a conception which in many respects derived from a misunderstanding of the Platonic dimension of Mallarmé's theory):

> We *lose* ourselves entirely in this [aesthetic] object ...; in other words, we forget our individuality, our will, and continue to exist only as pure subject, as clear mirror of the object ... and thus we are no longer able to separate the perceiver from the perception, but the two have become one. (I, 178)

It thus lies in the power of genius to 'discard entirely our own personality for a time, in order to remain *pure knowing subject*, the clear eye of the world' (I, 186). This dream of a perfectly transparent self was a fairly staple element of Romantic fantasy (Emerson, for example, spoke in similar terms of the self as a 'transparent eyeball', the conduit for 'currents of Universal Being'[17]), but Schopenhauer added to the theme an element of asceticism and renunciation which fired the decadent imagination. As the century moved towards its close, literature was dominated increasingly by tropes of withdrawal from the world and by extreme attempts to recover a lost spirituality in the realm of the aesthetic.

In line with what has already been said about the disappearance of a social language, it is perhaps not surprising to find that for decadents and Symbolists alike, music came to stand as the ideal form of 'disinterested' expressivity. Here again Mallarmé's influential poetics seemed to find philosophical confirmation in the work of Schopenhauer, for whom

> music is by no means like the other arts, namely a copy of the Ideas, but a *copy of the will itself*, the objectivity of which are the Ideas. For this reason the effect of music is so very much more powerful and penetrating than is that of the other arts, for these others speak only of the shadow, but music of the essence.   (I, 257)

In this version of Plato's shadow and essence, music offers freedom from imitation, since it expresses 'only the inner nature, the in-itself, of every phenomenon' (I, 261). As a figure for poetic form, such musicality also encodes a social purpose which coincides with the trope of artistic withdrawal – on the wings of a 'pure' music the artist may apparently escape the bonds of mimetic desire and ascend to a vision of genuinely original intensity.

These transcendental associations made music a suggestive model not only for poetry but for the other arts as well, a development which focused interest on ways of fusing the different media at the same time as it expressed a strongly hierarchical view of the relative status of the arts (in this circle, fiction tended to be denigrated as naturalistic and mimetic). Central to the elaboration of this aesthetic was the music of Wagner, which became the object of cultic fascination in France between 1885 and 1888. The brevity and intensity of this enthusiasm (Symbolist taste would soon favour the very different music of Debussy) corresponded to the life-span of the *Revue wagnérienne*, a magazine founded by Téodor de Wyzewa, Houston Stewart Chamberlain and Éduard Dujardin. The *Revue* was a tireless promoter of Wagner's ideas, providing translations of key texts, like the 1870 essay on Beethoven, and placing the composer at the centre of the French literary avant-garde. The *Revue* was also successful in recasting Wagnerian themes in Symbolist format – Wyzewa, says one critic, was always keen 'to cut Wagner to fit Mallarmé's suits'[18] – and at a time when, for po'·ical reasons, the composer's work could be heard in concert ʰ   ᵗʰᵉ French stage,[19] the appropriation of his music for liᶠ could proceed largely unhindered.

The main starting-point for French Wagnerism ᵗ the *Gesamtkunstwerk*, the total or synthetic work c theory of the music-drama was based. This idea ᵗ various arts in one great Work was a constant point of reference for the Symbolists, though, with the exception of Mallarmé, none of them was prepared to reckon with the logic of Wagner's thought, for which all the arts (including poetry) were fundamentally inferior to the music-drama. Wyzewa and his circle quickly blurred the edges of that logic, accenting the Schopenhauerian elements in Wagner's theory to produce the new slogan that all the arts must become 'musical'. Wagner thus became the focusing point for ideas which had already had some currency: Baudelaire quoted the composer to the effect that 'the most complete work of any poet ought to be the one that, in its ultimate form, was a perfect music' (*BSW*, 339), and, in England, Walter Pater argued along similar lines that 'All art constantly aspires towards the condition of music.'[20] What was really at issue here was not the complex 'musicality' of Mallarmé's theory, which was fundamentally hostile to sound-values and recitation,[21] but a conception of music as a register of emotional intensity, a convergence of extreme pitches of feeling, as in the tremendous finale of Wagner's *Tristan and Isolde* (first performed in France in 1865). Disregarding Wagner's view that 'the union of Music and Poetry must…always end in…a subordination of the latter',[22] the French Symbolists thus began to take over aspects of his theory to support their own conception of 'musical' language.

The original concept of the music-drama now began a strange mutation, with the *Revue wagnérienne* proposing the quite un-Wagnerian idea that 'a drama which is read will appear, to sensitive souls, more real, more living than the same drama acted in a theatre by living actors'.[23] Wyzewa's comment was actually more in line with Mallarmé's influential account of *Hamlet* as the prototype of what would become, in the hands of Villiers de l'Isle-Adam and Maurice Maeterlinck, the Symbolist theatre, 'the theatre of the mind alone' (*MSP*, 59). Mallarmé was keen to have theatre abandon its stage props and external devices, and along with this he envisaged a shift of focus from the mimetic forms of social dialogue to the metaphysical possibilities of monologue. In a later piece on *Hamlet* (1896), he explained that 'The play is the high point of the theater and, in Shakespeare's work, it lies halfway between the old multiple-action method and the Monologue, the drama of the Self, which belongs to the future' (*MSP*, 139). Mallarmé thus grasped the idea of music-drama as a means of creating a dematerialised tre – as he put it in his essay on Wagner:

Now that Music has been added, everything is completely
changed. The central principle of the old Theater has been anni-
hilated. Now stage performance has become strictly allegorical,
empty, abstract, impersonal; now, in order to rise up and resemble
truth, it must be revived in the life-giving breath poured out by
Music. (*MSP*, 74)

Poetry and drama certainly began to move closer together here,
though the hermetic emphasis in Mallarmé's theory was quite at
odds with the political intentions of Wagnerian opera. We may note
too how Mallarmé emphasised the 'impersonal' character of the
drama of the future – Wagner had remarked in his essay on
Beethoven that 'a drama does not depict human characters, but lets
them display their immediate selves',[24] and the evolving Symbolist
theatre connected the great spectacle of the Wagnerian *Liebestod* with
a formal rejection of representation and the drama of 'psychology'.

* * *

The preoccupation with the impersonal work of art as also the end
of Art was closely bound up with the theme of the embattled sensibility choosing death rather than compromise with the forces of
nature and modernity. The quintessential Symbolist drama in this
respect was Villiers de l'Isle-Adam's *Axël* (1890). Villiers had been
born an aristocrat but in his later years had been reduced to a life of
grinding poverty. His short stories, collected in *Cruel Tales* (1883),
display a taste for Romantic horror, complemented at times by a
mordant wit and scepticism, often directed at the world of 'industrial literature' which Villiers had been forced to enter.[25] *Axël*, his
last, unfinished play, offers a monumental statement of aristocratic
stoicism and worldly abnegation. Like his hero Wagner ('a genius
such as appears on earth once every thousand years'[26]), Villiers saw
himself writing for a theatre which had yet to come into existence,
but for Villiers this would be a 'metaphysical' theatre which would
spurn the conventions of the popular stage (hence his satirical
account of Eugène Scribe's theatre in the story called 'The Glory
Machine').

The technique of *Axël* was predictably uncompromising in its degree of stylisation, shifting between scenes of almost impossible symbolic intensity and passages of philosophical debate (the whole of the second Act, for example) which impose an intolerable burden even when the play is read privately. Seeing the first performance of *Axël* in Paris in 1894, W. B. Yeats caught its appeal to the contemporary imagination: Villiers, he observed, had 'created persons from whom has fallen all even of personal characteristic except a thirst for that hour when all things shall pass away like a cloud, and a pride like that of the Magi following their star over many mountains'.[27] This ideal of 'passing away' brought together the Symbolist and decadent strands of the period in a climactic denial of life. Villiers's occultism made the act of renunciation one of triumph, and each of the four Acts of the play centres around a refusal of temptation. In the first, Sara rejects the monastic life; in the second, Axël (her distant cousin) rejects the worldly life, only to turn aside from the ascetic way in the third; the climactic fourth Act brings Sara and Axël together, offering the temptation of hidden treasure and illicit sexual pleasure.

Echoes of Wagner abound: the theme of gold and love recalls *The Rhinegold*, which Villiers had seen in Munich in 1869; Axël and Sara are related, like Siegmund and Sieglinde in *The Valkyrie*; and, most obviously, the suicide which ends the play has a debt to the lovers' deaths in *Tristan and Isolde*.[28] But where Wagner's *Liebestod* is the tragic outcome of individual fates, Villiers meant the symbolic renunciation in his final Act to signify a repudiation of life itself. The complexity of the decadent tone is marked here: for while the ending of the play gives monumental expression to the absurdity of existence, the lyricism which, in the final lines, presents the 'hum of life' which the lovers are leaving behind seems fundamentally ambivalent. The choice of 'the Supreme Option' may affirm aristocratic distinction from the 'million unimportant people' and from the worldly and corrupt Commander ('a man of today'), but there is a sense, too, in which Axël's idealism is murderous, as negative in its way as the alternative options of wealth and seclusion which he has already rejected.

The refusal of life is a posture, as extreme and absurd as the artifice with which it is associated (Yeats remarked that, in the wake of *Axël*, 'The Latin Quarter had become virtuous, and notorious young women talked of their virginity'[29]). The absurdity of Villiers's play is, however, deadly serious: when Axël declares 'As

for living? Our servants will do that for us,' there is the sense too
that the nobility can now be noble *only* in death. 'Lost between
dream and life', Sara and Axël are the last representatives of their
line, and their final 'triumph' is at once ascetic and hedonistic. The
paradox here is the product of the tendencies examined in my previous two chapters: as art becomes more self-consciously anti-
social, so it is driven to adopt ever more extreme forms of artifice to
secure its own autonomy. Yet, as was clear from Baudelaire's
concept of the dandy, cruelty displayed towards nature and the
(social) body also entails cruelty towards the self and the 'aesthetic'
mutilation of what it shares with others. The only pleasure that
remains is to contemplate the horizon which spells the end of all
pleasure, and *fin de siècle* art shares with the baroque a preoccupation with death and decay which manifests itself in a stylistic extravagance and morbid excess of the aesthetic.

This art denigrates life and the body but at the same time,
vampire-like, it seems to appropriate human energies for itself, becoming monumental in just the proportion that its protagonists are
drained of energy and life.[30] Style is now associated with an inward
turn which signifies both aristocratic renunciation and a desperate
sense of exile to a claustrophobic and interiorised world. The motif
of the hot-house, which is everywhere in the writing of this period
– for example, in Zola's *The Kill* (1872), Joris-Karl Huysmans's
Against Nature (1884) and Maurice Maeterlinck's collection of
poems called *Hot-houses* (1889) – combines artifice and luxuriance
with this sense of suffocating richness. And the hot-house is not
simply the place of languorous sensuality: in decadent writing
artifice is increasingly wedded to cruelty, and the dandy's cultivation of tropical plants 'like hospital patients inside the glass walls of
their conservatory wards'[31] provides a 'sickly' reminder of the cor-
ruptness of sensual existence along with a notion of the 'perverse'
intelligence which nourishes itself upon them. In *Against Nature*, for
example, the unnaturalness of the blooms hints at a corruption of
the flesh which Huysmans persistently links to the virus of syphilis
which infects his hero, Des Esseintes. This artificial garden is a
scene of pain and degeneracy, a symbolic site which will receive
consummately horrific treatment in Octave Mirbeau's *The Torture
Garden* (1898).

These are not isolated cases of aesthetic violence, for the decadent
literature of this period, in France and in England, is nourished on
the legacy of the Marquis de Sade, whose work was appearing in

new editions during the 1880s. Swinburne, for example, was well-known in France for his fascination with the 'English vice', and the fiction of writers such as Jean Lorrain, Rachilde, Joséphin Péladan and Pierre Louÿs gluts itself on dreams of torture, destruction and sexual cruelty. In part this was a product of erotic fantasies of domination and transgression which reflected the fading claims to 'aristocratic' status of a now mundanely bourgeois literary elite. At the same time, though, the relentless misogyny of these texts – a misogyny ill-concealed by fantasies of female dominance and lesbian freedoms – was closely bound up with an anguished repudiation of the body and erotic desire. Everywhere in the literature and visual art of the period there is the association of women with death, and of erotic desire with murderous instincts.[32] Art becomes a form of morbid machination, mesmerised by the idea of a 'pure' intelligence freed from the bondage of bodily desire. In Gabriele D'Annunzio's *The Triumph of Death* (1894), for example, the hero Giorgio is obsessed with the possibility of 'detaching the individual will which confined him within the narrow prison of his personality, and kept him in perpetual subjection to the base elements of his fleshly substance'.[33] The intelligence in these works is characterised by its 'cruel lucidity' (289), by its truly Sadean way of making instrumental rationality the foundation of the aesthetic enterprise, so that Huysmans's Des Esseintes is forever 'experimenting' on other people, testing their susceptibility to corruption, while D'Annunzio's Giorgio undertakes the 'transformation, so intoxicating to a lover of intellect – the metamorphosis of the woman he loves to his own image' (141).

All of this would be merely material for the pathologist had it not had such a significant impact on conceptions of the aesthetic. Nowhere is that clearer than in the case of the most famous book of the period, Huysmans's *Against Nature*, that 'breviary of decadence', as Arthur Symons called it, and the 'poisonous book' which seduced Oscar Wilde's Dorian Gray. Here the pursuit of artifice is complicit with a violent rejection of sociality, and much of Huysmans's novel details Des Esseintes's project of 'hiding away far from human society, of shutting himself up in some snug retreat, of deadening the thunderous din of life's inexorable activity' (23). The elaborate construction of Des Esseintes's 'retreat' reflects the nineteenth-century preoccupation with privileged spaces and ideal interiors (the prototype is perhaps Poe's curious essay on 'The Philosophy of

Furniture'). Des Esseintes aims to turn his life into art by surrounding himself with artefacts from a remote past. The perfectly tuned ambience will thus free him from both the weight of objective history and the exigencies of the present – 'Travel, indeed, struck him as being a waste of time, since he believed that the imagination could provide a more-than-adequate substitute for the vulgar reality of actual experience' (35). This self-reflecting imagination is replicated in the decor Des Esseintes chooses for his retreat. In true Baudelairean style, everything 'corresponds' to everything else in a riot of synaesthesia, but these correspondences are now determined by personal needs and not by an order exteriorised in language or in reality. What, for Baudelaire and Rimbaud, had been a means of exploring experience now works to paralyse it, rather as Des Esseintes's jewel-encrusted tortoise dies beneath the weight of its artificial carapace. This is the real theme of Huysmans's novel, that the model of the Symbolist self will ultimately collapse under the pressure of the very devices in which it originated. Here the airy arabesques of Mallarmé's ballet dancer give way to the leaden movements of an enervated body.

Des Esseintes's withdrawal from vulgar economic reality is linked to his weakness and impotence, signs of a disastrous feminisation which represents the degeneration of his family line – 'the men becoming progressively less manly', as Huysmans informs us at the outset (17). This theme of the last scion has a peculiar pathos in the period – we find it in Mallarmé's *Igitur* and Villiers's *Axël*, for example, and it will continue to reverberate in modernist writers such as Rilke, Yeats and Thomas Mann. The fear of hereditary illness, which the decadents share with naturalists like Zola, spells the death of the family, which is now the locus of 'idiotic sentimentality' (176) rather than of authority. Where *Axël* is frozen in its feudal decor, Huysmans's novel is obsessed with modernity as a state of transition. *Against Nature* thus charts the decline of society from 'the aristocracy of birth' to the 'aristocracy of wealth' (217), connecting the failure of the family with the shift from an accumulative concept of wealth to one of expenditure and consumption.

Now we can begin to see how the 'unworldly' decadent posture is fundamentally shaped by the economic forces it disdains, and in particular by the phase of accelerated consumerism which was the achievement of the *belle époque*. In this new world the decadent sensibility has to rely on an ideal of its own disembodied intelligence to free it from the appetitive drives of modern society. Yet the 'pure' cruelty of the Sadean hero proves difficult to sustain in the democratic world of late nineteenth-century France, and it has often been observed that Des Esseintes's desperate aestheticism is in fact deeply implicated in the commercial world he despises.[34] But there is another irony too: for Des Esseintes's inability to adapt to the culture of modernity is due in part to his failure to *consume enough*; his decadent body lacks the power to constitute itself in the multiple forms required by a modern consumerism. Where an economy of consumption depends upon a rapid turnover of goods, the effeminate Des Esseintes simply cannot keep pace. On one level, this becomes another book about being ill: in a paroxysm of inwardness the body seems to consume itself – something noticed by one famous dandy of the time, Barbey d'Aurevilly, who remarked that Huysmans's hero is 'a mechanism breaking down. Nothing more.'[35] Much as Des Esseintes tries to overcome 'the bodily reality in all its crudeness and urgency' (110), it is finally the weakness of his physical constitution which sets limits to his idealistic flights of aesthetic fantasy. An ailing body comes increasingly to occupy the centre of this novel, and its inertness is paralleled by the increasingly leaden privacy of the aesthetic interior.[36]

The central trope of the novel, then, is of a world turning in on itself, with the aesthetic interior characterised by its claustrophobic spaces and the 'heaviness' of its artefacts. *Against Nature* in this way projects the ultimate failure of the Symbolist imagination to make desire the guarantee of visionary distance. What is absent here is that narcissistic appropriation of the world through which everything external offers itself as an opportunity for consciousness. Des Esseintes's effeminacy is bound up with his failure to project himself as something different from what he is:[37] the self-fashioning on which this aesthetic project depends is blocked by the dead 'weight' of the decadent body which, inadequate to the challenge of an insistent consumer world, can finally seek comfort only in 'the impossible belief in a future life' (219). Either this 'impossible belief' or the terrible temporality of the body, 'the dull, persistent, unbearable drum-beat of his arteries, pounding away under the skin of his neck' (117): such, for Des Esseintes, are the only choices offered by modernity.

*　　*　　*

But there *is* another option, of course, the 'Supreme' one, as Villiers calls it, and in D'Annunzio's novel (a work much indebted to *Against Nature*) Giorgio finally leaps to his death from the hill-top. He has been in love with death all along – 'death attracts me', he remarks early in the novel (66) – but his suicide tells us two important things about the decadents' 'cruel' aesthetic: first, that the refinement of the Supreme Option requires an other to be 'worked' upon as well (Giorgio drags Ippolita down with him, 'locked in that fierce embrace' [315]), and secondly, that the sadistic drive of the decadent aesthetic always in the end recoils upon the self. Just as Des Esseintes cannot escape the 'weight' of his body, which continues to affirm his likeness to others, so the turning back of cruelty upon its instigator constantly undermines the fantasy of the disembodied intelligence.

At the levels of both theme and literary style, these decadent fictions are indelibly marked by a reflexive displacement of affect or backward turn which is akin to what Freud will later call a 'turning round upon the subject's own self'.[38] This gives us a rather more complicated view of decadent self-immersion and solipsism, as we find it, for example, in Villiers's remark that 'I do not get outside myself. It is the story of Narcissus.'[39] The underlying drama is actually closer to Freud's view of sadism as rooted in a masochistic identification with its object:

> When once feeling pains has become a masochistic aim, the sadistic aim of *causing* pains can arise also, retrogressively; for while these pains are being inflicted on other people, they are enjoyed masochistically by the subject through his identification of himself with the suffering object.[40]

The death of the decadent protagonist is perhaps the least interesting feature of this reflexive movement, for as the cruel intelligence inflicts its aesthetic violence on the world, forcing its elements into new, inorganic forms of order, so its sadistic energy is also turned back onto the language of artifice which constitutes its medium of expression. One cannot help thinking here of Freud's account of the death drive as the desire for a return to the inanimate,[41] for the decadent aesthetic projects a literal desire for death and dismemberment into the style itself, producing a peculiar petrifaction of language. Words are no longer connected to a world of objects, which can be dominated, but tend to become things in themselves, opaque and material.

Contemporary accounts of the style thus stress its likeness to jewelled ornamentation, brilliantly hard yet reified and atomistic. Wilde's Dorian Gray, for example, finds the 'poisonous' yellow book to be written in 'that curious jewelled style, vivid and obscure at once, full of *argot* and of archaisms, of technical expressions and of elaborate paraphrases, that characterizes the work of some of the finest artists of the French school of *Symbolistes'*.[42] His model, Des Esseintes, had thought in similar terms of Mallarmé

> refining upon thoughts that were already subtle enough, grafting Byzantine niceties on them, perpetuating them in deductions that were barely hinted at and loosely linked by an imperceptible thread.
>
> These precious, interwoven ideas he knotted together with an adhesive style, a unique, hermetic language, full of contracted phrases, elliptical constructions, audacious tropes.   (196)

The decadent style is, above all, excessive, always obsessed with local effect at the expense of overall sense. It is, in Gautier's memorable phrase, 'worked for all it is worth',[43] but the refinement of effect also produces a deliberate impurity of tone. This is already in evidence in some of Mallarmé's poems, where we find both 'Byzantine niceties' of vocabulary (*ptyx, nixe, lamphadore,* and so on) along with a use of words which suddenly shifts or lowers the tone (as in, say, 'The Jinx' and 'Alms'). The full-blown decadent style went far beyond this, however, as Huysmans notes in his description of Barbey d'Aurevilly's writing as 'full of twisted expressions, outlandish turns of phrase, and far-fetched similes, [he] whipped up his sentences as they galloped across the page, farting and jangling their bells' (164). This sounds boisterously carnivalesque, but the deliberate *over*-working of the style also testifies to the return upon the expressive self of that sadistic energy which had originally been exerted to ensure its transcendent superiority. The decadent style is gamy (*faisandé*, in a favourite epithet of the time), partly because its dispersive tendencies register the corruption of the self's relation to others.

This is especially clear in the decadent cult of the 'rare word'.

Such words have a closed opacity which makes the constant comparisons to jewels particularly apt. The tremendous power of the foreign or 'alien' word is frequently invoked in this style so as to create the effect of a language partially dead and not in any practical sense for use. This is the extreme reach of Mallarmé's linguistics and we can discern analogues everywhere in the period: in Stefan George's arcane vocabulary and eccentric coinages,[44] for example, and in the purple prose of Walter Pater. It was precisely this aspect of the new aesthetic which Paul Bourget focused on in a famous contemporary critique which Nietzsche would later draw upon for his own account of decadence.[45] Bourget drew attention to the decadent preoccupation with forms of decomposition, noting how its habitual intellectualism worked upon sensations 'with the precision of a prism breaking down light' (I, 7). This tendency towards fragmentation led to a breakdown of the unity of expression which ran parallel to an increasing atomisation of the social order:

> A decadent style is one where the unity of the book is broken down in favour of the independence of the page, where the page is broken down to allow the independence of the phrase, and [similarly] the phrase in favour of the word.   (I, 20)

A decadent literature sequesters the reader from a shared reality (Bourget noted that in *Madame Bovary* and in *Sentimental Education*, Flaubert attributed the 'disequilibrium' of the individual to exposure to fiction), and the high artifice of the style deepens that divide between spoken and written language which Mallarmé had opened. Decadence spells the end of the 'classical' ideal, and Bourget observed of the Goncourts' style that 'It delights in witticisms and couplings of terms which make the reader jump, while classical prose tries [to ensure] that no word of the phrase comes loose from the securely woven web of the style as a whole' (II, 173). The relational economy of classical prose has broken down and in place of the intersubjective 'web' of a social language we now have neologisms and eccentricities which bespeak the loss of any shared horizon. Bourget's point, put another way, is that we are now talking not about *discourse* but about language as an agglomeration of only loosely related words.

It is worth pausing for a moment to consider the implications of this critique. For Bourget's account of the decadent disruption of 'classical' style may remind us of nothing so much as Roland Barthes's description of how 'modern poetry destroyed relationships in language and reduced discourse to words as static things'. And Barthes's definition of 'the economy of classical language' also sounds remarkably like Bourget's: it is 'relational, which means that in it words are abstracted as much as possible in the interest of relationships. In it no word has a density by itself …'.[46] The comparison reminds us that if the principal qualities of decadent style – its sceptical view of representation and linguistic transparency, its mixed registers, its analytic intelligence – seem somehow familiar, it is because they would reappear in different guises in modernist style. Indeed, for Barthes as for Bourget before him, 'modern' writing perpetrates a kind of violence on language and on the forms of social cohesion it should promote. The difference between the two styles hinges, then, on their relative 'density', to use Barthes's word, for a decadent language seems to draw off human affect, locking up desire in the word and attracting erotic glamour to itself. Bourget's idea of decomposition confirms our understanding of the death-drive within the decadent style, and suggests again that the masochistic turning back makes the symbol the murder of both the thing and the self.[47]

This particular aporia is once more traceable to Mallarmé, whose verse, while subordinating local richness to a web of 'musical' relations, is much preoccupied with the capacity of language to take the place of the object of desire. In 'Herodias', for example, his heroine looks at herself in a mirror and, as she does so, she recognises the full force of her own sexual desire. Her triumph, of course, is to deny this desire, and her victory over natural inclination is registered when the mirror, too, reflects the purity of her resolve:

> … This mirror that reflects in sleepy calm
> Herodias of diamantine gleam …
> Yes, final charm! I feel, I am, alone.[48]

Herodias's sexual impulse is internalised, as unfulfilled desire, but the suggestion is that the masochistic denial of natural pleasure and fecundity is rewarded by their reappearance at the level of the words themselves. Inhibited sexual desire is thus in some way compensated by the hermetic depth and materiality of the language:

something of the self is extinguished so as to reappear in the 'chastened' forms of artifice (the *froides pierreries* of Herodias's closing lines).

The particular 'density' of Mallarmé's language is exceeded in true decadent fashion in the poetry of Swinburne, where the play of sadistic and masochistic desires is openly staged. In poems like 'Hymn to Proserpine' and 'Anactoria', Swinburne creates a religion of pain which draws erotic violence back onto the writing, rendering it as worked upon, as belaboured, as the object of the sadist's passion. The dream, as ever, is to 'consume' the loved one in an act of aesthetic passion:

That I could drink thy veins as wine, and eat
Thy breasts like honey! that from face to feet
Thy body were abolished and consumed,
And in my flesh thy very flesh entombed![49]

Yet the protracted act of cruelty can never really 'abolish' the body, and the hypertrophy of style in Swinburne's work – especially notable in the way sound habitually supervenes on meaning – finally makes the writing, like the body castigated by the rod, a dehumanised *thing*. This was in part to be T. S. Eliot's point when he later argued that language in Swinburne's work is somehow 'uprooted, [it] has adapted itself to an independent life of atmospheric nourishment'.[50] That sense of language as falsely material and fetishistic was in turn closely bound up with its identification as *feminine*. However structured, the sadistic fantasies of the decadents almost always embodied a strong misogynist drive, so there was a curious logic to the association of the dehumanised body of the female victim with the excessively material nature of a 'feminine' language. Furthermore, the masochistic turning back inherent in the decadent style necessarily encrypted within it a guilty and fascinated sense of the male's feminisation. If modernism was to be relentlessly masculinist, particularly in its opening phase, it was partly to block this tendency.

A passage from Remy de Gourmont's essay on 'Women and Language' (1901) indicates a gendering of terms which was shortly to become commonplace. Gourmont here designates as 'feminine' those linguistic effects which are 'the most musical, the most rhythmical parts of speech – some combination of phrases resembling those melopoeias repeated insatiably by Negroes'.[51] Where masculine language is exploratory, governed by the logic of concepts and syntax, women's language is tied to the repetitive and conservative rhythms of the oral tradition. Gourmont concludes that 'All mimetic art is the work of women', and that 'The whole woman speaks. She is language incarnate', a proposition which epitomises this way of connecting the material properties of language with the female body and with a degraded form of representation unable to articulate the more 'virile' energies of modernity. Such habits of thought would provide a sort of deep structure for the subsequent waves of modernism, eliding 'politics' with 'sexual politics' – Baudelaire's identification of Woman with a failed sociality continues to function here – and then construing the resulting tensions at the level of artistic 'style'.

4

Paths to the Future

The decadents were finally ruined – as, of course, they had known all along they would be – by the cynical cast of their aesthetic. The decadent self was nourished by the pride it took in recognising that its own values were false, a cynical superiority of view which was also, however, an acknowledgement of its powerlessness to make things otherwise. This art accepted the hollowness beneath its material display and with a kind of malicious joy resigned itself to a circular logic for which death was not an escape but a consummation.

Within *fin de siècle* culture there were, however, other tendencies at work which would suggest ways of avoiding this impasse. For the decadent writers the self proved to be inert and reified, but for others – notably for Tristan Corbière and Jules Laforgue – the distinctive feature of the modern sensibility was precisely its multiplicity and mobility. Corbière's collection *Yellow Loves* was published in 1873, a decade before the decadent phase, but its mordant pessimism and ironic polyphony both predict the mixed style of the decadents and point towards a way out of their introverted world. Des Esseintes caught something of the hybrid nature of Corbière's work:

> It was scarcely French; the poet was talking 'pidgin', using a telegram idiom, suppressing far too many verbs, trying to be waggish, and indulging in cheap commercial-traveller jokes; but then, out of this jungle of comical conceits and smirking witticisms there would suddenly rise a sharp cry of pain, like the sound of a violincello string breaking. (188)

Corbière's irreverence towards the French language and the delight he takes in indelicacies of style and phrase coincide with a boisterous distrust of all forms of heroic rhetoric. He is wryly suspicious of the excessive claims the poetic sensibility usually makes for itself, but his relentless clowning actually sacrifices nothing of the serious pessimism which underlies his thought. Instead, the act of self-dramatisation is a way of coming to terms with a self which cannot be expressed directly because introspection seems unable to disclose a stable core of being. Corbière's 'Épitaphe' for himself, for example, opens with a characteristically dismissive gesture:

> He killed himself with ardour, or died of laziness.
> If he's alive, it's from forgetfulness; he leaves himself this, no less:
> – His only regret was not being his mistress.[1]

The epitaph is for the writer – 'despite his verse' – but the elliptical quality of the poem works to undermine the still fashionable trope of the poet as seer: Corbière's artist is (conventionally) 'misunderstood', but 'by himself in particular', and this failure of self-knowledge points beyond comedy to the play of masks which now seems to constitute identity; Corbière's poet 'Was neither *someone*, nor something / A *pose* was his natural leaning.'

As Laforgue observed, no other French poet had departed so radically from conventional diction,[2] and while his own work would be less demotic in tone, he shared Corbière's disrespect for accepted poetic vocabulary and verse-forms. His first collection, *Complaints*, appeared in 1885 and is permeated with decadent elements, not least of which is a version of Schopenhauerian pessimism which Laforgue derived from Éduard von Hartmann's *The Philosophy of the Unconscious* (1869; French translation 1877). The Unconscious, for Hartmann, was an irrational life-force which had much in common with Schopenhauer's Will, and Laforgue found in it support for his own temperamental pessimism and his sense of random fate and accident. As he remarked, in essays not published until after his death, 'the world is destined for evil', and 'Beyond humanity, the Law follows its own course of reflexive development and the Unconscious blows where it lists.'[3]

Laforgue's poetry is almost exclusively concerned with relations between the sexes which he takes to represent the random workings of 'unconscious' desire. The vicissitudes of love provide him with a sensitive register of the ephemeral and impressionistic nature of modern life (the Unconscious, for Hartmann, is both a negative and a dynamic force). Sexual passion leads to all sorts of misunderstandings and bizarre posturings, most notable of which is the delusion of unique romantic love: 'If she'd initially met / A,

B, C or D, instead of Me, / She would have loved them uniquely yet!' (*PL*, 413). Love, too, blows where it lists, and the accidental nature of passionate attachment serves only to remind us that 'This lower world where scandal heaves / Is one of a thousand throws at dice' (*PL*, 205). Laforgue's pessimism couples the fatalistic decadent tone with a determinedly social sense of its effects:

> Cults and Literatures,
> Warm eyes, distant, bright,
> The cut-price infinite,
> The to-and-fro, nothing endures
> Of creatures quite,
> Oh, nothing ensures. (*PL*, 87)

As he puts it in one of the essays, art does offer an escape from illusion and from one's own self,[4] but only so long as we do not take it too seriously. Hence the title of his first published collection, *Complaints*, links sadness of tone to the lightness of the popular ballad form. The irony throughout is one of self-doubt and self-parody, just as his own version of *Hamlet*, in the *Moral Tales* (1887), emphasises not the metaphysical gravity of the hero's plight (that was Mallarmé's focus), but rather his awareness that, in one critic's words, he 'must live up to his artistic paternity' as a character of Shakespeare.[5]

The complex play of tones in these poems – Laforgue often builds a crossweaving of voices which are marked by quite different prosodies[6] – creates a mobile setting for the ironic, and ironised, self. There is all the decadent attachment to the 'rare word' here – Laforgue is a master of neologisms like *sangsuelle* and *voluptantes* and his metrical virtuosity is allied to a strong interest in word-play:

> Prolixe et monocorde
> Le vent dolent des nuits
> Rabâche ses ennuis
> Veut se pendre à la corde
>   Des puits! et puis?
>   Miséricorde. (*PL*, 86)

Yet the playfulness of the writing, however serious the underlying theme, prevents the self from rigidifying within its language. As in Corbière's verse, much of the irony is in fact turned against the pretensions of the conventional Poetic self, presenting the poet as 'poor and pale and pitifully unsublime / Who only trusts his Self in his spare time' (*PL*, 377) – and not surprisingly, since 'I know myself so little' (*PL*, 289), and 'that gentleman whom I call / Me is no more, they say, than a fatal octopus!'

Laforgue would be important to the later modernists mainly for this sinuous mobility of tone, which opened up a relation between self and other which the cynical deadlock of the decadent style left largely unexplored. In his work, irony became the very medium of the self's social engagement, making its mockery unconditional and independent of any particular object. No longer the death-driven decadent, the poet shuffles his different masks in these poems, creating kaleidoscopic effects from word-play which parallel the shifts and turns in the interior monologue he speaks. Laforgue thus renews one aspect of Baudelaire's poetics and inflects it towards developments which would be more fully worked out in later experimental fiction. Moréas, in fact, had already projected a form of Symbolist prose that would be governed by a conception of a multiplied self:

> The conception of the symbolic novel is polymorphous: now a single character moves through spheres deformed by his own hallucinations, by his temperament, and the only *reality* lies in these deformations. ... Thus, scorning the puerile methods of naturalism ... the Symbolic-Impressionist novel will build its work of *subject deformation*, strong in this axiom: that art can only seek in the *objective* a simple and extremely succinct starting point.[7]

Eduard Dujardin's *The Bays Are Sere* (1888), a novel highly regarded by Joyce, was the first work of fiction to explore this 'subjective deformation' of reality, in some places dispensing with orthodox punctuation to register the 'flow' of interior sensations.[8]

In different ways, Laforgue and Dujardin both offered dynamic views of the self's relation to external reality, and these complemented the 'plasticity' of the Parnassian strain in French writing which, running from Gautier through Leconte de Lisle and Verlaine, had not been extinguished by the 'gamy' decadent style (the Parnassian cult of the exotic had ensured that it was never quite eclipsed).[9] The *Odes* (1890) of the German poet Stefan George, for example, fused the Parnassian mode of presentation with lessons carefully learnt from Mallarmé, and the result was a verse which combined exotic mysticism with a sculptural lucidity:

The silver beeches linger hand in hand
Along the sands where crowding waves careen,
The yellow furrows verge on pasture-land,
A villa hides in gardens drenched with green.[10]

George's work would move increasingly towards an ornamental frigidity (even as it sank deeper into a turgid mysticism), but the incisive clarity of the early poems pointed the way towards Rilke's exploration of a new 'plasticity' in the writing of his *New Poems* of 1907–8.[11] Parnassian technique suggested, in fact, a way of freeing language from the ossified forms of decadence and anchoring it once again in the external world; the word would no longer be a thing valued for itself alone but a medium of passage between the poet and the world.

Faith in the 'rare word' certainly seemed harder to sustain as the century moved to its end. Austrian poet Hugo von Hofmannsthal, in an essay called *The Letter of Lord Chandos* (written around 1901; published 1903), expressed his sense of the breakdown and inadequacy of language in terms of precisely that atomisation which had been such a distinctive feature of the decadent style. Abstract terms, he writes, 'crumbled in my mouth like mouldy fungus':

> For me everything disintegrated into parts, those parts again into parts; no longer would anything let itself be encompassed by one idea. Single words floated round me; they congealed into eyes which stared at me and into which I was forced to stare back – whirlpools which gave me vertigo and, reeling incessantly, led into the void.[12]

This sense of language 'congealing' to produce a narcissistic fixity rather than enacting the movement of thought ('a medium more immediate, more liquid, more glowing than words'[13]) led Hofmannsthal to give up lyric poetry in favour of the more popular medium of musical theatre. That renunciation was prefigured, though, in the critique of aesthetic hedonism in his early play *Death and the Fool* (1893). There the Fool, or aesthete, recognises too late the price paid for his denial of life: 'Too much attracted to mere artifice / I saw the sun with eyes long dead', and 'Always I dragged along that awful curse / Which made my life a book, some twice-told tale'.[14]

The key to Hofmannsthal's own renunciation of poetry lay in his increasing sense of a need for empathy or identification with others which the essential privacy of the lyric seemed to prevent. 'If we wish to find ourselves', he wrote, 'we must not descend into our own inwardness; it is outside that we are to be found, outside'.[15] That rediscovery of an 'outside' to the febrile interior of the decadent imagination would be fundamental to the various forms of modernism. At the same time, the preoccupation with musicality as a measure of the arts would gradually yield to a stronger sense of the visual image as a leading component of a new poetics. We can find this prefigured in the attention to the plastic arts in Walter Pater's *The Renaissance* (1873), a sequence of essays which manages to combine most of the principal features of the later decadence with a sophisticated (and prescient) concept of form and abstraction. Pater was responsible for one of the strongest expressions of the 'musicality' of the arts, but he was also powerfully responsive to the capacities of sculpture and painting to 'project in an external form that which is most inward in passion or sentiment'.[16]

Strongly influenced by modern science and its relativistic accounts of experience, Pater looked to past works of art to provide the 'finite images' (164) which expressed a desired balance of idealist and empiricist elements. Much of his interest in remote periods, and especially in Greek antiquity, derived from Pater's sense of the growing abstractness of modern thought, which he saw as 'committed to a train of reflexion which must end in defiance of form, of all that is outward, in an exaggerated idealism' (164). In contrast, 'the thoughts of the Greeks about themselves, and their relation to the world generally, were ever in the happiest readiness to be transformed into objects for the senses' (163). As Pater imagines it, the Hellenic Golden Age is strikingly different from the *fin de siècle* images of Byzantine and Roman decadence: there are no murky, perfumed interiors here, but rather 'a condition of life in which, by the nature of the case, the values of things would, so to speak, *lie wholly on their surfaces*'.[17]

Pater's conception of style had much in common with that of the decadents, and he, too, conjured with images of sadistic Medusas and the 'fascination of corruption' (83), but at the same time his work was animated, often nervously so, by a desire to burst the limits of the self, to escape that 'narrow chamber of the individual mind' (187) which would become the decadents' sole domain. This was the central problem in the notorious 'Conclusion' to *The Renaissance* (withdrawn from the second edition lest it 'mislead some of those young men into whose hands it might fall' [186]). In these pages, Pater tried to meet the challenge of a relativistic world by offering a gospel of aesthetic hedonism – 'To burn always with this hard, gem-like flame, to maintain this ecstasy, is success in life' (189). If everything solid in our universe actually amounts to little more than 'impressions, unstable, flickering, inconsistent, which burn and are extinguished with our consciousness of them' (187), our only hope is to dwell in the moment as intensely as we can. '[W]e may well grasp at any exquisite passion', Pater concluded, thereby opening up possibilities more radical than any he himself would have explored, but which his more extrovert disciple Oscar Wilde would make central to the new aestheticism.

Pater's own passions were more exclusively literary, and in fact the main argument of the 'Conclusion' was really that the great works of the cultural tradition would allow us 'a quickened, multiplied consciousness' (190) through a sense of continuity and community with moments other than our own. Here lay the power of the image: while it need have no particular moral 'message' (104), it could produce a 'momentary conjunction' of elements (118) which, like the Mona Lisa, seemed to have a synoptic or encyclopedic fullness of implication (evoking 'some brief and wholly concrete moment – into which, however, all the motives, all the interests and effects of a long history, have condensed themselves, and which seem to absorb past and future in an intense consciousness of the present' [118]). Such images have a singular power of suggestion, combining a sense of felt concreteness with that freedom for fantasy which the 'sharp and importunate' reality of contemporary experience (187) seemed to deny. Pater's writing has plenty of decadent features, but his concern with an outwardly focused aesthetic offered an early alternative to a death-driven art, indicating a way of expanding our 'interval' rather than of hastening its closure.

* * *

This sampling of different strands within *fin de siècle* writing cannot convey the full richness of international contact during the period. Certainly the cosmopolitanism of the modernist phase was prefigured by the level of cultural exchange and cross-influence which took place in the last decades of the nineteenth century. The work of Rossetti and Swinburne, for example, was widely known on the Continent and in America,[18] while developments in England were shaped by a growing interest in Symbolist and decadent writing, especially that of Verlaine and Mallarmé.[19] French fashions were quickly transplanted to other cultures, with Schopenhauerian pessimism and Symbolist drama unexpectedly taking root in American bohemianism.[20] This was the time of the great mediators: George Moore's *Confessions of a Young Man,* (1888), Arthur Symons's *The Symbolist Movement in Literature* (1899) and James Gibbons Huneker's *Egoists: A Book of Supermen* (1909) brought the names of Symbolists and European philosophers into intellectual conversation in England and America and created a need for translations of their difficult works.

American writers were also becoming known in Europe: Poe and Emerson had become standard points of reference in France, and as we move to the end of the century the figure of Whitman begins to loom large. In the less developed countries it took longer for Symbolism to become part of the cultural currency. Spanish poet Rubén Darío published his first collection, *Azul,* in 1888, while Russian Symbolism was a phenomenon of the nineties and extended into the pre-war decade. In Italy, the impact of Symbolism is sometimes dated from Ardengo Soffici's 1911 pamphlet on Rimbaud,[21] though Marinetti had translated Mallarmé well before this. In Germany, Symbolism was harder to track, though we have already noted Stefan George's debt to Mallarmé and Verlaine, to which we can add Rilke's lasting interest in French writing and the influence of Rimbaud on Trakl and Brecht in the new century.[22]

France, however, remained at the leading edge of literary developments, and even as her European neighbours conducted their own experiments in the new writing, French culture was beginning to move in a different direction. One of the first indications of that change came from an unexpected source, Jean Moréas, who had launched the 'official' Symbolist movement in 1886. Moréas's own work had actually never been fully Symbolist, and when, in September 1891, he announced that 'Symbolism, which has been of interest only as a transitional phenomenon, is dead',[23] this was the first move in an attempt to return to a classicism which had strong connections with the Mediterranean and especially with Greece, the country of his birth. This return was to the 'graeco-latin' tradition which Moréas saw as the 'fundamental principle' of French letters, a tradition of clarity and order exemplified in the work of writers such as Ronsard and Racine.

Moréas christened the new tendency the 'romanic school' [*l'école romane*], and his announcement soon drew the attention of other writers now seeking an alternative to the prevailing Symbolist fashion. These writers were minor talents, most of whom need not detain us here – Maurice du Plessys, Raymond de La Tailhède, Ernest Raynaud, Charles Maurras – and the productions of the new 'school' were not generally of major significance (the rather cold and sober verse of Moréas's *Stanzas* [1899–1920] is, however, often thought to be his best). The move towards a form of neo-classicism is important, though, since it initiated that close connection between conservatism and literary nationalism which was to have lasting reverberations within international modernism. The rejection of Symbolism and the Romantic inheritance on which it was now seen to be founded marked an attempt to return to an idealised Hellenic world of order and perceptual clarity – a poetics ostensibly of the finite rather than of the infinite. For Moréas and his group, this was the authentic strand in the French tradition from which Symbolism had effected a potentially disastrous deviation. Charles Maurras, for example, argued that the Symbolists 'have forged words with no breeding [*race*], they have used a syntax which is too slack and wantonly distorted'.[24] In the 1886 manifesto, Moréas had stressed the value of devices such as pleonasm and anacoluthon, but the new 'call to order' promised an ideological rejection of these and inaugurated a sort of hellenic renaissance in French letters after 1892. The one-time Symbolist Henri de Régnier, for example, returned to classical themes with *Medallions of Clay* in 1900, and Pierre Louÿs had a major success with his 'translations' from a fictional Greek text in *The Songs of Bilitis* (1894).

This neo-classical repudiation of Symbolism was not, however, the only one. The 1890s also saw the publication of Max Nordau's sensationalist *Degeneration*, a treatise which claimed that Symbolism was rooted in insanity and hereditary disorders. More serious objections were advanced by Leo Tolstoy in *What is Art?* (1897), an attack on recent forms of writing in which 'obscurity is exalted to a dogma'. Tolstoy complained of Baudelaire's habit of 'exalting coarse egoism into a theory, and replacing morality with an idea of beauty indefinite as a cloud'. Obscurity was the index of moral and political irresponsibility in Tolstoy's view, and he stressed that 'The business of art consists precisely in this, to make intelligible and accessible to all what might be unintelligible and inaccessible in an intellectual form.'[25] The interest of French readers in such views ran parallel to the growth of social reform movements at this time and to the wave of humanitarian thought which was fuelled partly by the new enthusiasm for the Russian writers which E.-M. De Vogüé's *The Russian Novel* (1886) had initiated. As the fashion for decadence began to decline, social issues returned to prominence, and readers looked to the theatre of Henrik Ibsen and Gerhart Hauptmann and to works like Oscar Wilde's *The Soul of Man under Socialism* (1891) to revive discussion of collective identity. For some, though, and especially for those writers who felt themselves to be part of an emerging avant-garde, a more radical dissolution of the Symbolist aesthetic was required. It was in the 1890s that Nietzsche's thought began to be known in France, making available a powerful concept of the heroic will with which to overcome the pessimism and inaction now associated with Schopenhauerian decadence. Nietzsche's demolition of the metaphysical illusion of 'truth' led him not to nostalgia for some lost plenitude of meaning and unity, but to a new oppositional energy which rejected the past in an 'heroic' effort to confront a modernity emptied once and for all of sacred values. This, then, was the definitive twist which Nietzsche gave to the notion of decadence, seeing it not as summation and aporia, but as the ashes from which a new, regenerative culture might rise. Writers seeking a way out of the impotent postures of decadence were quick to grasp the implications of this form of modernism. Freedom from the illusion of an external, transcendental 'truth' meant freedom to construct one's own meanings, and in that claim to independence lay a fundamental redefinition of the self as active, dynamic, and confrontational. Where the decadent writers had grasped too easily at the Mallarméan aesthetic of 'failure' as a justification for their secession from the modern, the new Nietzschean man would seek to harness the transformative energies of the modern to his own project of self-renovation. The present could now be regarded not as impasse and decline, but as a moment of decisive change.

The impact of this proposed shift of perspective on writers coming of age within the Symbolist milieu can best be seen in the work of André Gide. Gide's early books, which include the significantly named *Treatise of Narcissus* (1891) and *The Poetry of André Walter* (1892), are strongly coloured by the work of the older generation (and especially by that of Verlaine and Laforgue). In an almost paradigmatic way, Gide's development lay in freeing himself from these influences: as he notes in the autobiographical *If it Die* (1926), it was crucial to overcome the once-fashionable pessimism of Schopenhauer and the ponderous Wagnerian aesthetic of the 1880s ('I hold the person and the work of Wagner in horror', he observed in his *Journals*, 'This amazing genius does not exalt so much as he *crushes*'[26]). The hot-house poetics of the previous era had now lost its erotic attraction – Gide's friend Paul Claudel wrote to him of 'that special atmosphere of suffocation and stagnation ... breathed from 1885 to 1890'.[27] Claudel and Gide were not alone in seeking a way out of this oppressive atmosphere. Marcel Proust, for example, had already launched his own attack on the obscurity of Symbolist writing, and a new edition of *The Flowers of Evil* would soon carry Guillaume Apollinaire's strictures against Baudelairean pessimism.[28]

Gide's reading of Nietzsche was instrumental in his handling of the dilemma, suggesting a return to the clean air of 'life' and a healthy sensuality. In fact, in a later preface to his lyrical *Fruits of the Earth* (1897), Gide described the writing of the book as a recovery from an illness. The source of the 'illness' was clear enough; Gide went on to explain that 'I wrote this book at a time when our literature was terribly imbued with a close and artificial atmosphere, and it seemed to me urgent that it should be brought down to earth once more.'[29] Coming back to earth again meant literally a return to nature, to sensuality and liberation through pleasure. The Laforguian attention to the ephemeral is here translated into a doctrine of momentary experience ('I fell into the habit of *separating* each moment of my life in order to fill it wholly with a complete and isolated joy' [43]), but significantly these brief intensities usually lead not to fragmentation of the self but to a sense of its participation in the rhythms of a larger whole: 'my body', Gide recalls, 'seemed at times to have no limits; it was prolonged outside myself – or sometimes became porous; I felt myself deliciously melting away, like sugar' (55).

Pleasure is here redeemed from its associations with a guilty privacy, and Gide's plunge into the 'real' is motivated by a desire to expand the limits of experience through contact with others: 'I have turned prowler in order to rub shoulders with all that prowls; my heart has melted with tenderness for all shelterless creatures, and I have passionately loved the vagabonds of the earth' (96). The posture of the reclusive aristocrat has yielded to that of the impulsive extrovert for whom 'experience' connotes both sexual freedom and voluntary *déclassement*. In a passage in his *Journals*, Gide makes an interesting reference to the 'Constant *vagabundance* of desire', and this coinage, from 'vagabondage' and 'abundance' neatly connects those ideas of errancy, risk, and 'excessive' pleasure which would play such an important part in the propaganda of the new modernism.[30]

Rimbaud had been the first to explore this kind of 'subversive' identification, initiating a thematics of life at the periphery which we can trace in the work of later writers such as Blaise Cendrars, Henry Miller and Jean Genet. For Gide's generation, though, the main inspiration for this particular fantasy came from the work of Walt Whitman, now something of a cult figure amongst European literati. French interest in his work had grown steadily since the appearance of an introductory article in 1861. Émile Blémont and Thérèse Bentzon published further accounts in 1872 (Rimbaud may have read these[31]), and the first translations from *Leaves of Grass*, by Laforgue, appeared in *La Vogue* in 1886. Laforgue, however, died before he could complete the work, and France had to wait until 1909 for Bazalgette's version (two years after Italian and Russian translations of the work).

How is Whitman's massive influence in Europe to be explained? Partly it was due to a convergence between aspects of his work and the main preoccupations of Symbolism: his bardic idealism echoed the Symbolist poetics of vision, and the preference expressed in the 1855 'Preface' to *Leaves of Grass* for forms of 'indirectness' (a poetry 'not direct or descriptive or epic'[32]) coincided with French techniques of suggestiveness. But Whitman's poetry also had its own distinctive cosmic ambitions, proclaiming a new optimism, a faith in science, technology and democracy which, when coupled with the openness and muscular expressivity of his free verse, offered a radical vision of human solidarity in place of decadent introversion. Whitman's 'open road' seemed to lead directly into the modern world, substituting the 'body electric' for the jaded 'mechanism' of Des Esseintes and making its rugged rhythms the vehicle of a collective experience. Nineties America found it hard to assimilate Whitman's brash assault on gentility, and his influence there produced hybrid work like Bliss Carman and Richard Hovey's *Songs from Vagabondia* (1895), in which the dandy still stalked the open road. In Europe, though, the fashion for decadence was beginning to yield to what has been called 'social Symbolism', a new

development associated particularly with the Belgian poet Émile
Verhaeren.[33]

Like Whitman, Verhaeren was an uneven, often clumsy writer who
had a fondness for the declamatory style. At the same time he was
often able to adapt the Symbolist style to a social content which had
so far been foreign to it. Two of his best-known volumes – *The
Hallucinated Countryside* (1893) and *Tentacular Cities* (1895) – chart a
complex response to the late but very rapid industrialisation of
Belgium, trying to reconcile a socialist faith in the future with a pessimistic response to the depopulation of rural regions. His imagery of
mist and stagnant rivers is suggestive in the Symbolist mode, but it
also seeks to articulate a collective experience of radical social change.
In an interview which he gave in 1905, Verhaeren proposed a strikingly new image of the poet as one who would 'live in harmony with
the present, as close as possible to the future; he will write with au-
dacity, no longer with prudence; he will not fear his own intoxication
and the red and fiery poetry which will express it'.[34]

Modern readers may feel more at ease with the poems in which
Verhaeren reveals the darker side of technological progress, but it
was this note of rather strident evolutionary optimism which galvanised many of his contemporaries. Verhaeren had in fact caught
the wave which was to sweep a succession of avant-garde movements into the new century, a wave of dynamic, prospective energy
captured in one of his most famous poems, 'Toward the Future'.
Here the presentation of 'The fury to discover more' which animates modernity is freed from the stigma previously attaching to
bourgeois progress:

> In the leaven, in the atom, in the dust,
> Vast life is sought and appears.
> Everything is caught in an infinity of nets
> Which immortal matter compresses or distends.[35]

This rhapsodic materialism is far removed from the Platonic
impulse of Symbolism, and the urban landscape evoked elsewhere
in the poem is not just the spectral backdrop for some drama of the
self but presages change, 'red strength and new light'. Verhaeren's
expansive optimism equates technological progress with human
liberation, generating an unequivocal excitement in the face of the
new. It is hard to appreciate the full force of such poetry as an inauguration of the modern – Verhaeren's work is now largely forgotten, a voluminous footnote in nineteenth-century literary history –

yet an English critic writing in 1913 could still describe him as 'a man who both in thought and technique is indisputably the most modern and the most massive force in the whole of European poetry'.[36]

The intellectual climate, then, had suddenly changed: the fashion was now for energetic and outspoken expressions of faith and, above all, for manifestos. Between Moréas's announcement of his *école romane* in 1891 and the opening of world hostilities in 1914, writers and intellectuals vied with each other to name the new tendency. Movements surfaced with a loud fanfare and then disappeared almost without trace (Henri Meschonnic lists fifty 'isms' invented in the period between 1886 and 1924[37]). Many, like 'integralism' and 'impulsionism' were little more than attempts to upstage competitors and are long since forgotten. Others, though, give a clearer sense of the energies at work in the Parisian scene and also suggest a context in which to understand the emergence of Italian Futurism, the first definitively modernist movement.

A tendency like 'Naturism' (1895–8), for example, was characteristic both in its assemblage of relatively minor talents – the poets Francis Jammes, Paul Fort, the Comtesse de Noailles – and in its strident claims for social action and a return to 'nature'. Typical too was its rejection of Mallarméan obscurity; as Jammes put it, 'The poet gets to a time when he says: the sky is blue, and this expression is enough for him.'[38] The manifesto of the movement (issued in January 1897) had, like that of the *école romane*, a strongly nationalistic base, dismissing Symbolism as the product of a 'German' influence which 'disfigures the spirit of our race'.[39] Along with a rather sentimental identification with 'sailors, [and] workers born in the bowels of the earth' (60) the naturists express a love of dynamism, which is the most distinctive feature of the period: since this is a time of peace, 'military intoxication ... is transformed amongst us into a kind of cult of energy' (59). The same set of emphases appears in Fernand Gregh's 'humanist' manifesto of December 1902. His movement is not, says Gregh, opposed to Symbolism as such, 'but it must be clear. We are tired of a certain kind of impassivity and incoherence' (73). Once again, formal clarity and precision are directly linked to masculine energy: 'Poets of today and tomorrow,' cries Gregh, 'let us be men!'

* * *

The masculine tones of these avant-garde manifestos connect, of course, with that gendering of literary language which we observed in Remy de Gourmont's essay. If, by the turn of the century, femininity was felt to have strongly negative cultural associations, it was mainly because of that decadent legacy which linked sexual and linguistic excess to social decline and the unsettling of the gender divide. Zola's *The Kill* (1872) provides a relatively early statement of the theme in its presentation of Maxime as 'a strange hermaphrodite making its entrance at the right moment in a society that was growing rotten'.[40] Nowhere is the association clearer than in an influential polemic by Charles Maurras against the 'feminine romanticism' of a new group of women poets which included Renée Vivien and the Comtesse de Noailles. Part of the argument of the set of articles Maurras published under this heading in 1903 hinged on an opposition between a masculine classicism and a feminine romanticism which he traced to dubious foreign (i.e., German) origins.

More interestingly, Maurras attempted to locate this gender opposition within specific practices of writing. The women writers, he claimed, had at least one thing in common: in their work, 'words acquire that material weight, that physical value, that tone, that *carnal pleasure* which must, of necessity, slow down movement, but increase the power of suggestion'.[41] Maurras was seeking a return to 'reason' and to the relational economy of classical verse, and in doing so he attacked the familiar modes of Symbolist writing – musicality, colour, synaesthesia, even metaphor – as both disruptive of 'signification' and indicative of feminine self-absorption. Maurras thus drew a fundamental contrast between a 'womanly' preoccupation with the material (especially phonic) properties of language on the one hand, and a virile literature of action on the other. 'It is', he concluded, 'a womanly pleasure to handle words like material [*étoffes*]. Subtle analogies of sentiment and sensation, poorly discerned or fleetingly conceived by coarse manly intelligences, are here, on the contrary, natural and commonplace elements of the soul's life.'[42] Where the decadents had associated Woman with death, now the new avant-gardes began to couple femininity with decadence, a move already made in Nordau's *Degeneration* (1895), where a polemic is mounted against Wagner ('all [of whose] ideas revolve around women') and the Symbolists, who 'make of the word, that conventional vehicle of a conception, a musical harmony, by whose aid they endeavour to awaken not an idea, but a phonetic effect'.[43]

Maurras's backward-looking neo-classicism would have a particular relevance for Anglo-American modernists, some of whom would soon express a similar distrust of 'feminine' inwardness and the instability of a decadent language. In France, though, the characteristic tropes of the new avant-gardes were ostentatiously modern ones of dynamism and global simultaneity which had less to do with the issues of social justice that had occupied writers like Tolstoy, Ibsen and Verhaeren than with Nietzsche's declaration that

> we 'conserve' nothing, we will return to no past, but we are in no sense 'liberal' either, we do not work for 'progress'...we rejoice in all that like us loves danger, war, adventure, all that is never satisfied, never fenced in, reconciled, emasculated.[44]

These 'masculine' themes of risk and self-exposure were soon developed as a general avant-garde programme intended to challenge not only a decadent aesthetic but those social structures whose inertness was powerfully symbolised in the decadent interior.

Where Des Esseintes felt himself to be imprisoned in an ailing body, the avant-gardist would bank everything on an attempt to transcend the boundaries of the self. Bearing in mind the economic tragedy of *Against Nature*, we might say that the modernist ambition was now to *consume* reality rather than to represent it as an image of the bodily self. Gide's idea of exceeding the limits of the body, of 'deliciously melting away, like sugar', and of somehow exteriorising the self, also began to take on an explicitly political dimension, as fantasies of dynamism and spatial conquest found expression in a rhetoric of imperialist aggression (the literary journal *Montjoie!*, for example, carried the sub-title 'Organ of French artistic imperialism'[45]). This 'activist' stance converted Gide's luxurious self-transcendence into an irreverent and openly destructive attitude towards the body and the various pieties – aesthetic and philosophical – associated with it.

Yet it is strangely characteristic of modernism that the now much-vaunted repossession of a public sphere should coincide with the rejection as 'anti-modern' of a whole mass of social material which had provided the focus of nineteenth-century fiction. The hostility to narrative which we shall find in so much modernist writing has its origin in this major shift in perspective. The world of human production explored in the work of writers like Dickens and Zola now largely disappeared, as an intricate thematics of domestic manners tied to the accumulation and transfer of capital gave way before a culture increasingly deriving its values and concepts from the realm of consumption.[46] In the boom years of the *belle époque*, society seemed to present itself as mobile and self-transforming under the power of a rapidly expanding capitalism. Modernity, as the new generation perceived it, was conditioned less by stratification and class than by an all-embracing consumerism – in Antonio Gramsci's words, an increasingly powerful bourgeoisie offered itself as 'an organism in continuous movement, capable of absorbing the entire society, assimilating it to its own cultural and economic level'.[47] That illusion of a seamless social *totality* is of fundamental importance to an understanding of this early modernism; for where the aim of the nineteenth-century avant-garde had been to situate itself somewhere *outside* the bourgeoisie it derided, the new generation was mesmerised by modernity as an all-embracing *condition* (as Des Esseintes had discovered to his cost, there is ultimately no space untouched by modern capital).

What was especially important about the widespread search for expanded, spatial figures for the self – figures seen as antithetical to an over-cultivated, self-absorbed and 'feminised' culture – was that it seemed to be driven by the power of modernity itself. Whereas nineteenth-century writers had followed Baudelaire's lead in spurning the economic as the domain of 'natural', bourgeois values, the new avant-gardes looked to the process of global modernisation and imperialist expansion for tropes with which to shatter the confines of the decadent interior. It was not merely the spectacular advances in the technology of communications and transportation which produced the new fantasies of mobility and dynamism, but a different sense of the economy itself as an awesome driving force. If we can speak of a metaphysics of the modern here, it is because the literary pursuit of 'dynamism', which seems to have been a preoccupation of almost every pre-war avant-garde movement, was conceived as an attempt to penetrate the deep structures of modernity, those structures of capital flow and circulation which suddenly seemed homologous with the drives of the newly 'liberated' imagination.

None of this is to suggest that writers were suddenly interested in the detail of economic process, but rather that the mystique of capital which is everywhere in this period coincides with the expanded operation of finance capitalism. As the Marxist economist Rudolf Hilferding noted in 1910, 'the specific character of capital is obliterated in finance capital. Capital now appears as a unitary power which exercises sovereign sway over the life process of society...'.[48] International finance thus comes to seem something superhuman, a force working according to its own laws and having no clear connection to the mundane sphere of production: a fetishism of capital which structurally complements a fetishism of the commodity.[49] This helps to explain why so many fantasies of power and mobility during the period are emblematised by the adventures of consumerism, since to purchase is, in these terms, to 'liberate' oneself into the cycle of capital's reproduction. The space of modernity thus provides the occasion for a peculiar *disembodiment*, with the spectacle of endless consumer desire abolishing the 'merely human' limits of the ailing body in *Against Nature*. It is as if the erotic aura of the body is displaced within an expanding consumerism so as to reappear in the form of a depersonalised libidinal energy which invests the commodity and its rituals.

Now we may begin to see how the spectacle of modern consumerism might instigate a new practice of writing: for we are dealing here not with concepts of lack and compensatory form but with a plenitude which seems always mystically to reconstitute itself in and through the experience which consumes it. This consumer world is an increasingly dematerialised one, and as categories of production, use and need appear to diminish in importance, so modes of engagement with commodities become less direct, a matter of visual flirtation rather than the fetishistic possession which motivated Des Esseintes. Advanced consumerism thus depends as much upon the mobility of desire as it does on actual purchase: while capitalism presents itself as an overwhelming visual spectacle, specific commodities are less important to this particular consumer fantasy than the circulation of exchange value, which, even as it operates as the general equivalent of all things, seems itself to exceed the possibility of stable representation.

An early and partial exploration of some of these new themes can be found in the work of Valéry Larbaud, whose *Poems of a Rich Amateur* was first privately published in 1908. Larbaud was, like his protagonist, a wealthy 'amateur', and the poems record a life of international travel and pleasure, striking a deliberately modern note in their celebration of speed and movement:

Lend me thy great noise, thy powerful, gentle gait,
Thy delicate nocturnal glide across illuminated Europe,
O luxurious train! And the agonizing music
Running the length of thy gilt, embossed corridors,
While behind the brass knobs of lacquered doors,
Millionaires slumber![50]

For Larbaud's character Barnabooth (a South American by birth), Europe is truly a 'new world', with 'its railways and its theatres / And its constellation of cities'.[51] The listing of places in the poems, part of the tourist's itinerary, recalls the catalogues of Whitman, from whom Larbaud has learned the lesson of the open road as an authentic alternative to the 'narrow life' (30) of those who, like Des Esseintes, remain in one place. But this is no fantasy of simple vagabondage: the freedom to travel is nothing without the ability to purchase, and Barnabooth is horrified by the thought of 'colonial countries' where days have to be spent in 'towns without shops', with nothing to look at but 'the marvels of nature' (76). For Barnabooth, to be is to consume; thoughts of his own death lead inevitably to the dreadful realisation that 'O shopwindows in the great thoroughfares of the capitals, / One day you will no longer reflect the face of this passer-by' (86).

This world of expanded horizons requires a new poetics, and Larbaud is one of the first writers to express that desire for 'reality' over representation which is a major preoccupation of early modernism: 'Enough words, enough sentences! O real life, / Artless and unmetaphored, be mine'.[52] Yet Larbaud's poems cannot quite achieve that full disembodiment which the consumer fantasy requires: reality here clearly *is* mediated by tone and ironic distance in ways which make us aware of the very social divisions that consumer mobility is meant to occlude. Barnabooth's worries about being 'too rich' (37) and his intermittent sense of 'social injustice' (36) are deftly managed as self-parody, but they serve also to remind us that something is still lacking.

Larbaud's search for forms of unmediated experience was given more extreme – and more influential – expression in another collection of poems published in 1908, Jules Romains's *La Vie unanime*. Unanimism – based on a fantasy of absorption into the 'total' life of the city – emphasised the decentring of the self: 'I scorn my heart and my personal thoughts / The city's dream is more beautiful than mine'; and, characteristically, 'I disappear. And the charming [*adorable*] life of everyone / Drives me out of my body, possessing every fibre'.[53] Romains returns again and again to mystical, semi-erotic fantasies of the self invaded by the city: 'The emanations of the city penetrate and transform the molecules of my body' (205).

For Romains, desire is closely linked to consumer mobility in the city ('My pleasure [*volupté*] subsides and increases according to / Whether it is dark or sunny in the shops' [138]); to consume is here to be consumed, to achieve a kind of disembodiment:

> I slowly cease to be myself...
> Jostled by the appearances of the street
> I am completely drained of interior life.
> My being diminishes and dissolves...
> Greedy city,
> I am like sugar in your mouth.   (133)

Romains's fantasy of self-transcendence gives a particular twist to these new notions of space:

> The eyes do not see separate forms
> ... Each thing prolongs another. The metal
> Of the rails, the dazzling squares, the entrances
> To the houses, the passers-by, the horses, the carriages
> Join each other and join my body.
> We are indistinct.[54]

Such passages evoke a new type of space which associates the visual image with a certain 'depth': 'To love the real as the realists do is not worthy of poets. The writers of whom I speak love the real in its depths [*en profondeur*].'[55] Romains thus seeks to go beyond what he calls the 'coloured surfaces' of Zola and Verhaeren to perceive the social as animated by diverse rhythms of permeation and cross-connection.

'Depth', in this sense, no longer connotes a stratified space, with mechanisms of power and subordination standing in a hierarchical relation, but rather, a 'phenomenological' space which transcends the limits of the individual body. 'Space is no one's possession', Romains argues. 'No one has succeeded in appropriating one scrap of space and saturating it with his own unique existence. Everything over-crosses, coincides, and cohabits.'[56] Romains's notion of an 'organic consciousness', coupled with Henri Bergson's even more influential concept of 'duration' (*durée*), entailed a 'compenetration' of forms which implied the dissolution of the 'merely' individual in a field of shifting and collective states of consciousness. From the vantage-point of unanimism the world of the decadent interior seemed remote indeed; the iconoclastic moment of Futurism had arrived.

5

A Metaphysics of Modernity: Marinetti and Italian Futurism

On 20 February 1909 the Parisian paper *Le Figaro* printed a bizarre manifesto which declared the beginning of a new art in much the same terms as might be used to declare war. The connection, as we shall see, was far from coincidental. The writer of the manifesto was an Italian, Filippo Tommaso Marinetti, author of Symbolist verse and editor of a literary magazine called *Poesia*. Marinetti had spent his childhood in Egypt, where his father had amassed a fortune which would later provide resources for the multifarious activities of Futurism. Educated in Paris, Marinetti had a close knowledge of the French language, in which he wrote most of his early work, and his acquaintance with the literary scene there gave *Poesia* a key role in promoting a range of writers from Moréas and Romains to Alfred Jarry. First and foremost, Marinetti was a form-idable cultural impressario, a tireless publicist of his own genius and that of his movement, Italian Futurism. Here was the writer not as cloistered man-of-letters but as performer, activist and knowing buffoon. The manifestos of Futurism would constitute a guide to almost every aspect of avant-garde activity to come; they would also encode some of its most problematic attitudes.

The intellectual origins of the movement are complex, mainly because it absorbed so many of the ideas we have already examined. Predicting the form of subsequent avant-gardes, Futurism was instinctively eclectic, its philosophical base formed from a wide range of elements in the contemporary intellectual scene. Key ideas of dynamism and flux, for example, were drawn from Nietzsche and Bergson, while Georges Sorel's theory of political violence contributed to Marinetti's advocacy of artistic aggression. The real brilliance of the first manifesto, though, lay in Marinetti's way of using these different ideas to ground a rejection of decadent poetics in a celebration of economic change. Futurism was the progeny of those northern Italian cities like Genoa, Milan and Turin where modernity was powerfully experienced as the everyday clash of cultural tradition with the forces of industrial innovation. Marinetti's basic insight was that such a struggle was relentless, unpitying, and weighted in favour of the modern; the first manifesto accordingly purged those strains of sentiment and unfocused humanitarianism which had clouded naturism and unanimism, and proceeded to *celebrate* the very inhumanity of the new machine age.

Marinetti was not, of course, the first to take an aesthetic interest in technology – Flaubert's friend Maxime du Camp had published poems about machines in the middle of the previous century, and Marinetti himself readily acknowledged the importance of Verhaeren as 'glorifier of machines and tentacular cities' (*F*, 68). There were also precursors he was less willing to notice. A Spanish movement actually calling itself Futurism had already been unsuccessfully promoted by one Gabriel Alomar, and this probably gave Marinetti the name for the new tendency he had originally planned to call *elettrecismo* or *dinamismo*. And closer to home, an Italian, Mario Morasso, had advocated an 'aesthetic of speed' some four years before Marinetti's manifesto. Perhaps more important than any of these, though, was the example of D'Annunzio – Marinetti would constantly deride him as decadent, but D'Annunzio's Nietzschean cult of action and energy shaped Futurism's most fundamental precepts.

The content of Futurism, then, was hardly original, but its extremism – formal and conceptual – certainly was. 'Let's give ourselves utterly to the Unknown, not in desperation but only to replenish the deep wells of the Absurd! '(*F*, 40). So, in the manifesto, Marinetti exhorts his comrades to commit themselves to the adventure of modernity. They have been up all night arguing 'to the last confines of logic', in an exotic room whose mosque lamps and metalled ornaments reflect their 'immense pride' and hardened spirits. Tired at last of words, they respond to 'the famished roar of automobiles' and race off into the night in their 'three snorting beasts'. The absurdity of all this is quite calculated, for the fantasy played out in the opening stages of the manifesto is a ludicrous fantasy of birth, of being born by an act of *self*-generation. Where the decadents had been mesmerised by endings and by the miserable plight of the last scion, the Futurists know only those beginnings in which the self emerges new-born, without father, mother, past. The triumph of the mechanical over the natural thus encapsulates the capacity of the modern subject to experience himself as pure origin, as uncontaminated by tradition.[1] When Marinetti crashes his car into a ditch full of factory waste he gulps down the 'nourishing sludge' and is freed from the centuries' dream of culture ('the horrible shell of wisdom') into the life of the present. Smeared with 'good factory muck', the rite of mock baptism is complete, christening the venture under the triple sign of technology, speed and occult sensualism. Chronology flows backwards, from baptism to birth: so in Marinetti's epic 'novel' *Mafarka the Futurist* (1910), the 'absolute and ultimate power of the will' triumphs over 'Love' with an act of titanic parthenogenesis (*TIF*, 224, 223).

The rhetorical inflation which accompanies such fantasies carries us to the brink – and frequently over the brink – of total absurdity, thus undermining the marmoreal gravity of the decadent cult of death. '[O]ur frank optimism thus neatly challenges the pessimism of Schopenhauer', declares Marinetti (*F*, 92), and that decisive break with the *fin de siècle* mood is also a rejection of the masochistic self-wounding which accompanied it. In a deliberately grandiose gesture, the Futurists now confront Villiers's 'Supreme Option' with ironic contempt, turning upon death as if it were a beast to be hunted down:

> And like young lions we ran after Death. ...But we had no ideal Mistress raising her divine form to the clouds, nor any cruel Queen to whom to offer our bodies, twisted like Byzantine rings! There was nothing to make us wish for death, unless the wish to be free at last from the weight of our courage!   (*F*, 40)

Freed from the worship of death and the 'ideal Mistress', the Futurist strives to abolish a culture of romantic love in an aesthetics of deliberate brutality: 'Art, in fact, can be nothing but violence, cruelty, and injustice' (*F*, 43), partly because culture, like life, is a war of one generation against another. 'They will come against us, our successors', acknowledges Marinetti, but the recognition brings with it none of the pathos of the Oedipal drama, since, as Futurist architect Sant'Elia puts it, 'Each generation must build its own city.'[2] Each avant-garde, then, is born with the delirious knowledge that 'We stand on the last promontory of the centuries!' (*F*, 41), a vantage-point which commits art to a pure present defined by the necessity of struggle: 'Except in struggle, there is no more beauty! No work without an aggressive character can be a masterpiece' (*F*, 41).

The 'struggle' was in part against literary tradition, but the particular force of the various manifestos lay in their repeated suggestion that cultural inertia was the symptom of a deeper malaise in the nation as a whole. The nationalistic thrust of Futurism actually provided its main momentum, though contemporary observers often tended to caricature it as merely a form of Latin excess. The *Manifesto of Futurist Painters* (1910), for example, hammered home the connection between cultural rebirth and national regeneration: 'In the eyes of other countries, Italy is still a land of the dead, a vast Pompeii, white with sepulchres. But Italy is being reborn. Its political resurgence will be followed by a cultural resurgence' (*FM*, 25). The promotion of violence and war has to be understood in the context of the Italian desire to break free from the Triple Alliance with Germany and Austria and to claim its rights as an autonomous, modernising power. It is also significant that Futurism came of age alongside the nationalist movement in Italy (founded in 1910 by Enrico Corradini), reaching its apogee in the interventionist moment prior to Italy's entry into the war in 1915 ('our much-prayed-for great war' [*F*, 123]). Even before this, however, Marinetti's own work was closely bound up with the theme of war, and specifically with Italy's move against Libya in 1911–12 and its seizure of Tripoli and Cyrenaica, and with the war in the Balkans, which he followed as a reporter.

Yet it was not the foreign yoke alone which held Italy back – in the Futurists' view, their rich cultural past had left Italians marooned as curators of a vast tourist museum, as 'singers of serenades, as ciceroni or beggars' (*F*, 108). If anything symbolised the burden of this tradition it was Venice, and in an outrageous 'Futurist Speech to the Venetians', Marinetti urged them to transform this 'greatest bordello in history' into a vibrant industrial port. Venice, with its 'leprous, crumbling palaces' and its gondolas, those 'rocking chairs for cretins', was the supreme denial of the modern Italian spirit: 'you want to prostrate yourself before all foreigners', roared Marinetti from the top of the Clock Tower, 'Your servility is repulsive!' (*F*, 56–7).

In the new world of 'holy Electric Light' and 'metal bridges and howitzers', the moonlight in which Venice had always seemed so seductive to the tourist signalled all that was backward-looking in Italian culture. In Marinetti's writing, such 'moonlight' also connoted Futurism's prime literary target, the decadent, Symbolist tradition (the two terms were now becoming inextricably linked for the purposes of polemic). Yet French Symbolism was too deep and complex an influence simply to shrug off, and Marinetti's injunction to 'hate the intelligence' (*F*, 89), for example, was essentially just a toughened up version of the Symbolists' emphasis on intuition and the irrational. Since such ideas quickly proved indispensable to the Futurist project, Marinetti deftly turned his guns against 'decadence', a concept which in this context had both cultural and political implications. Given the decadent obsession with sexuality and deviance, the polemic now acquired a usefully sensational aspect at the same time as it assumed a heroic 'masculine' tone.

In thus connecting aesthetic radicalism with the struggle of the sexes, Futurism both extended the sort of thinking about language promoted by Gourmont and Maurras, and made the whole context of an emerging modernism a strongly gendered one. To attack practices and institutions which stood in the way of modernisation was, it now turned out, also and necessarily to attack Woman: 'We will destroy the museums, libraries, academies of every kind, will fight moralism, feminism, every opportunistic cowardice' (*F*, 42). The presence of 'feminism' in this list was by no means an afterthought; indeed, the most notorious proposal in the manifesto reads: 'We will glorify war – the world's only hygiene – militarism, patriotism, the destructive gestures of freedom-bringers, beautiful ideas worth dying for, and scorn for woman.' This 'scorn for woman' was to permeate the thought of other modernist avant-gardes, and it clearly amounted to something more than either a class-based misogyny or an attempt to promote a 'manly' sense of pride in Italy's technological and imperialist potential. For a recurrent theme in modernist polemic – a theme given definitive form in the Futurist manifestos – would be that Woman is 'anti-modern', that the feminine denotes a particular psychological formation which is in some sense resistant to the new.[3]

On one level, of course, the Futurist contempt for 'feminine' values arose from an attack on outmoded structures within Italian society. This explains a set of fundamental contradictions in Marinetti's various pronouncements, for along with the flamboyant chauvinism for which he is well known there developed an equally outspoken propaganda on behalf of some feminist concerns. The so-called 'Manifesto of the Futurist Political Party' (1918) numbers among its main proposals the facilitation of divorce, universal suffrage, and the right to equal salaries; elsewhere Marinetti mounted a bitter attack on the family, which he saw as little better than 'a legal prostitution powdered over with moralism' (*F*, 77).[4]

The Futurist 'scorn for women' was thus rather more complicated than it has often seemed, for it was closely related to the
Nietzschean desire for a transcendence of the 'merely' human.
From that perspective, Marinetti saw past cultures (and Italian
culture in particular) as locked into social and political roles which
were deeply repressive. He could thus afford to be quite ambivalent about the 'woman question' since the principal Futurist objective was ultimately 'the creation of a nonhuman type': 'This
nonhuman and mechanical being, constructed for an omnipresent
velocity, will be naturally cruel, omniscient, and combative' (*F*, 91).
Although this fantasy of a new heroic existence amounted to a
dream of supermasculinity, it thrived on the 'paradox' that the lack
and inadequacy which it aimed to abolish were the entailments not
merely of traditional femininity but of sexual difference itself.
Something more complicated than a conventional chauvinism was
involved, which perhaps explains why Marinetti was actually prepared to retract the manifesto's derogatory reference to women – in
the August/September issue of *Poesia* of the same year he complained of

> the terrible nausea we get from the obsession with the ideal
> woman in works of the imagination, the tyranny of love amongst
> latin people, and the monotonous *leit-motif* of adultery! A nausea
> which we have expressed in a perhaps too laconic way by these
> words: *Scorn for women*.[5]

And in his preface to *Mafarka the Futurist* (1910), Marinetti further
emphasised that his real object of attack was 'the sentimental
significance' attributed to women (*TIF*, 217). In view of these
qualifications, it is a little less surprising to find that the Futurist
movement, which we tend to think of as a male avant-garde *par excellence*, actually included a number of women writers. As Claudia
Salaris has shown, the war years saw a lively dialogue about feminism within the movement, and it is clear from some of the writings
of the women involved that the *anti-passéisme* of Futurist theory
could be appropriated for potentially progressive political positions.[6]
   The repudiation of the feminine was, however, more clear-cut at
the cultural level: here 'woman' provided the symbolic focus of an
attack on those attitudes towards language, subjectivity and sexual
difference which seemed to characterise a Symbolist or decadent
poetics. Marinetti listed 'four intellectual poisons', which, as usual,

he attributed to D'Annunzio, a writer always to be found, with the French Symbolists, 'hovering above the naked female body':

> (1) the sickly, nostalgic poetry of distance and memory; (2) romantic sentimentality drenched with moonshine that looks up adoringly to the ideal of Woman–Beauty; (3) obsession with lechery, with the adulterous triangle, the pepper of incest, and the spice of Christian sin; (4) the professorial passion for the past and the mania for antiquity and collecting.   (*F*, 68)

The passage brings together a number of major elements, all in some way types of a 'false' embodiment: the nineteenth-century tropes of memory and displacement, forms of deviant sexuality, excessive sentimentality, and an academic reclusiveness and fetishism. The female body is the symbolic centre of this set of negative and disabling forces since it is the traditional cultural focus of desire and deferred pleasure, the emblem whose unattainability is conventionally the guarantee of its transcendent power.

Note that the emphasis is on the passivity and immobility induced by a romantic fetishism of femininity – not only does the false religion of *amore* effeminise the male, producing 'impotent voyeurs *à la* Huysmans' (*F*, 69), but it also creates a poetics of reflection and solipsism, a hoarding of internal riches against an ever-present sense of lack and incompleteness. Futurism, in contrast, pledges itself to the open spaces of the public domain, abandoning the psychic investment which motivates the symbol (and fetish) in favour of a lavish expenditure worthy of a new consumer age. Now we can understand the rejection of history as the all-important founding gesture of Futurism, since 'history' blocks both libidinal and monetary economies by conjoining the fetishistic and mimetic: 'History, in our eyes, is fatally a forger, or at least a miserable collector of stamps, medals, and counterfeit coins' (*F*, 67).

Here we might speak with some precision of a poetic economy, for Marinetti comes back on numerous occasions to this association between hoarding (collecting, investing) and the decadent use of language which, not untypically, he finds epitomised in Mallarmé's verse. Thus we find him writing in his 1913 manifesto on 'Words-in-Freedom':

> I oppose the decorative, precious aesthetic of Mallarmé and his search for the rare word, the one indispensable, elegant, sugges-

tive, exquisite adjective. I do not want to suggest an idea or a sensation with passéiste airs and graces. Instead I want to grasp them brutally and hurl them in the reader's face.　(*FM*, 105)[7]

What Marinetti objects to is Mallarmé's 'static ideal', his fetishistic attention to the single word rather than to 'the beauty of speed' which is the objective of the Futurist 'destruction of syntax'. Of course, Marinetti is perversely inattentive to the rhythmic articulation of Mallarmé's poems, focusing instead on the decadent preoccupation with the 'rare word' (we recall that Mallarmé's style had impressed Des Esseintes because it 'avoided dispersing the reader's attention over all the several qualities that a row of adjectives would have presented one by one, concentrating it instead on a single word, a single entity').[8]

The critique of Mallarmé's style now inserts itself into a much larger context, for what Marinetti objects to is the connection he discerns between inhibited sexual impulse and the hermetic depth and materiality of language which seems to be its compensation. But 'compensation', of course, only in the mirrored world of a text like 'Herodias', for in Marinetti's terms the closely-worked opacity of Mallarmé's language falsely attracts to itself the allure and corporeality of that eroticised body whose claims it strives to deny. The absorbed inward gaze is, as it were, crystallised in the 'rare word', which becomes a fetishistic object whose material 'weight' inhibits movement and expressivity, confining the imagination to a world of artifice whose law is one of perennially unfulfilled desire. For Marinetti, this is the world of the pre-modern, a world where an economy of accumulation and repression blocks access to any immediate sensual experience of the new (he writes, for example, of the characters in D'Annunzio's play *The Dead City*, that they are 'swollen with interior life'[9]). As so often with Marinetti's thought, Nietzsche lurks in the background; the following passage from *On the Genealogy of Morals* (1887) is especially relevant:

All instincts that do not discharge themselves outwardly *turn inward* – this is what I call the *internalization* of man: thus it was that man first developed what was called his 'soul'. The entire inner world, originally as thin as if it were stretched between two membranes, expanded and extended itself, acquired depth, breadth and height in the name of measure as outward discharge was *inhibited*.[10]

Once again we have the theme of a false embodiment or material-isation which inhibits the 'outward discharge' which is modernity. The implied analogy between the fulfilment of male desire and the drive of modernisation suggests, too, a parallel tendency to associate a sense of introversion and 'deep' materiality with a notion of femininity.

The Nietzschean figure of 'discharge' is especially suggestive here, partly because it implies that idea of explosive energy which the Futurists constantly define as *simultaneity*, the desired condition of the new arts; and also because it epitomises the redirection of affect which governs the Futurist aesthetic. As we have seen in earlier chapters, the model of split subjectivity which originated with Baudelaire had led to the construction of an increasingly masochistic art in the last decades of the nineteenth century. Marinetti's polemic against 'feminine' or reified language is part of a larger strategy which invents modernism through the act of *directing violence outwards*, away from the self. The literary manifestos thus urge an assault on all linguistic structures and the smashing of that 'jewelled' language of inwardness whose remnants must now be 'hurled in the reader's face'. The audience for the work becomes a target rather than a recipient – the Futurists speak of their plays as having been 'victoriously imposed on crowded theatres' (*FM*, 196) – and the public's complete understanding is neither sollicited nor desired.[11] 'Art', declares Marinetti, 'is a need to destroy and scatter oneself' (*F*, 89), a need which can be met only, as we shall see, by the simultaneous annihilation of others.

* * *

The invention of 'words-in-freedom' (*parole in libertà*) was essentially a means of cancelling 'psychology' or 'the inner life' (*FM*, 129). Where the Mallarméan text had achieved its effect by an intricate reticulation of surface whose echoes and reflective deferrals project a syntax of desire and dream, the Futurist 'destruction of syntax', with its rejection of 'inevitable echo-play, internal and external' (*FM*, 99), employs juxtaposition and analogy to create a fast-moving surface which denies the Symbolist imagination a foothold.

Emotion now tends to be depersonalised: the linear trajectory of the text brutally suppresses any opportunity for introspection, and in place of the structures of syntax Marinetti opts for 'very brief or *anonymous* mathematical and musical symbols' (*FM*, 104). Movement here is not that of Symbolist dream, but something apparently external and absolutely enjoined, the movements of 'objects' rather than of the contemplative sensibility: 'To render the successive motions of an object, one must render the *chain of analogies* that it evokes' (*F*, 86).

In place of the vertical relations presupposed by the symbol (the real as imperfect embodiment of the ideal), the scatter-gun effect of Futurist analogies is intended to produce a horizontal cross-weave of images which brings together different, initially unrelated zones of experience. This is, according to Marinetti, writing which banishes both 'materialism' and 'psychology', operating somewhere between the two in a kind of hyper-reality where the Nietzschean will-to-power is caught up into the newly liberated forces of the industrial world. The result of this self-transcendence is 'Man multiplied by the machine. New mechanical sense, a fusion of instinct with the efficiency of motors and conquered forces' (*FM*, 97). Such 'fusion' occurs when man is 'able to externalize his will' (*F*, 96), thereby overcoming the 'feminine' tendency to inwardness; hence Marinetti's injunction to 'Destroy the *I* in literature: that is all psychology. ... To substitute for human psychology, now exhausted, the lyric obsession with matter' (*F*, 87).

Perhaps not surprisingly in view of the strong element of performance in Futurist aesthetics, the fullest realisation of these ideas came in experimental theatre. Art and life converged as the Futurists tried to drive their audiences into a frenzy of outrage and indignation (Marinetti's favourite trick was to 'sell the same ticket to ten people' in order to ensure a fracas [*F*, 121]). During 1915–16 the Futurists toured Italian cities presenting the highly compressed 'plays' they called *sintesi* or syntheses. Often lasting only a few moments, and eschewing narrative and 'psychology', the *sintesi* provoked enigmatic confrontations with the very nature of the theatrical medium. In Francesco Cangiullo's *Lights!*, for example, the performance begins in a darkened auditorium with the curtain raised. Actors planted among the audience shout for lights, leading what is intended to become a general complaint. After several minutes, 'The stage and auditorium are illuminated in an EXAGGERATED way. At the same moment, the curtain slowly falls.'[12]

Such ironic play with dramatic conventions is coupled with a calculated lack of interest in character. In one *sintesi* by Arnaldo Corradini and Bruno Corra, 'Alternation of Character', the dialogue shifts without logic from one emotional extreme to another,[13] and devices such as this work towards a mechanisation of theatrical illusion. The actor, rules Marinetti, must 'Completely dehumanize his voice, systematically doing away with every modulation or nuance. Completely dehumanize his face. ... Metallize, liquefy, vegetalize, petrify, and electrify his voice' (*F*, 144). Such dehumanisation was more fully explored in Futurist experiments with scenography. Influenced partly by theorist Gordon Craig, stage designers such as Enrico Prampolini began to develop kinetic sets capable of producing a 'drama' of light, movement and sound which would not require human actors at all. As Prampolini put it, 'the intervention of the actor in the theatre as an element of interpretation is one of the most absurd compromises in the art of the theatre'.[14]

Futurist poetry was a rather more elusive thing, partly because the form itself was so conditioned by lyric expectations. One unsatisfactory solution to that problem was to meet the claims of the manifestos by freighting the poem with ostentatiously Futurist tropes and images. Enrico Cavacchioli's 'Let the Moon be Damned', for example, looses another volley against the seductive moonlight and enjoins the reader

> if you want to live, go get a mechanical heart,
> inhale the red-hot blast of furnaces
> and powder your lovely face with chimney soot;
> then shoot a million volts into your system![15]

Many of the poems in the early collections echo the rhapsodic materialism of the manifestos, coupling this with a recurring promethean gesture and an attempt to achieve cosmic implications through the imagery – Luciano Folgore's hymn 'To Coal', for example, from his *Song of the Engines* (1912):

> Ascend, great carbon, in towers of flame,
> and sweep your light across the Universe
> that readies, in time, our future.[16]

Such poems do free themselves from 'crepuscular' moroseness and sentimentality,[17] but our expectations of 'telegraphic lyricism' (*FM*,

104) are not often met – there is little typographic experimentation in these volumes, and if the 'I' is undermined it is more often through the relatively conventional irony of a poet like Aldo Palazzeschi than through the acts of 'destruction' envisaged by Marinetti. Of course, the most significant of these poets – Corrado Govoni, Paolo Buzzi, Palazzeschi – passed through Futurism, splicing it with other forms and drawing energy from it rather than seeking its pure expression.

Others, like Ardengo Soffici, were broadly concerned with an art of modernity rather than with any particular modernist tendency.[18] Soffici thus coupled Futurist motifs with a Cubist cityscape, cutting between different times and languages. His 'Crossroads' is arguably one of the better poems we can class as Futurist and brings together most of its main elements:

Crossroads

To be dissolved, a mote of dust, in the sheen of evening:
sudden clamor of electricity gas-light acetylene the lamps
flaring in the window-panes
as in the airplane of the firmament
and shoes dripping diamond and gold on the pavements of
    Spring
like the lips [and] the glances of all these women hysterical with
    loneliness
automobiles converging from everywhere
regal carriages trolleys screeching like wounded birds
Nous n'avons plus d'amour que pour nous-mêmes enfin
'Do not talk to the conductor'
Oh to drift, a fish enamoured, drinking emeralds
among these nets of fragrances and fire![19]

Here, again, is the desire for disembodiment, which the poem figures partly through the deliberate suppression of the 'I'. Characteristically, the lack of punctuation (a device here learnt as much from Apollinaire as from Marinetti) allows a loose assemblage of elements, though the poem constantly hovers on the brink of mere impressionism, and the 'I' still lurks in the desire 'To be dissolved'. The 'nets of images or analogies' which Marinetti proposed as a principal poetic technique are in operation here (Soffici seems to allude to them directly in the last line), with the light of the lamps caught in multiple reflections which weave together the cosmic 'airplane of the firmament' with the 'dripping diamond and gold' on the women's shoes.

We may still feel, though, that Soffici's poem does not meet the full requirements of Marinetti's 'destruction of syntax' or, indeed, the kind of violence against language which he advocates: 'The rush of steam-emotion will burst the sentence's steampipe, the valves of punctuation, and the adjectival clamp. Fistfuls of essential words in no conventional order' (*FM*, 98). Marinetti's own work shows a quite deliberate development from the sadomasochistic movements of an early poem like *Destruction* (1904), where the desire for heroic transcendence competes with a decadent desire to be crushed by the sea,[20] to the programmatic Futurist prose of *Zang Tumb Tuuum* (1914), an evocation of the siege of Adrianopolis during the Balkan War. Two years earlier, Marinetti had advised his fellow Futurist poets that 'your strict nets of metaphor are too disgracefully weighed down by the plumb line of logic' (*F*, 88), and we might take *Zang Tumb Tuuum* as his own attempt to work towards 'a yet more essential art, when we dare to suppress all the first terms of our analogies and render no more than an uninterrupted sequence of second terms' (*F*, 89). Certainly, the text moves at a greater speed than any of the poems mentioned above:

> exploding roasting + speed + ferocity of the tires coal dust of the street thirst thirst of the rubber cactus[21]

Marinetti purges out metaphor and substitutes his mathematical signs for conventional syntax ('This intermediary must be suppressed, in order that literature may enter directly into the universe and become one body with it' [*F*, 89]). The result is an elliptical and staccato chain of nouns and sensory impressions, the whole marked by a strong lateral movement:

> earthquake of walls–mud   feel-
> ing the sea as a sum of different
> weights   navigating = addition
> 200,000 blocks beams ropes barrels
> (**ploooom**) + a million sacks blue rotten
> ceilings green doors yellow cabs
> + 2,000 steam pregnancies **tataploom-
> ploom flac flac**   against the prow-

stomach   holding in its mouth the
entire   ROUND SEA = swimmer juggler
+ porcelain dish (6 Km. in diameter)
between the teeth   (63)

Marinetti's deliberate reduction of literary figures to strings of
nouns is intended to dissolve those private intensities of the
reflective imagination and eroticised body whose 'feminine' inscriptions – as 'depth' and materiality – offer resistance to the
mechanised currents of modernity.[22] The aim in *Zang Tumb Tuuum*
is to create a language which does not so much represent as
present, which does not reproduce an absent reality but which produces its own reality (it does not yearn for the absent body of the
beloved, but, as he says in those remarks on syntax, strives instead
to 'become one body' with the material universe). Yet, as Marjorie
Perloff has observed, such passages of words-in-freedom are little
more than lists, and the destruction of the lyric ego is achieved by
'rendering sensations at a level so generalised that anyone might
feel them'.[23] The 'one body' is accordingly a highly abstract one
since Marinetti's assault on the lyric 'I' also tends to deprive his
words of any social ground.

Marinetti's characteristic emphasis on flux and movement registers the impact of Bergson's idea of personal time, though here it is
as if duration (*durée*) has been 'spatialised', equated with the
rhythms of technological and communicational process which
mark out the dimensions of the modern life-world.[24] If man is 'multiplied' by the machine it is because his limitations seem to vanish
in a prodigious surrender to the machine which cancels subjectivity
at one metaphysical stroke: 'We already live in the absolute,
because we have created eternal omnipresent speed' (*F*, 41). While
the machine embodies a harsh productivist logic, it is one which
abolishes the traditional dialectic of private and public, inner and
outer, in order to institute a self whose thorough dehumanisation is
the mark of its triumph over the lack and incompleteness associated with sexual difference:

> We systematically destroy the literary *I* in order to scatter it into
> the universal vibration and reach the point of expressing the
> infinitely small and the vibration of molecules. ... Thus the
> poetry of cosmic forces supplants the poetry of the merely
> human. (*F*, 98)

Marinetti's aim was thus to cancel that association of desire with lack on which avant-garde poetry since Baudelaire had been founded. Lying behind the Futurist destruction of the 'I' is, in fact, a conception of desire which is strangely close to that which Gilles Deleuze and Félix Guattari have more recently proposed:

> Desire does not lack anything; it does not lack its object. It is, rather, the *subject* that is missing in desire, or desire that lacks a fixed subject; there is no fixed subject unless there is repression. [25]

This way of connecting desire with reality, liberating the artist from the tyranny of representation and 'the lost Object' (*FM*, 198), transforms the Futurist self into the functional conduit of external rhythms. Sexuality is freed from the law of desire to become a purely mechanical genital contact,[26] the body 'metallised' in its transcendence of sexual difference. Desire becomes a kind of 'non-human' force, as Valentine de Saint-Point claims in her *Futurist Manifesto of Lust* (1913): 'Lust, when viewed with moral preconceptions and as an essential part of life's dynamism, is a force' (*FM*, 70). Futurist theory thus entails a kind of 'decentring': when Marinetti calls for '*strict nets of images or analogies*' (*F*, 86), the structural model of the net suggests, as Umberto Eco notes in another context, 'no centre, no periphery, no exit, because it is potentially infinite'.[27] No longer a stable centre, subjectivity drains through the holes in the net, denied a 'materialisation' in the hermetic word.

What Marinetti was proposing was thus a kind of 'unbinding' of romantic erotic fantasy through a breaking down of the social institutions in which desire is contained. An aesthetics of simultaneity dissolves consciousness in the 'real', conflating social and psychic in a fantasy of disembodiment which relegates the oedipal narrative to 'history'. Where the family had once functioned as bridge and mediator between the self and the social body, now capitalist modernity offers a space of unrestricted desire which has no object because nothing has been 'lost'. Marinetti's attack on the past thus goes much further than his desire to dynamite museums, since it repudiates the main oppositional thrust of nineteenth-century poetics. For if the development of Symbolism, from Baudelaire on, had been an attempt to open up the divisions in subjectivity in order to call into question bourgeois ideals of rational progress and self-presence, Futurism, in its celebratory dissolution of the self, was really nothing less than an attempt to repair those divisions, to make the subject a transparent vehicle of capitalist modernity. Futurism, we might say, collapsed the distinction between aesthetic and bourgeois modernities which Baudelaire had made the founding condition of avant-garde activity. In this sense, the dialectic of destruction and creation on which the Futurist transcendence of self and culture depended actually embodied the larger, more devastating logic of capital – a logic which modern theorists were beginning to explain as a necessary relation between ever-increasing productivity and the ensuing competition for markets. So, while the Futurist exaltation of war was hardly unique in its time, it did exceed the forms which this took in the work of other avant-gardists. The pre-war passion for violence generally tended to result either from purely nationalist loyalties or from a more confused desire to destroy a conservative and academic culture. Futurism contained both of these elements, but the deeper rationale of its apparently irrational metaphysic was quite simply that of the market. A cruel aesthetic now sought its own reflection in the bourgeois society which it celebrated.[28]

Not, of course, that Marinetti would have thought of this in such rationalistic terms: for him the circuit of capital was ultimately as inscrutable as the Bergsonian *élan vital* and it was precisely in this measure that it supported a fantasy of modernisation as liberating because absolute. As he put it, with his usual bluntness, 'Progress…is always right even when it is wrong, because it is movement, life, struggle, hope' (*F*, 82). As that inversion of Baudelairean principle suggests, the early Futurist preoccupation with speed soon yielded to a celebratory sense of the mobility of capital. According to this view, capitalism has no 'logic' as such, but merely articulates a process of never-ending evolution and global expansion. War is 'hygienic' because it encapsulates in the most extreme form the productive and destructive drives within the process of modernisation. If, as Walter Benjamin argues, Marinetti 'expects war to supply the artistic gratification of a sense perception that has been changed by technology',[29] this is indeed 'the consummation of *l'art pour l'art*' – an ironic outcome for an aesthetic which repudiates decadence in the name of 'action'. For Benjamin, this contemplative, disengaged stance signifies the conversion of political values to aesthetic ones, and Futurism in this respect prefigures the fascism it will later endorse. Mankind's 'self-alienation has reached such a degree', continues Benjamin, 'that it can experience its own destruction as an aesthetic pleasure of the first order'. But we should qualify this by noting that Marinetti's thematics of war is once again generated from a reversal of decadent aesthetics: the 'metallisation' of the Futurist body protects it against the masochistic drive of decadent art by cancelling the sense of bodily finitude and by exorcising the fear of death through the death of *others*.

The extremity of this exteriorising aesthetic is likely to conceal the familiar structure contained within it, for this is, in part, a legacy of Hegelian subjectivity which, in Jessica Benjamin's words, 'posits a self that has no intrinsic need for the other, but uses the other only as a vehicle for self-certainty'.[30] With the failure of a properly mutual recognition, the other is reduced to the status of an object; Benjamin concludes that

> The image of the other that predominates in Western thought is not that of a vitally real presence but a *cognitively perceived object*. In this sense 'false' differentiation has been a constant component of the Western version of individualism. Recognizing the other has been the exceptional moment, a moment of rare innocence, the recovery of a lost paradise.[31]

But for Futurism (and, as we shall see, for many subsequent avant-gardes), it is precisely that 'moment of rare innocence' which is repudiated as romantic and narcissistic, since it opens the way to forms of identification and imitation which seem to threaten the very existence of a modernist art. War thus provides the apocalyptic occasion in which the other can be obliterated rather than recognised, while the self is absorbed (and absolved) by the 'cosmic' movements of modernity. As one critic puts it, war thus conceived is

> a *festival* in a psychological sense – as the abolition of norms and as a dispersal of energy – , in a sociological sense – as a magnificent cycle of production and expenditure of goods – , in a political sense – as a pattern of a new order generated from the violent break with the past.[32]

Yet the reference to production and expenditure may remind us that war is the extreme summation of a logic which permeates modernity – the logic of consumerism. This logic the Futurists welcomed as the perfect antidote to a decadent economy of accumulation and repression. Art would no longer be fetishised for its aloofness but would be thoroughly integrated into the fast-moving circuit of commodities: 'To the conception of the imperishable, the immortal, we oppose, in art, that of becoming, the perishable, the transitory and the ephemeral.'[33] Instead of the display-case of the museum we should look instead to the shop-window, since, according to Giacomo Balla, 'Any store in a modern town, with its elegant windows all displaying useful and pleasing objects, is much more aesthetically enjoyable than all those passéist exhibitions which have been so lauded everywhere' (*FM*, 219). The Futurists may have approached the masses with scorn and cynicism – that after all was the technical discovery of both their manifestos and their performances – but they did so in the knowledge that their field of operation was that of the consumer. As Germano Celant has observed:

> Art became 'socialised', following not the utopian paths of revolution but rather those of consumption and disposability, an attitude that implies the final disappearance of the 'avant-garde' as value and the advent of a social statute of culture.[34]

To externalise the self in the public domain was to open it to the manifold stimuli of the market, where a new range of pleasures awaited the consumer. As one Futurist work, called *The Death of Woman* (1925), put it: 'Love as sentiment is therefore absurd, an enemy to modern existence where there are no differences between male and female and where the atmosphere is so rich in sensual sensations.'[35] Replacing desire by commodification, Futurism conflated economic expenditure with a celebratory expenditure of the *self* which promised freedom from the limits and incompleteness of a gendered ('pre-modern') identity.

The full force of this idea is clear when we compare the use of the concept of 'expenditure' in the work of Georges Bataille: for where Bataille affirms waste and expenditure as the transgression of the limits of the purposive world of labour and consumption,[36] Futurism called for an ecstatic and impersonal submission to the homogenising process of exchange and consumption. So we find Bruno Corradini and Emilio Settimelli, in their manifesto of 1914, *Weights, Measures and Prices of Artistic Genius*, insisting that

> The producer of artistic creativity must join the commercial organisation which is the muscle of modern life. Money is one of the most formidably and brutally solid points of the reality in which we live. It is enough to turn to it to eliminate all possibility of error and unpunished justice.   (*FM*, 149)

Just as the rapid production of verbal analogies would dissolve subjectivity in its 'net' of images, so money could be grasped as a 'solid point' because it promised the abolition of difference, the perfect metonymic logic in which every element referred inexorably and transparently to the total system. Here, once more, we find that metaphysics of modernity which conflates abstraction and amnesia in a desperate attempt to 'forget' the material realities which confront it. Futurism, we might say, seeks to redeem aesthetic cruelty from its decadent associations with masochism, to purify and refine it so that it appears as the cutting edge of modernity itself. Yet amnesia is rarely total, and the consumer fantasy in which Futurism invested so heavily needed fast-talking words-in-freedom to keep at bay the spectre of the suffering bodies which haunted its margins.

As if to emphasise that persistent materiality, the literary experiments themselves remained tied to the 'bodily' effects which the manifestos derided as feminine and *passéiste*. For the attachment to performance, to eloquence and rhetoric, worked ultimately to restore the body as source of expressivity by stressing effects of sound and voice. As the Russian Futurists observed critically, Marinetti's technique was heavily dependent on onomatopoeia, and while his polemic for words-in-freedom connected the anti-mimetic with a rejection of 'feminine' materiality, his dependence on sound-effects led ultimately to a calculated *elision* of sign and referent rather than to their separation. This was more likely to be successful in the Futurist theatre, where the dehumanisation of the body could be carried out in spectacular fashion. The literary text, however, presented problems of its own: having banished both syntax and rhythm, Marinetti's words-in-freedom tended, as we have seen, to produce merely a linear sequence of sensory impressions – a cumulative registration of effects which reminds us of the strong positivist background of Futurist aesthetics. That is not in itself surprising, since Marinetti's main preoccupation as a writer was with evoking multiple sensory impressions rather than with visual images. What is important, though, is the way in which the paradoxical return to a form of representation disrupted Futurism's fantasy of a disembodied consumer world. For the reappearance of the body here brought with it the full material 'weight' of class relations: Marinetti's 'metallised' man turns out to be man in chains, the wage-slave of modernity rather than the 'liberated' consumer of the future.[37]

*   *   *

Futurism ended its most original phase around 1915 with Italy's entry into the war. Later there would be a 'second wave', as Marinetti tried to sustain the momentum of his movement with a string of new fads like 'tactilism' and 'aero-painting'. Yet the 'much-prayed-for great war' had depleted the ranks of the Futurists (according to Marinetti, thirteen lost their lives, including Boccioni and Sant'Elia[38]), and perhaps the most significant feature of the post-war period was Futurism's difficult relation to Italian fascism. Between 1915 and 1919, Marinetti was close to Mussolini, standing as parliamentary candidate for the Fascist Party in 1919 and going to prison with its leader after the loss of the election to the Socialists. Yet as Mussolini began to ease his swing to the Right by making strategic compromises with the Monarchists and the Church, Marinetti found himself unable to follow. For his part, Mussolini soon had little need of the volatile Futurists, and after the successful March on Rome in 1922 he ditched them without ceremony. It might seem that fascism, with its *passéiste* cult of the Roman past and its attachment to traditional family values, was far removed from the manifesto commitments of Futurism, but Marinetti's veneration of dynamism and the productivist fantasy at the heart of his particular modernism kept him within the orbit of Mussolini's movement. Notwithstanding the Duce's coldness, Marinetti would later join the Accademia d'Italia and become a diehard supporter of both the Italian campaign in Ethiopia and the puppet regime of Salò.

What of those Italian writers who did not align themselves with either Futurism or fascism? It is ironic, perhaps, that the three poets now commonly thought to be the greatest of this period worked for the most part outside the avant-garde. The writings of Umberto Saba, Giuseppe Ungaretti, and Eugenio Montale show in different ways a complex mix of highly innovative thought and technique alongside a deliberately anti-Futurist sense of continuity and tradition. This is not to minimise the large-scale reverberations produced by Futurism – in terms of its advocacy of the new, Marinetti's movement coloured almost all literary experiment of the period, and technical play with ellipsis, typographical layout and lack of punctuation generally had some debt to Futurism. Yet what is especially notable in these poets, none of whom had particularly close contact with Futurism,[39] is the interest taken in traditional verse-forms and the undaunted commitment to those concerns of the lyric ego which Marinetti had sought to prohibit. Saba's principal work, *Song-book* (1945), for example, plots the writer's life across a number of volumes, often in homely and decidedly non-cosmic detail, while Ungaretti had no hesitation in calling his collected poems, many parts of which have the character of an intimate journal, *The Life of a Man* (1947). Montale's verse may seem more calculatedly impersonal, but he too observed that 'It is probably an illusion to think that explicit subjectivity or the use of "I" makes poetry more precarious and less universal.'[40] Montale sums up a strand of thought shared by these poets when he remarks in an essay on Ezra Pound that

> the Imagists imported modern poetry into America, while remaining extraneous to that poetry of Virgilian and Petrarchan origin which thanks to Leopardi and Baudelaire is still the core of the European lyric. Perhaps they misunderstood this tradition, which for them signified Swinburne whom they detested.[41]

A certain subjectivism, then, is central to the tradition of European lyric, and Montale, along with Saba and Ungaretti, regarded Futurism as but a momentary deviation from that broad path.

The Futurist rejection of the lyric 'I' was not, however, the only avant-garde move which these poets refused to accept. There was also the theatrical dimension of Futurism, the element of performance which, as we have seen, led to Marinetti's dependence on onomatopoeia and sound-effects. Here was an irony which opponents were not slow to notice: Futurism, the avant-garde movement *par excellence*, was still tied to forms of representation. This would become a familiar taunt, one considerably sharpened by the success of its principal competitor, French Cubism. Ungaretti, who had studied in Paris and been close to its leading painters and poets, mobilised the usual contemporary arguments against Marinetti: Futurism limited itself simply to *imitating* machines, and this capitulation to immediacy was reflected in its practice of words-in-freedom, which exhibited a 'blind faith in raw material, in sensation, in chaotic impressions'.[42] Futurism opted for the 'brutal' exteriority of the machine, 'not waiting for memory to transform it into a morally recognisable fact'.[43] Ungaretti's criticism shows how distant he was from the essential goals of Futurism: not only was memory to play a central part in his writing, as in that of Saba and Montale, but private recollection was to be part of a larger rhythm of cultural memory which set the new poem in relation to the echo chamber of literary tradition. This temporal dimension allowed a distance from the chaos of immediate experience, creating an imaginative space in which the elements of reality could be recombined into a new whole. In the thirties, this emphasis on the internal space of the poem would lead to Ungaretti's work being labelled 'hermetic'.[44] The word was somewhat inaccurate in suggesting that his writing was governed by hidden or secret meanings, but it did register the particular difficulty attaching to metaphor and analogy in many of his poems.

Analogy, we recall, had been a prominent device in Futurist writing, and Marinetti had longed for the time 'when we dare to suppress all the first terms of our analogies and render no more than an uninterrupted sequence of second terms' (*F*, 89). In reacting against what he saw as the excessive 'objectivism' of Marinetti's writing, Ungaretti adopted a similar approach to analogy but with the aim of heightening the subjective element. In a poem from *The Joy* (1919), for example, 'Roses in flames', we have the following image (the poem is quoted in its entirety):

On an ocean
of ringing bells
suddenly
there floats another morning[45]

The poem does not refer directly to the village or town whose bells usher in another morning; that first term of the analogy is suppressed, leaving us only with the second, distanced one of the 'ocean', whose implications are not fulfilled until we reach the morning, which 'floats' in the final line. Poems like this are remote indeed from the 'positivism' of Marinetti's *Zang Tumb Tuuum*, with its chain of sensory notations. In fact, the brief but highly concentrated structures developed by Ungaretti in his early volumes give the reader a sense of both fullness of meaning and of something left unspoken.

Ungaretti seems to have had this in mind in a much later interview with Denis Roche in which he explained that 'This poetry is born from the idea that you can't represent things poetically, that's to say that you can only grasp them in their most profound reality when they don't exist; and it's at that moment only that they become ours.'[46] One might think of Mallarmé's flower, which is 'absent from all bouquets', and indeed *The Joy* opens with the following two-line poem:

Eternal

Between a flower gathered and the other given
the inexpressible nothingness[47]

It is in that space that the poet must operate, according to Ungaretti, knowing all the time that the natural ('given') flower can never be adequately represented but only sought in the figure which signifies its absence. This is, then, a poetry which endeavours to avoid the trap of the mimetic, knowing that 'We have recourse to the mental world to feel the existence of things.'[48] It is that transposition of the real to a different imaginative space which connects Ungaretti with Mallarmé and at the same time puts him outside the Futurist aesthetic.

The poems in *The Joy* which record Ungaretti's wartime experience in the Carso and in France explore the violence and inhumanity of that world in terms which are very different from those of Futurist heroics. (Ungaretti observed of the 1916 volume *The Buried Port* that 'it certainly was not a book exalting heroism. It was a book of the poet's compassion for himself, for his companions, for human destiny. It was a cry, an offering, an invocation of fraternity.'[49]) The poems are marked by place and date, and these specificities give the volumes something of the character of an intimate journal. Yet the 'cry', acutely personal as it may be, is subordinated to the tightest of disciplines. Ungaretti's lines often carry only one word, and these sparely organised structures descend the page with a Mallarméan sensitivity to their surrounding spaces (again, this verticality contrasts strongly with the pronounced lateral movement of Marinetti's texts). 'Vanity', for example:

Suddenly
high
on the ruins
the limpid
stupor
of immensity

And the man
bent
above water
surprised
by the sun
revives
a shadow

Rocked and
slowly
split[50]

Ellipsis and lack of punctuation focus attention on each word in succession as Ungaretti breaks his rhythmic form into smaller and smaller units (one critic aptly terms this a 'molecular scansion'[51]).

Such reverence for the word has a markedly mystical feel in these early poems, and indeed Ungaretti recalls that

> it suddenly dawned on me how the word (*parola*) ought to be called to birth through an expressive tension that loaded it to overflowing with the fullness of its meaning. ...If the word were made naked, if one stopped at each cadence of rhythm, each beat of the heart, if one isolated moment after moment each word in its own verity, this was because in the first place one felt oneself a man, religiously a man, and it seemed that this was the revolution which under these historical circumstances [the war] necessarily had to be initiated by and from the words themselves. [52]

Ungaretti seems to imply that this reverential sensitivity to words gives some access to 'being' (the cadence unfurling in time with the heart-beat), and poems like 'Vanity' seek to explore those moments when inside and outside are locked in some extraordinary tension. 'Vanity' registers both the exhilaration of the scene, the 'immensity' of a landscape which preserves its neutrality amidst man-made violence, and the psychic fragmentation of those caught within it. The moment seems as if frozen in 'the stupor of immensity', until the 'splitting' of the soldier's reflection suddenly brings violence back into the picture.

The characteristic mode of *The Joy* tends towards such brief, concentrated, and self-contained moments of lyric intensity. Like 'Vanity', some of these express exhilaration, the most famous being the two-line poem called 'Morning': 'I flood myself with light / Of the immense' ('M'illumino / d'immenso'[53]); others work towards some moment of common sympathy and identification. In 'Watch', for example, the poet spends 'An entire night / thrown close / to a comrade / massacred'; in the final lines of this brief poem he finds that

> in my silence
> I have written
> letters full of love
>
> I have never been
> so
> tied to life[54]

In his next main collection, *Feeling for Time*, published in 1933 but including poems from as far back as 1919, Ungaretti seeks to develop the sense of connection with others through an exploration of 'the infinite complexities and obligations of memory'.[55] As memory intersects with the larger memory of the cultural tradition, so the presentation of the self becomes more complex; in a note to the new collection, Ungaretti observes that 'The poems of *The Joy* are all in the first person: *I* spoke.' In *Feeling for Time*, he seeks instead 'a more objective content, which would put a certain distance between the poet and his inspiration'.[56] This new direction is occasioned by Ungaretti's intensive meditation on the Italian literary tradition. He is concerned above all with a perception of 'duration' or, we might say, psychological as opposed to linear time (he had attended Bergson's lectures when a student in Paris). No longer can there be a present suspended out of time, for each moment is permeated by memories of what is past. It is this recognition which makes Leopardi's work of such importance for Ungaretti:

> Leopardi wonders whether we are not reduced – since time exists no longer, or only consumed or defunct time – to no longer being able to evoke the reality of our being, to no longer being able to set it in motion, save through the efforts of memory.[57]

Memory thus becomes Ungaretti's 'substantial theme', as he puts it,[58] a development which is accompanied by a growing interest in ancient myth (as, for example, in the *Legends* section of *Feeling for Time*). The major theme becomes, as he explains in a note to one of the poems, 'the tragic sense of time's flight', and this time creates a highly particular psychic dimension:

> Internal duration is composed of time and space beyond chrono-logical time; the internal universe is a world where reversibility is the rule. This time never flows in a single direction, never orientates itself in the selfsame manner; one can trace back its course to one knows not what inaccessible source, yet it is at the same time immediately present within us.[59]

Ungaretti's notion of temporal 'reversibility' is extremely sugges-tive, not least because it might lead to a fundamental distinction between avant-gardism and what some critics have called, by way of distinction, 'modernism'. Certainly, the difference between Marinetti's writing and that of Ungaretti is not simply one of em-phasis or content. What is involved is actually structural, for the Futurist concept of the avant-garde is premissed on a moment of absolute rupture with what has gone before. It has often been argued, and with particular force by Peter Bürger, that the achieve-ment of the avant-garde (he thinks primarily of Surrealism) is to call into question the very institution of art, to undermine aesthetic autonomy by seeking to make art part of the 'praxis of life'.[60] The disadvantage of this strategy, as we saw with Futurism, is that it can grasp the present only as a moment of destruction – destruction of the other or, ultimately, of the self. As Henri Meschonnic remarks, Futurism cannot conceive of the present in any other way since its internal logic compels it endlessly to manipulate the two self-contained 'blocks' of past and future time: the 'mythical' time of the avant-garde, says Meschonnic, using a particularly damning word in this context, is 'linear'.[61]

If the dominant psychic figure of Futurism is the Nietzschean one of 'discharge', then Ungaretti's idea of temporal 'reversibility' seems to hint at an alternative conception of the self as complex and dynamic, but in an important sense also as historical. The inner life is thus conceived as an unending interaction of present experience with memories of the past; time flows away, carrying with it expe-riences which cannot be lived again, though they can become present momentarily as memories. Such a conception allows pre-cisely that space in which the 'morally recognisable fact' may emerge – in contrast to the essentially passive though grandiose self of the Futurists, Ungaretti's concept of psychic temporality offers resistance to any amnesiac dreams of a perpetual present. Instead he draws from Vico and Leopardi a sense of a fundamental 'antinomy' between humanity's innate desire for transcendence and the temporal and spatial limits by which it is constrained.[62]

That sense of limits has an almost 'classical' feel, in contrast to the Futurist fantasy of effortless transcendence, and it is shared by Eugenio Montale, whose first book of poems, *The Bones of Cuttlefish*, appeared in 1925. Montale's verse is at first sight more convention-ally discursive than Ungaretti's, employing complex and extended syntactical structures in contrast to the fragmented forms of *The Joy*. The two poets share a quality of inwardness, though, and in each case this is complemented by a writing which draws strength from resistant forms. In Montale's case, the ruggedness of the Ligurian coastline, which is the principal setting for these poems, instigates a language which is equally hardbitten, defeating easy lyricism with its awkward packing of consonants:

> Lazying pale and thoughtful at noon
> along a scorching orchard-wall,
> listening amid the thorns and the scrubs
> to the crackles of blackbirds, to the rustles of snakes.[63]

The poem offers its objects quite dispassionately – in the original most of the main verbs are in the infinitive – and the clinching 'philosophical' observation in the final stanza is at once reticent and ironic:

> And while moving in the dazzling sun
> feeling with sad bewilderment
> how all of life and its labour is
> in this following alongside a steep wall
> topped with sharp bits of broken bottle.

Even Antonino Mazza's fine translation cannot quite convey the re-barbative quality of that final line, 'che ha in cima cocci aguzzi di bottiglia', where the dry abrasiveness of the language conveys the literal quality of the landscape even as it hints at some internal limit or obstacle which the poet cannot cross. Here we may recall Ungaretti's observation that 'you can't represent things poetically', for Montale's poem seems similarly to signify some failure within representation itself.

He expresses something of this in a retrospective account of his first collection:

> I obèyed a need for musical expression and wanted my words to adhere more closely to what I was expressing than was the case with the other poets I knew. I seemed to be living under a glass bell, and yet I felt myself close to something essential. A thin veil, a mere thread, divided me from that definitive *quid*. Absolute expression would have meant the tearing of that veil, the breaking of the thread: an explosion, the end of the illusion of the world as a representation. But such an end was unattainable, and my desire for adherence remained musical and instinctive, not programmatic. I wanted to wring the neck of the eloquence of our old courtly language – even at the risk of counter-eloquence.[64]

'Absolute expression', the removal of any distance separating discourse from its object, was certainly one primary goal of Italian Futurism, and we shall find it in different forms in other avant-garde movements. Montale's own work, however, accepts that language always interposes itself between the world and the poet, and the contradictory sense of feeling 'close to something essential' is inscribed in the grain of the writing, which couples an almost provincial alertness to local detail with an exacting and highly sophisticated commitment to formal rigour. Montale constantly implies that there can be momentary flashes of truth and vision, but that poetry is also grounded in a fundamental negativity. As he puts it in the last stanza of the poem which opens the collection:

> Do not ask us for the formula which could open worlds for you,
> yes, some twisted syllable and dry like a branch.
> This alone nowadays can we tell you,
> what we are *not*, what we do *not* want.[65]

Unlike the Futurists, Montale's poet does not 'already live in the Absolute' (*F*, 41), and while the strand of negativity in his work entails a constant recognition of limits, it also provides an equally constant safeguard against totalitarian fantasies of presence and the grand 'formula'.

6

Other Spaces: French Cubism and Russian Futurism

The extremism of the Futurist aesthetic leaves us with the question as to whether there could in fact be no ecstatic modernism, as we might call it, which did not tread the same path, no modernism which did not make the celebration of a dynamic modernity the ground of a radically anti-social aesthetic. An alternative route did lie in conceiving of modernity less as a content to be represented than as an instigation to *form*, and indeed we find that Ungaretti's criticism of Futurism for its failure to move beyond representation was widely echoed by modernists elsewhere. Guillaume Apollinaire, for example, impressario of French modernism and a formative influence on Ungaretti's early work, voiced the same complaint:

> The Italian futurists declare that they will not abandon the advantages inherent in the subject, and it is precisely this that may prove to be the reef upon which all their artistic good will will be dashed to bits. (*AOA*, 199)

The emergence of Cubism after 1907, the year of Picasso's pathbreaking *Les Demoiselles d'Avignon*, was to give French modernism a strong anti-representational bias. Futurist painting was profoundly affected by these developments, which in Italy were first discussed in Soffici's 1911 article on Picasso and Braque for *La Voce*,[1] but where the French scene differed from the Italian one was in the close working alliances forged between Parisian writers and artists. Here literary modernism was radically shaped by the non-figurative developments in Cubism, and the result was a very different construction of modernity.

Cubism had plenty of things in common with Futurism, of course, namely its love of the dynamic and simultaneous, and its fascination with types of duration, which issued here in the exploration of multiple points of view and the abandonment of unitary perspective. Where the two tendencies differed was in their respective conceptions of dynamism – while the Futurist ideal was one of constant movement, the Cubist interest in simultaneity led to a freezing of time so as to explore the interlocking of multiple perspectives.[2] Cubist simultanism thus implied almost from the outset a certain analytic grasp of experience, as opposed to what was constantly seen as the Futurist immersion in the flux of mere sensation. Maurice Raynal, for example, writing in the wake of the Futurist exhibition in Paris in 1912, argued that 'The movement which the futurists have perceived is therefore only relative to our senses and is in no way absolute. Here, then, is one error of reasoning due to our senses.'[3] It was not enough, claimed Raynal, to base painting 'solely on external perception'; what was needed was a painting attentive to 'forms as they are conceived in the mind'. The same point was made in the first major defence of Cubism by Albert Gleizes and Jean Metzinger, whose talk of 'the lucid region forbidden to those who are blinded by the immediate'[4] also implied a critique of Futurism.

Apollinaire's own relation to Futurism was more ambivalent. In 1912, for example, he dismissed its painting as 'a kind of art of fragmentation, a popular, flashy art' (*AOA*, 255), while the next year found him publishing his own manifesto *Futurist Antitradition* in *Lacerba*; Marinetti, it has been suggested, helped him with the typographical layout. Critics disagree as to whether or not the manifesto was actually a spoof at Marinetti's expense, but the things which Apollinaire condemned or praised ('mer ...de aux' and 'rose aux') were familiar from the principal Futurist manifestos – negative: syntax, punctuation, *ennui*, museums, Wagner, Venice; positive: 'plastic dynamism', words-in-freedom, and artists such as Picasso, Soffici, Kandinsky, and, of course, Marinetti.[5]

Apollinaire was clearly drawn to Futurism for its sheer energy and love of scandal, but his own work was increasingly bound up with the evolution of Cubism, a tendency which he himself was partly responsible for defining and promoting in *The Cubist Painters* (1913). Crucial to that aesthetic was the break with representation:

> If painters still observe nature, they no longer imitate it, and they carefully avoid the representation of natural scenes observed directly or reconstituted through study. ...Verisimilitude no longer has any importance, for the artist sacrifices everything to the

composition of his picture. The subject no longer counts, or if it counts, it counts for very little.   (*AOA*, 197)

Apollinaire's lack of concern for the subject-matter of the painting is quite different from a Symbolist interest in states of mind: Walter Pater, for example, had seemed to find a comparable transcendence of subject in the landscapes of Alphonse Legros – 'mere topography', he remarked, 'the simple material, counts for so little' – but Legros's modulation of elements to 'one dominant tone'[6] was far removed from the 'analytic' scrutiny of elements carried out by the Cubist. 'A Picasso', observes Apollinaire, 'studies an object the way a surgeon dissects a corpse' (*AOA*, 198), a comment which associates an ideal of dispassionate technique with a repudiation of the rhapsodic materialism of the Futurists – the Cubists return to 'nature', but it is 'dead', a source for living *aesthetic* forms.

Now we can see the full implications of the Cubist rejection of mimesis, for where words-in-freedom were supposed to provide 'a marvellous bridge between the word and the real thing' (*TIF*, 120), the art for which Apollinaire speaks is constantly exploiting the *difference* between its medium and the objects to which it alludes.[7] The theme and techniques of modernist 'cruelty' here undergo a profound development – where the Futurist figure of 'discharge' had embodied a dream of self-transcendence at the expense of the other, the Cubist concept of mastery attaches primarily to an ideal of aesthetic form. The new modes of perception it offers transfigure the world and in doing so conjoin primitive and modern in an explosive union which links the 'cruelty' of seeing to a 'barbarism' which exceeds Western conventions of representation. There is a sort of violent joy in the discovery of forms which disrupt figurative expectations, as if such experiments tap the primitive energy latent within the modern. If Futurist histrionics never quite transcend decadent posturing, here the celebration of enlightened perception brings together lucidity and objectivity under the sign of simultaneity, at once the condition of modernity and the formal means by which new and old may cohabit.

The association of aesthetic form, violence and 'objectivity' recalls Rilke's fascination with Baudelaire's poem about 'Carrion' ('with its legs in the air like a lewd woman's'[8]): 'I am of the opinion', he confides to his wife in 1907, 'that without this poem the whole trend towards objective expression, which we now think we can discern in Cézanne, could not have begun at all; first *this* had to be there in all its pitilessness.'[9] In part, Rilke retains a deca-dent interest in Baudelaire's scandalous subject-matter, but his way of associating it with Cézanne's 'objectivity' also connects 'pitiless-ness' with the idea that modern art is intensely *analytic*, a dissection (in Apollinaire's word) of the natural world.[10] There is a powerful conjunction of ideas here: 'form' and the move towards the non-figurative are bound up with notions of quasi-scientific mastery and 'diagnosis', with an objectivity which mocks the humanist fetish of the unified body.[11] The avant-garde rejection of mimesis is now clearly linked with a dismemberment of the body and its translation into inorganic form as a prerequisite of 'original' aes-thetic perception; at the same time, that subordination of the natural to form releases an energy which in some way exceeds rep-resentation, exerting a kind of simultaneous pressure against the conventions by which it alludes to the real. With these conceptions of form we enter a space which results from the collision of archaic and modern – a space which we may say with certainty *had not existed before.*

Apollinaire's 'Zone', from the 1913 collection *Alcohols*, provides a resonant evocation of the tensions set up by this particular modernism. The long poem begins with the definitively modern gesture – 'You are tired at last of this old world'[12] – as Apollinaire seeks to reckon with his loss of religious faith. Now the new and the old seem to converge in a sweep of feeling motivated by the poet's nostalgia for a spiritual world to which he can no longer belong.[13] In the juxtapositional mode which characterises so much of his writing, different times intersect. 'O shepherd Eiffel Tower the flock of bridges bleats at the morning': the pastoral merges seamlessly with the cityscape of modern Paris as the poet's wanderings, temporal and spatial, evoke the spiritual vagrancy of contemporary life. With a debt, perhaps, to Marinetti's fantastic poem called 'The Pope's Monoplane', Apollinaire links the continuing force of Catholicism to the development of modern aviation ('Religion alone has remained entire fresh religion / Has remained simple like the hangars at the airfield' and 'It is Christ who soars in the sky better than any aviator'). The poem now launches into a powerful celebration of modernity, Apollinaire delighting in 'Lettering on signs and walls / Announcements and billboards shriek like parrots / I love the charm of this industrial street'. Yet the colourful confusion of the city, with its chaos of signs and images, corresponds too to the poet's sense of his own psychic instability. The title 'Zone' may refer to a district of

Paris known for its poverty, but in a more general way it also alludes to the imaginative space in which memories weave together.

So the poet recalls moments from the past, yet without any expectation that together they will reveal authentic continuity. The self is, characteristically, unstable, and this is registered dramatically in the poem as the declarative 'I' of the opening lines yields to the 'you' of reminiscence ('Here is the young street and you are once again a little child'). Identity splits and mutates, as Apollinaire complicates the Futurist fantasy of the disembodied self by setting it adrift within this maze of temporal and spatial locations. We notice above all the complexity of tone: here there is nostalgia and celebration, pathos and streetwise toughness, sensuality and spiritual lament; above all, there is a sense of energy and desire which constantly border on violence, since modern life is something 'you drink like an eau-de-vie'. With the final lines of the poem, that sense of intoxication produces a vivid image of brutality and illogic as Apollinaire sees Christianity starkly outlined against a primitivism which is at once ancient and modern:

> You walk toward Auteuil you want to walk home on foot
> To sleep among your fetishes from Oceania and Guinea
> They are all Christ in another form and of another faith
> They are inferior Christs obscure hopes
>
> Adieu adieu
>
> The sun a severed neck

Images like this work by violent juxtaposition (as one critic puts it, Apollinaire produces a 'dissolving of symbol in image'[14]); there is an element of literalism here (a legacy of Rimbaud, no doubt) which tears the lyric convention and collapses the high style into a deliberately mundane register (the moon as symbol of romantic desire is now 'the moon which fries like an egg in the pan'[15]).

Such moments may prepare us for Apollinaire's invention of a particular term to define a modern art freed from the constraints of the mimetic image – 'surrealism'. The coinage appears in the late preface to his play *The Breasts of Tiresias* (1917): 'When man wanted to imitate walking, he invented the wheel which doesn't resemble a leg. He thus produced surrealism without knowing it.'[16] As Apollinaire envisages it here, 'surrealism' entails a play of different tones – 'melancholy, satire, lyricism' – and it is the resulting discontinuity which shocks the reader or audience out of the realistic attitude. The position of the reader is, in other words, never secure – simultaneity produces a collision of moods and ideas, of fantasies and memories, or, we might say, another space in which it is the contradictory present tense which is at issue rather than the destructive opposition of past and future, as in Marinetti's programme.

If it makes any sense to talk of Apollinaire's poetry as 'Cubist' it is because it shares with the art of Picasso and Braque a refusal to make of the work a transparent window on the world. The artistic material – paint, lines, words – assumes a new kind of self-sufficiency and we are not invited to look beyond the work for something to explain or legitimate it. It is easier, perhaps, to grasp the implications of this view for painting than for poetry, for how can words *not* refer to the things they name? One answer is that poets can exploit ambiguity to create an excess of meaning; they can also disrupt conventions of syntax and grammar so that discursive continuity is lost. Beyond this they might also try to block the illusion of reference by emphasising the material nature of language, the marks and spaces which make up the words on the page; sounds rather than ideas might become the principal matter of the poem. The result would carry the reader away from a discoverable, unitary meaning toward what Umberto Eco has called 'unlimited semiosis'.[17] In the remainder of this chapter we shall see how developments in painting led writers to experiment with all these ways of regarding language as a sort of physical medium (like paint); and we shall also see how the celebration of the modern in the work of Apollinaire and Blaise Cendrars was often bound up with the idea that it was somehow intractable to 'normal' language. In France, the modernist tropes of dynamism and simultaneity thus seemed to find their first authentic embodiment in a vocabulary that was both alien and unrecognisable, that of primitive art-forms.

* * *

Picasso's interest in Iberian and African art must be distinguished from the vitalism of the Futurists, for whom 'Our own primitivism

⅃ have nothing to do with antiquity.'[18] And where the
ⴖan Expressionists tended to discover a potent sense of origin
a⸜ ⅃ human continuity in these primitive artefacts, Picasso and the
Cubists were intrigued by the explosive *conjunction* of archaic and
modern (as, for example, in the use of that pastoral image in
Apollinaire's 'Zone' or in Blaise Cendrars's *Prose of the Trans-
Siberian* (1913), where the poet proposes to build an aircraft hangar
of mammoth bones[19]). For Picasso, this conjunction led to the en-
coding of the archaic within the modern not merely as a binary
'other' to be dialectically assimilated to Western modes, but as a
network of desires capable of deforming representation from
within.[20]

The primitive thus had a two-fold appeal: most conventionally, it
evoked those libidinal energies apparently repressed by Western
forms of social order (this is the version of primitivism celebrated
in, for example, the later fiction of D. H. Lawrence and further trivi-
alised in a work of imitation like Sherwood Anderson's *Dark
Laughter* [1925]); more interestingly, it could function as the correlative of experiences and emotions which were felt to lie beyond representation, to resist sanctioned Western modes of expression and
to precede the Futurist opposition of past to future. This eclipse of
'history' could take the artist beyond Western conventions (and
also beyond troublesome questions about Western imperialism); as
the Russian critic Victor Shklovsky explained, 'the aim of creating
new art is to return the object from "recognition" to "seeing"'.[21]
Hence, perhaps, Picasso's way of emphasising that Negro art provided him not with just a range of formal *models* which could be
used again and again, but with a kind of 'magic' which impelled
him to produce 'exorcism-paintings' like *Les Demoiselles
d'Avignon*.[22] Viewed from the perspective of primitive art, modernity now seemed to contain energies and desires which were
violent and dionysian, and which could be expressed only through
formal deviations from every norm.

This fascination with the apparently unrepresentable energies in
African masks and sculptures made Picasso's exploration of non-
objective forms partly contingent upon new ways of conceiving the
body. Critics have often commented on the vein of anti-humanism
in his work, noting how a 'bilious vision of the flesh' relates to a
violence frequently practised upon the image of the female body.[23]
Certainly it is a commonplace to remark on the violence attaching
to Picasso's early exploration of primitive forms, in terms of both

the deformation of the human figure and the techniques used (the aggressive hatching employed, say, in his *Head of a Man* of 1907[24]).

Much of the impact of these works derives from the way in which the dislocation of the body expresses the primacy of composition over motif.[25] D.-H. Kahnweiler observed, for example, that a Wobé mask, one of Picasso's early acquisitions, suggested a way of disrupting the conventional representation of the face, the recessed eye being here transformed into a cylinder. This inversion of mass and void had powerful implications.[26] At one level, as Kahnweiler notes, it creates a definitive break with naturalism, allowing the artist to invent his own system of signs. At another, it proposes a sort of turning outward, an exteriorisation of the human image which substitutes formal self-sufficiency for the implied presence of an occulted inner meaning or spirit. Daix and Rosselet observe that what attracted Picasso to African art was 'the radiating form, the way the shapes seemed to spread out into the atmosphere',[27] and it is clear that the various experiments in conflating inner and outer volumes were aimed at the production of a visual field structured by a radically new relation of desire to representation – a relation based on open forms which evoked another version of that de-limiting of the self which we observed in Unanimism and Futurism.

In a series of developments initiated by Cézanne's technique of *passage*, the internal rhythms of surface now become increasingly important.[28] Space is redefined so that materiality is made equivocal and the old hierarchy of figuration is abolished (the spaces between objects now rank as equal in importance with the spaces which delineate the objects themselves). This new relation of figure to ground opens the possibility of a painting where mobile surfaces subordinate individual objects to larger pictorial units, thus suspending recognition of subject in a weave of traces and echoes.[29] Our current habit of talking about painting – and especially about Cubist painting and collage – in semiotic terms, as systems of *signs*, is initially suggestive here.[30] Yves-Alain Bois, for example, discussing Kahnweiler's comparison of the Wobé mask and Picasso's *Guitar*, concludes that the artist realised here 'for the first time that a sign, because it has a value [within a system of differences], can be entirely virtual, or nonsubstantial'.[31] I want to suggest, however, that the interest taken in the new painting by writers like Apollinaire and Cendrars was a product of Cubism's exploration of simultaneous and sensible elements which *escaped* the temporal and differential structure of language. In fact, when Cendrars later became critical of academic and formalist tendencies within Cubism it was precisely the loss of a certain unrepresentability which he lamented in Picasso's later work: 'In neglecting colour,' he argued in 1919, 'the cubist painters neglected the emotive principle that, to be alive (alive in itself, super-real), every work should include a sensuous, unreasoned, absurd, lyrical element, the vital element that hoists the work out of limbo.'[32]

Even Apollinaire, tireless promoter as he was of the new art, had reservations about some aspects of Cubism. He mainly admired the Picasso of the blue and pink periods, and if his response to Braque was somewhat cool, his view of Gris was actually quite negative.[33] Similarly, Cendrars was drawn primarily to the work of Léger and the Delaunays, and while he retained an admiration for Picasso, he showed little enthusiasm for the canvases of Braque, whom he saw as prime instigator of a 'cold' rationality which marred Cubism.[34] In the terms of Apollinaire's *The Cubist Painters* (1913), it was not the geometric tendencies of 'scientific cubism' or the representational elements of 'physical cubism' which appealed to the two men, but rather, what Apollinaire called 'Orphic cubism'.[35] With this awkward term he meant to indicate an 'art of painting new structures out of elements which have not been borrowed from the visual sphere, but have been created entirely by the artist himself, and been endowed by him with fullness of reality'.[36]

Of the various painters Apollinaire listed under this heading (Léger, Picabia, Duchamp, Delaunay, Picasso), it was Delaunay who would become the central point of reference. Delaunay shared the two poets' enthusiastic response to the forms of modernity, and his fascination with contemporary urban themes stood in sharp contrast to the deliberately 'academic' subject-matter increasingly favoured by Braque and Picasso; and Delaunay was also intent on exploring powerful effects of colour at a time when Cubism was working with a deliberately restricted palette. Where Picasso's art tended to retain a strong graphic discipline which fostered certain patterns of 'recognition', Delaunay shifted the emphasis to rhythm and colour: 'The line', he argued, 'is the boundary. Colour gives depth (not perspectival, not successive, but simultaneous) and its force and movement.'[37] Delaunay rejected the arbitrary constraints of the perspectival grid (the 'syntax' of space, we might say), and looked instead to colour, light and rhythm to create spaces with a certain 'depth' that resists assimilation to 'a known and defined order'.[38]

This 'depth' results from Delaunay's theory of 'simultaneous contrasts', which in not perceiving gaps between colours offers a concept of difference which is not locatable in the oppositions of visual or verbal language.[39] It is in these terms that Delaunay characterised his 1914 painting *Blériot*, observing that 'It's all roundness, sun, earth, horizons, fullness of intense life, of poetry which can't be put into words.'[40]

The impact of these theories on Apollinaire's work is relatively easy to discern. In 1912, the year in which *simultanéité* entered the Cubist vocabulary,[41] we find him stitching together quotations from Delaunay and concluding that 'Simultaneity is life itself, and in whatever order the elements of a work succeed each other, it leads to an ineluctable end, which is death; but the creator knows only eternity' (*AOA*, 265). The collection of poems called *Calligrams* (1918) pursued this struggle against narrative on several different fronts: there were the so-called 'conversation poems', like 'Windows' and 'Monday in Christine Street', which developed the structural discontinuities of *Alcohols* by incorporating snippets of dialogue overheard:

Three gas burners lit
The proprietress is consumptive
When you've finished we'll play a game of backgammon
An orchestra leader who has a sore throat
When you come through Tunis we'll smoke some hashish[42]

As his translator remarks, 'The intention seems to be to face the reader with a mass of unintegrated details, not unlike the profusion of planes that, at first sight, obscure the overall design and organization of a cubist painting.'[43] We have only the barest indication of how to integrate these different elements as signs (of something else), and Apollinaire's concept of simultaneity seems to immerse us in the event he evokes so as to prevent us from immobilising its components in a recognisable form.

This is even more obviously the case with the 'calligrams' themselves, where playfully inventive typographical layouts are used to create spaces outside the regulated spaces of language. This is the legacy of Mallarmé's 'simultaneous vision of the Page', for these texts hover between figurative and non-figurative printed shapes, either creating tension between the typographical 'image' and the discursive meaning of the poem, or leaving the eye to find its way in an abstract maze of possible paths. Such examples of 'visual lyricism'[44] powerfully make the point that an authentic response to modernity requires an art which situates itself, as it were, on the outer limit of language, though Apollinaire's equally strong attachment to the elegiac mood gives this clearly modernist position a certain ambivalence. As Roger Shattuck remarks, 'When Apollinaire did not succeed in rising above time to occupy it all, he was its most despondent victim',[45] and those emotional extremes might be felt to accord with the striking mix of avant-garde and neo-classicist elements in the famous essay he wrote at the end of his life, 'The New Spirit and the Poets' (1918).[46]

For a less equivocal exploration of the idea that modernity is 'excessive' and somehow resists signification we may turn to the work of Blaise Cendrars. Outside Italian Futurism, Cendrars is perhaps *the* poet of modernity, with his celebrations of urban life and the new media, from film and radio to advertising. He is also the author of the first 'simultaneous' book, an edition of his long poem *The Prose of the Trans-Siberian and of Little Jeanne of France*, published in 1913 in an accordion format with designs by Sonia Delaunay. Characteristic of the tone of his work is the 1917 prose poem 'Profound Today', which, as the title indicates, has a deliberate debt to Delaunay's concept of 'depth'. In fact Delaunay's well-known phrase 'Everything is colour in movement, depth'[47] is constantly cited by Cendrars as a figure for his own poetics. The text has a debt to Futurism, not only in its evocation of machines and 'the sexual frenzy of factories',[48] but also in its identification of the modern experience as one of centrifugal dispersion. Here Cendrars expresses the same modernist desire for a dissolution of the self in modernity, and the dismemberment of the body which is everywhere in the text is closely connected with an idea of the simultaneity of a new consumer world which allows it to be assimilated to a conception of painterly space.

Cendrars's surrender to the lure of the commodity as something powerful and 'profoundly' liberating is accompanied by a twisting and fragmentation of syntactical forms:

> Like a religion, a mysterious pill hastens your digestion. You lose yourself in the labyrinth of stores where you give up your identity to become everyone. You smoke with Mr. Book the Havana at twenty-five cents, which is on the poster. You are part of that great anonymous body which is a café. I no longer recognize

myself in the mirror. Alcohol has clouded my features. He marries the department store like a bridegroom. We are all the hour which strikes.

Cendrars shares with the Futurists a sense of the modern as the occasion for a spectacular disembodiment – once penetrated and expanded by capital, the body no longer offers itself as a privileged object of representation, but exists instead as a source of discrete sensory intensities which elude symbolisation.

The transformations of the self in this passage, from 'I' to 'you' to 'we', are bound up with references to colour and rhythm which are intended to evoke the 'simultaneous contrasts' of Delaunay's work: 'A blue eye opens. A red one shuts. Soon there's nothing but colour. Interpenetration. Disk. Rhythm. Dance. Orange and violet eat each other up.' Delaunay's paintings of Paris and the Eiffel Tower seem to Cendrars to offer an *experience* of the modern rather than an image of it, the modern as an 'event' whose instantaneity language can never properly express. The idea of 'depth', then, is one which appears to situate modernity in terms of being rather than of consciousness; this is the *profondeur* of reality, a 'depth' of experience at which all conventional barriers between discourse and its objects have been overcome – like Larbaud, Cendrars dreams of the 'First Poem with No Metaphors'.[49] Such a conception can only dramatise the incommensurability of language to a simultaneous world, though for Cendrars this falling short simply expresses the awesome nature of the 'real' and does not lead to any Mallarméan pathos of failure.

It is just this aspect of Delaunay's theory which the philosopher Maurice Merleau-Ponty has emphasised:

Depth thus understood is, rather, the experience of the reversibility of dimensions, of a global 'locality' – everything in the same place at the same time, a locality from which height, width, and depth are abstracted, of a voluminosity we express in a word when we say a thing is *there*.[50]

In this simultaneous world, where commodities testify not to the rule of exchangeability but to 'everything in the same place at the same time' – 'Produce, from five parts of the globe, united on the same plate, in the same dress', as Cendrars puts it – in this world, writer and painter must strive to convey not 'the reality of the object' but 'reality itself'.[51] As Cendrars tells us in an account of the cinema, 'We drink. Drunkenness. Reality has no meaning. No significance. Everything is rhythm, word, life. There's no longer any [need for] proof. You commune.'[52]

*   *   *

Cendrars's evocation of modernity as painterly space typifies his fascination with 'wordless levels of being'.[53] A text like 'Profound Today' thus carries us towards what the French psychoanalyst André Green has termed a 'writing of the body', a writing in which

> representation no longer lays the foundation of a structured fantasy; it becomes fragmented into short-lived, evanescent bodily states, the writer failing repeatedly to communicate through the writing process this incommunicable reality because neither the spoken nor the written word can yield a rendering of it.[54]

If this is one limit-case of modern writing, another, suggests Green, would be the kind of text

> which strives to say nothing beyond the mere statement of the writing process. This writing style is non-figurative in the same respect as the preceding one, which was not so much concerned with representing the body as in making it come alive in chips, in fragmented form and piecemeal. Here the absence of figurability makes the script the only representation.

In this second case, Green concludes, 'The only desire left is the desire to write without object.' Such a desire may help us to understand the further development of the Cubist aesthetic as it passes into the very different world of Russian Futurism.

The name of this avant-garde is likely to mislead, for the Russian writers and artists who grouped themselves as 'Futurists' after 1913 had less in common with their Italian counterparts than their shared title suggests. Relations between the two tendencies were, in fact, strained and competitive, and the Russians were quick to argue not only that their movement pre-dated the Italian one, but also that their essential aims were starkly opposed to the modernolatry of the Futurists.

· Yet the Russians clearly did learn something from Marinetti's movement. In their literature, Symbolism remained influential until the end of the first decade of the new century and although experimental work began to appear from 1910, the appearance of Italian manifestos in Russian translation in 1912 gave such developments an added impetus.[55] The group involved first called themselves Cubo-Futurists to distinguish their aims from those of the Italians. These writers and artists had in fact worked together since 1910, when they had formed a group known, after the old Greek name of their region, as Hylaea, land of the Scythians. In that year three brothers, David, Vladimir and Nikolay Burliuk, made up the core of the group along with Benedikt Livshits and Velimir Khlebnikov. In 1911 they were joined by Aleksei Kruchenykh and Vladimir Mayakovsky. By the next year they were ready to produce their first manifesto, and *A Slap in the Face of Public Taste* duly appeared over the signatures of David Burliuk, Kruchenykh, Mayakovsky and Khlebnikov. The pugnacious tone was certainly reminiscent of Marinetti – 'We alone are the *face* of *our* Time' (*RFM*, 51) – and the manifesto went on to deplore the 'perfumed lechery' of the Symbolist poet Constantine Balmont and to exhort its readers to 'Throw Pushkin, Dostoevsky, Tolstoy, etc., etc., overboard from the Ship of Modernity.'

The four may have spoken 'from the heights of skyscrapers' but they made little direct reference to technology and to the new experiences of modernity. This was to be one main point of divergence between Cubo-Futurism and the Italian movement – for most of the Russians had little time for what Kruchenykh dismissed as 'that extremist twaddle about contemporaneity as a patented panacea for all misfortunes and ailments – this theme is no more elevated than any other' (*RFM*, 66). Not that Russian poetry was devoid of urban subject-matter; Verhaeren's influence had been felt by the Symbolists and city-imagery had already featured in the poems of Alexander Blok and Valerii Briusov.[56] The technological revolution was, however, less in evidence here than in Northern Italy, and, partly for this reason but also as a matter of artistic policy, the Russian writers celebrated the machine age not for the new experiences it made available but rather for the kind of model it offered for aesthetic form.[57] Kruchenykh and Khlebnikov emphasised this in one of their most important manifestos, *The Word as Such* (1913):

A work of art is the art of the word.

From which it followed automatically that tendentiousness and literary pretensions of any kind were to be expelled from works of art.

Our approximation was the machine – impassive, passionate. (*VK*, 255)

The machine provides a model, an 'approximation', and the Russians have no desire to follow the Italian habit of 'making imitation art'.

The competitive nature of such polemic made Marinetti's 1914 visit to Russia an unexpected failure. 'Marinetti did not see a single Russian Futurist in Moscow', jeered Livshits in his autobiography,[58] and it is true that most of the writers the Italian had expected to meet were elsewhere during his visit. The episode caused a break in the Russian group, with Khlebnikov abandoning Hylaea because of some of its members' tolerance for Marinetti.[59] Not satisfied with that, Khlebnikov wrote to him in abusive terms ('man of the future, born a hundred years too late'), going so far as to challenge him to a duel! (*VK*, 85–6). In part this hostility was due to the rivalry of East and West – Khlebnikov in particular dreamed of wedding Russian Futurism to a campaign for pan-Slavic unity. Yet the two movements did have some things in common. If Russian writers showed little interest in technology until Mayakovsky's involvement with *Lef* in the twenties, there was nonetheless, within this avant-garde, a deep current of pro-war enthusiasm which had surfaced in 1908 at the time of the Austrian annexation of Bosnia and Hercegovina and which would continue to make intermittent appearances. So too, while Livshits joked about Marinetti's '100 h.p. phallic pathos',[60] the Russians also tended to associate avant-garde language with masculinity: Kruchenykh declared that 'because of a foul / contempt for / women and / children in our / language there will be / only the masculine / gender' (*RFM*, 66), a principle he tried to put into effect in the libretto of his opera *Victory over the Sun* (1913).

The two movements were more clearly at odds in their conceptions of the past. While Khlebnikov could declare that '20th century man is dragging around a thousand-year-old corpse (the past)' (*VK*, 261), his own work was strongly marked by an interest in an archaic and mythical past. The manifesto in which these words appeared was titled *!Futurian* (1914), and Khlebnikov's coinage of an alternative to 'Futurist' was meant to designate 'the action of the future on the past' (*VK*, 280). The past, then, was not to be destroyed but reshaped, an objective which made sense only when referred to the Russians' highly original theories of language. For, like the Italians, these writers had no time for the old lyric 'I': 'Is a poem not a flight from the *I*?', asked Khlebnikov (*VK*, 371), and Livshits explained that 'We consider it impossible to create in a vacuum, to create "out of oneself" ' (*RFM*, 79). Yet while the two movements coincided in their repudiation of inwardness and 'psychology', the Russians sought to externalise the self not in the cosmic rhythms of capital, but in the space of signification. Here the battle between past and future is fought out in terms of language: the avant-garde asserts 'Freedom to create words and form words', as Mayakovsky puts it, and authentic Futurism must be generated from a 'Hatred for the language that existed before us' (*RFM*, 89). Such an objective is arguably more extreme than anything to be found in Italian Futurism, partly because the founding principle of the Russian group is to reject not only previous literary convention but the language itself in its current condition: 'to depict the new – the future,' declares Kruchenykh, 'one needs *totally new words and a new way of combining them*' (*RFM*, 72).

This brings us to the most important difference between the two Futurisms. As Livshits put it, there was in the Italian movement an 'indifference towards material', by which he meant that content invariably seemed to take priority over medium. The 'material', in Livshits's sense, comprised the graphic and phonic elements of language, which offered sources of meaning quite independent of any expressive function of the voice (hence his dismissal of Marinetti's onomatopoeia which, he observed, simply restored traditional sentence structure to words-in-freedom[61]). Like Apollinaire and Cendrars (some of whose work was known here), the Russian writers constantly took their cue from the visual arts and most of them had either trained originally as painters or worked consistently in both media. Given the range of emphases in Russian Futurism, from Khlebnikov's Slavic populism to Mayakovsky's urbanism, the only real common denominator would seem to be this close connection with painting.[62] Furthermore, since Italian painting was not exhibited in Russia during this period, it was through the study of French Cubism that the Futurists arrived at their valuation of medium and form over content.[63] As painter Kasimir Malevich put it, 'the artist, enslaved by utilitarian reason, wages an unconscious struggle, now submitting to an object, now distorting it',[64] and this idea of visual distortion seems to have lent support for what Khlebnikov called 'painting with sound' (*VK*, 49). In each case, emphasis is placed on the potential of the medium to determine content; Roman Jakobson observes of Khlebnikov's similes, for example, that 'they are hardly ever motivated by an impression of real similarity of objects, but are simply compositional effects'.[65]

How do such effects differ from those of, say, Marinetti's *Zang Tumb Tuuum*? In Marinetti's work the meaning of the sound, its connection to the object it represents, is made through the force of vocalisation. His aim is thus to forge an absolute identity of word and referent. What Khlebnikov envisages has, in contrast, no need of a performer; additionally, language is not called upon to articulate some prior experience, and signification occurs, as it were, internally; it is generated from language deployed for its own sake rather than as the instrument of thought. The word here floats free of any referent; it is, to use the term favoured in numerous manifestos, 'self-sufficient'. The resulting idea of sound *painting* is in deliberate contrast to Symbolist musicality, emphasising the materiality of language by its emphatic attention to consonants rather than euphonious vowels. Just as Picasso dismembered the classical body in order to discover new spaces, so the Russian Futurists disarticulate language, breaking it down into ever smaller units of meaning and rhythm. In 'The Word as Such' (1913), Kruchenykh and Khlebnikov explain accordingly that

> the Futurian painters love to use parts of the body, its cross sections, and the Futurian wordwrights use chopped-up words, half-words, and their artful combinations (transrational language), thus achieving the very greatest expressiveness, and precisely this distinguishes the swift language of modernity, which has annihilated the previous frozen language. (*RFM*, 61)

'Cruelty' is not now thematised at all, but is taken to be the creative–destructive motivation of style; and if this constitutes an attack on language it is one which does not move in the direction of nonsense, like the European sound-poetry of Kurt Schwitters, Hugo Ball and Francesco Cangiullo, but rather splinters words into new meanings, just as Picasso's assault on the body had yielded new spaces. As Yury Tynyanov observes of Khlebnikov, 'For him, no sound is uncoloured by meaning.'[66] This way of regarding language removes it from the obligation to represent; indeed, we may produce a new subject-matter by manipulating language, since new words will create new content. Kruchenykh puts it like this:

Invent new native words!
A new content *becomes manifest only* when
new expressive devices are achieved, a new form.
Once there is a new form, a new content follows;
form thus conditions content.   (*RFM*, 77)

Neologism is viewed by both Kruchenykh and Khlebnikov as the deflection and modification of existing linguistic structures so as to reveal hidden, 'primitive' meanings through the forgotten roots of words. 'Transrational language [*zaum*]' is based on the principle that letters have a meaning independent of the words in which they appear. They can therefore be recombined to produce words which, while they belong to no known language, still mean something; as Tzvetan Todorov observes, 'We must distinguish what is *comprehensible* to reason from what is *significative*.'[67]

Shapes on a canvas may not remind us of recognisable objects in the world, but they do signify in relation to the other shapes to which they are related; similarly, words which may seem to have no semantic relation in the dictionary can display phonemic connections which in turn can produce flashes of new meaning. So, for example, Kruchenykh 'would sooner say that laughers [*smekhiri*] and swordsmen [*mechari*] share the same sense than say that swordsmen [*mechari*] and gladiators [*gladiatory*] do, because it is the phonetic composition of the word which gives it its living coloration, and the word is perceived and keenly affects you only when it has that coloration' (*RFM*, 71). Following this logic, Khlebnikov's most famous poem, 'Incantation by Laughter', plays an amusing sequence of variations on the root of the word for laughter (*smekh*): 'Laughters of the laughing laughniks, overlaugh the laughathons! / Laughiness of the laughish laughers, counterlaugh the Laughdom's laughs!'[68]

As we see from that poem, the Futurists are intrigued by what happens when endings alter or when a vowel is changed within a word – one of Khlebnikov's favourite examples was the transformation of the word for sword (*mech*) to *myach*, playing ball, a minute alteration with portentous implications.[69] This is an example of what he called internal declension' or 'case endings inside the word':

the words of the same family have widely disparate meanings. ... For instance, *bobr* in Russian means beaver, a perfectly harmless rodent, while *babr* is a tiger, a terrifying beast of prey – but each represents a different case – accusative and genitive – of the common stem *bo*. (*VK*, 277)

Khlebnikov's theory of language is radically at odds with that of Saussure, for whom the example of *bobr/babr* would demonstrate that 'in a language there are only differences, and no positive terms'. For the Saussurean sign, 'what matters more than any idea or sound associated with it is what other signs surround it'.[70] Khlebnikov certainly has an acute sense of linguistic environments,[71] but his interest in sound–meaning units is determined by the connection they apparently reveal between word and meaning, signifier and signified. So in the *bobr/babr* example, he assumes that particular sounds are meaningful in themselves, here because the phonemes *bo* and *ba* can be interpreted as case endings: the accusative case expresses action toward something, while the genitive expresses action whence; so, concludes Khlebnikov, 'the very structure of the words demonstrates that a beaver is something to be followed, hunted like game, while a tiger is something to be feared, since now a man may become the game and be hunted by the animal'.

This is the crux of Khlebnikov's version of *zaum*, that the 'very structure' of language encodes primaeval truths about the world, and that whole systems of relations lie hidden beneath the rationalised taxonomies of the dictionary. Look at and listen to the word, say Khlebnikov and Kruchenykh – it is a plastic and transformative entity whose unlimited freedom to be reshaped liberates us from 'the bookish petrifaction of language' (*VK*, 382). Hidden etymologies are lines of force which reveal the primitive world of myth and heroism. 'Words that begin with an identical consonant share some identical meaning' (*VK*, 384): such a discovery opens up 'the beauty of language set free from its ends' (*VK*, 234), and once we have moved beyond language as instrument we may receive intimations of a 'self-sufficient language [which] stands outside historical fact and everyday utility' (*VK*, 147). In Khlebnikov's case, *zaum* offered a way of activating the roots of words 'so as freely to fuse all Slavic words together', and as his attention moved from phonemes to individual consonants so he made what he called his 'second approach to language [which] was to find the unity of the world's languages in general, built from units of the alphabet' (*VK*, 147).

This 'Futurian' dream of a universal language led Khlebnikov into increasingly bizarre speculations designed to exploit 'the action of the future on the past' (*VK*, 280), a dynamic hitherto concealed in the fact that ' "Fate" has the double meaning of destiny and that-which-is-spoken [*fatum*]' (*VK*, 297). Experiments with mathematical theories of history, coupled with utopian projects organised around his group of fellow 'inventors/explorers' called Presidents of the Planet Earth, led to a late work called 'The Tables of Destiny', where Khlebnikov proposed his own 'science' of fate. A multidimensional view of language thus culminated in a vision of a new world space which would no longer be the property of the 'investors/exploiters' (*VK*, 321).

Khlebnikov's later writings constantly ventured into what we would call science fiction (see, for example, the remarkable piece called 'Ourselves and Our Buildings'), and if the apocalyptic tone often seems self-deluding that is partly because of a conviction that meaning is everywhere (just as words beginning with the same consonant seem semantically connected, so the sequence of events in history can apparently be understood in terms of multiples of 317 years). Kruchenykh's development of *zaum* tended, in contrast, to produce patterns of sound which were arbitrary and logically meaningless but which would set up unexpected associations.[72] Hence the famous sound-poem:[73]

> dyr   bul   shchyl
>   ubeshshchur
>   skum
> vy   so   bu
> r   l   èz

The poem has no meaning, though its separate elements hint at units of sound which could be used to generate words. Kruchenykh shares Khlebnikov's idea that sounds are intrinsically meaningful, though he seems to be less interested in exploring large-scale semantic patterns than in creating a pronounced sense of verbal texture or *faktura* (the word was much used by contemporary painters). The aim was to produce a roughened combination of sounds, often ugly and glutted with awkward consonants. Kruchenykh's experiments with this aspect of *zaum* were complemented by the interest he shared with the other Futurists in calligraphy and typography, which yielded the many small, often deliberately shoddy books which brought the avant-garde to the public.[74]

Kruchenykh's aim was to shock, and the emphasis given to the materiality of words often produced unexpected and scatological associations. To this end he invented what he called 'shiftology', from the word 'shift' or 'dislocation [*sdvig*]' which was usually applied to effects of distortion in Cubist painting. The Russian language is rich in affixes and polysyllabic words, and Kruchenykh's 'shiftology' entailed a close attention to meanings produced accidentally as the last syllable of one word hooked up with the first syllable of the next. Markov gives the example of the phrase 'gro*my* *lo*mayut', 'thunders break', in which the word 'mylo', 'soap', unexpectedly appears.[75] Once highlighted, 'shifts' of this kind were disastrous to the sense of the original (Kruchenykh delighted in finding them in Pushkin), and those with a scatological meaning – *kak* is the Russian conjunction 'as' or 'like' – seemed to hint at repressed unconscious elements.[76] As the 'word as such' became increasingly opaque, Kruchenykh's 'shiftology' seemed progressively to deny the classical dream of reason working through language, for these unintentional shifts thwarted expressivity by catching the eye on the actual marks of which the words were made. The linear continuity of discourse thus gave way to a sort of simultaneity as consonants and vowels began to slip into discordant, spatial relationships: 'INTRODUCING NEW WORDS, I bring about a new content WHERE EVERYTHING begins to slip (the conventions of time, space, etc.)' (*RFM*, 68). Here, according to Kruchenykh, we may pass into a new space, the '4th dimension' discovered by the Cubist painters, which produces 'a new perception of the world' (*RFM*, 72–3).

Four years after Kruchenykh wrote those words, the October Revolution did indeed precipitate Russia into a new social and political dimension. The Futurists based in Moscow welcomed the bolsheviks and a shortlived alliance was forged between them. Strains and tensions were inevitable, though, given that the particular radicalism of Khlebnikov and Kruchenykh was hard to grasp outside a literary context – as Trotsky observed, 'The futurist break with the past is, after all, a tempest in the closed-in world of the intelligentsia which grew up on Pushkin, Fet, Tyutchev, Bryusov, Balmont, and Blok.'[77] The bohemian strain that Trotsky discerned running through Futurism was, however, more mixed in the work of Mayakovsky, who was doomed to become the official poet of the Stalin years.

Mayakovsky had been associated with Hylaea, and like Burliuk, Khlebnikov and Kruchenykh he had a strong practical interest in the visual arts. This was clear from the 'Cubist imagery' of his earliest poems. In 'Night' (1912), for example, Mayakovsky combined vivid colour-imagery with the intensive use of metaphor which would become one of his trademarks:

For boulevards and squares there was nothing bizarre in
the sight of the buildings in togas of blue.
Before that with bracelets of yellow, like scar-rings,
the street-lamps had wedded men's running feet too.[78]

Almost from the first, Mayakovsky's work couples urban imagery with a use of 'painterly' metaphor to create a heightened emotional effect ('I splashed some colours from a tumbler / and smeared the drab world with emotion', he writes in another early poem[79]). Mayakovsky shares the Futurist love of sound-effects, and like Khlebnikov and Kruchenykh he decomposes the word so as to give it a striking concreteness:

U-
litsa.
Litsa
u
dogov
godov
rez-
che.
Che-
rez[80]

The poem, 'From Street to Street' (1913), seems to evoke the view from a moving streetcar, but the rapid shifts in perspective are not handled in an impressionistic way, being instead internalised in the word-play of the lines, with inner rhymes and palindromic effects translating the pattern of images into something equivalent to an interleaving of planes.

A related and striking feature of Mayakovksy's style is his way of wrenching similes into literalism, an effect often used to explore the erotic energies of the cityscape:

A bald-pated street-lamp,
blatant,
lascivious,
pulls off the street's black stocking

Such hyperbolic figures predict the forms of the Surrealist city, though Mayakovsky uses them to embody contradictory strains within the self – his own self, that is, which always occupies the centre of his work. In his first major work, the long poem called 'A Cloud in Trousers' (1914–15), the principal elements of Mayakovsky's idiosyncratic style are assembled. Like Khlebnikov, Mayakovsky develops a declamatory style as a vehicle for a heroic, not to say titanic, version of the self. Here it is cut with constant irony as the poet oscillates between optimism and pessimism, strength and weakness:

No gray hair in my soul,
no doddering tenderness .
I rock the world with the thunder of my voice,
strolling, looking good –
twenty-two.[81]

Mundane detail is galvanised by the poet's 'thunderous' presence, which gives everything around him an inflated and ludicrous phys-icality. He waits for his mistress to arrive, but 'Eight. / Nine. / Ten.':

Then the twilight
spun around from the window
and stomped off into nightmarish darkness,
frowning,
decemberish.

The distance between literal and figurative disappears, and the wildest fantasies (the poet 'using the sun / as a monocle') consort with a polemical realism ('Who gives a damn for Faust ... I know / a nail in my boot / is worse than Goethe's fantasies!'). When his

mistress finally does arrive it is with traditionally bad news –
' "Guess what? / I'm getting married." ' How to sidestep conventional sentiment now, for the poet is, naturally, devastated. 'His
heart is on fire', but literally, 'like' a burning brothel: 'Here they
come! / Glittering / helmets! / But please, no heavy boots. / Tell
the firemen to climb / tenderly on a burning heart.'

Such extended and overblown similes make the image self-
sufficient (not the image *of* a state of mind) and at the same time
give Mayakovsky a way of handling the emotional extremes of his
own personality. For the Mayakovsky who abuses the deity in
thunderous tones ('I thought you were Mr Big once, / but you're a
jerk, a dwarf') and in another poem invites the sun to tea[82] is also
the Mayakovsky who is rejected by Maria and who is finally left
alone, confronting an indifferent universe:

The universe sleeps,
a paw on its huge ear
lousy with stars.

The image is at once cosmic and banal, a fitting conclusion to a
poem which veers between anguish, on the one hand, and what
Trotsky called 'the universalization of one's ego', on the other.[83]

If 'A Cloud in Trousers' seems to convey the excitement of
modernity more effectively than, say, *Zang Tumb Tuuum* it is
because its play of tones grounds Mayakovsky's version of modernity in exactly the kind of 'criss-crossing of differently oriented
social accents' of which Vološinov would soon speak.[84] Indeed,
Mayakovsky's account of his own poetics in *How Are Verses Made?*
stresses the public function of writing and its dialogic relation to
an audience. While the 'printed text speaks in rather dispassionate
tones', the voice may adapt to the needs of a particular occasion:
'The larger part of my things are based on a conversational tone',
he observes, 'But despite all my careful planning this tone isn't a
fixed thing, established once for all, but a stance that I quite often
change in the course of reading, according to the kind of audience I
have.'[85] Mayakovsky thus gave an almost unique twist to the
'painterly' view of modernist language, making the thematics of
unrepresentability the basis for a shift away from language as a
means of referring to things and towards language as the medium
of social relations. It would be left to Bertolt Brecht, several decades
later, to develop the full implications of that view.

7

Cruel Structures: The Development of Expressionism

In previous chapters we have seen Paris emerge as a magnetic cultural centre, as the very hub of European modernist activity. Here a sense of energy and dynamism brought art and metropolitan life into powerful association – the Paris of Delaunay was preeminently the city of light, colour, and movement, the city where expanding consumerism had acquired an exciting erotic aura. If that sense of erotic modernity was connected, *via* the new painting, with an attack on forms of representation, it was above all because the Symbolist preoccupation with desire as the response to *loss* was now being called into question by the sense of modernity as an experience of plenitude and abundance. In this respect, dynamism and simultaneity expressed what the Russian writers referred to as the 'self-sufficiency' of the medium, be it paint, stone, or language. Delaunay's vision of Paris caught exactly that sense of self-sufficiency in its association of non-figurative forms with a vividly coloured expression of energy and confidence.

Yet not all visitors to Paris saw it like this. In a partly autobiographical novel published in 1910, the Austrian poet Rainer Maria Rilke has his narrator begin with a strikingly gloomy question: 'People come here, then, to live? I should have thought that they came here to die.'[1] For Rilke's protagonist Malte Laurids Brigge, Paris is a city of poverty and disease – 'I have been out, and I saw hospitals,' he continues. Malte's view of modernity has more in common with that of Huysmans's Des Esseintes than it does with the erotic fantasies of Cendrars and Apollinaire. For him, the new is threatening and invasive – 'The electric street-cars rage through my room with ringing fury. Automobiles race over me' (4) – and where this interpenetration of inner and outer spaces might put us in mind of Futurist images like Umberto Boccioni's vibrant *The Street*

Enters the House (1911), for Malte the permeability of self and other is a source of real terror. Not only does this Paris connote the mortality of the body rather than its pleasures, but Malte's isolated existence shows him cut adrift from others. 'I belonged among the outcasts,' he concludes, with the sick of the Salpêtrière and with those who, like the man he sees afflicted with St Vitus Dance, experience life as some sort of terrible invasion of the self.

This novel shows no trace of those unanimist fantasies of disembodiment and loss of self in the crowd; Malte finds himself confronting not an exciting future but an exhausted past. Rilke sets his story against the declining fortunes of his protagonist's aristocratic family – Malte is, like Des Esseintes, its last scion – and the complex mood of the novel reminds us that German-language modernism is much less sanguine about the loss of narrative and genealogical continuities than its French and Russian counterparts. As Malte's *Notebook* shows, the family retains its hold and the new tensions and mutations within it provide the most sensitive register of the condition which is modernity. The family may now be seen as 'decayed', as Hanno puts it in Thomas Mann's *Buddenbrooks* (1901),[2] but it remains the matrix of the conflicting economies which structure the present. In Germany and the Austro-Hungarian Empire, the Futurist sense of *rupture* with the past did not figure in the same way, even though by 1914 Germany had become the greatest industrial nation in Europe. The cultural effects of modernisation were felt differently here, as an unstable interpenetration of old and new, with the sentimental, semi-feudal past of conservative and military values drawn into alliance with the brutal realism of new capitalist power. Within German-language modernism, then, there was little libidinal investment in fantasies of technology and urbanism, even though the structures of patriarchal authority which persisted were often felt to be repressive and inhuman.

This was to be the world of Expressionism, and its underlying tension is predicted in Malte's *Notebook*, where the narrator recalls being comforted by his mother: 'we remained like this, weeping tenderly and kissing one another, until we felt that Father was there and that we must separate' (91). A moment of emotional unity is shattered by the arrival of the Father, but in line with the form of the Oedipal drama the moment retains its intensity, thus ensuring 'the unending reality of my childhood' (188).[3] For Rilke, as for the Expressionists, any dream of a future uncontaminated by the past will be undermined by the narrative frame which attaches to experience: Malte, for example, realises that if 'I persisted in think-ing that my childhood was past, then in that same moment my whole future also vanished' (188). What is most characteristic of this particular modernism is the way in which this sense of tension between past and present produces a parallel opposition between the social and the aesthetic. Where the French modernists had derived new art-forms from the novel world around them, the German-language writers tended to value a radical aesthetic for its capacity to bring release from a claustrophobic social environment.

The tension is pronounced in Rilke's work, where we find a con-stant preoccupation with death as the ultimate horizon of the aes-thetic. From this perspective, the family is regarded as a powerful nexus of desires and interests which always stands over against the autonomy and inwardness of the art-work. This is the moral of Rilke's version of the story of the Prodigal Son which closes Malte's *Notebook*, a parable which is here reshaped to become 'the legend of one who did not want to be loved' (235). The love of others always changes or 'consumes' the one who is loved, such is the text of Rilke's version; and if the Son is able to return after a long absence it is because he has realised that the members of his family do not really know him, for all their protestations of love: 'What did they know of him? He was now terribly difficult to love, and he felt that One alone was capable of loving him. But he was not yet willing' (243).

Rilke's preoccupation with the idea of 'a well-finished death' (8), which consummates the death we carry within us 'as a fruit bears its kernel' (9), links a major decadent theme to a new way of identi-fying art with death. With the decline of Christianity, the only au-thentic existence seems to be one which grasps death not just as part of the totality which is life, but as the final objectification of that absence of desire as self-interest which is, for Rilke, the condi-tion of the greatest art. Like other modernists, he finds models for writing in the visual arts – Rodin and Cézanne, in this case – but where Cubism had been drawn to forms of exteriorisation, here the emphasis is very different. In the first *Rodin-Book* (1902), for example, Rilke explains that 'This distinguishing characteristic of things, complete self-absorption, was what gave to plastic art its calm; it must have no desire nor expectation beyond itself, nor bear any reference to what lies beyond, nor be aware of anything outside itself.'[4] Rodin's objects seem to Rilke to embody 'this turning-inward-upon-oneself, this tense listening to inner depths'[5] which connote freedom from all desire, 'the great calm of objects which know no urge'[6]. Yet something more than just the interiorisation of elements of the external world is involved here: for while, as Malte knows, 'even the unheard-of must become an inward thing' (70), this becoming-inward allows things to retain their own shape because it is not motivated by desire or possessiveness. In another early piece on Rodin, Rilke imagines occasions

> when a bird-call in the open and in his inner consciousness were one, when it did not, as it were, break on the barrier of his body, but gathered both together into an undivided space, in which there was only one region of the purest, deepest consciousness, mysteriously protected.[7]

In contrast to Futurist fantasies of absolute presence, Rilke's 'undivided space' is marked by absence, as it maps the passage from outer to inner. This is the principal paradox which lies behind his development from the impressionism of the early poems of *The Book of Hours* (1905) and *The Book of Pictures* (1902, 1906) to the *New Poems* of 1907 and 1908. The 'new objectivity' of 'thing-poems' (*Ding-Gedichte*) such as 'The Panther' and 'Archaic Torso of Apollo' requires an attention not merely to the things themselves, but to the patterns of association which enable the mind to draw objects inward without interfering with them. The effect Rilke pursues here is akin to something he admires in Cézanne's still-life painting: the fruits with which the painter so often worked 'cease to be edible altogether', Rilke observes, 'that's how thinglike and real they become, how simply indestructible in their stubborn thereness'.[8] We might contrast the similar-sounding sense of 'thereness' in Cendrars's work (his emphasis on 'reality itself'), for in Rilke's case it is not a matter of remarking how the presentness of things eludes language but rather of seeing how that 'thereness' can be grasped only in the absence of all desire.[9]

This is the train of thought which will issue in the warning against 'that hidden, guilty river-god of the blood' in the Third of the *Duino Elegies* (written in Paris in 1913), prompting us to ask, perhaps, whether too high a price does not have to be paid for this type of aesthetic perception. Is there not a kind of ultimate cruelty precisely in the withholding of all desire? This is the poet who boasts that 'I have no beloved, no house, no place where I live',[10] the advocate of 'possessionless love' and one who shares Malte's confused ideas about the poor ('I know that if one tried to love them, they would weigh upon one' [201]). Rilke, however, seems to confront the issue in a poem of 1914 called 'Turning-Point':

> Work of the eyes is done, now
> go and do heart-work
> on all the images imprisoned within you; for you
> overpowered them: but even now you don't know them.[11]

In the great Elegies of the early twenties, this 'heart-work' is closely allied to the idea of praising the world, of transforming things into words. In the famous Ninth Elegy, inwardness is elided with the celebratory, not to say hymnic, function of language: 'For when the traveler returns from the mountain-slopes into the valley, / he brings, not a handful of earth, unsayable to others, but instead/some word he has gained, some pure word, the yellow and blue / gentian.'[12]

The Elegies thus exist in tension with a modernity increasingly tied to modes of objectification – 'Earth, isn't this what you want: to arise within us, / *invisible*? Isn't it your dream / to be wholly invisible someday?' The question is asked because language seems increasingly to lack its former intimacy with things; as Rilke put it in a letter to his Polish translator, 'The lived and living things, the things that share our thoughts, these are on the decline and can no more be replaced.'[13] This is an effect of modernity and, more specifically perhaps, of 'the unexperienced nature of technology', as Heidegger puts it in his discussion of Rilke,[14] a condition in which 'empty indifferent things ... counterfeit things' can only be restored to intimacy through making them 'invisible' within the human medium of language.

*   *   *

Rilke's work cannot be subsumed under the rubric of Expressionism, though it shares with that strand of German-language modernism a preoccupation with themes of inwardness, loss, death, and the family. Like Rilke, the Expressionists were also closely concerned with the interrelation of writing and the visual arts. 'Painterly' questions were thus very much to the fore, and it was with the XXII Berliner Sezession of April 1911 that the term 'Expressionist' came into general use; 1911 was also the year in which Reinhard Sorge's play *The Beggar* was first performed, an occasion which is sometimes taken to mark the beginning of literary Expressionism. As usual, though, we can detect precedents for the movement which was to take shape. A group of Dresden painters known collectively from 1905 as the 'Bridge' (*Die Brücke*), and including Ernst Kirchner, Otto Mueller and Erich Heckel, had explored aggressive effects of colour and a kind of 'savage' simplicity of form derived from Gauguin and Van Gogh. The Bridge painters felt a powerful affinity with all types of primitive art, placing a strong emphasis on self-expression through a vigorous use of line and a thematic and emotional association of the sensual and the spiritual.

In Munich, a second group, calling itself the 'Blue Rider', took shape in 1911 around the painters Franz Marc and Wassily Kandinsky. This group was also interested in primitive art, but largely at Kandinsky's instigation the work of the Blue Rider was to move in the direction of abstraction and angularity of form (Kandinsky painted what may be the first completely abstract canvas in 1911). The second group also had more to say about the theory behind their painting, and *The Blue Rider Almanac* (1912) provided an intriguing cross-section of a modernism as eclectic as it was internationally focused. Contributors to the *Almanac* were keen to stress that their new art would inaugurate a spiritual age no longer tainted by nineteenth-century materialism, and that their modernism would thus renew connections with the art of earlier epochs. So, for example, Franz Marc illustrated his essay on 'Spiritual Treasures' with images drawn from a wide range of traditions (they include German woodcuts, Chinese painting, Bavarian Mirror Painting, Picasso's *Woman with Mandolin at the Piano*, and two drawings by children). This eclecticism is both helpful and unhelpful when it comes to unravelling the complicated origins of Expressionism. On the one hand, it points to a grandness of purpose which situates this avant-garde within a broad Romantic tradition; on the other, it places an emphasis on what Kandinsky calls 'form', the outward manifestation of 'inner need', as he puts it in his most influential essay, *Concerning the Spiritual in Art* (1911).[15] For the artist to move away from 'mere representation' was, for

Kandinsky, to discover – or to re-discover – a spiritual dimension obscured by contemporary materialism.

There was always a danger, of course, that Expressionism might be equated with mere expressivity, since, as one critic puts it, what the new art 'seeks to render visible … are soul states and the violent emotions welling up from the innermost recesses of the subconscious'.[16] There are several reasons for the Expressionists' preoccupation with *violent* emotion, first among which was their generally shared view of modernity as a condition of servitude from which humanity must break free. In contrast to the Futurists, these writers and artists were obsessed with the infernal nature of the city, with its subordination of the individual to the mechanistic environments of tenement and factory. In Hermann Bahr's words, Expressionism was a product of 'the strenuous battle between the soul and the machine for the possession of man'.[17] Subjective emotion seemed to suffer a constant repression, and in its boldness and grandiosity Expressionist art sought to direct that emotion as a transformative energy against social constraints. In practice, Expressionism veered between an often decadent preoccupation with types of spiritual 'sickness' and an attempt to harness liberated emotion to this project of social renewal; humanity might thus be regenerated, bourgeois individualism might yield to an active sense of spiritual community, the dawn of the 'New Man' may be in sight.

These large-scale objectives led on the aesthetic front to a fundamental opposition of Expressionism to earlier forms of Naturalism and Impressionism. For these writers and artists, Impressionism simply reflected humanity's servitude, projecting the passive image of 'man lowered to the position of a gramophone record of the outer world', as Hermann Bahr put it in one of the most famous manifestos of the new movement.[18] Like the Cubists, the Expressionists were interested in arriving at unfamiliar images of the world through calculated modes of distortion, but where the French artists sought some kind of analytic distance and detachment from the objects to which they alluded, the Expressionist emphasis was always on an intensity of perception secured by infusing the world with violent emotion.

For painters like Kandinsky and Marc, colour was a measure of 'spiritual' intensity and had little or nothing to do with actual objects, which provided merely a starting-point. As another spokesman for Expressionism put it:

The world is here, it would be meaningless to reproduce it. To seek it out in its last convulsions, its intrinsic essence and to create it anew – that is the greatest meaning of art.[19]

We may note the apocalyptic implications here and the 'convulsive' energies associated with new creation. Expressionism is, characteristically, committed to an exploration of 'essence', penetrating beneath the veil of matter. The result is an art which takes pride in its 'self-sufficiency', grasping the outward world as merely 'a stimulus to improvise in colour and form', as Arnold Schönberg noted of Kandinsky and Oskar Kokoschka.[20] At the same time, though, the Expressionist painters stressed the importance of 'inner meaning', to use Kandinsky's phrase, a meaning which expressed spiritual intensity and thereby avoided the 'trap' of Cubist formalism. While the changing styles of Picasso and Braque would develop in the general direction of mastery and analysis, the Expressionists used primitive and naive forms as models for an art which sought a return to origin, to the instinctual and ostensibly 'innocent' springs of expression.

This trope of a 'return' reminds us once again of Expressionism's divergence from the main preoccupations of Futurism, a divergence all the more surprising in view of Marinetti's apparent success in promoting the movement in Germany. Two exhibitions including Italian painting were in fact held in 1912, the second attracting particular attention as it made its way from Berlin to Cologne, Munich, Karlsruhe and Dresden. Six Futurist manifestos were published in *Der Sturm* between March 1912 and March 1913, and Marinetti – here nicknamed 'Marionetti' – gave a reading of his work in Berlin in the Spring of 1913.[21] Yet for all this exposure (even a volume of Marinetti's poems appeared in German), few writers joined the Futurist camp. The anti-humanist thrust of the Italian movement was fundamentally at odds with the psychological and political preoccupations of Expressionism, and if the two avant-gardes had any common ground it amounted to little more than a shared fascination with art as an expression of energy (one contemporary American critic spoke aptly of German 'explosionism'[22]).

Of the Expressionist poets, only August Stramm sought to develop Marinetti's words-in-freedom as a kind of 'telegram style' based on a concatenation of nouns. In Stramm's hands, though, the technique yielded rather different results, with 'clenched' strings of participles and nouns creating moments of macabre intensity.

Poems like 'Melancholy', for example, which register Stramm's wartime experience, record a world for which previous maps, syntactical and otherwise, are painfully obsolete:

Striding striving
living longs
shuddering standing
glances look for
dying grows
the coming
screams!
Deeply
we
dumb.[23]

Of the Expressionist poets, Stramm was, however, the only one to carry experimentalism so far, and for the most part the violence of the new writing was more a matter of imagery and content than of linguistic 'distortion'. One of the first poems of the Expressionist wave, Jakob van Hoddis's 'End of the World' (1911), set the tone for much that was to follow. The first stanza evokes great winds and rising waters, and in the second, concluding one, we read:

The storm has come, the seas run wild and skip
Landwards, to squash big jetties there.
Most people have a cold, their noses drip.
Trains tumble from the bridges everywhere.[24]

The form is regular enough, and, as Michael Hamburger notes, the novelty of the poem resides mainly in its shifting viewpoint and its collaging of disparate elements.[25] The tone has a quality of lugubrious excitement which is typical of Expressionist writing and which colours the urban landscapes of so many of these poems.

Depravity lurks everywhere in the Expressionist city, peopled as it is by beggars, prostitutes and murderers. The mood of urban degeneration and apocalypse can lead, as in the poems of Georg Heym, to feelings of despair and doom, or, as in some of Ernst Stadler's work, to a sense of a new beginning.[26] What is common to the early Expressionist poets, though, is the sense of cultural emergency which makes personal anguish invest the larger scene. The loudness of such writing – both literal and figurative – constantly stresses the need for a return to that which is primal in humanity, a shedding of cultural inhibition ·in the name of the naked 'cry' (*Schrei*) rather than the 'intellectual' word. Such poetry is perhaps best taken in small doses, partly because of the strain imposed by its favourite devices of exclamation and repetition, but also because its cosmic ambitions lead to a calculated abstractness of theme. The subject headings of the principal anthology of Expressionist verse, Karl Pinthus's *The Twilight of Humanity* (1920), are revealing in this respect: 'decline and cry', 'the awakening of hearts', 'proclamation and revolt', 'the love of humanity'.[27] Published in 1920, the anthology encapsulates the two main phases of Expressionism: the first, running from 1911 to 1914, when the central concern is with themes of death and decline, and the second, from 1914 through to 1920, charting the phase of political or messianic Expressionism, which was finally wrecked on the failure of the November Revolution of 1918.

The major poetry of the movement was produced in the first phase, with many of its most significant talents – Stadler, Georg Heym, Alfred Lichtenstein, and Georg Trakl – perishing in the War. Of these, the Austrian poet Georg Trakl was the most important, as he was the most equivocal, figure. Pinthus published ten of his poems in the *Twilight* anthology, though Trakl's work is altogether quieter and ostensibly more passive in tone than the familiar declamatory mode of Expressionist writing. Trakl's poem called 'Occident' is thus somewhat unusual in the apocalyptic imagery of its final stanza ('Gruesome sunset red / is breeding fear / in the thunderclouds. / You dying peoples!'[28]); more customary is the gloomy landscape elsewhere in the poem, with its imagery of the 'rocky path', the 'evening pond' and 'nocturnal shadows' – a landscape haunted by a mythical figure called Elis. The motif of decline is everywhere in Trakl's verse, though it is generally evoked through a psychic landscape rather than being voiced rhetorically. The quality of inwardness in these poems is arguably more extreme than any we have looked at so far, though in contrast to mainstream Expressionism it is not the product of overt emotional pressure, of the exterior world distorted by a projected intensity. Trakl's poems disturb, rather, because any sense of a shared external reality seems to have been lost.

The characteristic mood is an autumnal one, the present tense of the poem poised between fading memories of an idyllic past and intimations of darkness and decay to come. The loud Expressionist

'I' is rarely in evidence – in fact Trakl described his work as an attempt 'to subordinate myself unconditionally to the object to be represented'[29] – and the burden of emotion resides almost wholly in a repertoire of recurring images. 'Evening Song' will provide an example:

> Walking along dark paths in the evening,
> Our pale shapes appear before us.
>
> When we are thirsty,
> We drink the white waters of the pool,
> The sweetness of our mournful childhood.
>
> Dead, we rest beneath the elder bushes,
> Watching the grey gulls.
>
> Spring clouds rise over the dark city
> Silenced by monks of nobler times.
>
> When I took your slender hands
> You opened your soft round eyes.
> That was a long time ago.
>
> Yet when a darker melody visits the soul,
> You appear, white, in your friend's autumn landscape.[30]

The poem is striking partly on account of its shifting perspectives. The two 'friends' appear first as 'pale forms', which may suggest either a trick of the evening light or that they are ghosts. With the third stanza we are told that they are dead (*erstorbene*), and the perspective then changes again to give an image of Spring against the 'dark city', which could be either regenerative or destructive. The tense now shifts to the past, linking a moment of shared emotion with 'the monks of nobler times'. The final stanza, with its suggestion that the friend (the 'white' one associated still with childhood) will reappear whenever a 'dark' (or 'gloomy', *dunkler*) 'harmony haunts the soul', makes another temporal shift, implying that the present tense of the opening lines is that of fantasy.

The combination of dark and light imagery in association with these ideas of childhood suggests that the perception of the past is somehow double, ambivalent. Trakl's work returns obsessively to a moment of loss which is generally understood in terms of his incestuous desire for his sister; 'Evening Song' was in fact part of a textual complex later refashioned as the long poem 'Helion', a work which connects the poet's 'madness' with the loss of his sister to marriage with an older man ('A pale angel / The son steps into the empty house of his fathers. // The sisters have gone far away to white old men'[31]). The poems pull constantly into the past of remembered experience, back to the 'dark stillness of childhood'[32], though the contrasting imagery of whiteness and paleness, associated with the conjoint figure of 'a dying youth, the sister',[33] suggests that behind this lies what Heidegger, in his account of Trakl, calls 'the earliness of stiller childhood'.[34] This seems to be the burden of the prose poem 'Dream and Derangement', where the narrator's childhood is recalled as 'full of sickness, dread and sullen darkness'. Yet running through this text are intermittent references to 'the white form of an angel' and to 'the starry face of purity' which contrast with the 'dark rooms' of the guilt-laden family tradition ('O blighted race, accursed genealogy').

These images refer to an impossible time before guilt, a time before the crime which seems to initiate an Oedipal history ('when in the flourishing summer garden he raped the quiet child, and reflected in the afterglow, saw that profound darkness, his own face'[35]). This moment of violence, real or imagined, inaugurates the rule of sexual difference, and the insistent figures of decline and descent in the poems, associated even as they are with evening and autumn, evoke a return to some primal oneness. In 'Western Song', for example:

> O the bitter hour of decline,
> When we regard a stony face in black waters.
> But radiant the lovers raise their silver eyelids:
> One kin. From rosy pillows incense pours
> And the sweet canticle of the bodies resurrected.[36]

'Ein Geschlecht': 'one kin', but the word has a range of interconnected meanings, 'sex, genre, family, state, race, lineage, generation'.[37] As Heidegger observes, a weight of emphasis attaches to 'one' in these lines, evoking 'The force which marks the tribes of mankind as the simple oneness of "*one* generation," and thus restores them and mankind to the stiller childhood', to 'the stiller onefold simplicity of childhood [in which] is hidden also the kindred twofoldness of mankind'.[38]

* * *

The full articulation of this theme in Trakl's work is too complex to be pursued here, but his fantasy of a 'stiller childhood' which does not yet know the 'curse' of genealogy and sexual difference is one which also governed the development of Expressionist theatre. In fact the play usually taken to inaugurate Expressionist drama, Kokoschka's *Murderer, Hope of Women* (1907), is a macarbre exploration of the negative power of sexuality, here understood in terms of a violent struggle of man against woman.[39] When Kokoschka's play was first performed in 1909, at a small outdoor theatre in Vienna, there were riotous scenes as soldiers fought with members of the audience. While these violent confrontations may have had no direct relation to the play, they accorded well enough with the electric atmosphere Kokoschka was trying to create. The players' faces bore heavily made-up mask-like expressions, while veins and muscles were vividly painted on their arms and legs. The stage-setting itself was at once starkly simple and dramatically coloured:

> Night sky. Tower with large red grille as door; torches the only light; black ground, rising to the tower in such a way that all the figures appear in relief.

As the play opens, a warlord enters, followed by a group of men; almost immediately a woman appears with her female attendants. The Woman is transfixed by sexual desire: 'Why do you bind me, man, with your gaze?', she cries, 'Devouring life overpowers me. O take away my terrible hope – and may torment overpower you.' The Man's response is to order his attendants to brand her as his possession – an old man steps forward, tears open her dress and marks her with a hot iron. In her pain and fury the Woman springs at the Man, wounding him in the side with her knife. It seems that the wound will be fatal, for the Man is placed in a coffin behind the bars of the tower. But while the rival factions of men and women now begin to sport in the shadows, the Woman is inconsolable. 'She creeps around the cage like a panther', trying to awaken the Man (she 'prods his wound, hissing maliciously, like an adder'). Suddenly, though, there is a crowing of cocks, and the Man seems to revive. In a bizarre tableau, the 'Woman covers him entirely with her body; separated by the grille, to which she clings high up in the air like a monkey'. A terrible struggle now takes place, the Man finally draining the Woman's strength ('you vampire, piecemeal you feed on me, weaken me'). With a 'slowly diminishing scream' she expires, leaving the Man to wreak havoc on the male and female attendants.

> CHORUS: The devil! Tame him, save yourselves, save yourselves if you can – all is lost!
> *He walks straight towards them. Kills them like mosquitoes and leaves red behind. From very far away, crowing of cocks.*

Perhaps not surprisingly, this curiously ugly play – or, more precisely, theatrical event (it runs to only a few pages of text) – is often regarded as a forerunner of Expressionist drama, and its subsequent 'revivals' show that it continued to occupy a place in the later repertoire.[40] Even my brief sketch of the play's action should indicate its proto-Expressionist qualities. Naturalistic psychology is jettisoned in favour of an extreme stylisation, and Kokoschka builds the play around a sequence of emotional intensities rather than according to a clear narrative logic. These intensities are coupled with a primitivism of setting and emotion which gives this conflict of the sexes the quality of a primal scene. As if to reinforce this sense of the primitive and its displacement of social by sexual conflict, the play foregrounds non-textual effects of gesture and *mise en scène*. The acting style demanded by the play prefigures that 'convulsive equation of body and soul'[41] which was to become the mark of Expressionist performance and which produced the notorious staccato sound-effects of 'scream-theatre' [*Schreidrama*]. In *Murderer*, there is a high-pitched lyricism which approximates to 'singing higher and higher, soaring';[42] indeed, the primacy of sound over meaning becomes the very mark of the violence and excessiveness of desire.

This connection between sexual violence and a kind of formal 'excess' epitomises that aspect of Expressionism which would prove least assimilable to Anglo-American notions of modernism. T. S. Eliot's idea of an 'objective correlative' is a useful way of gauging the difference, especially since the term derives from a consideration of a dramatic work, Shakespeare's *Hamlet*. The famous definition is as follows:

> The only way of expressing emotion in the form of art is by
> finding an 'objective correlative'; in other words, a set of objects,
> a chain of events, which shall be the formula of that particular
> emotion. [43]

It is this 'correlative' which *Hamlet* apparently lacks, the play failing
to ensure the 'complete adequacy of the external to the emotion'.
On closer scrutiny we find that Eliot's idea that the play 'is like the
sonnets, full of some stuff that the writer could not drag to light,
contemplate, or manipulate into art' is closely bound up with an
anxiety about the feminine as fundamentally intractable to representation.[44] Eliot's commitment to 'objectification' points up the
dissociation between inner and ·outer, subjective and objective,
which is central to his conception of art's power to transmute the
primitive 'stuff' of emotion. In producing a 'formula' for the
emotion, art is able to constrain that 'bodily' affect which he tends
to associate with a kind of pathology.[45]

Now, as the example of Kokoschka's *Murderer* will show, the pri-
orities of Expressionist drama are very different from those which
govern Eliot's reading of *Hamlet*. In this new theatre we find that
narrative indeterminacy and the hyperbolic pitch of emotion con-
spire to unsettle and exceed representation. Where, for Eliot, sexuality seems to threaten a moment of pure self-presence which
blocks Oedipal resolution and escapes formulation in the differential medium of language (sound is dangerously privileged over
meaning), in Expressionist drama a certain negativity attaches to
sexuality, not because it is intractable to the 'chain' of representation but *because it is already bound by it*. To put it another way, sexuality here always exists within a structure, whether it be one of
violent opposition or the Oedipal triangle itself.

So we find in *Murderer* a kind of imbalance between the perennial 'battle of the sexes' – a structure determined above all by narrative and repetition – and a countervailing use of dramatic effects to
elide distinctions between inner and outer, self and other, so as to
dissolve the symbolic in moments of pure 'bodily' affect. Eliot's
representational 'chain' of objects and events is, in fact, precisely
what the excessive modes of Expressionist drama seek to disrupt,
for to be bound by this 'chain' is to be bound by the law of secondariness – a law which the new theatre constantly strives to violate
in its struggle to establish itself as pure 'event' rather than as narrative, as 'scream' rather than speech. The difficulty we may have in

interpreting *Murderer* thus stems mainly from the way in which Kokoschka employs a range of formal intensities which are deliberately (in Eliot's phrase) 'in excess of the facts'. Light, sound, gesture, a strangely overdetermined symbolism – these elements create a slippage of meaning which substitutes spectacle for narrative. Are we, for example, to explain the ugliness of the play in terms of that misogyny which seems to pervade Expressionist writing, or is narrative indeterminacy a clue to subtler contradictions of attitude?

There are few close interpretations of *Murderer*, but even these are divided by some fundamental disagreements. Perhaps the most straightforward reading of the play is that given by Frank Whitford: 'the male, threatened by the woman's sexual desire, regains his strength by killing her'.[46] But if the play expresses a triumphant misogyny, why does it end, as two other critics have observed, on a note of pessimism and foreboding?[47] And to make matters worse, Kokoschka's own comments on the play tend to complicate rather than resolve problems of interpretation. In a letter of 1931, for example, he refers to *Murderer* as 'my expressionistic dawn chorus, sung in honour of an anonymous Penthesilea',[48] and in an essay of 1935 ('On Experience') he describes the play as striking 'a blow against the thoughtlessness of our male civilization with my fundamental notion that man is mortal and woman immortal, and that only the murderer tries to reverse this basic fact in the modern world'.[49] In his autobiography, however, Kokoschka describes the famous poster advertising the play in rather different terms: 'The man is blood-red, the colour of life. But he is lying in the lap of a woman who is white, the colour of death.'[50]

These apparent contradictions arise because *Murderer* actually focuses less on gender oppositions than on something violent and contradictory which undercuts them and appears as sexuality itself. This at any rate seems to be the implication of other remarks in the autobiography, where sexual conflict is linked with those 'Greek ideas of Eros and Thanatos' which are 'the counterparts of progress and enlightenment', ideas which, according to Kokoschka, he derived from the work of J. J. Bachofen and Robert Briffault:

> one thing was certain: the instinct for self-preservation which begins with the first movement in the womb and ends in death. … Fear makes for inactivity, but behind that shadow of Thanatos, which had dogged me from my childhood onwards, there lurked

the ever more enticing abyss of Eros. Here, in this new existence to which I began to seek the key, is perhaps the secret of my first stage play, *Mörder, Hoffnung der Frauen.*'[51]

In contrast to the superficially similar polemics of Italian Futurism against the 'feminine', Kokoschka locates a certain irredeemable negativity within sexuality itself (Eros is inextricably intertwined with Thanatos).

This line of thought clearly has its place in that view of 'the deathly hatred of the sexes'[52] which had already received definitive expression in the work of Schopenhauer and Nietzsche, but it does not solve completely the problem of the play's title. Why should Man as Murderer be the '*hope* of Women'? To conclude simply that *Murderer* ends with 'the victorious male passing through all who stand in his way'[53] is not only to miss the final association of Man with death, but also to underestimate the extent to which the flamboyant experimentalism of the play is, at one level, an effect of 'excessive' female desire.

One solution lies in Otto Weininger's *Sex and Character*, first published in 1903 and a work with which Kokoschka was almost certainly familiar. In this hugely influential book (twelve editions were published between May 1903 and May 1910), Weininger combined cultural evaluation with pseudo-science to create a sprawling monument to misogyny and antisemitism. Woman, for Weininger, is 'nothing but sexuality ... she is sexuality itself'.[54] In attempting to argue this case, Weininger assembles the main elements of traditional misogyny but gives them a polemical twist of his own: if woman's inferiority results from her failure to 'overcome the sexuality that binds her' (279), she can only be raised from her lowly status by the intervention of man, who, by denying her sexual fulfilment, will open for her the way to a new transcendence. Wagner's Kundry is, for Weininger, 'probably the most perfect representation of woman in art' (319) because she submits to the redemptive force of 'a sinless, immaculate man – Parsifal' (344).

Not surprisingly, perhaps, it has been suggested that *Sex and Character* can be read almost as an early Expressionist manifesto,[55] not least because of its habit of linking violence with regeneration. 'Love', says Weininger, 'is murder. The sexual impulse destroys the body and mind of the woman, and the psychical eroticism destroys her psychical existence' (249). But if 'sexual union ... is allied to murder' (248), the act of desired 'regeneration' is also linked to death: 'she must certainly be destroyed, as woman; but only to be raised again from the ashes' (345). Weininger's unpleasant but influential fantasies may thus explain Kokoschka's title and the withholding of sexuality, which is the play's major theme, but questions still remain to be answered. Woman, for Weininger, is incapable of conceptual thought or self-knowledge. She lives an 'unconnected, discontinous' life and represents 'negation, the opposite pole of Godhead' (146). Throughout the book, Weininger categorises the feminine as the realm of the body and the unconscious, and it is this aspect of his polemic which is directed at the 'feminised' and decadent art of the Secession, an art which, in privileging the 'material' values of sound and ornament, allegedly obstructs the conceptual clarity of male thought.[56] 'A being like the female, without the power of making concepts, is unable to make judgments. In her "mind" subjective and objective are not separated' (194); 'It is the conception which brings freedom from the eternally subjective' (192).

Here we can begin to see just how equivocal Weininger's influence was for the Expressionists, for their whole project was founded on a revaluation of subjectivity and its 'visionary' capabilities. An early essay by Kokoschka, for example, 'On the Nature of Visions', directly opposes any Weiningerian claims for 'logic': 'The consciousness of visions is not a mode of perceiving and understanding existing objects. It is a condition in which we experience the visions themselves.'[57] Kokoschka goes on to claim that

> This consciousness of visions has a life which derives power from itself. This power freely organizes visions whether complete or barely perceptible irrespective of how they relate to each other, and in complete independence of temporal or spatial logic.   (98)

As that last phrase suggests, verbal expression operates here according to very different criteria from those of Weininger:

> Thus we have to listen with complete attention to our inner voice in order to get past the shadows of words to their very source. 'The Word became flesh and dwelt among us.' And then the inner source frees itself, sometimes vigorously, sometimes feebly, from the words within which it lives like a charm.   (99)

To experience 'visions' is '[t]o be possessed', and Kokoschka uses a striking analogy to describe its effect: 'Suddenly an image will take shape for us, like the first look, like the first shriek of a child, newborn, coming from its mother's womb' (100).

Kokoschka's essay demonstrates the way in which Expressionism could assimilate Weininger's negative view of sexuality while at the same time exploiting those very non-conceptual qualities which he had derided as 'feminine' and anti-modern. An explanation for this lies in the essay's vocabulary of 'source' and 'origin', which points back towards primal intensities which pre-exist a modern sexuality contaminated by repetition and commodification; for early Expressionism is indelibly marked by the *fin de siècle* fascination with the figure of the prostitute and by that '"mechanistic" and sadistic imagination which separates love from a modern eroticism without aura'.[58] Kokoschka's reference to child-birth suggests a contrasting network of associations, linking the new and visionary with the pre-discursive and pre-Oedipal in a movement which seeks to rediscover the lost aura within artistic form itself. The connection with the maternal and (in Lacan's sense) the Imaginary not only runs counter to Weiningerian 'logic', but also suggests a domain which is unavailable to linguistic expression and which exists prior to structures of gender and family.

From this point of view it is perhaps not fortuitous that the earliest exponents of an Expressionist theatre, Kokoschka and Wassily Kandinsky, were both painters. Kokoschka's association of the visionary with a fantasy of uterine return certainly informs much painterly theory in this period, as we can see from the *Blue Rider Almanac* and the writings of artist Paul Klee. This is how Klee puts it in *On Modern Art*:

> Chosen are those artists who penetrate to that secret place where primeval power nurtures all evolution. There, where the powerhouse of all time and space – call it brain or heart of creation – activates every function; who is the artist who would not dwell there? In the womb of nature, at the source of creation, where the secret key to all lies guarded.[59]

For the dramatist, Klee's 'secret place' might arguably be the point at which narrative structure suddenly yields to dramatic event, the point at which theatre seems to attain an 'impossible' freedom from the trace of externality.

Yet as we can see from the late plays of Strindberg, commonly regarded as the precursors of Expressionism proper, this fantasy of origin and presence is constantly threatened by the transcendental pull of theatricality itself, a structure of re-presentation working tirelessly to absorb affective intensity and the movement of desire. Strindberg, too, was a keen admirer of Weininger, but the impact of *Sex and Character* on his theatre prefigured the Expressionist twist later given to this set of ideas: for while he fully endorsed Weininger's anti-feminism, the dream-like structure of his own 'station-dramas' [*Stationendramen*] had a surprising affinity with Weininger's contemptuous description of woman's life as 'discrete, unconnected, discontinuous, swayed by the perceptions of the moment instead of dominating them' (146).[60]

In a well-known preface to *A Dream Play* (1901), Strindberg outlines the technique at work here and in the earlier *To Damascus* (Parts I and II 1898):

> Everything can happen, everything is possible and probable. Time and place do not exist; on an insignificant basis of reality the imagination spins, weaving new patterns; a mixture of memories, experiences, free fancies, incongruities and improvisations. The characters split, double, multiply, evaporate, condense, disperse, assemble.[61]

Yet Strindberg's description, which bears a strong resemblance to Freud's later account of the 'primary process',[62] is in marked contrast to one of the major themes of *To Damascus* (and, indeed, of *A Dream Play* and *Ghost Sonata*), the theme of *repetition*. 'Why does everything recur?' asks the Stranger at the beginning of Part I, and as the plays unfold it becomes increasingly clear that sexuality and its domestic scene (the 'inferno' of Strindberg's life and art) are marked by interminable struggle. The Lady and the Stranger endlessly torment each other, as Strindberg evokes what is described in *A Dream Play* as 'the fairest of things, which is the bitterest: love, a wife and a home; the best thing, and the worst' (584). This drama is ultimately less a matter of 'weaving *new* patterns' than of concluding that, in the words of the Advocate, 'We must torture each other, then. What makes one happy, torments the other' (588). Sexuality here becomes 'the worst thing', standing as 'Repetition. Repeating the pattern' (606).

While there is a kind of heroism ultimately claimed in the knowledge that, as the Daughter concludes in *A Dream Play*, 'Strife between opposites generates power, just as fire and water generate steam' (629), the only real but intermittent hope lies elsewhere. In *To Damascus*, for example, the Stranger awakens in the Lady 'a feeling of motherhood which I had never known before' (201), and he confesses that 'I longed to sleep at a mother's breast' (204), a wish momentarily granted later in the play ('Come, my child, and I will repay the debt I owe you. On my lap I shall rock you to peace' [224]). It is therefore not by chance that this desire to return to the mother, to an original plenitude which precedes all repetitive strife, is articulated in a dramatic form in which the 'spinning' play of imagination and improvisation seeks to undermine the structure of representation. Indeed, this seems a decisive clue to some of the concerns of early Expressionism, opposing sexuality, as structure and repetition, to the 'timeless', non-sexual love of mother and child. If the episodic, dream-like form of Strindberg's late plays offers a model for a modernist drama, it is perhaps because it strives to couple the non-representational with a fantasy of fullness not predicated upon a lack or absence. In dramatic terms, then, the dream of the Mother is also the dream of a theatre with no 'outside', a theatre sufficient to itself and freed from the tyranny of both external reality and textual authority.

Kokoschka's *Murderer* seems to engage directly with these ideas and in so doing to test the limits of the dramatic medium itself. As several critics have observed, and as Kokoschka himself made clear in his autobiography, a decisive influence on his early work was J. J. Bachofen's *Mother Right* (1861).[63] The importance of Bachofen's thesis – it had a strong impact on writers as diverse as Nietzsche, Hauptmann, Klages, Rilke, Mann and Kafka[64] – lay in its imaginative account of three main phases of human development: the 'hetaerist-aphroditic' phase, characterised by female promiscuity and symbolised by the wild vegetation of the swamp; the Demetrian phase of mother-love and a settled, agricultural society; and finally the phase of father-right, of individual property and the division of labour. Bachofen concluded that 'Matriarchy is followed by patriarchy and preceded by unregulated hetaerism.'[65]

This evolutionary process might lie behind the attenuated narrative of *Murderer*, though Kokoschka hardly shares Bachofen's optimistic view of '[t]he progress from the maternal to the paternal conception of man'.[66] If Eros precedes or lies *behind* Thanatos, as Kokoschka suggests in his autobiography, the Man's final victory seems to represent the triumph of the deathly principle of patriarchal law, a principle governing desire and external to it. In the 'A text' of *Murderer*, the moment when the Woman covers the Man with her body is initially one of maternal affection – 'Who nourishes me?' the Man cries, 'Who suckles me with blood? I devour your melting flesh'[67] – but as the lurid allusions to vampirism indicate, the 'iron chains' of male desire can no longer be resisted. In the ensuing massacre, Kokoschka again hints through the sound of the cock-crow (the sign that Peter will betray Christ) that we have entered the age of theology and transcendence.

In the echo of that symbolic cock-crow, *Murderer* seems to perform a complex interrogation of the dramatic medium, its prefiguring of Expressionist modes bound up with a desire for the pre-figurative which defines an impossible and absolute theatricality. Indeed, the association here of closure with some form of patriarchal law recalls Jacques Derrida's rather similar sense of a theatrical 'evolution':

> The origin of theater, such as it must be restored, is the hand lifted against the abusive wielder of the logos, against the father, against the God of a stage subjected to the power of speech and the text.[68]

Derrida analyses Antonin Artaud's 'theatre of cruelty' as an attempt to escape repetition and the law of representation. Artaud's 'writing of the body', an ideal 'language without trace' (175), seeks to evade the absent authority of 'a primary logos which does not belong to the theatrical site and governs it from a distance' (235).

Artaud's is an 'impossible' theatre, founded, as Derrida observes, not only on an ideal of linguistic 'non-difference' but on a related fantasy of pure self-presence which abolishes Oedipal structure:

> Restored to its absolute and terrifying proximity, the stage of cruelty will thus return me to the autarchic immediacy of my birth, my body and my speech. Where has Artaud better defined the stage of cruelty than in *Here Lies*, outside any apparent reference to the theater: 'I, Antonin Artaud, am my son / my father, my mother / and myself'? (190)

Artaud may be the best-known exponent of these claims for an 'absolute' theatre, but the Expressionists, too, dreamed of a drama which might be said to 'shelter an indestructible desire for full presence, for nondifference: simultaneously life and death' (194). Yet the theatre is, as Derrida observes, an exemplary instance of the general rule by which 'all destructive discourses … must inhabit the structures they demolish' (194).

That paradoxical condition, endlessly affirming difference and exteriority, is the object of ritual confrontation in Expressionist drama, a confrontation staged (as we see in *Murderer*) between two theatrical limits: on the one hand, there is a theatre prefiguring the ideal of Artaud in its search for an immediate, pre-discursive reality; on the other, there is a drama endlessly preoccupied with Oedipal structure and with an ideal of transcending it (the theme of the 'New Man' which figures so prominently in the later theatre of Expressionism). That we should find few pure instances of either type both supports Derrida's case and reflects the peculiarly hybrid nature of so many Expressionist plays.

Of the first form of Expressionist theatre Kandinsky's *The Yellow Sound* (1909) is almost the only 'pure' example.[69] This brief dramatic event comprises six scenes or 'Pictures' (*Bilder*), as Kandinsky calls them. As that term suggests, the text of the play is not so much a script as a series of directions for movements, coloured lighting and musical effects. We are given few clues to the meaning of the 'characters' here (they comprise Five Giants, Vague Creatures, a Child, a Man, People in Flowing Robes, People in Tights, a Chorus, and a Tenor (backstage)). There seems to be some sort of progression from the indeterminate to the human, with timeless space giving way to recognisable objects, and it may be that the play has a utopian theme linked to Kandinsky's concept of spiritual form: 'This white ray leads to evolution, to elevation. Behind matter, within matter, the creative spirit is hidden.'[70] Ultimately, though, the play claims our attention less on account of some hidden narrative than for its radical break with the conventions of nineteenth-century drama, condemned by Kandinsky for remaining 'under the spell of external events'.[71] In contrast, *The Yellow Sound*, he suggests, 'finally consists of the complex of inner experiences (soul = vibrations) of the audience'.[72]

Kandinsky's play was, in fact, never performed, and perhaps for that reason the text published in the *Blaue Reiter Almanac* came to represent an extreme of experimentalism. It was an extreme, however, which subsequent Expressionist drama would only fitfully explore, for Kandinsky had moved far toward that apparently pre-linguistic 'ground' (*Urgrund*) of experience where all structure seemed about to dissolve in a play of purely physical effects:

The word, independent or in sentences, was used to create a certain 'atmosphere' that frees the soul and makes it receptive. The sound of the human voice was also used pure, i.e., without being obscured by words, or by the meaning of words.[73]

Colour was therefore of primary importance to this project, producing 'irrational pictorial spaces' which allowed a kind of 'spiritual' or psychic mobility, a freedom from determinate social and psychic structures.[74]

If Kandinsky's play in some sense anticipates what André Green has termed in another context a post-Freudian theatre,[75] the major plays of fully-fledged Expressionism are dominated by the imperatives of structure, and specifically by the binding forms of the Oedipal plot. Not only does sexuality imply ineluctable repetition, as in Strindberg and Kokoschka, but its controlling network of desires is deeply embedded within the family narrative. Here the Father returns to exercise control, governing theatrical expression either directly or 'at a distance', and while plays of filial rebellion, such as Walter Hasenclever's *The Son* (1914), strive to create a final, liberating sense of independence, this amounts in practice to little more than a familiar avant-garde fantasy of self-authoring.

Although critics have tended to disregard the determinism of psychological structure in Expressionist theatre,[76] it is not just the sensational cases like Sorge's *The Beggar*, Hasenclever's *The Son* or Arnolt Bronnen's *Parricide* (1915) which bring to the fore the Oedipal conflict between father and son. Bronnen's play, in which the son kills his father and is then wooed by his naked mother, may provide the most luridly memorable handling of the theme, but the family narrative is, in fact, everywhere in Expressionist theatre, working its effects in plays as diverse as Hanns Johst's *The Young Man* (1916), Fritz von Unruh's *A Family* (1916), and Georg Kaiser's *From Morning to Midnight* (1916).

One reason why critics have tended to underestimate the determining power of the Oedipal plot is that the recurring motifs of rebellion and parricide gesture towards a new independence, a freedom from the constraints of the past and the family, and accession to the status of 'new man'. This utopian attempt to refigure masculinity in terms of a transcendence of social roles caught in the Oedipal net is clearly expressed in an influential manifesto by Kasimir Edschmid:

Each person is no longer simply an individual bound by duty, morality, society and family. In this art, each becomes the most elevated and the most deplorable of things: *becomes a human being.*[77]

Such, then, is the dream of a new beginning (*Aufbruch*) which animates Expressionist drama, a recreation of the self which aims to purge it of any contact with the past, and, specifically, with the Father. For in these plays the force of repetition is derived from the law of the Father, and freedom can be found only in a regeneration equivalent to Artaud's idea of self-birth. The attempt to free theatre from mimesis is thus inextricably bound up with the generational struggle against paternity: representation is at once a theatrical mode which disastrously situates repetition at the heart of performance *and* that genealogical chain by which a son is bound to represent his father. Yet, as Richard Sheppard has shown in a discussion of four of these plays, 'the iron law that sons must succeed their fathers' is one which, finally, it is impossible to break. Each of these plays is, he concludes, 'caught in the classic double bind of castration by a yet secret dependence upon a more or less sadistic but absent Father'.[78]

As for the theme of salvation so much emphasised in readings of these plays (and, for example, in Hasenclever's description of *The Son* as 'the revolt of the spirit against reality'[79]), Sheppard concludes that

No sooner does an 'anoedipal' drive manifest itself in the plays, than it is assimilated into the Oedipal chain of lack and dependence, rendered harmless by being allowed to exhaust itself in aggression against part-objects or turned into a regressive flight to the mother. (376)

The importance which Sheppard attaches to the 'closed circuit of the Oedipal drama' certainly accords with what we have already seen of the relation between sexuality and structure in early Expressionism. Yet, as Kokoschka's *Murderer* shows, the tendency to 'excess' in Expressionism means that its drama is never quite as diagrammatic as this 'circuit' suggests. Sheppard argues that 'the *Ich-Dramen* cannot envisage an essential drive in the human personality which … can produce free individuals' (377), thereby leaving us with 'a loss that can never be made good' (378). It is the ideal of self-presence which is complicated here: on the one hand, it exists at the thematic level, as the desired escape from structure which, expressed in the familiar rhetoric of Expressionism, is ultimately re-contained in a discursive, Oedipal order; on the other hand, though, the curiously uneven, hybrid quality of these plays arises because this thematic 'circuit' is, as it were, broken by its production as dramatic event. Much Expressionist drama is, like Kokoschka's *Murderer*, governed by this fundamental tension between a narrative structure always already contaminated by sexuality and the Oedipal chain, and a displacement of libidinal energy into a form whose ecstatic 'bodily' rhythms strive to defer the return of the Father. To stress the compensatory effects of that form is not simply to engage in conventional critical pieties about performance values; for the tension between narrative and event, between sexuality and unstructured affect, is actually interiorised in the acting-style of Expressionism – interiorised, that is, as *strain* (at the level of voice, diaphragm, musculature) and a *straining after* the condition of 'pure', non-discursive theatricality.[80]

* * *

That quality of strain is something we now readily associate with Expressionism, but to follow the later mutations of its dramatic style is to see how such tension was increasingly resolved at the level of rhetoric. By 1920, the Oedipal theme was commonplace; as the Secretary puts it in Georg Kaiser's *The Coral* (1920), 'Father and son are drawn in opposite directions. It is always a life and death struggle.'[81] Yet while the opening phase had been characterised by acts of filial rebellion, plays of the twenties, like Franz Werfel's *Mirror-Man* (1920), focused increasingly on what Peter Gay has called the 'Revenge of the Father'.[82] In this changed climate the work of Ernst Toller affirmed the radical potential of theatre, but it did so through a political vision which transferred attention from the individual to the group. In *Transfiguration* (1919), for example, the way towards a 'true humanity' is seen to lie through the rejection of sexual love ('Can't you see that love and goodness are eternally separated by a hopeless gulf?'[83]), and Toller's search for a 'collectively valid subjectivity' led in his next play to the proposition that 'Only the Masses are holy.'[84] Toller thus offered one path out of what the Marxist critic Georg Lukács would soon be calling the 'self-trumpeting emotionalism' of subjective Expressionism.[85]

Toller was a revolutionary (he spent five years in prison as a result of the part he played in the November Revolution of 1918), and he was able to transcend the Oedipal narrative in favour of larger social and economic themes. Yet it was precisely the largeness of such themes which ultimately proved difficult to handle, and with the exception of *The Machine-Wreckers* (1922), most of Toller's work drifted too easily towards the purely didactic and allegorical.

By 1925, in fact, the whole Expressionist experiment had begun to seem dated and out of step with modernity. An exhibition held at the Mannheim Kunsthalle in the middle of that year gave a name to a very different tendency in the arts: *Die Neue Sachlichkeit*, the new objectivity. The principal artists contributing to the show – Otto Dix, George Grosz, Max Beckmann among them – announced a return to figurative painting and to a hard-edged style of social criticism. The second half of the decade would now see a swing against the subjectivism of Expressionist art and towards a new quality of formal control and cynical detachment which ran parallel to a fascination with technology and urban capitalism (America became in several senses a cultural lodestone during this period).[86]

The collision of these two very different artistic tendencies can be seen in the early, pre-Marxist theatre of Bertolt Brecht. In *Baal* (1922), for example, Brecht depicts a wandering poet whose hedonism and flouting of social convention deliberately parody the grand humanist aspirations of later Expressionist drama (at the literary dinner which opens the play, Baal gets outrageously drunk while a young lady reads her Expressionist verse: 'The new world / Exterminating the world of pain, / Island of rapturous humanity', etc.[87]). Baal rejects all moral constraints and dedicates himself to the pursuit of pleasure. Where Expressionist theatre had struggled with the deterministic thrust of narrative, Brecht's play, with its brief, loosely articulated scenes, enacts what one critic has called 'a dream of transience accepted, of conflict enjoyed and of contradiction sustained with equanimity'.[88] This 'acceptance' of contradiction produces a nihilistic tone in the early plays which couples a cynical realism with an indifference to political struggle. The best example is *Drums in the Night* (1922), in which the protagonist Kragler deliberately turns against revolution in order to win back his fiancée. Brecht later remarked that 'It seems just about the shabbiest possible solution, particularly as there is a faint suspicion of approval on the part of the author',[89] but the element of 'approval' is motivated by a deep distrust of communal relationships and the rhetoric in which they had been celebrated in much Expressionist drama.

In rejecting didactic and allegorical modes at this point in his career, Brecht was also formulating a scepticism about the tortured modes of 'deep' subjectivity which had recently dominated the stage. With *In the Jungle of Cities* (1924) and *A Man's a Man* (1927), his drama became harder and more 'objective', mingling elements from farce with a darkly pessimistic sense of oppression. In the 'jungle of the big city', supposedly Chicago in 1912, an 'inexplicable' struggle takes place between two men.[90] In his prologue to the play, Brecht warned his audience: 'Don't worry your heads about the motives for the fight, concentrate on the stakes.' As is clear from the play's opening scene, what is at stake is nothing less than the possibility of personal freedom: when the timber merchant Shlink meets the younger Garga, a bookseller, he requests his opinion of a book and then asks: 'Is that your personal opinion? I'll buy your opinion. Is ten dollars enough?' Shlink thus begins a series of challenges to Garga's sense of the inviolability of his personal life – if his literary opinions can be bought for cash, so perhaps can his private fantasies of a bohemian existence in Tahiti.

The 'fight' that ensues forges a powerful sadomasochistic bond between the two men, and Brecht seems to imply that, in contrast to the ineluctable and predetermined Oedipal struggles of the Expressionist theatre, the conflict between Garga and Shlink is *chosen* by them as the only authentic medium of social contact – at the very end of the play, after the death of Shlink, Garga concludes: 'It's a good thing to be alone. The chaos is spent. That was the best time.'[91] Here and in *A Man's a Man*, farce and dramatic irony destroy psychological depth, reducing social life to exploitative trickery and mechanical gestures. Brecht commented on the later play that 'Every single scene of the comedy is so far removed from the problem-play or the psychological type of play that any naive actor would be bound to be able to reproduce it simply from memory.'[92] So, in *A Man's a Man*, a completely new identity is forged for Galy Gay – as the Widow Begbeck puts it in her 'Interjection':

Mister Brecht appends this item to the bill:
You can do with a human being what you will.
Take him apart like a car, rebuild him bit by bit–
As you will see, he has nothing to lose by it.[93]

Brecht gave a similar account of the play in an interview in 1926: 'It's about a man being taken to pieces and rebuilt as someone else for a particular purpose.'[94] Brecht was on the verge of discovering Marxism, but the sardonic humour of *A Man's a Man* is already enough to make us feel that the tortured humanism of Expressionist theatre belongs to another time.

8

Modernity and the 'Men of 1914'

In its association of narrative with forms of psychic oppression and confinement, Expressionism provided an extreme statement of one of the main principles of early European avant-gardism. Where it differed from some of the other tendencies, though, was in its agonised sense of the ultimate impossibility of escaping from structure into some pure, pre-Oedipal origin. The drive towards metaphysical presence was, in this sense, always compromised by the more powerful demands of history, narrative, and repetition. When we turn to the Anglo-American modernists, we find once again that the problematic of time occupies a central place, but here temporality is explored not as a repressive genealogical structure, but rather as a discontinuous cultural memory conceived as the very matrix of the new modernism. There are many reasons for this difference in perspective, but one is surely that, while the Expressionists associated narrative forms with the stultifying reproduction of a domestic history, for many of the major figures of Anglo-American modernism, time was imaginatively experienced through the shock of 'exile' and cultural contrast.

It is this theme, which Henry James had handled with such nuance and intricacy in a sequence of major novels which became a primary reference point for a new generation of émigrés from America to Europe. In his late novel *The Ambassadors* (1903), for example: 'They walked, wandered, wondered, and, a little, lost themselves; Strether had n't for years so rich a consciousness of time – a bag of gold into which he constantly dipped for a handful.'[1] So James's hero finds himself experiencing the freedoms and pleasures of youth in his middle age: 'I never had the benefit at the proper time – which comes to saying that I never had the thing itself' (305), he later explains to his confidante Maria Gostrey. The key to the novel lies in this sense of grasping what has almost been missed, for Strether is, in James's words, a 'belated man of the world – belated because he had endeavoured so long to escape being one, and now at last had really to face his doom' (41). Yet James's genial tone often veils the traumatic import of this 'doom', for having seen Europe, the traveller will be doubly displaced, cut adrift from a once familiar homeland while at the same time lacking a cultural place in the old world. Such a traveller's feelings may veer from resentment to passive admiration; like Strether, he or she may have a 'sense of moving in a maze of mystic closed allusions' (262), the very buildings exemplifying 'survival, transmission, association, a strong indifferent persistent order' (199).

This complex of desire and disorientation lies at the heart of one type of Anglo-American modernism whose prime movers also found themselves regarding this 'persistent order' from the outside. For this later generation, though, the irony ran in both directions, and when Ezra Pound tells us that his imaginary poet Hugh Selwyn Mauberley was 'born in a half-savage country, out of date',[2] he is also reminding us that English modernism is not much more than the sum of its cultural imports from America and Ireland. None of the so-called 'Men of 1914' who will concern us in this chapter – Pound, Wyndham Lewis, T. S. Eliot, and James Joyce – was born in England, and their various contributions to a common modernism were thus highly sensitive to questions of exile and cultural displacement.[3] And although London became temporarily a metropolitan 'vortex' for Pound, Lewis and Eliot, their sense of belonging to a shared avant-garde was considerably more ambivalent than that of comparable groupings on the Continent. Partly as a result of this designedly loose alliance, London's principal contributions to the history of the avant-garde – Imagism and Vorticism – proved to be moments rather than movements, short-lived phases in a more complex history.

There were other factors at work here which made this form of modernism different from its European counterparts. Neither Britain nor America possessed a powerful *academic* culture on the European model, and this may explain why these writers felt little direct hostility towards art as an institution and, accordingly, no desire to dissolve the boundaries between art and life. Furthermore, in contrast to the 'ecstatic' tendencies of some European modernisms, the Anglo-American version developed in part as a *critique* of modernity. Here the 'new' was a highly equivocal category, since cultural renovation was frequently projected as a *return* to the values of a previous age (the nineteenth-century Pre-Raphaelites, Britain's first real avant-garde, had already sketched this model of cultural decline and a compensatory 'return'). The modernism presided over by Pound and Eliot (one among several, but arguably still the hegemonic one) thus issued a call to order in the name of values which were explicitly anti-modern, though it did so by developing literary forms which were overtly modernist.

One key to this particular combination of elements is the centrality within Anglo-American modernism of precisely this problematic of time. In contrast to Futurism and its derivatives, this modernism sought to correct the apparently amnesiac tendencies of modernity by reconnecting it to a valued cultural tradition. Here the avant-garde conception of a rupture between past and present was supplanted by a concern with figures of anachrony and temporal disjunction which put questions of narrative back on the agenda. This version of modernism ascribed fantasies of an absolute present to a decadent romantic tradition deluded by notions of originality and spontaneity. Forms of 'cosmic' experience and disembodiment thus exerted little attraction here, and these modernists were, as we shall see, more concerned with developing models of psychic order which reinstate the divide between art and life, frequently in terms of a parallel re-fixing of sexual difference. And where the Expressionists feared the power of the Father and the law of mimesis he imposed, for the 'Men of 1914' a renovated culture often carried a paternal sanction, with resulting forms of 'filial' emulation actually providing the condition of an authentic modernism.

* * *

Some of these elements can already be discerned in the early poetry of Ezra Pound. Collections from *A Lume Spento* (1908) to *Canzoni* (1911) exhibit a strong and reverent sense of literary tradition and a corresponding paucity of recognisably 'modern' subject-matter. Pound is ostentatiously indebted both to distant cultures – to the lyric conventions of Provence and Trecento Italy – and to the pre-modernist world of the Pre-Raphaelites. Almost from the first, his preferred poetic figures express a sense of anachronism, associating a response to a literal (and, of course, chosen) 'exile' from his American homeland with a more generalised, Paterian mood of 'homesickness' for an earlier age. The poems in the visionary mode are strongly influenced by Yeats – especially by *The Wind Among the Reeds* of 1899 – fusing remoteness with abstraction in line with Yeats's talk of 'images that remind us of vast passions, the vagueness of past times, all the chimeras that haunt the edge of trance'.[4] Poems such as 'In Durance' thus dramatise a feeling of alienation by evoking in Yeatsian style those 'far halls of memory'[5] in which the echoes of a more habitable past still seem to resonate.

To review Pound's early volumes with this theme in mind is to be struck by the convergence of stylistic pastiche with a sense of the poet's self not only as estranged and locked in '[e]xquisite loneliness',[6] but as the passive vehicle and conduit for images deriving from 'the great dead days'.[7] Such poems couple the imagery of a sensuous Platonism with the formal device of reminiscence or *anamnesis*, but derive their consolatory power from a capacity to efface the poetic self, which is otherwise felt to be trapped in the closed moment of modernity: 'How our modernity, / Nerve-wracked and broken, turns / Against time's way and all the way of things, / Crying with weak and egoistic cries!'[8] This view of the self is expressed almost programmatically in 'Histrion', where Pound conjures with the idea that 'the souls of all men great / At times pass through us, / And we are melted into them, and are not / Save reflexions of their souls.'[9] Here the romantic aesthetic of the arrested moment allows the past to return, but at the expense of the poet's sensibility, which is invaded or possessed in the act of imitation: 'So cease we from all being for the time, / And these, the Masters of the Soul, live on.'

This effacement of the self in the process of mimesis is, however, a paradoxical one since the complete identification of the writer with his model also has the effect of reducing the past to a repertoire of stimulating masks or *personae* for the modern writer. The contradiction is at its sharpest in Pound's practice of translation, which soon developed from a conventional idea of rendering the immanent meaning of the original to a much more complex sense of *interaction* between the translator's language and that of the text upon which he works. This is in contrast to the type of self-effacement imagined in 'Histrion', which dramatises the act of translation as the quite literal bringing back of the past, endowing it with a force of presence which is sufficient to abolish momentarily the actual present. Pound's early concern with themes of memory, exile and loss moves within the orbit of elegy, but it is only when he begins to conceive of a tensional relation between past and present – thus extending the function of anachronism from content to *form* – that he can explore the full implications of translation as a type of re-inscription.

It is the conjunction of different times which is important here, since it has the effect of opening a gap between language and its objects – a gap which, we recall, the European modernisms had sought to close by abolishing the temporal 'delay' in representation. This at any rate is one effect of the poetics of loss which pervades Pound's early work, and it may explain, too, his enduring attachment to Ovidian myths of metamorphosis since, as Peter Sacks remarks in his study of elegy:

> Ovid presents a condensed version of the [mourning] process, a metamorphosis in which the lost object seems to enter and become inscribed in the substitute, in this case the found sign or art. Of course only the object as lost, and not the object itself, enters into the substitute sign, and the latter is accepted only by a turning away from the actual identity of what was lost.[10]

As in mourning, the trope 'turns away' from the lost object in order to provide a substitute, and its consolatory power lies in the gap or difference which it opens between the two.[11]

We can see in this 'turning away' the germ of a new poetics which would ultimately carry Pound beyond the Paterian fascination with arrested moments ('the lacing-on of armour, with the head bent back so stately – the fainting lady', etc.[12]). In 1912 it received a name – Imagism – which Pound first applied to the work of two friends, Richard Aldington and Hilda Doolittle (soon to be known as H.D.). The following year Pound was ready to provide 'A Few Don'ts By An Imagiste', in the course of which he defined the image as the presentation of 'an intellectual and emotional complex in an instant of time'.[13] Three other 'rules' by poet and translator F. S. Flint complemented Pound's essay:

1. Direct treatment of the 'thing,' whether subjective or objective.

2. To use absolutely no word that did not contribute to the presentation.

3. As regarding rhythm: to compose in sequence of the musical phrase, not in sequence of a metronome.[14]

Imagism is an attempt to recover a stylistic purity, a 'welding of word and thing',[15] which Pound traces back to the 'plasticity' of Gautier's style and to the realism of Stendhal and Flaubert (note that Pound's modernism is in no way hostile to what he calls the 'prose tradition', which can provide models of a style freed from rhetoric).

It is easy to see how a certain 'directness' of presentation contrasts with a Symbolist *in*directness, but at first sight, Imagist poems like 'In a Station of the Metro' and 'Liu Ch'e' do not seem so different from the 'momentary conjunctions' of which Pater had spoken. Closer scrutiny of these highly compressed texts shows, however, how Pound's poetics of memory makes the moment a complex one, his continuing fascination with emptiness and things past suggesting that concreteness and precision are somehow won by an overcoming of absence. In 'Liu Ch'e, for example:

> The rustling of the silk is discontinued,
> Dust drifts over the court-yard,
> There is no sound of foot-fall, and the leaves
> Scurry into heaps and lie still,
> And she the rejoicer of the heart is beneath them:
>
> A wet leaf that clings to the threshold.[16]

The juxtaposition of times in the poem, the present tense of the rustling silk abruptly 'discontinued' by its sudden relegation to the past, sets the 'objectivity' of the presentation within the frame of elegy. The image which resolves the poem in this sense accomplishes a withdrawal of affection from the lost object and its subsequent reattachment to a substitute for that object. Hence, perhaps, Pound's way of talking about the image as an 'equation' for a particular mood,[17] for in such poems there is a subtle shift of attention away from the object itself towards something else which allows desire to be mediated by a tradition or a set of conventions.

Imagism thus begins to suggest a way of moving beyond a Paterian 'moment' freed from the continuum of normal experience, a moment which at the turn of the century had become the 'impression' of Joseph Conrad and Ford Madox Ford. It was precisely literary 'impressionism' which Pound was trying to avoid when he invented Imagism. The use of juxtaposition (or 'super-position', as he sometimes called it, 'one idea set on top of another'[18]) suggested a way of making a formal hiatus or pause – a gap between two parts of the poem – a space in which the reader might construe relationship. In contrast, impressionism, in Pound's view, seemed to depend on a certain intellectual passivity, the mind as 'the toy of circumstance, the plastic substance *receiving* impressions'.

Much of the subsequent history of modernism is foreshadowed in this at first sight rather trivial distinction between 'image' and 'impression'. Each suggests a way of suspending the linear drive of narrative and of achieving an unusual intensity of experience, but the 'impression' derives its power from its removal from any supporting context, as we can see from Conrad's famous account in his Preface to *The Nigger of the 'Narcissus'* (1898):

> To snatch in a moment of courage, from the remorseless rush of time, a passing phase of life is only the beginning of the task. The task approached in tenderness and faith is to hold up unquestioningly, without choice and without fear, the rescued fragment before all eyes and in the light of a sincere mood. It is to show its vibration, its colour, its form; and through its movement, its form, and its colour, reveal the substance of its truth – disclosing its inspiring secret: the stress and passion within the core of each convincing moment. In a single-minded attempt of that kind, if one be deserving and fortunate, one may perchance attain to such clearness of sincerity that at last the presented vision of regret or pity, of terror or mirth, shall awaken in the hearts of the beholders that feeling of unavoidable solidarity; of the solidarity in mysterious origin, in toil, in joy, in hope, in uncertain fate, which binds men to each other and all mankind to the visible world.[19]

It is necessary to quote at length because Conrad's account is sustained largely by its rhetorical momentum. The borrowings from Pater's *The Renaissance* ('movement', 'form', 'colour') give the moment an abstract dimension, but because the 'rescued fragment' is torn from its context Conrad can gesture toward its significance only by employing an inflated vocabulary of 'courage', 'faith' and 'sincerity'. Words such as these underline the association between the momentary impression and some sort of collective feeling which governs the passage; '[t]o arrest, for the space of a breath, the hands busy about the work of the earth' may awaken 'that feeling of unavoidable solidarity' which the narrative of modernisation works to undermine.

If Pound sought an alternative to impressionism it was partly because he was trying to avoid the rhetoric on which such expressions of collective sentiment seemed to depend, but also because the impression was, typically, unmixed. As Ford put it in his essay 'On Impressionism', 'to import into the record of observations of one moment the observations of a moment altogether different is not Impressionism. For Impressionism is a thing altogether momentary'.[20] The impression is thus merely the trace deposited in the mind by a previous experience, leaving art to re-present that trace so precisely that the intervening passage of time will be obliterated ('we saw that life did not narrate', says Ford, 'but made impressions on our brains'[21]). As we have seen, Pound's Imagist writing was already concerned to explore the collision of time-schemes, exploiting the gap or space between two momentary perceptions in order to prevent the poem from atrophying into an 'impression'.

As it happened, his hostility to impressionism found a target more fashionable than Ford, whose fiction and criticism Pound otherwise admired. That target was Marinetti's Futurism, which by 1914 Pound was labelling 'a sort of accelerated impressionism'.[22] The alternative was clear: 'There is another artistic descent *via* Picasso and Kandinsky; *via* cubism and expressionism', a descent, that is, which appeared to value form and design above speed and movement. This is not to suggest, however, that Pound's own poetics was not radically affected by his contact with the Italian movement. Between 1910 and 1915, Marinetti paid numerous visits to London, airing the first Manifesto shortly after its publication, and supporting the various exhibitions of Futurist painting.[23] The impact on writers and artists in Britain is hard to overestimate: the Futurists introduced London to the full panoply of avant-garde devices, promoting a scornful critique of conventional bourgeois art which outstripped anything that Pound and his associates had so far been able to muster. Here too was the outline of an aesthetic extolling the virtues of simultaneity and dynamism, and bringing with it a violent disrespect for an entrenched literary establishment. At the same time, though, Pound's sense of his own origin in 'a half-savage country, out of date' drove him in search of connections with precisely that older, Latin culture which Marinetti sought to destroy. Futurism was certainly exhilarating, but Pound could not subscribe to Marinetti's denigration of 'art' and his worship of the present.

Here we can detect a definitive parting of the ways, for Futurism exemplifies the project of modernism as Paul de Man has defined it:

> The continuous appeal of modernity, the desire to break out of literature toward the reality of the moment, prevails and, in its turn, folding back upon itself, engenders the repetition and continuation of literature.[24]

Yet far from having any desire to 'break out of literature', Pound regarded art as the means by which to give structure and value to an otherwise formless modernity; and the way to do this was always in some measure to restore a context to the chaotic 'reality of the moment', to disclose those cultural mediations which a mere impressionism would efface. Accordingly, the present is seen to have no particular value in itself, a point Pound's collaborator Wyndham Lewis was to hammer home:

> A space must be cleared, all said and done, round the hurly-burly of the present. No man can reflect or create, in the intellectual sense, while he is acting – fighting, playing tennis, or making love. *The present man in all of us is the machine.* The farther away from the present, though not too far, the more free.[25]

For Lewis, as for Pound, the epitome of such 'Presentism' is the Italian Futurist, whose 'life is such an eternal present as is matter's; only being a machine, he wears out'.[26]

Could there be, then, an alternative modernism able to respond to the exciting challenge of modern dynamism and technology without capitulating to the sentimental lure of modernity's 'eternal present'? To define such a modernism was to be the task of Lewis's *Blast* (1914–15), planned as a quarterly magazine of what Pound quickly christened the 'Great English Vortex'. In the event, only two issues of *Blast* were to appear, but its aggressive polemic, coupled with a strikingly innovative use of typographical effects (partly indebted to Marinetti and to Apollinaire's *Anti-tradition futuriste*), made it the flagship of a new modernism. Pound had first hit upon the word 'vortex' to describe London, but the term was also being used by the Futurists to designate forms of motion and concentration.[27] As Hugh Kenner puts it, 'a Vortex is a circulation with a still center: a system of energies drawing in whatever comes near',[28] and the word could thus combine a Futurist sense of dynamism with a rather different notion of bounded form ('Futurism', Pound declared in *Blast*, 'is the disgorging spray of a vortex with no drive behind it, DISPERSAL'[29]). Now Pound could distinguish the image from the arrested moment with more precision, a move which brought him closer to a poetics avoiding at once the linearity of conventional narrative *and* the tendency towards the static and purely ornamental which was the major limitation of Imagism: 'The image', he insisted, 'is not an idea. It is a radiant node or cluster; ... a VORTEX, from which, and through which, and into which, ideas are constantly rushing.'[30]

The painting of Lewis and the sculpture of Henri Gaudier-Brzeska provided, for Pound, the perfect types of a Vorticist art which released the imagination from the too-familiar world of mimetic representation into one of semi-abstract forms and 'planes in relation'.[31] The crucial move would then be to apply this juxtapositional, spatial model to ways of thinking about *time*. 'The Art-instinct is permanently primitive', declared Lewis in *Blast*,[32] thereby connecting his Vorticism with the dynamic drive of Expressionism and early Cubism, and at the same time dissociating it from the modernolatry of Futurism. For Lewis, the authentically modern would derive from the subordination of the technological to the aesthetic, and the resulting force of design would differentiate his art from both the facile 'automobilism' of Marinetti and the 'safe' domestic materials of Picasso's recent still-lifes and assemblages.[33]

Yet as Pound's essay on 'Vorticism' shows, the identification of the authentically modern with the non-mimetic was easier to grasp in terms of the new visual arts than it was in relation to literature. 'There is undoubtedly a language of form and colour', he mused, 'It is not a symbolical or allegorical language depending on certain meanings having been ascribed, in books, to certain signs and colours.'[34] Pound was struggling to find some connection between associative and juxtapositional contexts in language and the 'organisation of forms' in a visual art moving towards abstraction, but his work at the time of *Blast* continued to show a real uncertainty about what might constitute a properly 'modern' writing. The problem was painfully clear in the poems he contributed to *Blast*, a mix of rather lame satire and coy epigram which hardly matched the vigour of his polemical statement 'Vortex. Pound'. Lewis later recalled that 'It was with regret I included the poems of my friend Ezra Pound: they "let down", I felt, the radical purism of the visual contents, or the propaganda of same.'[35]

*   *   *

A partial solution to Pound's problem lay in his earlier techniques of pastiche and translation, and specifically in the questions these raised about the handling of temporal structures. For at the time of *Blast* he was also pondering the possibility of 'a long imagiste or vorticist poem',[36] a project whose feasibility seemed to grow in proportion to Pound's involvement with the Japanese Noh plays he was now beginning to work on with Yeats (between 1914 and 1916, he cited Noh as a model for a long poem no fewer than five times[37]). In one sense it was characteristic of Pound to pursue the spectre of the truly modern by the circuitous route of early Japanese theatre, but from 1913, when he came into possession of the papers of the sinologue Ernest Fenollosa, Pound was convinced that remote and alien cultures might provide a crucial antidote to an 'egoistic' and self-regarding modernity. This was partly a response to the level of stylisation cultivated by Noh, 'an art of splendid posture, of dancing and chanting and of acting that is not mimetic' (*NT*, 4). In Japan, Pound observed, 'The merely mimetic stage has been despised' (*NT*, 11), with the result that in place of 'the Western convention of plot' we find 'Unity of Image': 'the better plays', it seems, 'all are built into the intensification of a single Image' (*NT*, 27). Pound's way of emphasising the play-as-image was in line with his thoughts elsewhere on modern painting as a model for a non-mimetic writing, but the particular importance of Noh was that it suddenly seemed to offer a spatial embodiment of that anachronous sense of time which had become such a consistent feature of his own work.

Fenollosa had also been impressed by the formal 'concentration' of Noh, though his talk of 'a single clarified impression' (*NT*, 69) was not quite in tune with Pound's developing sense of the image. What Fenollosa had in mind was the capacity of a centralised metaphor to produce a unified, organic structure, and while this was in accord with Pound's original theory of the image as a sort of 'absolute metaphor',[38] he was now beginning to explore what he would later call the 'moving' as opposed to the 'fixed' image.[39] What that entailed would soon be clear from the first drafts of his long poem, *The Cantos*, where the image as static 'equation' for a particular mood would be recast as a device of reference and allusion which would hold in tension the various materials of the poem. Such a process is metonymic rather than metaphoric, and is clearly in line with Pound's recognition that 'The art of allusion, or this love of allusion in art, is at the root of the Noh' (*NT*, 4). The emotion expressed is, as Yeats puts it, 'self-conscious and *reminiscent*, always associating itself with pictures and poems' (*NT*, 160), and the 'intensification' of the Noh image prized by Pound thus produces results which are quite different from the centralising of a particular mood in the Imagist mode.

What then of the large-scale structure of Noh? According to Pound, 'The Noh service presents, or symbolizes, a complete diagram of life and recurrence' (*NT*, 11–12). The 'diagram' refers to the traditional presentation of five plays in sequence, though this does not entail any rigid closure. In contrast to linear Western concepts of 'form', the Noh cycle turns back on itself, always seeming to begin again (one critic observes that the last play in the sequence is not 'a final conclusion, but a temporary cutoff that might even be considered the beginning of an endless succession'[40]). Yet while this lack of closure is associated with the Buddhist theory of salvation, binding together natural and supernatural worlds in a rhythm of 'recurrence', Noh theatre also employs discordant structures which are quite removed from the fluid and predictable rhythms of a phantasmatic 'nature'. Indeed, 'recurrence' in this context has a second meaning, since many of the plays which Pound and Yeats presented embody the trope of a return, but a momentary return from death to life. This, then, is the time of the supernatural which, far from being cyclical and predictable, entails 'the suspense of waiting for a supernatural manifestation' (*NT*, 26). No wonder Pound was drawn to these plays, for, as he goes on to observe, they testify to the interpenetration of past and present, a theme with which virtually all his work, early and late, would be concerned.

What exactly does this 'interpenetration' entail? The question goes to the heart of Noh, one of whose two main forms, *mugen-noh*, or 'the Noh of spirits' (*NT*, 54), as Pound calls it, requires what Komparu terms 'the reflection-in-vision method (*mugen-kaisō-hō*), in which the flow of time within the play is reversed and takes place in a memory or dream' (75). This convention of reversed time produces a ritual (not to say 'diagrammatic') narrative structure. The leading figure of the play (the *shite*) appears as an old man or woman who is engaged in conversation by the secondary figure or *waki*, usually a priest. They discourse about a famous legend of the place, whereupon the *shite* reveals that he or she is in fact the character in the tale. The *shite* then disappears, only to return to the stage in the form of the legendary figure. The second part of the play – often preceded by a brief farce or Kyōgen performance – presents the *waki*'s dream, in which the *shite* dances. As Nobuko Tsukui observes, 'The highlight of the *mugen-noh* is the tale and dance of the Shite in both forms. … Its subject matter varies, but its form does not – the *mugen-noh* takes the form of a reminiscence of the Shite.'[41]

Tsukui's emphasis on *reminiscence* is very much to the point here, since a peculiarity of this type of Noh is that its main action takes place at once in the present of the play's performance *and* in the past of stylised recollection (the dream of the *waki*). The visionary second part of the play thus links the manifestation of the god or spirit with the irruption of the past in the present, making the point of greatest intensity that in which time flows back on itself and two moments are, as it were, superimposed or grafted together. The unity of the play is discordant in the sense that the action entails two different chronologies, even though the characters are the same. As Komparu puts it, 'dramatic time is split and revolves around two axes' (87–8). This 'splitting' involves more than a simple juxtaposition of past and present, for the reversal of chronology produces a sort of compound tense in which the past may seem open to change or revision. *Mugen-noh*, as Komparu observes, 'always follows a stream of consciousness … in which the remembered past and the actual present are fused into a whole *that advances both at the same time*' (77). The past, then, is not simply recalled (as a representation), but may be modified and transformed through its (re-)enactment. Komparu notes that 'We might say that a drama of reminiscence acts out the past after the present, and that time must overcome the natural flow and run in reverse' (86). The 'split' time of Noh thus offered Pound a model of a structure which folds back on itself, becoming in that movement a sort of allegory of its own process.[42]

One of Pound's favourite examples of this type of Noh was Zeami's *Nishikigi*. Here a priest meets a woman carrying 'a cloth woven of feathers' and a man with a 'staff or a wooden sceptre / Beautifully ornate' (*NT*, 77). The priest learns that this man's staff or charm-stick is a token, which may be left outside a woman's house as a sign of love for her. If, as is the case in *Nishikigi*, the woman refuses her suitor she ignores the stick; here, as Yeats observed, 'she went on weaving out of grass when she should have opened the chamber door to her lover, and woven grass returns again and again in metaphor and incident' (*NT*, 160). The priest is then taken to the burial mound of the man who had left charm-sticks outside the woman's house for three years and had still failed to win her love. As the second scene of the play opens, the ghosts of the couple appear in the priest's dream and the man dances to cele-brate the happiness he and the woman have found together in death.

In many respects, *Nishikigi* is, of the plays translated by Pound, the clearest example of Komparu's account of Noh times-schemes. Here the conjunction of past and present moves both into a new phase; the past, we might say, is transformed by being remem-bered. In reality, as the *shite* recalls in the first part of the play, 'We had no meeting together', but in the priest's dream, which provides the frame for the second part, the past can be, as it were, rewritten. As the ghost of the woman says, 'Now is there meeting between us, / Between us who were until now / In life and in after-life kept apart' (*NT*, 81–2).

As the play comes to a close it is as if we are caught between two times, a past of repetition and a present which celebrates its re-working. The austere stylisation of Noh is thus governed by a pro-found displacement of emotion, not simply as a translation of intensity into disciplined gesture, but by its habitual way of ex-pressing feeling through reminiscence. Emotion is felt retroactively, suggesting that the past can be completed only in the present. The analogy with the mechanism of translation is hard to miss, since it too functions to supplement its original, at once adding to and com-pleting the text on which it works.[43] Like Noh spirits, these texts 'come back' belatedly, *nachträglich*, in Freud's sense of the deferred action by which a traumatic experience takes on its full meaning only at a later stage ('the articulation of two *moments* with a time of delay', as one commentator puts it[44]). Since the shock of the first event is not felt directly by the subject but only through its later representation in memory, we are dealing with 'a past that has never been present'.[45] Belatedness, in this sense, creates a complex temporality which inhibits any simple nostalgia for origin and con-tinuity – the 'origin' is now secondary, deferred and made different by its repetition. That may seem an unnecessarily complicated gloss to Pound's famous injunction to 'Make It New', but seen from this perspective his catchphrase (borrowed from Emperor King T'ang) points not simply to an idea of cultural renovation but to a far more complex process whereby two different times are grafted together, each somehow 'supplementing' the other. *The Cantos* was to become a palimpsest in which, ideally, one text might overlay another without effacing it.

* * *

In this opening phase of Anglo-American modernism, Pound, Joyce and Eliot would share Lewis's definition of the artist as one who (as he put it in *Tarr* [1918]) 'turned away from the immediate world'[46] and from those romantic fantasies of 'presence' which had occupied the early European avant-gardes. The emphasis was close to that of Charles Maurras's neo-classicism, though its principal spokesman here was T. E. Hulme, whose aesthetic philosophy stressed 'a desire for austerity and bareness, a striving toward structure and away from the messiness and confusion of nature and natural things'.[47] This turning away ('toward structure') now began to imply two opposed conceptions of mimesis: on the one hand, mimesis as mere imitation (this was the social principle of a democratic modernity), and, on the other, mimesis as a process which somehow *supplements* its model. Where Futurism sought to embrace the real, the 'Men of 1914' turned to art in search of a productive mimesis, which may be defined in terms of intertextuality rather than by presupposing some relation between text and reality.

All this may seem quite opposed to Pound's insistence on 'objectivity' and 'direct presentation', but the habit of textual imitation (of pastiche, allusion, citation, translation) in his work, as in that of Joyce and Eliot, constantly undermined an aesthetic of spontaneous desire. While, as we shall see, the 'Men of 1914' all stressed the importance of the object as support for a properly 'externalised' desire, this emphasis was coupled with a powerful sense of that desire as mediated by existing literary models and conventions. It is indicative of Pound's early aestheticism that we have not yet had much occasion to remark about the possibilities of *irony* latent in such a conception of mimesis. When T. S. Eliot arrived in London in

September 1914, however, a reading of 'The Love Song of J. Alfred Prufrock' quickly gave Pound a glimpse of a new poetic manner. 'He has actually trained himself *and* modernized himself *on his own*', marvelled Pound.[48] The 'training' had begun as early as 1908, when Eliot discovered in the pages of Arthur Symons's *The Symbolist Movement in Literature* (1899) an enthusiastic account of Laforgue's 'subtle use of colloquialism, slang, neologism, technical terms, for their allusive, their factitious, their reflected meanings, with which one can play, very seriously'.[49]

Laforgue offered Eliot both a style and a means of self-defence, transforming his own temperamental pessimism and social unease into the basis for irony. Laforgue's 'inflexible politeness towards man, woman, and destiny', as Symons put it, allowed him to explore the terrors of life concealed behind social forms without dropping his own mask. When Pound talked of Eliot 'modernising' himself this is mainly what he had in mind, and as his own knowledge of Laforgue deepened, so he came to conclude that 'he marks the next phase after Gautier in French poetry'.[50] It is in some ways a remarkable judgement, reminding us that the enormously influential reading of nineteenth-century French poetry jointly proposed by Pound and Eliot was one which largely omitted Baudelaire, Rimbaud and Mallarmé! The route to this particular modernism apparently lay instead through the hard, 'plastic' qualities of Gautier and their reappearance in the supple ironies of Laforgue and Corbière.

If Eliot was more punctually 'modern' than Pound, it was partly because his early discovery of Laforgue allowed him to develop a *vers de société* able to confront both the aesthetic and the social implications of mimesis. Like Pound, he focused some of his unease and discontent on the salon – both wrote poems alluding in their titles to James's *Portrait of a Lady*, and both associated the figure of the older, cultured woman with empty social ritual and repetition ('In the whole and all, / Nothing that's quite your own', concludes Pound's poem[51]). The speaker in Eliot's poem is less sure of himself, his only hope lying in the sheer emptiness of his conformity ('And I must borrow every changing shape / To find expression'). That shapelessness is all that we can clutch at outside of art, for even there to be 'original' is to fall prey to self-aggrandising delusions of 'personality' – as Eliot puts it in the famous essay 'Tradition and the Individual Talent' (1919), 'the poet has, not a "personality" to express, but a particular medium ... in which impressions and expressions combine in peculiar and unexpected ways'.[52]

Poetry, then, offers the much-needed 'escape from personality', an escape from emotions which are immediate and shared by 'working them up into poetry' (21). It is this 'translation' of emotion rather than its actual *origin* which is important to Eliot; indeed, 'emotions which he [the poet] has never experienced will serve his turn as well as those familiar to him' (21), a view which reappears in his later praise of Pound's early work: 'The poem which is absolutely original is absolutely bad; it is, in the bad sense, "subjective" with no relation to the world to which it appeals.'[53] The 'personality', it seems, must always lack a cultural history; it is the essential expression of a modernity trapped in its own eternal present. But the way out of that cul-de-sac is not through a conventionally linear historical sense. Eliot does sometimes cast his concept of 'tradition' in a straightforwardly narrative mode (as 'an ideal order' modified by subsequent new works [15]), but he also insists on the imprecision of Wordsworth's idea of poetry as 'emotion recollected in tranquillity'; instead, he argues,

It is a concentration, and a new thing resulting from the concentration, of a very great number of experiences which to the practical and active person would not seem to be experiences at all; it is a concentration which does not happen consciously or of deliberation.   (21)

Eliot's 'new thing' implies the same effect of 'belatedness' as reinscription that we saw in Pound's early work, with the poet evading pressures of social conformity by his capacity to inhabit the 'other' realm of the cultural tradition. In some ways this is the most striking feature of *Prufrock and Other Observations* (1917), but where Pound's way of re-writing the past develops towards a dialogue of ideas, as in his *Homage to Sextus Propertius* (also 1917), Eliot's use of allusion and pastiche works to create a curiously empty poetic voice for which irony is a constant reminder of the self's instability, not to say intermittence. In 'The Love Song of J. Alfred Prufrock', for example, we learn much about what the speaker is not and what he should have been, but almost nothing about what he *is*. The reason for that is two-fold: first, Prufrock exists only in tension with the other voices that surround him. The poem does not presuppose a sensibility which dons and doffs different *personae* or masks, as was the case in Pound's early work: here, the 'I' evades all our attempts to 'formulate' him, with moments of dramatic self-interrogation ('Do I dare / Disturb the universe?') suddenly revealed as literary allusion (in this case, to a phrase from Laforgue[54]).

The second reason for Prufrock's notable absence from the poem is that Eliot is more interested in phrases than he is in psychology, with gauging the effect of fragments from earlier works, which are now drawn into the 'vortex' of the present. He therefore shows no nostalgia for a lost self (the Arnoldian 'buried life' of 'Portrait of a Lady'), but nor does he regard the resulting multiplicity of selves as anything more than the detritus of social role-play. Like many of the other poems in this collection, 'The Love Song' is like a thin skein stretched across a chaos of inchoate romantic desire. If such desire is always mired in imitation, the only salvation lies in finding some transcendent model, which is what 'classicism' seems to have meant to Eliot before his turn to Anglicanism in 1927; as he put it in 'The Function of Criticism' (1923), classicists 'believe that men cannot get on without giving allegiance to something outside themselves'.[55]

* * *

But if Prufrock had been an artist ...? Eliot would not 'presume', of course, but his other modernist colleagues did, each exploring this awkward intersection of the social and aesthetic by inventing an artist-figure of his own. Lewis's *Tarr* (1918) is particularly interesting in this respect, since it also investigates the relation of mimesis to sexuality, an area darkly present in Eliot's 'Love Song'. In *Tarr*, the whole question of imitative desire is grounded in social ritual, as we see in the following passage:

> Tarr bowed to Kreisler as Bertha said his name. Kreisler raised his hat. = Then, with a curious feeling of already thrusting himself on these people, he began to walk along beside Bertha. = She moved like an unconvincing party to a bargain, who consents to walk up and down a little, preliminary to a final consid-

eration of the affair. 'Yes, but walking won't help matters,' she might have been saying. = Kreisler's indifference was absolute. = There was an element of child's privilege in Tarr's making himself of the party, ('Sorbet, tu es *si jeune*'). There was the claim for indulgence of a spirit not entirely serious! = The childishness of this turning up as though nothing had happened, with such wilful resolve not to recognise the seriousness of things, Bertha's drama, the significance of the awful words, 'Herr Kreisler!' and so on, was present to him. = Bertha must know the meaning of his rapid resurrection – she knew him too well not to know that. = So they walked on, without conversation. Then Tarr enquired if she were 'quite well.'

'Yes, Sorbert, quite well,' she replied, with soft tragic banter.

(215–16)[56]

Lewis's fiction is full of such edgy moments, of encounters where hesitation and mutual suspicion underwrite his characters' laborious production of their social 'drama'. So the 'three-legged affair' of Tarr, Bertha and Otto Kreisler steps its clumsy way between concealment and histrionic self-display. Kreisler (the artist *manqué*) pretends indifference while wanting Bertha; Bertha meanwhile wants Tarr but is preoccupied with her preparations for the 'drama' necessary to achieve that end; and Tarr, who as the authentic artist-figure should have nothing to do with either of them, indulges himself by playing the naif.

Tarr, we quickly learn, is particularly bad at handling such 'sentimental' moments: his realm is that of the intellect ('He had no social machinery but the cumbrous one of the intellect' [23]) and, as Lewis would insist throughout his career, 'when reason speaks the language of feeling, it is liable to become a most muddled jargon'.[57] Once we have remarked Tarr's lack of 'social machinery' we will be prepared for another highly ambiguous word in Lewis's lexicon, 'personality'. In the awkward encounter recorded above, it is the 'personality' which is the medium of self-dramatisation, a chameleonic shifting of personal projections induced, like Bertha's 'soft tragic banter', by the changing social environment. 'Personalities' in this sense come and go (at one point Tarr and Bertha are caught 'posing for their late personalities' [220]), and if Lewis's fiction never handles drama or 'action' without irony it is because these modes of self-presentation, grounded as they are in habits of imitation, can never rise above the second-rate. Hence, too, his rejection of Eliot's rather confused notion of 'impersonality', with its proliferation of time-bound selves, in favour of some form of psychic stability:

> It *might* be a good thing – I do not say it is – for an artist to have a 'personality', and for a scientist not to have a personality: though here of course I am not using a 'personality' in the *Ballyhoo* sense – I do not mean an individualist abortion, bellowing that it wants at all costs to 'express' itself. ... I mean only a constancy and consistency in being, as concretely as possible, *one thing* – at peace with itself, if not with the outer world, though that is likely to follow after an interval of struggle.[58]

But this ideal of being 'one thing' is hardly likely to be valued in a world which makes a 'religion of impermanence'[59] and where 'personality' turns out to be something on loan from somebody else. So Lewis will later observe, in *The Art of Being Ruled* (1926), that the more 'individual' people think they are, the more they are expressing a 'group personality': 'If they were subsequently watched in the act of "expressing" their "personality", it would be found that it was somebody else's personality they were expressing.'[60]

In one sense, then, *Tarr* sets out to demonstrate the unoriginality of romantic desire. Bertha, we discover, is not really an object of desire for either Tarr or Kreisler; she is, rather, a stake in the game between them, 'an unconvincing party to a bargain'. The rivalry between the two competitors turns out to be more important than its ostensible object, just as the drama of Kreisler's ludicrous duel with Soltyk soon eclipses any thoughts of Anastasya. Lewis's way of structuring the narrative through markedly symmetrical relations between characters emphasises a kind of 'doubling' at work: envy springs from imitation rather than from competition for an object, and in a characteristic move Kreisler will strive to usurp Tarr's place only to discover that in the process he has lost his own.

This reading of *Tarr* will recall René Girard's account of the nineteenth-century novel, but with one significant difference, namely that the drama of rivalry at work in the fiction of Flaubert and Dostoyevsky has now degenerated into burlesque; as in Lewis's later novel *Snooty Baronet* (1932), tragedy gives way to black comedy. There is a calculated slide towards pastiche here, by which Lewis surely means to suggest that in his own time, in the world of mass politics and advanced consumerism, imitative desire produces not antagonism but passive identification. As he puts it in another early book, 'The life of the crowd, of the common or garden man, is exterior. He can live only through others, outside himself.'[61] In *Time and Western Man* (1927), the point is made more vividly:

> For our only terra firma in a boiling and shifting world is, after all, our 'self'. That must cohere for us to be capable at all of behaving in any way but as mirror-images of alien realities, or as the most helpless and lowest organisms, as worms or as sponges.[62]

The function of art must be accordingly to deny such osmotic identification by reviving the principle of active antagonism lost to modern social life. The artist will now become the Enemy.

*   *   *

This aspect of Lewis's writing is familiar and not widely liked, but it might help to understand the need for its particular asperity if we look briefly at another work of the time, which explores the theme of imitative desire in a very different way. In Ford Madox Ford's *The Good Soldier* (1915), Dowell's narrative provides a striking example of desire as identification. Dowell's ignorance of Ashburnham's affair with his wife Florence is so extreme as to hint at collusion. Ashburnham usurps his friend's position quite blatantly, but instead of reacting in a spirit of antagonism and rivalry, Dowell finds himself accepting Leonora's 'look of a mother to her son, of a sister to her brother ... she looked at me as if I were an invalid'.[63] It is not coincidental that family relations should be called upon to defuse aggression here, for only the family can sustain this residually feudal order (Ashburnham has been 'the good landlord and father of his people' [153]). The myth of the family is, in short, the bedrock of the 'sentimentalism' of an order doomed to disappear, an order in which masculine desire produces not open rivalry but envy. Ford's sympathies lie clearly enough with this order, but at the same time the novel cannot help exposing

Ashburnham's moral 'innocence' as a sort of socialised infantilism – Leonora 'was even taught that such excesses in men are natural, excusable – as if they had been children' (170) – and the regular association of Dowell with figures of weakness prepares us for that final moment of emotional identification which registers the full absurdity of imitative desire: thinking of Ashburnham, Dowell concludes that 'I love him because he was just myself. ... I am just as much a sentimentalist as he' (227).

Ford, no doubt, hoped that this remarkable moment of forgiveness might give substance to the 'sentimental' world of good soldiers, but viewed from the starker standpoint of Lewis's fiction, Dowell's passivity signals modernity's collapse into passive imitation. It is ironic indeed that the opening section of *The Good Soldier* should first appear in Lewis's *Blast* (under the title 'The Saddest Story'), for Ford's valedictory gesture towards a society in which 'tradition' and class-structure could still mask the drift towards psychic uniformity clearly placed the novel outside Lewis's own conception of the modernist avant-garde. That Dowell could allow his desires to be fulfilled by another and then convince himself of the moral fineness of his usurper would surely have expressed for Lewis the very essence of old lavender. And when Dowell tells us on the final page of the novel that Ashburnham was 'to the last, a sentimentalist, whose mind was compounded of indifferent poems and novels' (229), Ford (one might imagine Lewis remarking) has given the game away: the pathos of identification which the novel cannot bring itself to disavow is the reflex of large-scale *cultural* enervation.

This 'sentimental' elision of life and art would become the constant butt of Lewis's satire as he tried to dissociate the secondary forms of 'social' desire from the creative work of the artistic intelligence. Tarr's habitual response is thus, we assume, close to Lewis's own: 'He exalts Life into a Comedy, when otherwise it is, to his mind, a tawdry zone of half-art, or a silly Tragedy. Art is the only thing worth the tragic impulse, for him' (20). When life becomes 'tragic' we may be sure (according to Lewis) that sex is involved, for a vulgar ideology of romance has falsely transformed an 'appetite' (28) into something 'artistic' which masquerades as 'original' desire. So Tarr, for example, 'had a theory that snobbery and sex, like religion and sex, were to be found together' (23) – a theory founded on the idea that sexual desire is somehow based in imitation (just as Kreisler desires Bertha simply as a move in his struggle with Tarr). In other words, sexual desire produces a sort of lacuna in the subject, a lack which is made good by copying someone else's desire, by finding a relation with another by which one's own self might then be mirrored back in idealised form. Herein lies the most important difference between Kreisler and Tarr, for whereas 'Woman was the aesthetic element in Kreisler's life' (102), Tarr had always known that 'Surrender to a woman was a sort of suicide for an artist' (214).

There is misogyny here, but although Lewis, like the other 'Men of 1914', yields too easily to the temptation of this kind of bravado, something else is involved as well. For sexual desire is a kind of 'suicide' not primarily because it entails a surrender of the masculine to the female will, but because the romantic pursuit of the 'other' proves in fact to be the pursuit of the 'same'. For all its pretensions to 'drama', romantic desire amounts to not much more than a kind of infantile narcissism, and while there is plenty in Lewis's work to evidence chauvinism in these matters, there is also much to show that he was trying to uncover a process of social identification which went beyond the categories of gender. This is particularly clear in *The Art of Being Ruled*, where Lewis's attempt to deal objectively with feminism is based on the assumption that 'There is no mysterious *difference* between the nature of the sexes.'[64] Seen from this perspective, the doubling and symmetry within his narratives testifies to the inescapable specularity of desiring relations, to the narcissism which he locates as the structural compulsion of democratic (or communistic) societies for which the other must always prove to be the same. That drive towards the 'suppressing of *differences*'[65] expresses for Lewis the negative principle within modernity, for in finding itself elsewhere, the subject experiences a loss of the borders of the self, a loss of that psychic territoriality which stands over against the regressive and 'jellyish diffuseness' of those who display 'a lack of energy, permanently mesmeric state, and almost purely emotional reactions' (314).

*   *   *

Sexuality construed as (original) desire rather than as simple appetitive need thus seems to threaten the self by opening the way to fantasies of identification whose unreality derives from a narcissistic suppression of otherness. That such fantasies are especially damaging to the artistic intelligence is a view expressed not only by Lewis, but also, in different ways, by Joyce, Pound and Eliot; indeed, the dilemma expressed here is right at the centre of this particular form of modernism. In Joyce's *A Portrait of the Artist as a Young Man* (1916), for example, Stephen's youthful experience of desire introduces him to a range of troubling emotions including 'unrest', 'moodiness', 'loss of vitality', and 'sloth'.[66] 'Stultified only by his desire' (130), Stephen is rootless and drifting: 'Nothing stirred within his soul but a cold and cruel and loveless lust. His childhood was dead or lost and with it his soul capable of simple joys and he was drifting amid life like the barren shell of the moon' (125). The 'drift' of desire sets Stephen 'beyond the limits of reality' (122), leaving him with only 'phantasmal comrades' (115) and destroying family ties: 'He felt that he was hardly of the one blood with them but stood to them rather in the mystical kinship of fosterage, fosterchild and fosterbrother' (127).

Stephen's first attempts to write are similarly blocked by the narcissism Joyce associates with 'loveless lust' (125). His poem to Ellen, for example, registers '[s]ome undefined sorrow', effacing any hint of the occasion which produced it – 'There remained no trace of the tram itself nor of the trammen nor of the horses; nor did he and she appear vividly' (104). Having completed the poem, Stephen 'went into his mother's bedroom and gazed at his face for a long time in the mirror of her dressingtable' (105), a moment of narcissistic contemplation which sets Stephen's desire for Ellen in the inhibiting context of a failure to terminate his desire for his mother.[67] So it is when Stephen loses his virginity to the prostitute: 'His lips would not bend to kiss her. He wanted to be held firmly in her arms, to be caressed slowly, slowly, slowly' (129). In this respect, *Portrait* reflects an orthodoxly Freudian insistence on the need for the male to dissolve the maternal bond in order to accomplish a full differentiation of self and world. Hence the association Stephen makes between the reactionary power of the Church and his mother's injunction to make his Easter duty. Not only does Joyce place Stephen in a position (here and in *Ulysses*) where he has no authentic alternative but to refuse his mother's request, but Stephen's decision to leave family and home is first conceived as a necessary break with his friend Cranly, who 'felt then the sufferings of women' (246) and who in the closing pages of the novel is glimpsed 'Still harping on the mother' (250). Stephen cannot emulate

Cranly's sympathetic way with women: 'Away then: it is time to go. A voice spoke softly to Stephen's lonely heart, bidding him go and telling him that his friendship was coming to an end' (246). Joyce may give an ironic edge to Stephen's self-important rhetoric at the end of the novel ('I go to encounter for the millionth time the reality of experience ...' [252]), but no amount of irony will undercut the persistent association here of the artistic life with the father ('Old father, old artificer, stand me now and ever in good stead' [252]), and its pursuit with a freedom from the feminine and maternal.

The artistic intelligence comes into being over 'the grave of boyhood' (185), by which Joyce means not only to reject any romantic cult of childhood innocence, but also to emphasise the process of differentiation which must mark off the self from others. Further romantic stereotypes lie in wait, of course, and Stephen's progress to maturity will entail a translation of his early Hamletish 'moodiness' (104) into a capacity to objectify the non-self as an 'aesthetic image' (219). Stephen's awkward attempts to produce a Thomistic definition of this image are less persuasive, perhaps, than his version of Aristotle on tragedy in which he argues that

> The feelings excited by improper art are kinetic, desire or loathing. Desire urges us to possess, to go to something; loathing urges us to abandon, to go from something. ... The aesthetic emotion ... is therefore static. The mind is arrested and raised above desire and loathing.   (213)

Once again, art purports to save us from the 'drift' of desire by its capacity to 'impersonalize' personal emotion (221) and thus achieve the ecstatic perception Stephen associates with his vision of the wading girl. In that rather ostentatiously Symbolist 'epiphany', the feminine is somehow 'redeemed', no longer cast as the origin of 'stultifying' male desire: 'She seemed like one whom magic had changed into the likeness of a strange and beautiful seabird ... her eyes turned to him in quiet sufferance of his gaze, without shame or wantonness' (186). As usual, the passage is not immune from Joyce's retrospective irony, though the Yeatsian conceit is expressed with a metaphorical elaboration which is surely intended to distinguish it from the decadent fetishism of Stephen's earlier grasp of a language of the feminine ('it was only amid softworded phrases or within rosesoft stuffs that he dared to conceive of the soul or body of a woman moving with tender life' [173]). .

*   *   *

While Stephen's ideal of the impassive artist, 'invisible, refined out of existence, indifferent, paring his fingernails' (221), has palpable limitations and would soon be reviewed in *Ulysses* (1922), the concept of aesthetic form as a kind of defence against the 'drift' of desire was something Joyce shared with the other 'Men of 1914'. Pound's *Hugh Selwyn Mauberley* (1920), to take another influential example, presents an imaginary character who has more than a little in common with Joyce's Stephen. Mauberley is at times a distanced presentation of Pound himself and at others a satirical portrait of an ineffectual aesthete. The first main section of the poem presents an epitaph for 'E.P.' whose quixotic attempts to sustain the lyric tradition have foundered in a modernity which demands only a mimetic image of 'its accelerated grimace', 'a mould in plaster, / Made with no loss of time'.[68] Mass production is swiftly elided with the democratic masses, and a merely representational art equated with the equally hollow forms of contemporary politics. The poem's second section then focuses more directly on Mauberley, who is first presented as a sort of failed Poundian, a writer committed to 'the "sculpture" of rhyme', but whose productions seem minimalist and one-dimensional ('Firmness, / Not the full smile, / His art, but an art / In profile').

With the second poem in this section we learn that Mauberley's artistic failure is in some way the product of an infatuation: 'For three years … he drank ambrosia', the food of the gods which earlier in the poem Pound has associated with the Dionysian and phallic. Bewildered by the sexual desire he feels, Mauberley 'Drifted … drifted precipitate', thus recalling lines from Tristan Corbière's 'Épitaphe', one of the hidden models for Pound's poem: 'A lounger at large, – drifting, / Jetsam never arriving.'[69] The passage brings to a focus a series of earlier references to personal anachronism and postponement which connect artistic failure with sexual temptation. The opening 'Ode', for example, has already linked E. P. and Mauberley, who, it seems, have both 'Observed the elegance of Circe's hair / Rather than the mottoes on sun-dials', and the reference is, one assumes, to Odysseus's postponement of his departure from the enchantress's isle.

This same isle appears again in the next poem, 'The Age Demanded':

> The coral isle, the lion-coloured sand
> Burst in upon the porcelain revery:
> Impetuous troubling
> Of his imagery.

The 'porcelain revery' is linked in one of the preceding stanzas to Mauberley's contemplation of the woman, whose 'colour' is 'Tempered as if / It were through a perfect glaze'. This contemplative image is shattered by the force of desire which suddenly 'burst[s] in' on the poet's revery, 'Destroying, certainly, the artist's urge', and leaving him 'delighted with the imaginary / Audition of the phantasmal sea-surge'. Homer's grasp of actuality yields here to a sort of interiorisation of the aesthetic (the sound of the waves is purely 'imaginary' for Mauberley); sexual desire seems to frustrate the objectivising tendencies Pound associates with avant-garde art, producing 'utter consternation' in the artist.

The final poem of the sequence, 'Medallion', has caused particular disagreement, with some critics treating it as a 'bad' poem attributable to Mauberley, and others regarding it as a companion-piece to the earlier 'Envoi', in which Pound mounts his final critique of aestheticism.[70] There are plenty of suggestions, though, that the woman whose 'sleek head emerges / From the gold-yellow frock' is the same woman who has provoked Mauberley's hedonistic 'drift'. It is possible, too, that the tricky use of *personae* in the poem masks an account of Pound's own temporary digression into passionate rather than aesthetic affairs. Either way, it now seems probable that the woman who appears in 'Medallion' is modelled on the soprano Raymonde Collignon, a close acquaintance of Pound, and while most critics have taken the hard, ornamental imagery of the poem to signify an impoverished aestheticism, Pound's own accounts of her performances emphasise the ways in which her style shares in modernism's rejection of the mimetic:

No one has a more keen perception than she has of the difference between art and life; of the necessary scale and proportion required in the presentation of a thing which is not the photograph and wax-cast, but *a re-creation in different and proportional medium.* As long as this diseuse was on stage she was non-human; she was, if you like, a china image; there are Ming porcelains which are respectable; the term 'china' is not in this connection ridiculous.[71]

Mauberley's original 'mistake', of course, was to see the woman rather than the china image; hence his loss of the 'artist's urge' to a mundanely human one. If 'Medallion' suggests some way out of his 'anaesthesis', it is because the 'urge to convey the relation / Of eye-lid and cheek-bone / By verbal manifestation' signifies not a retreat into aestheticism but a form of 'armour' against 'utter consternation' and the 'drift' towards sensual indulgence. That implied notion of style as some kind of defence would place a politics of gender at the very heart of this modernism's developing preoccupation with forms of authority.

9

At a Tangent: Other Modernisms

Pound's way of pitting the 'armour' of style against the mere 'drift' of desire neatly encapsulates a turn against those fantasies of the disembodied self which had played such an important part in early European modernism. By way of contrast, the 'Men of 1914' were concerned with inventing strong and authoritative versions of the self, a difference in emphasis which grounded their claims for the autonomy of the avant-garde in a model of psychic development which to some extent paralleled the Freudian trajectory from primary narcissism to objectival desire. There was, however, no ac-knowledged debt to the new science of psychoanalysis here; in fact Freud was generally condemned by the 'Men of 1914' as a prime in-stigator of another 'romantic twilight', in Lewis's phrase.[1]

Such hostility was due, in part, to imperfect knowledge of Freud's writings, but there was also a sense that psychoanalysis produced an excessively rational account of areas which mod-ernism itself was exploring.[2] More fundamentally, though, it was perhaps the preoccupation with desire itself which occasioned modernist antagonism. Freud, we recall, spoke broadly of two forms of desire: on the one hand, sexual desire, desire for an object, and, on the other, that desire to be oneself which he began by con-struing as narcissistic desire but which, in his later work, was con-ceived as the foundation for forms of social identification.[3] For the 'Men of 1914', the first type of desire seemed simply reductive – 'Freud explains everything by *sex*', complained Lewis[4] – while the second epitomised the dangerous tendencies to introversion which were taken to characterise psychoanalysis generally. The recurrent trope of Woman transfigured (and displaced) by Art occupied a central place in this modernism since the alternative to the apparent cul-de-sac of 'Freudianism', where all desire appeared to end in mimesis, lay in the fundamentally non-mimetic art-forms of the new modernism.

The critical writings of Pound, Eliot and Lewis thus contain a sort of self-narration which associates formal experiment with a history of successful individuation: the modernist comes of age through his emergence from both the 'womanish introspection' which Yeats, for example, discerned in his own early work,[5] and from the habits of imitation on which contemporary democracy depends. The modernist will therefore go in search of objects sufficient to the task of stabilising the self, closing it to the turbulent movements of desire by discovering that desire as the property of some external object.[6] It is in comparable terms that Eliot recalls his early encounter with Romantic poetry:

> I took the usual adolescent course with Byron, Shelley, Keats, Rossetti, [and] Swinburne. … At this period, the poem, or the poetry of a single poet, invades the youthful consciousness and assumes complete possession for a time. We do not really see it as something with an existence outside ourselves; much as in our youthful experiences of love, we do not so much see the person as infer the existence of some outside object which sets in motion these new and delightful feelings in which we are absorbed. [7]

Eliot's snippet of autobiography provides a naturalised figure for the more momentous history of modernism, recapitulating the fear of 'possession' by an other (be it the past or Woman), and stressing the need for clear boundaries to be drawn around the self. We return, as if in one leap, to the defensive tactics of Baudelairean irony: once again, the absolute fixing of sexual difference, which is seen as the condition of the self's autonomy, makes the feminine a fantasised source of threat and aggression simply because of the independence which is symbolically assigned to her.

What is of interest about this otherwise conventional misogyny is its function as a criterion of literary style. Charles Maurras's rejection of Symbolism in the name of lucidity and articulation comes strongly into play here, bringing with it a familiar freight of conservative politics. We can trace this most easily in the writings of Eliot, an admirer of Maurras's aesthetic and political traditionalism.[8] Eliot's early essays return almost obsessively to the need for some sort of literary objectification. Emotion must be referred to 'a set of objects, a chain of events, which shall be the formula of that particular emotion';[9] lacking such a 'formula', we are left with an inarticulable excess, with the mere 'stuff' which in *Hamlet* Shakespeare was allegedly unable to 'drag to light, to contemplate, or manipulate into art' (144). This, says Eliot, is the stuff of pathology (146), the self unable to represent its feeling to itself and hence to understand it (145). The references here and elsewhere to materiality as a figure for some kind of deadly self-absorption produce a conception of poetic language as the record of successful objectification.

This is the burden of Eliot's essay on Swinburne, a poet who violates the fundamental premise that 'Language in a healthy state presents the object, is so close to the object that the two are identified' (327). For Swinburne's verse tends to eclipse the object altogether, and its language is 'morbid' because the weight of its own materiality (its value as pure sound) blocks any emergence into the 'healthy' world of objects. Swinburne, of course, is not an isolated case, and Eliot finds that Dante's 'lucidity and universality' give way to 'an opacity or inspissation' after the Renaissance (240). That failure of articulation can then be traced intermittently from Milton's rejection of 'common speech' in favour of 'personal style'[10] through to Joyce's *Work in Progress*, where the 'auditory imagination [is] abnormally sharpened at the expense of the visual'.[11] In these writers, language apparently loses touch with the visual world, thus leaving the self immersed in the 'opaque' processes of its own confused desires; by contrast, for a writer like Lancelot Andrewes, 'emotion is purely contemplative; it is not personal, it is wholly evoked by the object of contemplation, to which it is adequate' (351).

For Eliot, then, as for Maurras, a decadent language is one which has become somehow 'bodily', a condition which prevents 'objectivity' and which is quickly marked as 'feminine'. So, for example, Virginia Woolf's 'feminine type' of language is one which 'makes its art by feeling and by contemplating the feeling, rather than the object which has excited it or the object into which the feeling might be made';[12] and Mina Loy similarly 'needs the support of the image ... [otherwise] she becomes abstract, and the word separates from the thing'.[13] Eliot's suspicion of forms of writing which make the word somehow self-sufficient – 'feminine' or narcissistic forms, because language has not there become a register of differentiation of self from other – are shared in various ways by Pound and Lewis. Pound, for example, always understands historical decline in terms of a loss of clarity, a descent into the 'brown meat' of Rembrandt, the 'thickening line', and the increasing opacity of the word;[14] and Lewis, with his commitment to the 'external method' of satire and the values of the visual imagination, derides the 'heavy, sticky, opaque mass' of Gertrude Stein's writing and the 'stupendous outpouring of *matter*, or *stuff*' which is Joyce's *Ulysses*.[15] We could multiply examples, but enough has probably been said to indicate the powerful association here between a 'false' materiality and 'the intuitional, mystical chaos'[16] which is the world of desire and the unconscious. The 'true' modernist aesthetic is thus supported by a mechanism of reference and metaphor, and exhibits a related concern with outlines and borders which protect against the 'chaos' of subjectivity.

For the 'Men of 1914', and especially for Pound and Lewis, what really counted was the 'organisation of forms',[17] the power of design as the 'composition and symmetry and balance' of structures (98) which might function to order the flux and chaos of modern phenomenal life. Form and 'pattern' yield a 'motif', and that 'motif', as Pound discovers it operating in Lewis's art, is characteristically that of 'the fury of intelligence' working against the 'circumjacent stupidity' of a formless modernity (93). This is in part the analytic impulse of Cubism, which works in the middle ground between representation and abstraction. The 'furious' artistic intelligence Pound ascribes to Lewis is thus one which supplements the real but still refers to it. To articulate 'form' is consequently to effect that displacement by which we are able to 'contemplate' (in Eliot's word) the flux of sensation in which we are normally immersed. Hence, too, the agonistics of this particular avant-garde, and the stress it places upon technique as mastery, for 'form' must be seen to be won through what Pound calls the 'combat of arrangement',[18] a 'combat' only marginally less dramatic than man as 'the phallus or spermatozoide charging, head-on, the female chaos'.[19] The connection exceeds simple analogy, reminding us that this privileging of intellect above emotion, along with correlate activities of 'seeing' and 'knowing', leads not (as it did for Paul Valéry's famous Monsieur Teste) to forms of rigorous *self*-scrutiny, but rather to an often aggressive objectification of the other.

As we saw with Baudelaire, a curious double logic is at work here, by which a set of political views is not only inscribed within an aesthetic but thereby protected and legitimated by it. The avant-garde occupies by definition the higher ground, claiming legitimacy in the face of a self-evidently degraded *culture*, and retaining its masculine privileges whilst at the same time appearing to contain current debates about feminism at the purely aesthetic

level. Hence, for example, *Blast*'s sardonic support of the suffragettes and Pound's refusal of 'any digression on feminism' in his
'Postscript' to *The Natural Philosophy of Love*. This mix of unexam-
ined assumptions and deliberate manoeuvres is sustained throughout by the disavowal of 'personal' desire, thus making the
presentation of Eliot's 'world of objects'[20] seem contingent on a singular act of technical and ethical self-discipline, on an *ascetic* refusal
to collapse art into life. The 'clean', 'hard', inorganic values of
Imagism and Vorticism are the only ones which seem adequately to
represent an 'intelligence' which works by reduction, denying itself
the immediate pleasures of the 'caressable' and the mimetic.[21]

* * *

The literary values of this type of modernism are founded, then, on
an attempt to dissociate desire from any form of identification, and
on the appeal to the visual and objective which affirms distance and
difference. This is without doubt the most familiar form of Anglo-
American modernism, known to us largely through rehearsals of
its formal qualities – precision, refusal of sentimentality and
rhetoric, the visual image – rather than through the political entailments of these. Yet because these formal objectives were, as we
have seen, inextricably bound up with a politics of gender, the
'Men of 1914' version of modernism produced a set of literary reactions which we can best define as forms of 'anti-modernism'. This
aspect of the Anglo-American scene, which distinguishes it from
any form of Continental avant-gardism, is a relatively recent discovery and constitutes not simply another kind of modernism
('feminine' modernism) but rather a deliberate and often polemic
disturbance within the canonical version.

The force of dissociation is clear, if complicated, in the work of
Hilda Doolittle, or H.D. as she became known. H.D. had been
engaged to Pound prior to his departure for Europe in 1908. She
settled in London after 1912, becoming part of the circle which included Pound, Lawrence and Amy Lowell. It was a selection of her
poems which seems to have galvanised Pound's sense of Imagism
as a movement ('H.D. Imagiste', he famously signed her work).

H.D.'s first published collection, *Sea Garden* (1916), seems at first sight a perfect fulfilment of Pound's criteria for Imagism. The poems are compressed, hard-edged, shorn of sentiment and rhetoric, and anchored to precise notation of natural objects. H.D. evokes the harsh beauty of a Greek landscape dominated by the powerful movements of the sea and offering little comfort or conventional prettiness ('a hill, not set with black violets / but stones, stones, bare rocks, / dwarf-trees, twisted, no beauty / to distract'.[22]) The style is one of discrete nomination which links the hard-bitten texture of the landscape to an insistently informal syntax: 'The hard sand breaks, / and the grains of it / are clear as wine' (37).

Not only does this kind of writing conform to Pound's criterion of 'direct presentation', but it seems to go further in that direction than anything Pound himself had yet managed.[23] And when we look at these poems more closely we also find that their emotional register differs from that of Pound and the other Imagists in part because H.D. does not excise the poetic 'I'. For Pound, the format of 'objectivity' is threatened by the incursion of the (rhetorical) ego, whereas for H.D., poetry becomes itself the medium in which the 'I' constitutes and reconstitutes itself. Yet this 'I' carries no obtrusive burden of 'character' – in fact, the personal pronouns ('we', 'I', 'you') in these poems are singularly indeterminate, reflexively bound to the rhythms of the landscape which provides their location. If the images of Pound and Aldington are distinguished by a sense of cool detachment and balance, H.D.'s early poems are fraught with a kind of psychic violence. Objects are not held at a contemplative distance here, even though the clarity of presentation might seem to situate things and events at some kind of remove.

Even the element of mediation is problematic, for while Pound may have praised these poems as 'straight talk, straight as the Greek!',[24] H.D.'s version of Ancient Greece was no more 'authentic' than that of Victorian Hellenists like Swinburne. In fact, when she employed original models she tended, like Swinburne, to elaborate and expand them;[25] and the quality of visual detail which distinguishes the poems of *Sea Garden* impressed at least one contemporary classicist as singularly un-Greek.[26] What was important, though, was the conjunction of beauty and violence which H.D. (like Swinburne before her) discovered in the Greek tradition. For these poems offer us precisely that drama of desire which the 'Men of 1914' were keen to consign to Victorian decadence. The linguistic discipline of H.D.'s writing seems to carry it toward Eliot's 'world of objects', but the dominant figures of the poems make the energies of that world embody strains and tensions which threaten to tear the self apart. The most richly descriptive moments are constantly rent from within as beauty is seen to be the product of some internal violence. A poem called 'Sea Lily', for example, begins:

Reed,
slashed and torn
but doubly rich –
such great heads as yours
drift upon temple-steps,
but you are shattered
in the wind.   (14)

'Objectivity' is never complete, since, if only by intimation, the 'you' seems also to include the 'I', which is repeatedly 'shattered' and 'scattered' in these poems. The self is frequently seen in flight, as in 'The Helmsman', and as passive, the prey of some hunter, the shore on which the sea beats. H.D. appropriates Swinburne's sadomasochistic figuring of desire, though she does so in order to interrogate the act of writing in relation to problems of sexual identity. There is the decadent motif of self-obliteration and engulfment ('O be swift – / we have always known you wanted us' [7]), but the fantasy of being crushed, by sea or storm, is tied to a vocabulary of 'splitting', 'breaking' and 'cutting': 'the green crushed, / each leaf is rent like split wood' (36).

The word 'cut', which figures prominently in *Sea Garden*, focuses the rocky landscape ('clean cut, white against white' [26]), but it also refers to an act of incision ('it is written on the walls, / it is cut on the floor' [34]) by which the verse constantly enacts a centrifugal movement of the self:

The light beats upon me.
I am startled –
a split leaf crackles on the paved floor –
I am anguished – defeated.   (10)

This 'I' now witnesses its own objectification as it is 'torn' and dispersed:

A slight wind shakes the seed-pods –
my thoughts are spent
as the black seeds.
My thoughts tear me,
I dread their fever.
I am scattered in its whirl.
I am scattered like
the hot shrivelled seeds.

The 'scattering' here is desired as a release from 'thought' and a sense of self; elsewhere, the 'whirling', 'swirling' movement by which it is produced allows a rhythmic unity with the landscape (as in 'Oread', 'Whirl up, sea – / whirl your pointed pines ... cover us with your pools of fir' [55]). H.D.'s poems play with these forms of movement as 'the tides swirl' (8) and 'the wind swirls' (28), providing a powerful figure for the uncertain self 'caught in the drift' (5). And that whirling trajectory also makes the 'cutting' of the new poem from the old tradition an act conspicuously *lacking* in mastery; indeed, as H.D. puts it in 'Pygmalion':

    am I master of this
    swirl upon swirl of light?
    have I made it as in old times
    I made the gods from the rock?   (49)

If Pound's Imagism is all about modes of differentiation, H.D.'s would seem to be preoccupied with what seems other but turns out to be the same. The relation of self to world is a thoroughly mobile one, in the same sense that H.D. regarded Sappho as 'the sea itself, breaking and tortured and torturing, but never broken'.[27] This doubleness destroys that autonomy of the self which is so much prized by the 'Men of 1914', H.D. developing instead the decadent fantasy of engulfment so as to *open* the self to what is outside it. Many of the poems associate a sultry heat with a claustrophobic self-immersion, and verbs of 'cutting', 'rending' and 'breaking' ('shall I let myself be broken / in my own heat?' [48]) gesture towards an escape:

    O wind, rend open the heat,
    cut apart the heat,
    rend it to tatters.   (25)

Once the heat is 'cut', the speaker is capable of 'turning it on either side / of your path' (25), allowing desire to pursue its object. But what object, one might ask, given that other people are here spoken of only in their absence. Traces do remain: 'the sand on the stream-bank / still holds the print of your foot' (11), and elsewhere the 'Huntress' finds 'heel-prints'; but the 'you' of the poems is as elusive as it is ubiquitous ('I catch at you – you lurch: / you are quicker than my hand-grasp' [27]). In part, the pursuit of 'traces' is the pursuit of lost mythic divinities, and a poem like 'Sea Gods' bears, with Pound's 'The Return', a marked debt to the first chorus in Swinburne's *Atalanta in Calydon* (1865) ('When the hounds of spring are on winter's traces'). But the 'you' which tantalises as it evades capture is also the poet's self, which the 'cut' of writing reveals as a kind of double. This possibility is implied in the tricky pronouns of these poems, and while 'we' sometimes seems marked as exclusively feminine ('you will break the lie of men's thoughts, / and cherish and shelter us' [31]), H.D. also invokes the figure of 'an external objectified self, a thin vibrant and intensely sincere young sort of unsexed warrior'.[28] The quotation is from H.D.'s novel *Her*, which, while not written until 1927, deals with events of the years 1909–10 and provides an intriguing gloss on the themes already discussed.

Most notably, the encoded story of H.D.'s troubled relationship with Pound and her subsequent affair with Frances Gregg develops the association of a 'classical' landscape with the hunt for an other who mirrors oneself: 'A sister would run, would leap, would be concealed under the autumn sumac or lie shaken with hail and wind, lost on some Lacedaemonian foothill' (10). The hunting imagery now becomes clearer: '... the thing that would have had that other hound, twin hounds, fleet-footed, the half of herself that was forever missing' (16). H.D. had been interested in Freud since around 1911,[29] and this search for a 'twin-self sister' (16) is recognised from the first as a form of narcissism (17). Yet in contrast to the 'Men of 1914', who, as we have seen, share Freud's early negative view of narcissism, H.D. grasps it as an ideal construction of the self, one which might free her from the 'whirling' and 'swirling' of hysteria,[30] and allow her to 'Keep a marble self for a marble self, Her for Her, Her for Fayne exactly' (177).[31] Here the classical world offers H.D. a psychic landscape for forbidden kinds of identification, just as it had for Swinburne, who is a powerful presence in the novel.[32] The utopian fantasy of *Her*, a fantasy of

absolute wholeness and symmetry, thus gestures towards a dissolution of ideas of difference as opposition. That H.D. should invoke
Swinburne as a sort of presiding genius in *Her* suggests, too, that
the fantasy of sameness might produce a language which is self-
sufficient, no longer predicated on a lack.

* * *

That possibility is pursued definitively in the work of Gertrude
Stein. Like H.D., Stein was a lifelong expatriate, taking up residence in Paris in 1903. In her voluminous works, which comprise
novels, short stories, prose poems, plays, operas, and lectures,
Stein developed a modernism at odds in almost every respect
with that of Pound, Eliot and Lewis. Stein shares with H.D. the
desire to move beyond an object-based poetics which derives its
force from a repudiation of the feminine, and to discover in its
place a form of writing that reveals continuities between self and
world. If the entry into (modernist) language no longer presup-
poses a break with the feminine, then the form of mastery which
derives from a conception of writing as the supervention of sign
on event loses its force. H.D. remarks of the mother that 'If one
could stay near her always, there would be no break in consciousness',[33] and once the feminine is no longer marked as 'other', the
way is open to a use of language which does not require it to represent what is absent.

Even in her early work, Stein's focus of attention travels consistently away from meaning to the texture of writing. Language
begins to assume a new opacity, blocking any easy passage
between words and Eliot's 'world of objects'. Stein, we might say,
invents another version of modernism by circumventing the
image altogether and by exploring precisely that self-sufficiency
of language which had seemed decadent to the 'Men of 1914'.
Stein took her model from contemporary painting (especially from
that of Picasso), but while there has been much ingenious speculation about her precise debts to Cubism, the link between writing
and painting is actually clearest in some late remarks about
Cézanne:

Up to that time composition had consisted of a central idea, to which everything else was an accompaniment and separate but not an end in itself, and Cezanne conceived the idea that in composition one thing was as important as another thing. Each part is as important as the whole.[34]

To apply this concept of 'composition' to fiction would be revolutionary indeed, suggesting a displacement of theme or motif in favour of what Stein goes on to call 'this background of word-system'. It is this 'background' which Imagism was concerned to whittle away so as to yield a clear view of objects. Stein, however, begins her experiments by trying to do without nouns, focusing instead on the grammatical elements which structure the 'composition' as a whole: 'I like to write with prepositions and conjunctions and articles and verbs and adverbs but not with nouns and adjectives' (*LMN*, 128). In Stein's view, nouns tie us to the world of thought, providing counters which are endlessly familiar and denying us the excitement of immediate perception. 'A noun is a name of anything, why after a thing is named write about it' (*LMN*, 125), asks Stein; 'if you feel what is inside that thing you do not call it by the name by which it is known. Everybody knows that by the way they do when they are in love and a writer should always have that intensity of emotion about whatever is the object about which he writes' (*LMN*, 126). Stein's example is carefully chosen, for her writing will deliberately court the naive in its refusal of irony and of that privileging of intellect over emotion which characterises one strand of Anglo-American modernism.

For Stein, then, writing is a passionate activity, and her shift away from representation deliberately invests language with 'bodily' values. William Carlos Williams, for example, who learned much from Stein, remarks in his *Autobiography* that 'It is the making of that step, to come over into the tactile qualities, the words themselves beyond the mere thought expressed that distinguishes the modern.'[35] It is important to note that Stein is making this 'step' at the beginning of the century, well before *Ulysses* and antedating by some twenty years Samuel Beckett's recognition that Joyce's writing 'is not *about* something; *it is that something itself*'.[36] Furthermore, it is a 'step' deliberately taken to open a new horizon for women's writing: if Stein's work lacks the anxiety and ambivalence of H.D.'s it is partly because (in the words of a recent critic) Stein's radical way with language 'represents an attempt to bring the female world into her writing without having to ensure its absence through figuration'.[37] For Stein, then, language is to be grasped not as a means of reference to a world of objects which can be dominated, but as a medium of consciousness. Here desire is continuous with a syntax of cognitive perception rather than being counterposed to an object of knowledge or attention.

Stein's early work falls into two main phases as she develops this new poetics: in the first, which can be represented by *Three Lives* (written 1904–5, published 1909) and *The Making of Americans* (written 1906–8, published 1925), Stein attempts to redefine the values of an authentically modern prose, concerning herself with questions of time, memory and character; in the second, epitomised by the 'poetic' prose of *Tender Buttons* (written 1911, published 1914), she turns her attention to the object. In the first phase, Stein explores the possibility of what she calls 'a continuous present' and, as her remarks on Cézanne suggest, a written composition will approach a segment of time much as the modern painter regards a composition: 'This brings us again to composition this the using everything', remarks Stein in a lecture, 'In these two books [*Three Lives* and *The Making of Americans*] there was elaboration of the complexities of using everything and of a continuous present and of beginning again and again and again' (*LMN*, 26). This concept of a 'continuous present' is usually traced to Stein's work as a student of William James at Radcliffe College, and particularly to his concept of a 'stream of consciousness'. James proposed a decisive break with traditional empiricism and its view of experience as a series of isolated sensations or impressions; a truer account, he argued, would regard consciousness as 'nothing jointed, it flows'. This 'stream' is, however, closer to the work of Dorothy Richardson and parts of Joyce than it is to Stein. Richardson, for example, explains that 'Feminine prose, as Charles Dickens and James Joyce have delightfully shown themselves to be aware, should properly be unpunctuated, moving from point to point without formal obstructions.'[38]

What this tended to mean in Richardson's huge novel-sequence called *Pilgrimage* was an interior narrative whose continuity was registered partly by an extensive use of ellipses:

> She found a bulging copper hot-water jug, brilliantly polished, with a wicker-covered handle. The water hissed gently into the wide shallow basin, sending up a great cloud of comforting

steam. Dare's soap ... extraordinary. People like these being taken in by advertisements ... awful stuff, full of free soda, *any* transparent soap is bad for the skin, must be, in the nature of things ... makes your skin feel tight.[39]

The characteristic movement of Richardson's prose is, as here, between authorial 'objectivity' and the inner world of the novel's principal character. Compare this passage from Stein's *Three Lives* (1909):

> Jeff Campbell was never any more a torment to Melanctha, he was only silent to her. Jeff often saw Melanctha and he was very friendly with her and he never any more was a bother to her. Jeff never any more now had much chance to be loving with her. Melanctha never was alone now when he saw her.[40]

The effect is quite different, for Stein's tactic of 'beginning again and again' creates exactly what Richardson calls 'formal obstructions' to the flow of the narrative. Each sentence adds to our knowledge of events, but the sense of linear progression is broken by the 'layering' of one phrase against another. Far from being a stream of impressions, Stein's passage draws attention to the words themselves; with each repetition of 'never', 'anymore', 'now' we are drawn deeper into this strange tense which Stein calls the 'continuous present', a tense where things seem to move on but in the same plane, as it were (notice too how this 'continuous present' is actually constructed using verbs in the *past* tense).

Like Pound and Eliot, then, Stein rejects mere impressionism, but where they create a collision of tenses to reveal the anachrony of (re-)writing, she frees the supplementary process of repetition from the assumption of mastery and embeds it in the differential process of language itself. The clue to this development lies in Stein's repudiation of memory and the thematics of time and identity which it governs. How do I know who I am? asks Stein: 'I am I because my little dog knows me but, creatively speaking the little dog knowing that you are you and your recognizing that he knows, that is what destroys creation' (*LMN*, 149). Identity in this sense connotes a fixed and closed self which Stein's little dog will never fail to recognise. But why should we desire this obedient recognition? Stein's reply is mischievously ironic: 'I once said what is the use of being a boy if you are going to grow up to be a man, the boy and the man have nothing to do with each other, except in respect to memory and identity' (*LMN*, 153). Time, then, is not continuity but difference (unless, of course, we wish to construe time simply as the imaginary history of strong male egos), and this proposition calls in question the whole notion of repetition. For narration always changes its object: 'No matter how often what happened had happened any time any one told anything there was no repetition. This is what William James calls the Will to Live. If not nobody would live' (*LMN*, 101). Not repetition, then, but 'insistence' is the force of desire within language as it is within life: 'there can be no repetition because the essence of that expression is insistence, and if you insist you must each time use emphasis and if you use emphasis it is not possible while anybody is alive that they should use exactly the same emphasis' (*LMN*, 100).

In writing, then, there must be 'neither memory nor repetition' (*LMN*, 107), but instead a present whose continuity is a product of differences (here we are closer to Derrida than to Futurist fantasies of a pure present): 'each sentence is just the difference in emphasis' (*LMN*, 119), as Stein observes, and 'insistence', which, like desire, goes on and on and is never completely satisfied, yields a model for a writing which similarly adds but does not conclude ('After all the natural way to count is not that one and one make two but to go on counting by one and one' [*LMN*, 136]). This is the mode of *The Making of Americans* (1925), Stein's novel of almost a thousand pages in which she pursues her early intuition that 'after all description is explanation, and if I went on and on and on enough I could describe every individual human being that could possibly exist' (*LMN*, 88). Here she studies the repetitive habits of her characters to reveal their 'bottom nature' ('the movements of their thoughts and words endlessly the same and endlessly different' [*LMN*, 86]).

Again, though, this approach to 'character' yields nothing like the interior narratives of Richardson's *Pilgrimage*; in fact, as one critic puts it, Stein's own 'discourse constantly engulfs the narrative and its individual characters in the ongoing "now" of her synchronic understanding of "kinds"'.[41] One example:

As I was saying Mary Maxworthing had gayety in living. She had very little fighting in her living but fighting in her was as attacking. She had very little fear in her. She had very little bottom to her, she had a little sensitive bottom to her enough to make her a little yielding to attacking. She had very little stupid bottom in her, most of the stupid being in her was of the impatient being always in her.[42]

Stein uses the conventional past tense of narrative, but the writing focuses our attention on the present tense in which the author narrates. The awkwardness of phrasing ('fighting in her was as attacking') thus combines with Stein's way of substituting participles for nouns to prevent the text from falling back into the comfortable past tense of conventional fiction ('it is this element of remembering that makes novels so soothing' [*LMN*, 108]).

With *The Making of Americans* complete, Stein suddenly switched course. If her prose has to do with paragraphs and 'insistence', and is 'strictly American' in its ability 'to conceive a space that is filled with moving' (*LMN*, 98), she now began to attend to objects: 'in doing very short things I resolutely realized nouns and decided not to get around them but to meet them' (*LMN*, 137). The 'very short things' became *Tender Buttons* (1914), a collection of prose pieces in which Stein playfully encountered the objects of domestic life. This turn from 'prose' to 'poetry' (the latter entailing 'a vocabulary entirely based on the noun as prose is essentially and determinately and vigorously not based on the noun' [*LMN*, 138]) would allow Stein to explore the continuity between self and world. For poetry is apparently 'doing nothing but using losing refusing and pleasing and betraying and caressing nouns' (*LMN*, 138); we cannot help remembering Pound's dismissal of the 'caressable' in art, but although Stein's words in *Tender Buttons* do assume a 'bodily' allure, blurring divisions between inside and outside and undermining any contemplative position of knowledge, her writing is also rigorously antimimetic. As in Cubist painting (a consistent point of reference in this volume), no one perspective offers itself as definitive, and while aesthetic form is clearly valued above the object which provides its occasion, the pleasure taken in the artistic medium is the result of a sense of felt connection with a world rather than of mastery over it.

The collection begins with this piece:

A CARAFE, THAT IS A BLIND GLASS

A kind in glass and a cousin, a spectacle and nothing strange a single hurt colour and an arrangement in a system to pointing. All this and not ordinary, not unordered in not resembling. The difference is spreading.   (*LMN*, 161)

This is more difficult than Stein's earlier prose, partly because of its way of heaping clauses together without any clear syntactical structure, but also because she is now intent on driving a thicker wedge between language and its objects. The resulting verbal artefact is distinct from but related to the real (it is a 'cousin' to the actual carafe, while not literally 'resembling' it). It is not, though, some sort of 'equation' for a state of mind, like Pound's 'image', but is adequate to itself. Stein seems, in fact, to imply that words do not evoke concepts of things so much as things provoke patterns of words.[43] We begin with the idea of a carafe but the words that follow are often produced by associative contexts which are triggered by the words themselves ('blind' sets up an echo for 'kind', for example).

The movement of the text, then, the manner in which 'The difference is spreading', assumes (again in contrast to the protocols of Imagism) that it is only by a sort of *indirect* presentation that we can hope to grasp the object – 'indirect', because as soon as we name it, call it a 'carafe', our sense of a vital particularity is eclipsed in the generic blankness of the noun. The nouns which it is a pleasure to 'caress' are therefore not those which seem simply to name their objects – when nouns function in that way they belong to the dead language of memory rather than to the praxis of 'looking' which structures this collection. As Stein remarked in an essay on Picasso, 'remembered things are not things seen',[44] a view which leads elsewhere to a new distinction between writing and description:

> And the thing that excited me so very much at that time and still does is that the words or words that make what I looked at be itself were always words that to me very exactly related themselves to that thing at which I was looking, but as often as not had nothing I say nothing whatever to do with what any words would do that described that thing.   (*LMN*, 115)

We have moved far from the particular precision of Imagism; compare, too, Eliot's account of 'naming':

> Try to think of what anything would be if you refrained from naming it altogether, and it will dissolve into sensations which are not objects; and it will not be that particular object which it is, until you have found the right name for it.[45]

For Stein, however, the domain of writing is precisely that of 'sensations which are not objects': once released from the instrumental duties of 'naming', language begins to take on a polymorphous life of its own, generating 'excitement' as it becomes a thing to be enjoyed for itself. It is perhaps not surprising that so many of the pieces in Stein's *Tender Buttons* are concerned with food, for eating epitomises that fundamental association of linguistic materiality with oral pleasure – locutionary and sexual – which runs throughout her work. We may recall here a passage in Freud's *Jokes and Their Relation to the Unconscious*. Freud is discussing jokes which depend upon word-play, cases where, he says, 'the (acoustic) word-presentation itself takes the place of its significance as given by its relations to thing-presentations'. We experience a particular pleasure on such occasions, and Freud concludes that

> It may really be suspected that in doing so we are bringing about a great relief in psychical work and that when we make serious use of words we are obliged to hold ourselves back with a certain effort from this comfortable procedure.[46]

Freud implies that a 'serious use of words' always entails a kind of repression, that if words are savoured in the mouth rather than being put swiftly to work, meaningful tasks will never be accomplished. To lift this repression, to abolish the lack on which a descriptive language is founded, is to discover a poetry in which the mind, like Melanctha in *Three Lives*, can 'wander'. Thus, to take just the first sentence of 'A Box' in *Tender Buttons*: 'Out of kindness comes redness and out of rudeness comes rapid same question, out of an eye comes research, out of selection comes painful cattle' (*LMN*, 163). Our reading has no clear place from which to begin (what sort of box is it?), and we can only allow our minds to wander through a maze of possibilities ('redness' coming from 'kindness' suggests 'kindred', 'rudeness' implies an etymological connection to 'redness', while 'rapid' is associated with seizing and tearing away – embarrassment, pain, selection, extraction, breeding, already we are launched into a set of possibilities all of which, we may note now with some surprise, are loosely connected to what we might expect to do with a box (take something out of it). We may be mistaken, of course, in this reading but, as Stein says about her fondness for verbs and adverbs, 'they have one very nice quality and that is that they can be so mistaken' (*LMN*, 126). Error, errancy, drift, sensual 'wandering': these are qualities quite opposed to those of what Stein later calls 'Patriarchal Poetry' (1927): 'Patriarchal poetry makes no mistake in estimating the value to be placed upon the best and most arranged of considerations ...': and 'patriarchal poetry', with its obsession with 'origin and history', is thus confounded by any lack of priority and hierarchy.[47] In Stein's world of lesbian desire, however, 'I double you, of course you do. You double me, very likely to be.' As in H.D.'s *Her*, this 'twin-self' abolishes any notion of 'male firstness',[48] opening the way to a continuous relation between self and other which does not depend upon Eliot's 'right' word to bring a world into being.

* * *

The erotic and textual pleasures indulged in Stein's writings were conspicuously alien to the small-town America shortly to be memorialised in Sinclair Lewis's satirical *Main Street* (1920). Stein accordingly stayed away, but her work nonetheless began to reach a small avant-garde audience in her homeland. The appearance of two of her 'portraits', of Matisse and Picasso, in *Camera Work* in 1912 probably brought her to the attention of William Carlos Williams at a time when New York was about to become a 'vortex' of artistic activity. Williams had known Pound at university, but, while he would remain a strong admirer of his friend's energy and invention, Williams was set to develop a form of modernism with specifically American objectives. He made visits to Europe, of course, but his working life was to be spent as a doctor in his hometown of Rutherford, New Jersey. It was a moment of large-scale cultural change for America: the country had seemed 'half-savage' to Pound when he left in 1908, but by 1912 he was able to declare his belief in 'the imminence of an American Risorgimento'.[49] Williams's proximity to New York put him right at the centre of an unexpected explosion of avant-garde activity.

Like the London 'vortex', the New York scene was centred around the visual arts: the great Armory Show of 1913 brought the new French painting to America (notably the work of Picasso and Marcel Duchamp), but Alfred Stieglitz's journal *Camera Work* had been in operation since 1903, exhibiting forms of the new visual and literary arts. In the years between 1908 and 1917, Stieglitz's '291' gallery also gave young enthusiasts like Williams an opportunity to savour the foreign and exotic,[50] and by 1915 there was sufficient sense of a New York 'scene' to attract Francis Picabia and Duchamp (it was also, of course, an attractive place in which to sit out the war). In loose alliance with the American Man Ray, the two French artists instigated the phenomenon which has come to be known as New York Dada. A lively and often bizarre magazine, named *291* after Stieglitz's gallery, expressed the new aesthetic – or anti-aesthetic, for in advance of the Zurich Dada of Tristan Tzara and Hugo Ball, whose exploits at the legendary Cabaret Voltaire would not begin until February of the next year, the New York group was already moving towards the black humour, anti-traditionalism and aleatory method which was to characterise full-blown Dada.[51] Yet while Duchamp's 'ready-made' works would be the most advanced expression of a disenchantment with Art, New York Dada was also bound up with an emerging machine-aesthetic which could combine both nativist and constructivist elements.

Williams's early writings are littered with allusions to Dada, but he seems to have been uncertain whether to give a full welcome to its dismissal of art, just as he oscillated between a celebration of America's energies and a condemnation of its small-mindedness. Like many writers of his generation, though, Williams's associated America's lack of a flourishing avant-garde tradition with its traditional moralism. Growing knowledge of Freud, who had made the transatlantic crossing in 1909, led to the hypothesis that the nation suffered in some deep sense from a 'repression' which was the legacy of the Puritan founders.[52] The cultural 'awakening' of the second decade, with its rash of often risqué little magazines – *Rogue* (1915), *The Pagan* (1916–22), *The Blind Man* (1917), *Rongwrong* (1917), and, most important, *Others* (1915–19) – thus associated moral constraints with outmoded artistic conventions. Free verse and free love were reactions to the same enemy;[53] Williams would later speak of 'the imagination drunk with prohibitions' (*I*, 93), a phrase which reminds us that this same decade saw the outlawing of alcohol, a 'prohibition' which would give added incentive to another generation of expatriates in the twenties.

But Williams, as we have noted, stayed at home to write about America, a decision which led, almost inevitably, to his antagonism towards a modernism which seemed to nourish itself exclusively on things European. Hence his now famous outbursts against Eliot and Pound, 'Men content with the connotations of their masters', settling for 'rehash, repetition' (*I*, 24). Williams had particular objections to poems like Eliot's 'La Figlia Che Piange' – 'just the right amount of everything drained through, etc., etc. ... the rhythm delicately studied and – IT CONFORMS!' (*I*, 25) – for the light Laforguean touch ('I should have lost a gesture and a pose') appeals to irony to conceal a secure because thoroughly conventional, self. 'Drained through' other cultural contexts, the poem comes to interpose itself as a barrier between self and world. So Williams concluded that

> the thing that stands eternally in the way of really good writing is always one: the virtual impossibility of lifting to the imagination those things which lie under the direct scrutiny of the senses, close to the nose. (*I*, 14)

Williams knew the problem well enough, for his early poems in *The Tempers* (1913) had been self-consciously literary and, like Pound's apprentice work, visibly in search of a properly modern content. 'I should have written about things around me,' Williams mused much later, 'but I didn't know how. ... I knew nothing of language except what I'd heard in Keats or the Pre-Raphaelite Brotherhood.'[54] Imagism, of course, offered one way forward, and from 1914 into the early twenties Williams was looking for ways to connect its criteria of accuracy and directness with contemporary developments in photography and painting. The connection was crucial since the Precisionist painting of the artists Williams most admired, Charles Demuth and Charles Sheeler, celebrated a distinctively American subject-matter, coupling a new form with a new urban and industrial content. 'Nothing is good save the new' (*I*, 23) was Williams's watchword, and in the poems of *Al Que Quiere* (1917), originally subtitled 'The pleasures of democracy', he began to expand the range of the image, showing less interest in modes of juxtaposition than in the capacity of direct presentation to defamiliarise that which lay 'close to the nose'.

The range of tone and mood is striking: increasingly, Williams takes his subject-matter where he finds it, and the stately lyricism of 'Spring Strains' ('In a tissue-thin monotone of blue-grey buds / crowded erect with desire against / the sky') can quickly yield to the demotic tone of 'Divertimento' ('Miserable little woman / in a brown coat – / quit whining!'). Williams constantly sets himself the challenge of 'redeeming' the prosaic matter of the world, not by aestheticising it, but by exposing it to the force of what he terms the 'imagination'. Where art provides the 'beautiful illusion', as he puts it in *Spring and All* (1923), the imagination allows us to see the commonplace as if for the first time. This is like Stein's 'looking without remembering', but what especially interests Williams is the way that the movements of the imagination produce a 'composition' which is already there if we are prepared to look:

> In brilliant gas light
> I turn the kitchen spigot
> and watch the water plash
> into the clean white sink.
> On the grooved drain-board
> to one side is
> a glass filled with parsley –
> crisped green.[55]

These are things 'close to the nose', and while the poem conceals a narrative of a sort (the poet arrives home late, his wife is in bed, preparations have been made for the next day), the pleasure taken lies in recognising certain objects simply, without assigning 'associational or sentimental value' to them (*I*, 14). Already we observe the strong propulsive movement which characterises so many of Williams's poems, the short lines, often with run-over, leading our attention forward, as 'The imagination goes from one thing to another' (*I*, 14). Thus conceived, the imagination is a cohesive field of force, magnetising the 'particles of dissimilarity' which come within its purview (*I*, 18). Yet we miss the complexity of this if we fail to see how, for Williams, the imagination 'lifts' things into language – not that the spigot and parsley are aestheticised in the way that, say, women are aestheticised as art-objects in *Hugh Selwyn Mauberley* and *A Portrait of the Artist*, but rather that we are now free to construe relations between things as relations between words. As in Stein's carafe poem, we are liberated from the meaningless contingency of real objects into a world of formal values. And to do this we must renounce our pragmatic attachment to 'meaning' and consider 'writing' instead. That, at least, seems to be the lesson Williams quickly learned from Stein, and it led him, not unpredictably, to regard the image as tied to mere simile.[56] Beyond this, 'writing' also suggested a Steinian break with 'sense', and, as

Williams later put it, his principal discovery now was that 'All you have to know is the meaning of the words – and let yourself go.'[57]

Here was a radical alternative to the neo-classicism flourishing on the other side of the Atlantic, and Williams chose to pursue it in prose, the very medium which Pound had adduced as a *corrective* model for an overly romantic, 'spontaneous' poetry. *Kora in Hell: Improvisations* (1920) is a radically discontinuous sequence of pieces interspersed with 'commentaries' which are sometimes more obscure than the passages which occasion them. Williams now 'lets himself go' by improvising, recording his 'day-to-day notations, off the cuff, thoughts put down like a diary in a year of my life'.[58] This procedure predicts the later Surrealist interest in automatic writing at least in so far as Williams is trying to give the imagination its maximum freedom to '[go] from one thing to another': 'The attention has been held too rigid on the one plane instead of following a more flexible, jagged resort. It is to loosen the attention, my attention since I occupy part of the field, that I write these improvisations' (*I*, 14).

This 'poet's prose', as Stephen Fredman calls it, takes speech as its model, and produces a 'fluidity and syntactic playfulness' which would subsequently allow Williams to move beyond established metrical forms in his verse.[59] The jocular tone registers this sense of new freedoms:

> There's force to this cold sun, makes beard stubble stand shinily. We look, we pretend great things to our glass, rubbing our chin: this is a profound comedian who grimaces deeds into slothful breasts.   (*I*, 78)

The wintry sun seems to make the beard grow, though it stands 'shinily', in the mirror's reflection; so we pretend and posture in such private moments, imagining great deeds while merely contemplating ourselves. Williams's prose characteristically denies itself the grand gesture, cultivating instead the 'disjointing process' (*I*, 285) by which the imagination recognises the tension between its own power ('There is no thing that with a twist of the imagination cannot be something else') and the 'finality' of 'the particular thing' which 'dwarfs the imagination … [and] sends us spinning through space' (*I*, 81).

It is this tension which lies at the centre of Williams's first major collection of poems, *Spring and All* (1923). After the descent into hell in the *Improvisations*, the new volume announces that Spring has at last arrived. The poems here are interleaved with a Dadaist 'commentary' again, though this time it is more clearly tied to the book's overall aims. Williams's target is, he reminds us on the first page, the 'constant barrier between the reader and his consciousness of immediate contact with the world' (*I*, 88). But it is time for the 'beautiful illusion' (*I*, 89) to be blasted away once and for all, and the following pages indulge in a fantastic carnival of violence, the imagination rising 'to drunken heights to destroy the world' (*I*, 91). Only through this Dadaist act of destruction can we achieve the new (not, most definitely not, says Williams, with the Sanscrit and Latin allusions of Eliot's *The Waste Land* [*I*, 90]); and the new heralds the end of that 'great copying' which has defined the mimetic (or 'plagiaristic') arts hitherto. In breaking with mimesis, Williams proposes his own version of modernism: the poem is not an 'equation' for a state of mind, nor is it a statement somehow 'backed' or stabilised by reference to a 'world of objects'. For Williams, the poem is quite simply one object among others, continuous with them, hence the necessity of avoiding 'complicated ritualistic forms designed to separate the work from "reality"' (*I*, 102). Such poems articulate a two-way process, with things 'energized by the imagination' (*I*, 138) 'revealing the oneness of experience' and 'showing the individual, depressed before it, that his life is valuable – when completed by the imagination' (*I*, 107).

It is easy to feel the force of the contemporary machine aesthetic in *Spring and All*, and the relation Williams everywhere assumes between triphammers, electricity and motorcars (*I*, 125) and the imagination's violent way with the world. For to make something new is to 'separate things of the imagination from life' (*I*, 107), a separation which throws us into an unexpected relation to familiar things. In 'The rose is obsolete', for example, a poem indebted, Williams says, to 'the fragmentation of Picasso',[60] the conventionally sensuous rose is shorn of its usual connotations and cast in 'metal or porcelain'. Suddenly the rose can become an object of clear perception ('The rose carried weight of love / but love is at an end – of roses'); with its new 'cold, precise' quality it sponsors an alternative visual and conceptual 'geometry'. Here and in the other poems which stand out against the deliberately inchoate and 'spontaneous' prose of *Spring and All*, Williams affirms his commitment to a poetics which literally transforms the world.

This is not in any sense, then, a poetry of ideas, but an exploration of the syntax which maps the mind's engagement with its objects. Like Stein, Williams asks us to read literally, to remain close to the surface of the words, and in this way our construction of the lines should enact a process not of interpretation but of continuous perception. Take the first four stanzas of Poem VIII:

> The sunlight in a
> yellow plaque upon the
> varnished floor
>
> is full of a song
> inflated to
> fifty pounds pressure
>
> at the faucet of
> June that rings
> the triangle of the air
>
> pulling at the
> anemones in
> Persephone's cow pasture –   (*I*, 109)

Sunlight, concentrated on a varnished floor: an image which Williams goes on to 'inflate' by connecting an intensity of heat and light first with the power of 'song' (the poem itself, we assume) and then with 'fifty pounds pressure', a specificity which hangs in metaphorical suspension until the faucet appears in the seventh line. My sentence stops, but Williams's still moves forward, the faucet which contains this pressure in its pipe now named as the month of June 'that rings / the triangle of the air'. But the subject of this verb is not in fact June, but the song of the second stanza; yet when we reach the fourth stanza the subject of 'pulling' could be the song or the triangle. As in *Tender Buttons*, our expectations of syntactical closure are constantly frustrated, and Williams creates complex connections which a conventional grammar could hardly sustain (is the triangle, whose 'ringing' is the air's vibration in the heat, the 'plaque' of the first stanza?). To read literally here is to see how Williams, like Stein, makes syntax an articulation of desire in language rather than a means of curbing it or holding it back. If the fourth stanza hints finally at the return of Persephone/Kore from her stay in Hell, then the force of growth and fertility which tugs the anemones from the soil is equally the power of song and sunlight (later in the poem Williams will associate it with other rapacious forms of desire which the 'expulsive emotion' (*I*, 111) of his own song sets out to challenge).

* * *

Williams's campaign on behalf of the imagination thus entailed a version of the Romantic relation between self and world, emphasising their interaction but making the poem articulate it rather than reflect upon it. As the poems in *Spring and All* show, that could be a risky business, and Williams's favourite image, of things seen from a moving car ('I went spinning on the / four wheels of my car' [*I*, 119–20]), was a way of characterising the poem as a series of chances taken, 'headlong composition'[61] combining with verbal precision to create dynamism rather than consolation. Williams's friend Wallace Stevens also centred his theoretical account of modern poetry on a concept of the imagination, but, as is clear from a letter which Williams published in his Introduction to *Kora in Hell*, Stevens' understanding of it was rather different. After reading *Al Que Quiere*, Stevens writes that 'What strikes me most about the poems themselves is their casual character.' 'Casual', partly because Williams refuses to adopt a consistent point of view: 'to fidget with points of view', warns Stevens, 'leads always to new beginnings and incessant new beginnings lead to sterility' (*I*, 15).[62]

Stevens's own concept of the imagination is tied to a more meditative and abstract poetics. Aspects of his early work may remind us of Baudelaire and (especially) Laforgue, and his understanding of poetry as a sort of necessary 'fiction' echoes the late nineteenth-century preoccupation with a loss of religious faith. In a late essay, for example, Stevens explained that

in an age in which disbelief is so profoundly prevalent or, if not ⸢disbelief, indifference to questions of belief, poetry and painting, and the arts in general, are, in their measure, a compensation for what has been lost.[63]

This idea of loss is different from anything in Williams's work, as is the ironic but 'stoic' acceptance of poetry's adequacy as a 'supreme fiction'[64] but *in*adequacy as a rival belief-system – 'Poetry does not address itself to beliefs.'[65] And while Stevens shares Williams's lack of reverence for the past ('Know that the past is not part of the present', he admonishes in one poem[66]), his early sense of art as a kind of compensatory artifice leads to a bohemian eclecticism which can borrow from the tradition while ironically presenting its discoveries as exotic and ornamental.

The poems of *Harmonium* (1923) are thus playful and highly coloured, exhibiting a sensibility which is both elusive and exquisite. Yet in contrast to the exploration of language in the work of Stein and Williams, the pleasure taken in Stevens's early poems is in a sort of surface glamour, the meditative conventions of the Romantic ode now adapted to a ritual comedy:

> The fops of fancy in their poems leave
> Memorabilia of the mystic spouts,
> Spontaneously watering their gritty soils.
> I am a yeoman, as such fellows go.[67]

The dandy walks a tightrope, but if he falls it will be a lapse in taste, not much more; Kenneth Rexroth remarks acutely of Stevens that 'If the mind can be so constructed, the sensitivity so attuned, principle so unfalteringly adhered to, it is quite possible to produce poetry in which there are no mistakes.'[68] The poise of Stevens's verse is certainly notable, even though the irony which colours it has tragic implications. Stevens's principal concern, if not his only one, is at first sight with the relations of self to world: 'The subject-matter of poetry', he argues, 'is not that "collection of solid, static objects extended in space" but the life that is lived in the scene it composes; and so reality is not that external scene but the life that is lived in it'.[69] Like Williams, Stevens regards the continuity between them as guaranteed by the imagination, and he too insists that 'The mind has added nothing to human nature. It is a violence from within that protects us from a violence without. It is the imagination pressing back against the pressure of reality.'[70]

In contrast to Williams, though, Stevens's objective is to find in poetry some sort of equilibrium between these interacting pressures, for 'it is not only that the imagination adheres to reality, but, also, that reality adheres to the imagination and that the interdependence is essential'.[71] Comments such as these have led critics to stress the dialectical shape of many of Stevens's poems, a point which serves also to demonstrate his dependence on rhetorical modes. A poem like the much-anthologised 'The Emperor of Ice-Cream', for example, is full of characteristically brilliant imagery (of big cigars and 'concupiscent curds'), but the task it sets itself – to arrive at a balanced and 'realistic' attitude towards death – is ultimately managed as an ironic rhetorical 'proof': 'Let be be finale of seem. / The only emperor is the emperor of ice-cream.' The balance is finely sustained, in part because of the complex play with images of cold and desire which Stevens is then able to resolve as a profound attitude – profound, that is, in the sense that the reader may finally include the glimpse of the corpse's 'horny feet' within a curve of attention which also contains the naked objectivity of the lamp's beam and the triumphant act of obeisance to the emperor of ice-cream.

It is this complexity of register and tone, coupled with a zest for the unusual and recondite word, which reveals Stevens's particular debt to Laforgue. Yet to stress only the ironic dandyism of *Harmonium* is to miss the range of his subsequent work, just as to be guided purely by Stevens's 'philosophical' concerns is to overlook the complex linguistic questions which the poems raise. For the recurring problem of the mind's relation to the real seems ultimately of less importance to the poems than the parallel problem of the relation of the literal to the metaphoric. The real for Stevens is not so much Eliot's 'world of objects' as it is what he calls 'the structure of reality', a structure which is constituted from the discovery of 'resemblance' between things.[72] Equivalent to neither 'identity' nor 'imitation', 'Resemblance in metaphor is an activity of the imagination; and in metaphor the imagination is life.' Stevens thus proposes not a binary division between mind and the world, but a condition of metaphor which dramatises 'resemblance' through the interplay of literal and figurative meanings. The object of such a poetics is quite different from Pound's ideal of a 'welding of word and thing', and Stevens's later poems, like 'Credences of Summer' and 'Notes toward a Supreme Fiction' would situate themselves in that uncertain intermediary space in which (as Paul Ricoeur puts it) 'metaphorical sense not only abolishes but preserves the literal sense'.[73]

* * *

Pound, then, might have placed Stevens's work in the category he called 'verbalism' (a term which the *OED* defines as the 'predominance of what is merely verbal over reality or real significance'). According to Pound, there are two types: 'Bad verbalism is rhetoric, or the use of *cliché* unconsciously, or a mere playing with phrases. But there is good verbalism, distinct from lyricism or imagism, and in this Laforgue is a master.'[74] It was not, however, Stevens but Marianne Moore and Mina Loy who became examples of 'good verbalism' or what Pound now began to call 'logopoeia', a term to distinguish from Imagism and 'melopoeia' ('poetry which moves by its music') a 'poetry that is akin to nothing but language, which is a dance of the intelligence among words and ideas and modification of ideas and characters'.[75] Pound regarded the 'arid clarity' of Moore and Loy as reflecting 'le tempérament de l'Américaine' (he did not know that Loy was British). It is a positive review ('I intend this as praise', he says), though 'arid' is an unusual word of commendation. For Pound, this type of 'verbalism' represents a writing he admires (particularly in the work of Laforgue and Eliot), but it is not his own, and one may feel that that is partly due to his sense of its non-lyric 'dryness': 'In the verse of Marianne Moore I detect traces of emotion; in that of Mina Loy I detect no emotion whatever.'

Reading both poets now, however, one might want to reverse Pound's judgement, for it is Moore's work which seems most formal and restrained. Her extensive use of allusion and quotation produces a collage-like effect which combines with a frequently exaggerated *enjambement* to create a sense of impermeable surfaces:

> Black in blazonry means
> prudence; and niger, unpropitious. Might
> hematite –
> > black, compactly incurved horns on bison
> > > have significance? The
> > soot-brown tail-tuft on
> > > a kind of lion
>
> tail; what would that express?[76]

The wit of such lines has much to do with pace and pause, as the poet weighs her words like rare exhibits. 'More apparently inhuman poetry has probably never been written', observes Kenneth Rexroth, but the inhumanness carries all the pathos of the acutely personal, so deeply is the latter hidden.[77]

Mina Loy's 'verbalism' is very different. Like H.D. and Stein she appropriates certain features of decadent writing – notably its particular forms of linguistic opacity and its preoccupation with psychic disunity – but uses them in the service of a satirical and outspoken feminism. In contrast to the polished ironies of Moore's work, Loy's writing has a deliberately rebarbative quality, with its contorted, often verbless constructions and its recondite and latinate vocabulary:

> Spawn of Fantasies
> Silting the appraisable
> Pig Cupid
> His rosy snout
> Rooting erotic garbage
> 'Once upon a time'
> Pulls a weed
> White star-topped
> Among wild oats
> Sown in mucous membrane[78]

The decadent 'rare' word returns, but this time with a compressed and epigrammatic cadence which gives the poems a calculated sense of posturing: 'Pure purposeless eremite / of centripetal sentience // Upon the carnose horologe of the ego / the vibrant tendon index moves not' (10).

It is probably this opacity and 'jamming' of the line which led Pound to find no emotion in her work, though such a judgement holds only if we ignore Loy's deliberate use of such decadent effects to foreground contingent and deliberately artful figures of the self. As in the lines just quoted, the high artifice of the writing complements Loy's satirical sense throughout her work of the ego as construction – but not as some kind of defence or stability within a world of flux: rather as the self-aggrandising disguises adopted in that 'masquerade sex' (14) which is the outward form of an ideology of romantic love ('We have been taught / Love is a god' [37]). Loy's satire has more than a little in common with Lewis's, though of course her critique of love as 'the preeminent littérateur' (107) entails an attack on male fictions of authority and on the ways in which 'fashions in lechery' (58) produce constructions of the feminine. 'Woman' here becomes simply a false sign – 'I catch the thread of the argument / Immediately assuming my personal mental attitude / And cease to be a woman' (39) – gender thus detaching itself from nature, and prompting the question 'are you / Only the other half / Of an ego's necessity' (96).

This is quite different from the more conventional 'impersonality' of Moore's work or, indeed, from the *personae* favoured by other modernists, for Loy seems to reject any coherent model of the self as something both imaginary and conventional. So, in *Love Songs* (1915–17) and her long poem *Anglo-Mongrels and the Rose* (1923–5), modernist irony is fundamentally reformulated, as the reflexivity of her style turns the force of critique back upon the self instead of directing it outwards, against other people. It is not, of course, that her satire lacks an object, but that the impulse of negation works also to reduce self to style, so that when she writes in her 'Feminist Manifesto', for example, that 'Woman must destroy in herself the desire to be loved' (271), she is invoking a form of aggressivity which the poems explore as 'a diurnal splintering of egos' (89). Where Pound's Hugh Selwyn Mauberley found in aesthetic style a form of 'armour' for the self, Loy discovers in its very fictionality a release from the ideological 'truths' of gender.

Here the frame of what we normally think of as Anglo-American modernism is turned inside out, as style is grasped not as the privileged vehicle of avant-garde authority but rather as witness to its metaphysical pretensions. In this respect Loy's work prefigures the playful transgressions of Virginia Woolf's *Orlando* (1928) and the more darkly baroque underworld of Djuna Barnes's *Nightwood* (1936). But while such later texts seem to stand outside 'modernism', effecting as they do such a fundamental break with the gendered aesthetics of the various avant-gardes, Loy's poems retain a connection with that first phase, partly through her critical relation to Futurism, but especially through her association with New York Dada. For Dada, as we shall see in the next chapter, produced an aesthetic of negation designed to undermine all forms of authority – especially that of the self.

10

From Fantasy to Structure:
Dada and Neo-Classicism

In her 'Feminist Manifesto' (1914), Mina Loy warned women that 'as conditions are at present constituted you have the choice between Parasitism, Prostitution, or Negation'.[1] That third possibility, Negation, reminds us of Loy's connections with New York Dada, and particularly with the forms of irony and black humour which Picabia and Duchamp had introduced into the American cultural scene. The invention of Dada proper, however, along with the discovery of its talismanic name, took place elsewhere, in Zurich. Switzerland's neutrality made it a natural haven for artists and intellectuals seeking refuge from war-torn Europe; Zurich especially became 'an island, isolated in the middle of a war',[2] an oasis of bourgeois normality from which to launch a critique of the reigning political madness. Here German intellectuals previously affiliated to Expressionism – Hugo Ball, Emmy Hennings, Richard Huelsenbeck, Hans Arp – were joined by Romanians Marcel Janco and Tristan Tzara.

Zurich Dada began with the opening in February 1916 of the Cabaret Voltaire by German poet and stage-manager Hugo Ball. In contrast to the other main European avant-gardes, Dada came into being as a direct response to the war, and while it drew freely on the innovations of Futurism, Cubism and Expressionism, it was, from the first, characterised by a spirit of outrage and negation. The modernist tendencies which preceded Dada had, as we have seen, depended heavily on fantasies of violence and aggression, which the outbreak of war had suddenly shown to be devastatingly misjudged. Dada would not disavow violence – by now the very notion of the avant-garde seemed unthinkable without it – but it would redefine antagonism as a form of absolute scepticism which called into question the political pieties concealed within the iconoclastic aesthetic programmes of movements like Futurism and Expressionism. Almost from the first, the Dadaists would occupy a deliberately ambiguous position, condemning the barbarity of war while drawing on those same destructive energies to fuel their own anti-culturalism.

Surrealist André Breton would later remark that 'Cubism was a school of painting, futurism a political movement: DADA is a state of mind.'[3] The comment is helpful in so far as it warns us not to expect to find a clear aesthetic programme motivating Dada. Of more importance is the ironic habit of mind, an expression of anger, deliberate stupidity, nonsense and black humour which prevents the Dada intelligence from settling comfortably into conclusions and convictions. The tone is there in Hans Arp's retrospective account of Dada's inception:

> In Zurich in 1915, losing interest in the slaughterhouses of the world war, we turned to the Fine Arts. While the thunder of the batteries rumbled in the distance, we pasted, we recited, we versified, we sang with all our soul. We searched for an elementary art that would, we thought, save mankind from the furious folly of these times.[4]

As the apocalypse plays itself out, the Dadaists immerse themselves in the 'Fine Arts', fiddling while Europe burns. But this turn to culture is also a turn against it, and the 'elementary' forms which Arp and his colleagues seek are ones which unleash a primal energy against the 'civilised' world's lust for self-destruction. For the 'Fine Arts' enshrine those same moral and religious principles for which 'the batteries rumbled in the distance'. Like Pound in *Hugh Selwyn Mauberley*, the Dadaists revile this cultural tradition (the war fought for 'a few thousand battered books'), but unlike Pound, they find themselves '*losing interest* in the slaughterhouses of the world war'. The war brought home to Pound the need for far-reaching political and economic reforms, but for the Dadaists it demonstrated only the complete bankruptcy of the West's intellectual tradition, leaving a posture of absolute indifference as the only one worth adopting.

'Introduce symmetries and rhythms instead of principles. Contradict the existing world orders. ... What we are celebrating is at once a buffoonery and a requiem mass': so writes Hugo Ball in 1916.[5] In contrast to the later, more clearly negative turn given to Dada by Tristan Tzara, Ball's particular 'buffoonery' had from the first an affirmative, not to say mystical dimension. In 1917, for example, he wrote in his journal: 'Dadaism – a mask play, a burst of laughter? And behind it, a synthesis of the romantic, dandyistic and – daemonistic theories of the 19th century.'[6] The sense of Dada as Dionysian lay behind Ball's experiments at the Cabaret Voltaire, as he drew together elements from the European avant-garde scene to create a distinctive performance art. Dada, Richard Huelsenbeck would recall in 1920, 'was to be a rallying point for abstract energies and a lasting slingshot for the great international artistic movements'.[7] The ammunition consisted of those simultaneous forms which had fascinated Apollinaire and Cendrars, along with the 'bruitism' or noise-music with which Luigi Russolo and the Italian Futurists had scandalised their audiences. Ball thus had no interest in conventional drama: during the period of the Cabaret, only two 'plays' were presented, and these were hardly orthodox works (Kokoschka's *Sphinx and Strawman* and Tzara's *The First Celestial Adventure of Mr. Antipyrine*[8]). The main aim of the early Dada performances was, in Ball's view, to create a mood of primitive spontaneity: simultaneous readings were supported by what he called 'stupendous negro music (toujours avec la grosse caisse: boum boum boum boum – drabatja mo gere drabatja mo bonoooooooooo').[9] At this stage, though, Dada was not yet openly destructive, shaped as it was by Ball's romantic sense of 'Childhood as a new world, and everything childlike and phantastic, everything childlike and direct, everything childlike and symbolical in opposition to the senilities of the world of grown-ups.'[10]

Performance was closely linked to Ball's interest in sound poetry – here Dada connected with that move against signification which we have already traced in Futurism and Expressionism. He also knew something of the work of Russian Futurists Khlebnikov and Kruchenykh,[11] and the early Cabaret Voltaire experiments in simultaneity exploited pure sound to demonstrate 'the value of the human voice'.[12] 'The poet', said Ball, 'crows, curses, sighs, stutters, yodels, as he pleases',[13] and that release of language from its normal transactional duties discloses 'the innermost alchemy of the word', a rediscovery of what he called 'the evangelical concept of the "word" (logos) as a magical complex image'.[14] Similarly, Ball remarked in his journal that 'I have invented a new genre of poems, "Verse ohne Worte" [poems without words] or Lautgedichte [sound poems], in which the balance of the vowels is weighed and distributed solely according to the values of the beginning sequence.'[15] Such poems approximate pure sound, creating waves of incantatory rhythm intended to release us from the pragmatic obligations of ordinary language. There is something in this which may recall Freud's account of the psychic 'relief' attaching to sound and word-play,[16] but Ball's own theory is mainly coloured by his earlier association with Kandinsky, who had written of the way in which

> pure sound exercises a direct impression on the soul. The soul attains to an objectless vibration, even more complicated, I might say more transcendent, than the reverberations released by the sound of a bell, a stringed instrument, or a fallen board. In this direction lie great possibilities for the literature of the future.[17]

Like Kandinsky, Ball saw in such experiments a means of achieving spiritual regeneration through art, and in this respect his contribution to the founding stage of Dada was strongly marked by Blue Rider primitivism.

At the Cabaret, though, Ball's mystical intentions often took second place to the scandal provoked by the performances. It is this aspect which comes through so strongly in Tzara's recollections and indicates the particular emphasis Dada would carry under his leadership:

> ... the big drum is brought in, Huelsenbeck against 200, Ho osen-latz accentuated by the very big drum and little bells on his left foot – the people protest shout smash windowpanes kill each other demolish fight here come the police interruption. Boxing resumed: Cubist dance, costumes by Janco, each man his own big drum on his head, noise, Negro music/trabatgea bonooooooo oo ooooo/5 literary experiments: Tzara in tails stands before the curtain, stone sober for the animals, and explains the new aesthetic: gymnastic poem, concert of vowels, bruitist poem, static poem chemical arrangement of ideas. ...[18]

For Tzara, the performance is above all a catalyst leading to violence and even to a confrontation with the law. The Dadaists had learned from the Futurists that the audience must be taunted and abused to such a degree that it is finally driven into a frenzy of anger and outrage. Not only would unwitting spectators come to realise that they were being deliberately exploited, but they would begin to collude in their own exploitation. When the audience's sense of outrage reached its peak, usually accompanied by a hail of insults and missiles, it would have effectively constituted itself as 'Dada', and the vicious circle of Dadaist irony would be satisfyingly complete.

Not for nothing does Tzara speak of this audience as 'animals', for the performer knowingly places himself at risk before a crowd soon baying for his blood. A dangerous transformation is worked on such occasions, the cultured bourgeois suddenly becoming the raving, chair-hurling spectator, and in that moment Dada seems to confound the conventional divide between culture and nature. If Dada begins as a storm in a teacup, a purely bohemian extravagance, its implications turn out to be far-reaching: for it is above all a denial of art as consolation, and to that degree it perfectly encapsulates the tensions of the avant-garde moment as Jürgen Habermas has described it:

> The 'alter ego' of the commodity owner – the 'human being', which the bourgeois could at one time encounter in the solitary contemplation of a work of art – thereupon split off from him and confronted him in the artistic avant-garde, as a hostile power, at best a seducer.[19]

In the turbulent present of the Dada performance, both past and future are denied, the aim being, as Walter Benjamin later put it, to guarantee art's 'uselessness for contemplative immersion'.[20] Art is, as it were, hollowed out; deprived of its traditional power to redeem and legitimate the social order, its mask of 'humanness' falls away.

It has frequently been said that Dada is anti-art, that it strives to abolish the art-work as such. Yet Dada is as deliberately contradictory in this respect as in every other, and as French Dadaist Georges Ribemont-Dessaignes observes, 'Dada created anti-aesthetic values. So then it created art.'[21] This was certainly an 'internal contradiction', but not one from which Dada necessarily suffered. Even in the aggressive 1918 manifesto we find Tzara declaring that 'the only basis of understanding is: art' (*SML*, 10), a statement which indicates that Dada rejects not art *per se*, but art which supplies an egotistical bourgeois culture with its halo of metaphysical, quasi-religious meanings. Such art performs the vital ideological function of mystifying bourgeois self-interest as disinterested rationality and individualism. As Hugo Ball put it, 'They are trying to make the impossible possible and to pass off the betrayal of man, the exploitation of the body and soul of the people, and all this civilized carnage as a triumph of European intelligence.'[22] Hans Richter recalled similarly that 'We would have nothing to do with the sort of human or inhuman being who used reason as a juggernaut, crushing acres of corpses.'[23]

Accordingly, Dada finds the cultural tradition thoroughly corrupted by its association with 'reason'. As Peter Sloterdijk observes:

> Dada does *not* revolt against bourgeois 'institution art'. Dada turns against art as a technique of bestowing meaning. Dada is antisemantics. It rejects 'style' as pretense of meaning just as much as the deceitful 'beautifying' of things. ... As antisemantics, Dadaism systematically disrupts – not metaphysics but the talk about it: The metaphysical domain is laid bare as a festival ground; there, everything is allowed, except 'opinions'.[24]

So we find the Dadaists attempting to dissolve 'art' in what they variously term 'nature' or 'life', a principle of pure energy which simply *is* and does not *mean* anything: 'the roar of contorted pains, the interweaving of contraries and of all contradictions, freaks and irrelevancies: LIFE' (*SML*, 13). Style becomes arbitrary, no longer tied to either theme or the writer's personality, avowedly 'public' and incorporating methods and motifs from popular entertainment. Dada assumes no coherent world to be mirrored in art – in this universe exceptions are the rule – and the success of the work itself will be measured by the degree to which, as sheer 'monstrosity' (*SML*, 16), it contravenes accepted notions of symmetry and intelligibility ('What we need is works that are strong straight precise and forever beyond understanding', declares Tzara [*SML*, 19]). The Dadaists are, in this sense, 'people who deliberately severed the process of communication, the causal nexus between payment and ware, between expectation and fulfillment, insecurity and affirmation'.[25] As Huelsenbeck's comment suggests, the Dada work refuses to become an art-work in the usual sense of an artefact which can enter the circuit of capitalist exchange. It refuses, we might say, to become a finished product, coupling formal abstraction with a commitment to instantaneity which together inhibit the emergence of art as commoditised object. And as for the artist's own investment in his craft? 'I write', says Tzara, 'because it's natural like I piss like I'm ill' (*SML*, 16).

Supplanting 'reason' and 'logic' by chance, Dada jettisons the traditional view of culture as nature translated into art. In fact Dadaists like Kurt Schwitters would soon develop Cubist forms of collage to show how the real might remain recalcitrant to artistic sublation as bits of actual objects were affixed to the 'imaginary' plane of the work. Hence too Tzara's hostility to dialectic ('an amusing machine that leads us ... to the opinions we would have held in any case' [*SML*, 9]) and Louis Aragon's later evocation of 'A universe in pieces, abandoned, without any hope, an image of the real'.[26] The 'real', for Dada, is closely bound up with the unconsciousness of the body – the Dadaist's 'culture is above all of the body', observes Huelsenbeck[27] – and instinct is accordingly prized above intellect.

Where Ball's sound poetry had sometimes seemed to assume 'the age-old cadence of the sacerdotal lamentation',[28] Tzara's own sense of an affective or 'bodily' language is blatantly scatological: 'DADA remains within the framework of European weaknesses, it's still shit, but from now on we want to shit in different colours' (*SML*, 1). This excremental language resists conceptualisation, suggesting once again the polymorphous freedoms of the nursery. Hence the aptness of 'Dada' as a name, for whatever its provenance, the word catches precisely this sense. According to Huelsenbeck, Ball lit upon it while perusing a dictionary:

> 'Dada,' Ball read, and added: 'It is a children's word meaning hobby-horse.' At that moment I understand what advantages the word held for us.
> 'Let's take the word dada', I said. 'It's just made for our purposes. The child's first sound expresses the primitiveness, the beginning at zero, the new in our art. We could not find a better word.'[29]

'Hobby-horse' in French, 'father' in English, 'yes, yes' in Romanian, a 'cube' and a 'wet-nurse' in Italian – suggestively connected as they are, the various meanings of the word are secondary to its sound, which, as Huelsenbeck observes, expresses a primitive inarticulacy, a phonic babble at the threshold of meaning. In equating the paternal with the nonsensical, 'Dada' also reduces semantic authority to a 'noisy primitivism' (*SML*, 4), to the insistence of some primal force of expressivity like the mindless pounding of the big drum. As one critic puts it, 'the word Dada was felt as a linguistic toy',[30] a bit of phonemic *matter* which, like a child's favourite object, would unfailingly meet the needs of fantasy. And this is perhaps the crux of Dada's sense of 'the plasticity of the word', as Ball called it,[31] for language in this state is infinitely malleable, both instigating and responding to desire. 'DADA DOES NOT MEAN ANY-THING', Tzara insists in his manifesto (*SML*, 4); equally, it can mean everything, expressing 'the fantasy of every individual' (*SML*, 8) and evading the straitjacket of conventional usage – 'One can say that the word Dada lends itself easily to puns', observed André Breton, 'That is why we selected it.'[32]

Tzara's own experiments with sound poetry explored such effects by working closely with African texts (his *Negro Poems* appeared in the first issue of *Dada* in July 1917). Tzara drew on the review *Anthropos* for his originals, which he did not attempt to translate but instead used as models for phonetic constructions of his own.[33] In this way, the African poems simply provided occasions for a fantasised primitivism, and Tzara quickly lost interest in them when they became declamatory and stylised, rather than 'the expression of a desire'.[34] At the same time, though, such experiments supported Tzara's own strategy of negation, and while his appropriation of primitive models exhibits a political insensitivity common to the period, it is clear that he, like Picasso, discerned in them a means of exploding the stable self-images which seemed to govern Western culture.

Now we may began to grasp the object of 'the great negative work of destruction' which Dada had set out to accomplish (*SML*, 12). For while Dada's spirit of negation is generally understood as merely anti-bourgeois polemic, it actually entails a more complex unleashing of violence *against the self*. Certainly, Dada revels in its own 'cruelty', thus perpetuating that decadent bequest to the avant-garde which associates a radical aesthetics with a certain 'sadism'. In the case of Dada, such cruelty manifests itself in a relentless 'honesty' and a corrosive laughter.[35] Yet since Dada is founded in a spirit of absolute contradiction, such cruelty must also be turned back against the self which inflicts it; so 'Punch yourself in the face and drop dead,' advises Tzara (*SML*, 28); and 'The principle "Love thy neighbour" is hypocrisy. "Know thyself" is utopian, but more acceptable because it includes malice. No pity' (*SML*, 5).

The death drive of the decadent phase seems to reappear here, but where for the *fin de siècle* writers this had led to fantasies of literal self-extinction and mutilation, for the Dadaists it is the ego, the self's imaginary identity, which becomes the ultimate object of violence. This begins as moral critique directed against the predatory nationalisms dismembering Europe. So Arp, for example, in 1915 defines visual works 'constructed with lines, surfaces, forms, and colors. They strive to surpass the human and achieve the infinite and the eternal. They are *a negation of man's egotism*';[36] and Ball offers a similar critique of 'individualism':

The accentuated 'I' has constant interests, whether they be greedy, dictatorial, vain or lazy. It always follows appetites, so long as it does not become absorbed in society. Whoever renounces his interests, renounces his 'I'. The 'I' and the interests are identical. Therefore, the individualistic-egoistic ideal of the Renaissance ripened to the general union of the mechanized appetites which we now see before us, bleeding and disintegrating.[37]

Tzara takes this one step further, aligning 'instinct' with the principle of unresolved contradiction to create a force which liberates the psyche by destroying its stable identity. For that stability belongs to an art which dutifully reflects to the bourgeois an ideal image of self-unity and bodily coherence, a 'cultural' personality, we might say, which seems purged of appetite and desire. In his construction of Dada, Tzara seems to recognise that aggressivity towards others actually originates in a primordial aggressivity *towards oneself*,[38] and the implication of his thought is that 'instinct' (or 'nature') is capable of destroying the cultural fabrication which is the 'ego'. The instincts, in this sense, may perform a work of disarticulation comparable to the death drive as Freud would shortly define it in *Beyond the Pleasure Principle* (1920); and for Tzara, as for Freud, this drive towards dissolution would also produce a paradoxical pleasure as it worked to overcome the constraints of the ego.[39]

The 'great negative work of destruction' on which Dada set its sights thus went far beyond the Futurist attack on cultural tradition. As Sloterdijk acutely observes, 'the Dadaist hatred of culture is logically directed inwardly, against the culture-in-me that I once "possessed" and that now is good for nothing'.[40] So, records Tzara, 'We have done violence to the snivelling tendencies in our natures' (*SML*, 10), rooting out 'culture' to reveal 'the new man', 'Uncouth, galloping, riding astride on hiccups' (*SML*, 7). Nature and life are 'idiotic' and 'Dada is senseless like nature', as Arp puts it,[41] a situation which stalls any dialectic and denies the dream of analytic mastery. We are left with Tzara's own terse expression of absolute contradiction: 'Order = disorder; ego = non-ego; affirmation = negation' (*SML*, 7).

Just as ego 'is' what it is not (nature), so nature, according to this 'logic', is a perfect expression of the mechanical – a chain of association which makes the self not only a mechanism devoid of 'sense', but one which seems to desire above all things its own extinction. This type of thought is 'made in the mouth', according to Tzara (*SML*, 35); that is, it articulates itself as a process of self-contradiction and refuses to countenance 'illusory conclusions and centres' (*SML*, 11). Dada thus goes out of its way to produce a kind of conceptual deadlock, leaving absolute irony as the only valid mode of self-consciousness. The effects of this reduction are powerfully felt in the works of Picabia and Marcel Duchamp, where the human lingers only as a sort of metaphorical trace in a world otherwise refined (or debased) to pure mechanism. In Picabia's mecanomorphic drawings and Duchamp's *Large Glass* (1912–23), for example, humour is joined to a rigorous asceticism; in contrast to Tzara's scatological vision of the fragmented body, these works produce a mechanisation of the erotic whose irony lies precisely in its failure to satisfy desire. For in marked contrast to the technological fantasies of the Italian Futurists, Duchamp's machines do not work, their mechanism often providing no clue to their function and thereby presenting a scandal to the pragmatic intelligence.[42] As with his famous 'readymades', these machines separate object from meaning, forcing the spectator to consider them from two completely different points of view at the same time. As Octavio Paz observes in his account of Duchamp, 'The essence of the art is contradiction; it is the plastic equivalent of the pun',[43] and it is precisely that sense of discontinuity which seems to make the non-fulfilment of desire in this 'celibate machine' a testimony to the power of the ironic intelligence.[44]

*   *   *

Duchamp's own form of irony – 'meta-irony', as he later called it[45] – was, however, of a particularly complex kind, being, as Paz explains, 'an irony that destroys its own negation and, hence, returns in the affirmative'[46]. That aspect of Duchamp's irony pointed forward, to Surrealism, but, by way of contrast, Tzara's brand of ironic negation was coming to seem increasingly like a dead end. Returning to Berlin in 1917, Huelsenbeck quickly became the most outspoken of his critics, arguing that Tzara's version of Dada negation remained purely aesthetic: 'While Tzara was still writing: "*Dada ne signifie rien*" – in Germany Dada lost its art-for-art's sake character with its very first move.'[47] In contrast to neutral Zurich, Berlin was now 'the city of tightened stomachers, of mounting, thundering hunger, where hidden rage was transformed into boundless money lust, and men's minds were concentrating more and more on questions of naked existence'.[48] The revolution of November 1918, focused around workers' action in Kiel, Munich and Berlin, produced a general strike in January of the next year and an attempted communist revolution in Berlin. The Left was, however, quickly crushed (Karl Liebknecht and Rosa Luxemburg were assassinated) and the new republic came into being under the aegis of the Social Democrats. Huelsenbeck and Dadaist colleagues like Raoul Hausmann, Wieland Herzfelde and John Heartfield now took a defiant stand as polemicists and satirists. Here Dada made a decisively new turn, shifting away from the aesthetic preoccupations of the Zurich group towards the political photomontage of Heartfield and the biting satire of George Grosz. Outside Berlin, Dada adopted different, less overtly political forms, centring around the visual art of Max Ernst in Cologne and Kurt Schwitters in Hanover.

While German Dada thus moved away from specifically literary concerns, Tzara was now busy transplanting his own anti-aesthetic from Zurich to Paris, where he took up residence in January 1920. 'Europe was accessible again',[49] and Tzara was only too ready to follow the suggestion of André Breton to move his operations to Paris. The next three years saw another burst of Dada activity, though one which was increasingly torn by disagreements and internal rivalries. The strains were due in part to the sheer receptiveness of post-war Paris, and while Berlin was torn by civil war, the French capital soon 'spoiled Dada to death',[50] as outrage became increasingly a matter of expectation and routine. In the brief moment before it was eclipsed by Breton's Surrealism, though, Paris Dada made its own distinctive contribution. Following Tzara's lead, the emphasis was not primarily a political one, though the interest in theatre during this phase linked Dada negativity to that anti-Oedipal strain which had already run so deep in avant-

234 *Modernisms: A Literary Guide*

garde drama in France and Germany. Now Tzara's concept of subversive 'fantasy' acquired clearer objectives as theatre became once more a site in which to contest patriarchal power.

The shift may be understood in terms of Tzara's quarrel with psychoanalysis, which he had dismissed in the 1918 manifesto as 'a dangerous disease, it deadens man's anti-real inclinations and systematises the bourgeoisie' (*SML*, 9). In so far as psychoanalysis seems to Tzara to inhibit the impulse to fantasy, so it shares the limitations of conventional theatre:

> every bourgeois is a little playwright, who invents different subjects and who, instead of situating suitable characters on the level of his own intelligence, like chrysalises on chairs, tries to find causes or objects (according to whichever psychoanalytic method he practises) to give weight to his plot, a talking and self-defining story. Every spectator is a plotter, if he tries to explain a word (to know!). From his padded refuge of serpentine complications, he allows his instincts to be manipulated. Whence the sorrow of conjugal life. (*SML*, 4)

Dada's brutal intervention in 'this little cerebral domestic scene' (*SML*, 90) aims to sweep away the narrative forms of the bourgeois drama by harnessing the energy of an 'unconscious' which escapes both representation and the bounds of the Oedipal scene: 'there is no common basis in humanity's brains', declares Tzara, 'The unconscious is inexhaustible and uncontrollable. Its strength is beyond us. It is as mysterious as the last particle of the brain cell. Even if we are familiar with it, who would dare state that we could reconstruct it as a viable generator of thoughts?' (*SML*, 109).[51] The implication is that a Dada theatre would employ free-floating fantasy to undermine the fixity of the Oedipal plot and in so doing would attack the ego by releasing the self from the trammels of the family narrative.

While French avant-garde dramatists had very little contact with or knowledge of the obsessive plots which dominated the German stage,[52] lack of familiarity with Expressionist theatre did not stop the Dada writers from contesting some of its main preoccupations. In fact contempt for the family as both social institution and dramatic scene quickly became part of the avant-garde posture in France, leading to the creation of a theatre in which a polemical confrontation with the Oedipal plot was closely bound up with a programme of formal innovation. By the mid-1920s there was little to surprise in Louis Aragon's claim that

> Today there is no longer material for even a vaudeville skeleton in the Oedipus story: should any author use it, he would be hissed off the stage. The same holds true for other stories of this kind. No one conceals his incestuous loves any longer. ... In fifty years, under the influence of DADA, parricides will be acquitted with the congratulations of the jury.[53]

Aragon's attitude to the Oedipal story seems contradictory (he dismisses it only to reappropriate it for its potential to shock) until we observe that he rejects it primarily as a model of *concealment*. The idea of something hidden connects the narrative workings of destiny (the fate of Oedipus) with a theatrical form of representation which is based on something standing for something else.

Aragon's dislike of 'stories' resonates with a general Dada and Surrealist distrust of narrative structure – a distrust of forms which subordinate the immediacy of presentation to some kind of external textual authority. And it is not simply that the story of Oedipus re-tells a series of past events, but that Oedipus himself seems to act out of an obligation to the requirements of narrative structure (as Jonathan Culler puts it, 'Oedipus becomes the murderer of his father not by a violent act that is brought to light but by bowing to the demands of narrative coherence and deeming the act to have taken place'[54]). The Oedipal story seems, then, to be deeply implicated in the logic of narrative – and vice versa.

Dada theatre and performance might be seen as the summation of previous attempts in France to create a drama in which fantasy and the absurd were means by which to challenge the narrative logic of authority. So in place of the shadowy recesses of the Expressionist stage, reminders of a deferred and hidden presence, French avant-garde drama cultivated what Fernand Léger invoked as 'a stage with the minimum of depth' ('Keep to the vertical plane as much as possible', he advised[55]). From the pioneering work of Alfred Jarry and Apollinaire, to the Dada experiments of the early twenties, such 'depthlessness' would be attempted in a variety of ways.

Like Expressionism, these new forms aimed to remove 'psychology' from the stage, substituting intense emotional states or fluid identities for the drama of 'character'. The difference, though, lay in the French hostility to narrative – a legacy of the 'static' Symbolist theatre still in vogue in the twenties – and a related preference for the discontinuous forms of popular culture. Léger was simply summarising a major concern here when he went on to use the circus as his model for the new theatre. Kandinsky, for example, had already opposed the circus to the narrative structure of conventional drama, arguing that 'Clowns, in particular, build their composition on a very definite alogicality. Their action has no definite development, their movements are incongruous, their efforts lead nowhere and, indeed, they're not meant to.'[56] Lack of motivation and of clear direction: these elements contributed to a 'depthlessness' and play which disputed the absent authority of the 'paternal' text.

If French avant-garde theatre begins with Alfred Jarry's *Ubu Rex* (1896) it is because in that work, with its deliberately schematic, one-dimensional *mise en scène*,[57] the repudiation of the Father seems the very condition of formal innovation. In the person of Pa Ubu, Jarry both lampooned the bourgeois patriarch and, more importantly, reduced the father figure to the quintessential expression of all that is weak and bestial in ordinary humanity. This dehumanisation of 'Man' – Ubu acts, says Jarry, 'with all the authority of the Ape'[58] – made theatre a sort of child's revenge (as it was, literally, in Jarry's own case), a return to ludic forms and a refusal of the closed structures of the 'historical dramas' Jarry loathed.[59] Playful this may be, but Pa Ubu cuts a monstrous and in many ways terrifying figure: in portraying him, Jarry has destroyed the transcendent privilege of the Father and made submission to his law a mark of degeneracy rather than of accession to maturity.

Jarry's opposition of theatrical fantasy to the constraints of social identities reappeared in the 'surrealism' of Apollinaire's *The Breasts of Tiresias* (1917) and, even more extremely, in Tzara's *The First Celestial Adventure of Mr. Antipyrine*, originally presented in Zurich in 1916 and revived in Paris in 1920.[60] On this occasion, the performers appeared in large coloured paper sacks, carrying their names on placards.[61] Their 'speeches' were punctuated by what Tzara later described as 'a diabolical machine composed of a klaxon and 3 successive invisible echoes', and the play included a long manifesto-speech by Tzara himself.[62] The decor was minimal, comprising a bicycle wheel borrowed from Marcel Duchamp, some ropes stretched across the stage, and placards carrying what one contemporary reviewer described as 'hermetic inscriptions'.[63]

Just what Monsieur Antipyrine's 'adventure' is remains difficult to say, for the dynamic of the piece derives not from any kind of narrative development but from an outpouring of language. The result is a flux of sound and rhythm, intelligible words and phrases cross-cut with words and sounds modelled on the African poetry which Tzara was translating at this time:[64]

> il n'y a pas d'humanité il y a les réverbères et les chiens
> dzin aha dzin aha bobobo tyao cahiiii hii hii
> héboum
> ièha ièho   (288)

Perhaps for the first time, theatre used language but dispensed with dialogue, the 'characters' becoming enmeshed within the general flow of sound. This was Tzara's ideal of a poetry 'made in the mouth', of 'language [as] a utopia' of liberated bodily energies. The scene seems to be set in a circus, with the 'characters' acting as clowns, but the tricks performed are purely linguistic ones which exploit the material properties of language:

> les chansons des saltimbanques se réunissent familièrement
>   avant
> le départ
> l'*acr*obate *cach*ait un *crachat* dans le ventre
> rendre prendre entre rendre rendre prendre prendre
> en*dran dran*dre
> iuuuuuuuuuuuuupht   (291; my emphases)

In his own speech, Tzara compares this play of sound to that of children's games, where meaning is generated by uncontrolled patterns of similarity and difference within language:

> Art used to be a game of nuts in May, children would go gathering words that had a final ring, then they would exude, shout out the verse, and dress it up in dolls' bootees, and the verse became a queen [*reine*] in order to die a little, and the queen became a whale [*baleine*], the children ran till they were out of breath [*haleine*].   (*SML*, 2, translation modified)

Tzara's challenge to the authority of the absent text is thus conducted on very different ground from that chosen by the early Expressionists. Where their theatre had been locked in a dualistic struggle between discursive order on the one hand, and the lure of a non-linguistic affect on the other, Tzara's Dada theatre seeks to undermine representation from within language.

The First Celestial Adventure was clearly connected with the wave of interest in sound poetry in the pre-war period, but in extending that line of experiment to the theatre Tzara was preparing the ground for a distinctively new form of drama. Sidestepping the dualistic tension between discourse and *mise en scène* which had characterised Expressionism, Tzara opened the possibility of a kind of deconstructive practice within the theatre. His use of sound and rhythm has to be distinguished from that of the *Schreidrama* in so far as that form either employed the purely expressive 'cry' or engaged in emotive distortion of a still recognisable language. Tzara also took care to dissociate his own use of sound from the Futurist tendency to simple onomatopoeia.[65] In *The First Celestial Adventure*, the voice is no longer the bearer of a 'message', but announces the immediate presence of the body. Language becomes a raw material, the 'shit' which is Dada, and the voice is returned to its 'primitive' functions. As Régis Durand observes in another context, 'The voice has to do with flows and desires, not with meaning.'[66] This desire bursts the bounds of the Oedipal triangle, becoming 'social' rather than familial, and making writing itself a form of 'pure' libidinal energy.

If it is apt to term Tzara's theatre 'deconstructive' it is because it does not seek to negate the authority of some absent text through recourse to 'absolute', non-linguistic effects, but rather puts in question the terms of textual authority while continuing to operate within them. This may explain the development within Dada and Surrealist drama which is usually regretted – namely, the emphasis there on linguistic effects at the expense of – those more obviously 'theatrical' innovations to be found in the plays of Apollinaire and Cocteau.[67] From this point of view, *The First Celestial Adventure* is a kind of limit-text, in terms of Tzara's own development and that of the other Dada and Surrealist dramatists. In contrast, *The Second Celestial Adventure of Mr. Antipyrine* (1920) has a tenuous but identifiable thematic 'centre' – a grotesque evocation of child-birth – though the general direction of the piece remains indeterminate (one critic, for example, discerns a 'poetics of rebirth' in the conclusion, while for another *The Second Celestial Adventure* is distinguished from its predecessor by the 'nihilistic tirade' with which it ends[68]). Tzara exploits sound-effects here, though the 'African' idiom is no longer present.

With *The Gas Heart* (1920), Tzara moves from short performance to a parody of the three-act play ('the greatest three-act hoax of the century' [*MFT*, 133]). The 'characters' who appear on stage (Eye, Mouth, Nose, Ear, Neck, and Eyebrow) were originally dressed in vividly painted cardboard costumes (designed by Sonia Delaunay), a visual clue to their one-dimensionality. One main 'theme' of the play seems to be the courtship of Mouth by Eye, and the speeches in the play shift beween deliberately tedious and clichéd exchanges and a more lyrical expression of desire (the Gas Heart suggests, perhaps, the power of love as a kind of life-force). But the 'theme' is once more secondary to the workings of language. Tzara again undermines dialogic connections between the performers, and the movement of the piece derives mainly from the capacity of linguistic items and figures to suggest further development. As Michel Corvin observes, one of the main features of Tzara's language is its literalism:

> If Eye *falls down* after Mouth has left (Act III) it is because he is *struck* by despair before the indifference of his loved one; if Nose and Neck show such calmness, if they demonstrate a superior attitude (notably in Act III), it is because they enjoy an *elevated* position, one of them above the audience, the other above the stage.[69]

Similarly, the peculiar transformation of Mouth into a race-horse (called Clytemnestra!) is triggered by an 'accidental' association earlier in the play:

EYE: Imagine that my dear friend I no longer love her.
EAR: Which one do you mean?
EYE: I mean the one I've loved too long.
EAR: Me too I've lost an illusion. The prize horse in my stable has lost his energy.   (*MFT*, 144)

Thematic development in this way is seen to be generated from the *process* of signification rather than from a set of events reenacted through narrative.

In the other main plays of Paris Dada we find a similar association between the project of an avant-garde theatre and the attempt to negate the Oedipal plot, with its interconnection of father, family, narrative and text. *If You Please* (1920), by André Breton and Philippe Soupault, provides the most programmatic example of the attack on narrative, with each of its three acts quite separate from the others (the authors conclude the play by noting that they 'do not want the fourth act printed' [*MFT*, 173]). The play – an early experiment in automatic writing – parodies boulevard themes, but is less radical than the work of Tzara (in a later interview, Soupault described it as '"a loosening of the theatre." One act had nothing to do with the other'[70]). Each act gives us an illusion of 'plot': Act I deals with a love triangle and ends inexplicably with the lover murdering the woman; Act II centres on the exploits of a detective and is full of unresolved 'clues'; Act III brings together a man and a prostitute in a bar. The play is deliberately discontinuous ('Perhaps only desire exists', observes Valentine at the end of Act I).

Soupault later recalled that the play had 'an extremely simple staging – "giving the importance to the text" – there was no stage setting'.[71] This apparently straightforward dependence on the text was, however, complicated by the non-dialectical conception of dialogue which André Breton was to develop further in the 1924 *Manifesto of Surrealism*. In dialogue, he argued, 'My attention, prey to an entreaty which it cannot in all decency reject, treats the opposing thought as an enemy; in ordinary conversation, it "takes it up" almost always on the words, the figures of speech, it employs; it puts me in a position to turn it to good advantage in my reply by distorting them' (*MS*, 34). The aim of the Surrealist dialogue, he continued, was to free 'both interlocutors from any obligations of politeness':

> Each of them simply pursues his soliloquy without trying to derive any special dialectical pleasure from it and without trying to impose anything whatsoever on his neighbour. The remarks exchanged are not, as is generally the case, meant to develop some thesis, however unimportant it may be; they are as disaffected as possible.   (*MS*, 35)

Something more than non-communication is involved here, for it is as if these soliloquies are spoken from somewhere else. Yet we are hearing this voice neither as a mark of self-presence nor as some absent textual authority; it is, as Breton puts it in the second manifesto (1930), 'a voice which converses with us most specifically about something other than what we believe we are thinking, and upon occasion assumes a serious tone when we feel most light-hearted or deals in idle prattle when we are unhappiest' (*MS*, 158). The voice of the unconscious, then, but less the unconscious as a

Surrealist repertoire of images and scenes than the unconscious as Dada violence and negation: the unconscious as a pre-individual source of violence and energy rather than of subjective representations of what is hidden.

'Perhaps only desire exists ...': this desire is close to what Antonin Artaud would later call 'the Force of Nature' ('The Force of *Nature* is the Law, and this Law is the *Nature of things* ...' [*AA*, 406]); it underlies the dark irony which is one of the most distinctive features of Dada theatre. In Georges Ribemont-Dessaignes's *The Mute Canary* (1919), for example, comedy is bred from Dada 'indifference' to the meaningless 'Nature of things'. Catching this tone, a contemporary critic astutely related this play to the French vogue for early American cinema (especially that of Chaplin), comparing Ribemont-Dessaignes's irony with 'those improbable [cinematic] adventures in which man is like the sport and resigned victim of the malignity of the elements'.[72] *The Mute Canary* shares with other Dada and Surrealist plays this strain of macarbre comic cruelty, a black humour which invests all relationships with violence – and, more importantly, a violence generated not by some transcendent narrative design, but by the force of a desire which speaks through the characters.

If the claims of narrative are constantly disputed in this drama, it is because no social structure exists to contain such violence, which is to say that no Father can produce that transcendent law which will set in place the forms of order. Hence the scandal which the impotent paternal word provokes in these plays; and hence, too, the irony which asserts itself as the only alternative to a belief in either structure or vacuum. In Ribemont-Dessaignes's short play, for example, the mutual hatred of man and wife (Riquet and Barate) leads to the accidental killing of wife and lover. Riquet, a pompous, Ubuesque figure, spends most of the play sitting 'majestically' on top of a ladder (the only prop to be used), indulging in fantasies of power and government, while Barate (or 'Messalina', as she prefers to call herself) pursues her 'insatiable' desires with Ochre, a Negro who believes himself to be the composer Gounod. *The Mute Canary* develops themes of illusion and delusion, with characters locked into themselves, and in each case (female) desire collides with violent (male) tyranny. Such darkly ironic views of the domestic scene gain in intensity from the playful vaudeville forms through which they are developed. In fact, 'play' here begins to assume again that 'cruelty' which it had in *Ubu Rex* and it is now directly related to the way in which these writers use theatrical fantasy to subvert the authority of father and text.

*   *   *

This form of irony had its limitations, though, amply summed up in Ribemont-Dessaignes's own litany of questions: 'What is beautiful? What is ugly? What is great, strong, weak? ... What am I? Don't know, don't know, don't know.'[73] Once a radical gesture, that 'don't know' had come to represent what André Breton now criticised as the 'intellectual poverty' of Dada, its confinement to a 'vicious circle' of its own making.[74] Other artistic currents were circulating, and in addition to Breton's own move towards Surrealism a certain neo-classicism was making its mark on the Parisian scene. The complex interplay of different aesthetic elements at this time is clear from Apollinaire's essay on 'The New Spirit and the Poets', published shortly after his death in 1918.[75] The piece voices some now familiar avant-garde concerns – the importance of experiments in 'visual lyricism', the view that 'Surprise is the greatest source of what is new', the commitment to the 'everyday event' as a source of poetry – but rather unexpectedly these are presented as examples of a 'new spirit' which 'strives above all to inherit from the classics a sound good sense, a sure critical spirit'. This spirit is French – after the war, 'art increasingly has a country', in Apollinaire's view – and 'France abhors disorder. She readily questions fundamentals, but she has a horror of chaos.' The lyricism of the 'new spirit', then, is remote from 'the excesses of the Italian and Russian futurists', whose verbal experiments Apollinaire now sees as merely 'imitative harmony', 'the imitation of a noise to which no lyric, tragic, or pathetic meaning can be attached'.

The conflation of classicist and avant-garde elements in Apollinaire's essay reflects certain tensions in his own work, but it also points to the diverse currents circulating within the Parisian milieu. The important journal *North–South* (1917–19), edited by Pierre Reverdy, exemplifies this interweaving of Cubist, Dadaist and neo-classicist strands, its contributors including Apollinaire, Breton, Tzara, Aragon, Soupault, Paul Dermée, Max Jacob and the

Chilean poet Vicente Huidobro. Cubism continued to be a major force for many of these writers, though it too had begun to move in a new direction. The war had brought calls for a stronger national identity, with Cubist painting coming increasingly under attack as a species of 'Munich' art.[76] Works like Jeanneret and Ozenfant's *After Cubism* (1918) and Severini's *From Cubism to Classicism* (1921) exemplified a critical turn against Cubism, and those who sought now to defend avant-garde painting did so by identifying it with the 'Latin' virtues of clarity, order and proportion.[77] By 1917, even Apollinaire was affirming the essential 'latinity' of Cubism,[78] and in the same year *North–South* was launched, with Paul Dermée's programmatic claim that 'A period of exuberance and force must be followed by a period of organisation, stocktaking, and science, that's to say a classicist age.'[79] That sense of a new period was instigated in part by the changes wrought within Cubism itself, as painters like Picasso, Severini and Juan Gris showed a stronger interest in ideas of restraint and design, with precision of line preferred to more 'painterly' effects.[80]

The desire for some sort of return to 'classical' values had, in fact, pre-dated the war, and we have already remarked Charles Maurras's campaign against 'feminine' Romanticism. With the new vogue for classicism, however, and the increasing prominence in the Parisian scene of Maurras's political movement *Action française*, the terms of this conservative aesthetic gained a second lease of life (by 1918 even Maurras's poetry would be praised by Apollinaire[81]). Aesthetic discussion now resounded with calls to order, as critics launched a series of attacks not only on Dada, but on the forms of *dynamism* which had animated the arts before the war. The Cubist and neo-classical perspectives converged here, in an attack on romantic habits of confusing art and life. Cendrars's earlier declaration that 'Literature is part of life. It is not something separate'[82] suddenly seemed to some to epitomise a degraded Romanticism, as did earlier Futurist fantasies of a rhythmic 'compenetration' of subject and object.

The influential critic Julien Benda may have had Cendrars in mind when, in *Belphégor* (1918), he dismissed claims for 'an abolition of the distinction between the artist and things, for a dissolution of his personality in their soul, for the disappearance of all judgement, of all its power of transcendence in relation to things'.[83] Benda was deeply contemptuous of 'that gluttonous thirst for immediacy which characterises the moderns' (15), and he may well have been thinking of a work like Cendrars's *Profound Today* when deriding 'the desire for a sort of sexual invasion of things' (9) and 'the aphasic union with the soul of reality' (14) which the modern 'veneration for art which conveys *life itself*' (84) seemed to him to produce. For Benda, the modern sensibility took two main forms: either it could be 'plastic', in which case it was 'centred' and 'collected', or it was 'musical', a condition marked by 'a sort of decentring of consciousness, in diffused and scattered sensation, a major source of intoxication and vertigo' (41). Modernity, in Benda's view, was afflicted by this second type of sensibility, whose purest expression he discerned in the twentieth-century obsession with the 'empathetic' modes of *theatre* (82).

People were now beginning to talk about a new literary tendency, 'Cubist poetry', which seemed quite at odds with both dynamism and Dada. The phrase had already been used occasionally, with critic Georges Polti predicting a 'Cubist poetry' as early as 1912.[84] But it was only in 1917, with the publication of a volume of essays by Frédéric Lefèvre, that writers as different as Apollinaire, Reverdy, Cendrars, Cocteau and Jacob were grouped together as 'Cubist'.[85] Lefèvre's account proved controversial, and while Jacob, for example, had no objection to the term, Reverdy was quick to insist that 'Cubist poetry doesn't exist' (*NS*, 145).[86] Most critical discussions which have taken the designation seriously have tended to make largely metaphorical use of the analogy with painting, suggesting, for example, that the multiple perspectives of Cubism are paralleled in the movements of Apollinaire's poems, that the writing of 'Cubist' poets operates like collage, that Reverdy uses prepositional phrases to 'suggest arrangements of abstract horizontal and vertical lines'.[87] The important thing, however, is perhaps the simplest, namely that these writers all had close connections with contemporary painters, and that their work was profoundly shaped by the questioning of representation in the visual arts.

Different writers, of course, drew different lessons from the painters: while, as we saw in Chapter 6, Apollinaire and Cendrars used the analogy to explore certain forms of unrepresentability, for writers like Reverdy, Jacob and Huidobro the principal discovery of Cubism is that of art's essential *autonomy*. Reverdy's sense of a 'plastic' writing requires, as he puts it, 'a certain *distance* between its own terms and *objects in reality*. This is exactly what the Cubist painters have the supreme merit of having done for the first time in history.'[88] Max Jacob's preface to his 1917 book of prose poems, *The*

Dice Cup, similarly emphasises that 'the work of art must be distant from the subject. That's why it must be *situated*.'[89] And 'situatedness' for Jacob is equivalent to 'transplanting' experience from the real world to an aesthetic one ('To surprise is nothing, one must *transplant*'). The work becomes hermetic and self-sufficient: 'The situation distances, that is, it excites the artistic feeling; one recognizes that it's situated by the little shock that one gets from it or again from the margin which surrounds it, the special atmosphere where it moves.'[90] That idea of *framing* a chaotic reality rather than immersing oneself in it is also the motive behind Vicente Huidobro's concept of 'creationism'. Huidobro was trying to invent what he called 'created poetry, without relation to the external world' and his encounter with the Parisian writers and artists led him to share some of their conclusions. As he put it in a preface to *Square Horizon* (also 1917), his main objective was 'To create a poem by taking the elements of life and transforming them to give a new and independent life of their own. Nothing descriptive or anecdotal. Emotion must be born from the creative strength alone.'[91]

With that shift of emphasis went a new interest in defining the aesthetic; and Reverdy observes that in the pre-war period 'it wasn't a matter of aesthetics; no one thought about it, especially in poetry where fantasy and the widest possible freedom were the only rules given and allowed' (*NS*, 167). Then, in 1916, 'the moment came when one could talk about aesthetics … because the period was concerned with organisation, with the mustering of ideas, because *fantasy gave way to a greater need for structure*' (*NS*, 173–4). This comment epitomises Reverdy's break with forms of dynamism and Dada, both of which seem to him to degrade art to unconscious 'fantasy'. That word occurs in numerous places in his essays, always with a strong negative implication. In 'On Cubism', for example, he explains that Cubist painting seeks not to represent objects but to deploy them as 'elements' within a composition so as to detach 'what is eternal and constant … and to exclude the rest'. It is this aim rather than 'the arbitrary fantasy of the painter' which governs Cubist techniques of 'deformation' (*NS*, 19).

Reverdy's use of this word 'fantasy' seems to denote a form of unregulated imagination (the French word can apply to both the activity of mind and its product) which deals in the currency of the immediate and 'anecdotal'. The word also, of course, carries associations of 'trivial', 'whimsical', and so on. But in the period between 1914 and 1925, *fantaisie* had several other connotations.[92] Since

Reverdy pits it against the 'intelligence', we might suspect some link here to an idea of the unconscious. In French psychoanalytic theory, the term usually employed for Freud's *Phantasie* is *fantasme*,[93] though early works, such as Samuel Jankélévitch's influential *Introduction à la psychanalyse* (1922), regularly employed *fantaisie*.[94]

It is unlikely that Reverdy was familiar with such texts, but the vogue for neo-classicism in France was very closely bound up with a rejection of all things 'Teutonic', not least amongst which was, of course, the work of Freud. Psychoanalysis in this respect seemed the very antithesis of 'latinity'; as the psychologist Angelo Hesnard complained in 1924, there was a general tendency in France to compare *Freudisme* to 'a mental epidemic which has already swamped the Anglo-Saxon countries and which is coming to beat with its rising waves the fortunately unshakeable base of the latin spirit'.[95] In this context, *fantaisie* came to be associated not only with a kind of impressionism and self-indulgence, but with dementia, anarchy and Teutonic depravity.[96] Right-wing nationalism hardly lies behind Reverdy's use of the word, but he does seem to associate it with an uncontrolled immersion in sensation – an immersion which, like Cendrars's 'plunge' into modernity, leads to an apocalyptic conflation of life and art:

> To create a work of art which has its own independent life, its own reality, and which is an end in itself, seems nobler to us than any sort of whimsical [*fantaisiste*] interpretation of real life, which is hardly less slavish than faithful imitation.... (*NS*, 41)

Note the rather unexpected alignment here of fantasy with a form of mimesis. If *fantaisie* implies an unconscious process of image-making, in contrast to the careful selection and combination of 'elements' from the real, Reverdy is arguing that the danger of unconsciousness is that it leaves us in an immediate and 'slavish' relation to reality.

For 'Cubist' writing, 'Reality does not motivate the work of art. One moves away from life in order to reach another reality' (*NS*, 117). That other reality is quite distinct from both the external world and the domain of the poet's own feeling; the poem becomes a completely self-sufficient construction rather than an expression of something else. Reverdy is firmly opposed to the kind of free association often favoured by the Dadaists and, later, the Surrealists,

emphasising instead the importance of composition and formal reduction. Yet his commitment to 'steadiness, immobility, structure'
(*NS*, 179) and his view that 'there is no art without discipline' (*NS*,
121) are coupled with a concept of juxtaposition which is far
removed from Maurrassian traditionalism:

> The poet thinks in unconnected fragments, separate ideas,
> images formed by contiguity; the prose writer expresses himself
> by developing a series of ideas which are already in him and
> which remain logically bound together. He unfurls them. The
> poet juxtaposes and rivets, in the best instances, the different
> parts of the work whose main merit is precisely that of not indi-
> cating too clear a reason for being thus associated.[97]

This later comment recalls Reverdy's influential concept of the
image:

> The image is a pure creation of the mind.

> It cannot be born from a comparison but from a juxtaposition of
> two or more distant realities.

> The more the relationship between the two juxtaposed realities is
> distant and true, the stronger the image will be – the greater its
> emotional power and poetic reality. ...   (*NS*, 73)

Reverdy's theory is quite different from Pound's: the power of the
image is not gauged in relation to the thing compared, and the
image is not in any sense an 'equation' for something else.[98]
Juxtaposition also functions differently as a technique: here the
poet proceeds like the Cubist painter, as Kenneth Rexroth explains:

> There is one subject, a still life, the *Pont Neuf*, a girl with a guitar.
> The elements of that subject are broken up and dissociated both
> in space and time and recombined in a new, more esthetically
> powerful whole, but still the same subject.[99]

Where the collage techniques of Pound and Eliot are, says Rexroth,
allusive and evocative, 'held together by an armature of narrative
and mood', this Cubist method deals with elements deprived of
any context beyond that of the poem's emerging syntactical

structure. Such poetry parallels the Cubist 'deformation' of the real by its assault on the sequential and causal logic we associate with ordinary experience. Where the habit of allusion in Pound's and Eliot's work always invokes a larger narrative order to which the fragment may ultimately be referred, here the only significant relationships lie within the poem's own field, in that 'invisible or subliminal discourse which owes its cogency to its own strict, complex and secret logic', as Rexroth puts it.[100]

Jacob's prose poems exploit this discovery in a deviously playful way, with the structure of the text shaped less by reference than by phonetic and semantic association. The focus of these short works is constantly changing as Jacob allows assonance and rhyme to create a flow of puns and internal allusions. Jacob chooses material of an anecdotal or descriptive kind and then sets himself the challenge of 'situating' it, of distancing it through artifice from any explanatory context. In the long sequence 'The Cock and the Pearl', for example:

> Mille bouquets de bosquets, mille bosquets de bouquets et mille camomilles. Si tu veux, ma gentille, tu mettras ta mantille. La mare a, dans la nuit, des vertèbres aussi profondément vertes que les mousses de mes pistils.

> (A thousand bouquets of groves, a thousand groves of bouquets and a thousand camomiles. If you wish, my sweet, you put on your mantilla. The pool has, in the darkness, vertebrae as deeply green as the mosses of my pistils.)[101]

The first two words provide the basis for a series of lyric variations, with the hyperbolic 'mille' (a thousand) setting up a chain of seductive implications (camomiles, the mantilla, the pistils all held together by assonance). Running behind that chain of phonetic associations are several others: 'tu met*tras*'/'La ma*re a*', 'vertes'/'vertèbres', and the sequence of sounds in 'que les mousses' seems an inverted reprise of the 'mille bosquets/bouquets' theme of the first sentence. Such effects make the poem seem like an object with planes and facets, inducing pleasure as it weaves elements from reality into new and unexpected forms.

Although equally concerned with this type of poetic autonomy, the work of Reverdy is more austere, less receptive to the playful and bizarre than Jacob's. Reverdy, much preoccupied with questions of religious faith and belief, is constantly concerned with the relation of perception to reality, and with the 'barrier' that seems to interpose itself between the poet and the real. A certain Platonism attaches to his sense of a 'static' art which can penetrate beyond appearance and express something 'eternal',[102] but this aesthetic is also coloured by a kind of humility, which makes most of Reverdy's poems explorations of the 'barrier' itself rather than of some revelatory vision. In Reverdy's deliberately reduced poetic lexicon, words associated with liminal spaces play a major part (thresholds, doors, windows, holes, borders, the horizon, walls, curtains), and the attempt at some kind of passage or movement across the barrier between perception and reality functions not simply as a figure for a desired transcendence but as a constant reminder of lack and incompleteness. In fact, in one of his later essays he defines poetry as 'an absence, a lack in man's heart',[103] and the implication is that the autonomy of the work which is so fundamental to Reverdy's aesthetics depends on an internal lack which needs to be supplemented by an 'outside' (that which has either been excluded from the poem or cannot be encompassed by it). So while Reverdy's poems seek to 'frame' a chaotic reality, any totalising claims for mastery or 'intelligence' are compromised by an alterity which creates the structure which appears to exclude it.

Perhaps this explains the curious combination of control and fragmentation which characterises his work, for the lacunary structure of the poem seems to arise at the point of 'intersection of two planes with a cruelly sharp edge, those of the dream and reality' (*NS*, 211). This way of talking of an 'intersection' shows again Reverdy's deliberate refusal of any uncontrolled fantasy. The combination of elements is deliberate and calculated, suggesting (in marked contrast to Dada) not only that the unconscious has a structure but also that it exists as an alternative scene *within* thought. The poem then entails a mapping of that complex and ambiguous space which is what Rexroth calls 'the syntax of the mind itself'.

Take, for example, 'False Door or Portrait', one of the best-known poems in *Roof Slates* (1918) and, with its reduced phrasing, spatial layout and deictic indeterminacy, highly characteristic of the work as a whole:

> In the space which lies there
> Between four lines
>   A square where white plays

The hand which held your cheek

Moon

A face which lights up

The profile of another

But your eyes

I am the lamp guiding myself

Finger on damp eyelid

In the midst

The tears flow in this space

Between four lines

Mirror[104]

The square 'Between four Lines' is at once the space of the door (mentioned only in the title) and the frame of portrait and mirror; it is also, in a typically self-reflexive move, the 'framing' of experience which the poem itself attempts. The portrait seems to be a 'false door' because it promises access to a stable image of the self, but even though the poem finally reveals that the frame contains a mirror, the 'space' obstructs any simple sense of identity, diffusing the self in the play of pronouns ('your eyes', but 'I am the lamp guiding myself'). The frame, then, does not lead us to the place of safety and coherence we crave, but triggers instead a sense of loss ('The tears flow in this space'), for the speaker pursues himself only to discover 'The profile of another'.

Here, as in many of these poems, fragmented phrases under high syntactical tension produce a world tipped towards hallucination, a world of part-objects and half-glimpsed presences. This is the medium in which, for Reverdy, the unconscious speaks: not in the 'bodily' outpourings of Dada fantasy, but in a syntax whose gaps and breaks mark the passage of desire through language. This articulation of what we might call the textual unconscious would soon allow Reverdy's version of neo-classicism to become the springboard for André Breton's Surrealism, an aesthetic which might seem at first sight its diametric opposite.

11

Other Times: The Narratives of High Modernism

On the other side of the Channel, the post-war years also saw a growing concern with 'order' and 'structure', though here its results would be very different. As we have seen in earlier chapters, the 'Men of 1914' version of modernism derived much of its energy from an attack on modernity. The polemical thrust given here to an anti-mimetic art was directed against the imitative tendencies associated with the mass politics of a democratic age in which, as Lewis put it, 'the life of the crowd' forces man to 'live only through others, outside himself'.[1] One of the first moves of this modernism had been to reconstitute the self as closed, autonomous, and antagonistic. At the same time, though, this construction of the self eschewed any form of romantic individualism: notions of authenticity and spontaneity were discarded as so many trappings of the democratic age, and the 'Men of 1914' stressed instead the self's *un*originality, its embeddedness in a complex cultural tradition. Having made the self autonomous, then, these modernists had no great desire to explore its interior – that was associated with the 'twilight' romanticism of Freud's chaotic unconscious – and the aim was, rather, to avoid a narcissistic individualism by restoring art to the public sphere.

It is worth emphasising the attachment to *public* values since modernism has so often been defined in terms of a turn to subjectivity. For these writers, however, the private life is commonly thought of as the domain of the 'sentimental' unconscious, a place in which, paradoxically, imitative behaviour is the rule. The resulting preference for the 'public' indicates an important new emphasis, as we can see by comparing Henry James's complaints about the 'complete proscription of privacy' in America.[2] James's disorientation in the new public spaces of hotels contrasts markedly with, say, Lewis's preoccupation with bars and *pensions* in his early Breton stories.[3] For Lewis, these are privileged spaces of adult hospitality, spaces freed from the claustrophobic constraints of the domestic scene, and his subsequent critique of modernity focuses on the disappearance of an authentically public sphere. For '[t]he present age is a private age in-the-making',[4] with genuine sociality now overtaken by the 'personal life': 'Each individual, when he got the chance, became a little universe to himself of exclusive personal life.'[5] The irony, of course, is that this 'personal life' is now thoroughly mediated by a culture of consumption in which, Lewis argues, as work becomes less important than play, 'this part of life into which all the cultural activities would be pressed would now become the *serious* part'.[6]

A society defining itself in terms of leisure is thus one in which life becomes increasingly aestheticised: 'art' provides the collective representations of a 'private' life which is founded in the rituals of imitation. Hence the indictment in *Tarr* of life as 'a tawdry zone of half-art' (20), for it is not simply that modern existence has been invaded by 'artistic' values, with the process of commodification governed more and more by the criterion of the 'beautiful'; to this we must add that modernity's degraded aesthetic produces an iconography bound by the frozen time of passive identification. As Lewis puts it:

> The world in which Advertisement dwells is a one-day world. It is necessarily a plane universe, without depth. Upon this Time lays down discontinuous entities, side by side; each day, each temporal entity, complete in itself, with no perspectives, no fundamental external reference at all.[7]

The lack of 'external reference' and the idea of claustrophobic enclosure ('each day ... complete in itself') connect Lewis's critique of advertising with his campaign for '*public* values, in contrast to the *private* values of the half-lighted places of the mind'.[8]

A developing consumerism thus conspired with the traumatic disruption of the war years to create the paradox of a timeless culture obsessed with 'timely' presentations of itself. Lewis's view – and it was one shared by the other 'Men of 1914' – was that modernity's aestheticisation of life called for an antagonistic art which would save history from being dissolved in mere style. Exactly what 'history' might entail was to be a bone of contention amongst these modernists, but there was broad agreement about the need to re-invent constructive social narratives at a time when politics seemed to be being overtaken by a hegemony of fashion and advertising.[9] In different ways, Pound, Eliot, Joyce and Lewis now set out to redefine the self as the narrator of what I have previously called a 'belated' history.[10] As in Freud's account of the Wolf Man (1918), an event in the past requires a second event to release its traumatic force. The first event belongs to the subject's past but is experienced as something foreign when it is restructured through memory.[11] This model of interactive temporalities seems exceedingly sugges-tive in view of the intense cultural allusiveness which distinguishes Anglo-American modernism from its European counterparts. Where the continental avant-gardes had defined modernism as a phenomenon of rupture, the absolutely 'new' appearing over the corpse of the old, for the 'Men of 1914' (with, as we shall see, one major exception), modernism is inextricably enmeshed with cultural tradition. Eliot's *The Waste Land* (1922) begins with the burial of the dead, but those first lines make it clear that desire will remain shack-led to memory, that no fantasy of the 'absolutely modern' can be en-tertained here. This modernism, we might say, is concerned primarily with the new rather than with the original, with the re-constituted rather than with the immediate.[12]

Here modernism begins to fulfil the possibilities explored in Pound's early work (and particularly in his Noh plays), for writing becomes a re-writing, the self saved from the passive mimesis of modernity by imitation of a higher order. Where other avant-gardes had chafed against the constraints of a paternal tradition, this strand of modernism casts the self as the bearer of a troubled history and makes writing a medium in which different temporal-ities intersect. Writing now comes to occupy a space between his-torical memory and imaginative construction – a space which these writers begin to define as 'myth' and 'epic'. Eliot's evocation of April confusing memory and desire does therefore have an oblique relation to Freud's account of trauma, since in each case it is the ar-ticulation of past and present together which promises release from a merely repetitive history and from a perpetual present lacking any hope of transformation.[13]

At least two main lines of development now begin to appear in twenties modernism: one which makes this interplay of historical times the means by which to ensure a certain authorial 'impersonal-ity'; the other (perhaps best represented by Virginia Woolf) is characterised by an interest in the contents of consciousness and the self's labile existence in time. Belatedness, we might say, defines the first, and stream of consciousness the second. The two forms are not, of course, mutually exclusive, and a late modernist work such as William Faulkner's *Absalom, Absalom!* (1936) would explore convergences between the two.

* * *

The different tendencies at play within 'High Modernism' are clear in the varied reactions to Joyce's *Ulysses* (1922), a work to which almost all the leading figures assigned landmark importance. Joyce's narrative of twenty-four hours in Dublin was structured in an intensely programmatic way, its major narrative form taken from Homer's *Odyssey* and supplemented by a wealth of internal corre-spondences and codes. As a writer, Joyce was ostentatiously com-mitted to the Flaubertian ideal of precision, with the result that the large-scale structures of the work were paralleled by an intensive technical concern with the individual sentence.[14] This double focus in the writing may now seem one of the most striking aspects of Joyce's achievement, offering a cogent response to the usual avant-garde objections to 'descriptive' narrative. The other 'Men of 1914', however, paid remarkably little attention to this aspect of *Ulysses*. Pound, for example, while praising the structure of the novel (it 'has more form than any novel of Flaubert's') emphasised its satirical power and its place in the great tradition of realist fiction.[15] Lewis, on the other hand, recognising that the novel must put Joyce 'very high in contemporary letters', found it nonetheless a sort of dead monument to naturalist fiction. *Ulysses* was, for him, a 'time-book', an 'Aladdin's cave of incredible bric-à-brac in which a dense mass of dead stuff is collected'.[16] And where Lewis discerned 'a monument like a record diarrhoea', Eliot's 1923 review in *The Dial* celebrated Joyce's discovery of 'the mythical method': 'a way of controlling, of ordering, of giving a shape and a significance to the immense panorama of futility and anarchy which is contemporary history'.[17]

Eliot's memorable comment condenses several of his own devel-oping preoccupations. First, modernity is anarchic and lacking in any sense of direction; secondly, something which is not 'history' and which is alien to modernity may be invoked as an *external* principle of order; and thirdly, in his discovery of this 'mythical method', Joyce has killed off the novel once and for all – it is, says Eliot, 'a form which will no longer serve' and which effectively 'ended with Flaubert and James' (177). Fiction, it appears, is disabled by its continuing association with forms of realism and this powerful nineteenth-century legacy prevents the novelist from adopting a sufficiently distanced or external view of that modernity which is his subject. In contrast to the 'mythical method', fiction cannot make the modern world 'possible for art' (178) because it remains trapped within it, its moral edge blunted by those nineteenth-century vices of 'cheerfulness, optimism, and hopefulness' ('words [which] stood for a great deal of what one hated in the nineteenth century').[18]

The 'mythical method', it turns out, will reveal what is lacking in a modernity increasingly degraded by the imitative forms of mass politics and consumer culture. Like Pound and Lewis, Eliot is contemptuous of romantic models of authenticity and expressivity – models which, for a writer like D. H. Lawrence, could still offer vital alternatives to an imitative culture – and his appeals to myth and tradition are governed by a desire for an antithetical form of mimesis, one which (as we saw in Chapter 8) might be said to *supplement* its model. In this sense, *Ulysses* appears to add to or exceed its original Homeric narrative even as it signals a lack or incompleteness in the world of modern Dublin.

Such, at any rate, seems to be the fundamental assumption behind Eliot's praise of the 'mythical method'. But how does this negativity relate to what has already been said of this modernism's attempt to constitute a strong subject? Eliot's famous essay on 'Tradition and the Individual Talent' (1919) warns us not to confuse self with 'personality':

> the poet must develop or procure the consciousness of the past and ... should continue to develop this consciousness throughout his career. What happens is a continual surrender of himself as he is at the moment to something which is more valuable. The progress of an artist is a continual self-sacrifice, a continual extinction of personality.[19]

The poet 'surrenders' any delusory sense of the self as original, escaping from his immediate emotion by referring it to the complex articulations of the 'tradition'. Yet while this version of modernism is so much preoccupied with ways of stabilising the self, with fixing it in relation to boundaries and objects, these writers entertain a parallel anxiety about being trapped *inside* the self, in its inchoate and unconscious driftings.

Myth, in contrast to a history bound on the wheel of 'progress', now seems to offer the desired passage between private and public. The result in *The Waste Land* is effectively to freeze history – as Franco Moretti puts it, 'History must no longer be seen as irreversible as regards the past, and mainly unpredictable as regards the future, but as a cyclical mechanism, which is, therefore, fundamentally static: it lacks a truly temporal dimension.'[20] The different movements of the poem, from 'The Burial of the Dead' to 'What the Thunder Said', do not establish a strong forward-moving trajectory but tend rather to create a simultaneity of effect. We might expect that the weave of allusions and citations in the poem would establish a sense of cultural relativity, compelling us to contemplate Western decadence in the context of other cultures. Yet, as Moretti observes, the poem's timelessness works in the opposite way, making it 'the place where a single and immutable structure of values, with negligible variants, establishes itself'.

What the poem seeks to invoke is the voice of an absent authority – later Eliot will discover this in Anglo-Catholicism – but in *The Waste Land* there are only written words, the fragmentary inscriptions in which this distant order may resonate. Yet it is the very secondariness of these words, their removal from any pretension to immediacy and 'presence', that gives them value, for in the absence of any authentically redemptive voice they testify to a refusal of romantic egotism. 'Poetry ... is not the assertion that something is true, but the making that truth more fully real to us', Eliot later remarks in an essay about propaganda, 'Poetry proves successively, or fails to prove, that certain worlds of thought and feeling are *possible*.'[21] *The Waste Land* certainly harbours its fantasy of an alternative order, of a culture in which things of the intellect are not alienated from sensuous lived experience, and where social classes co-exist in a peacefully 'organic' relation, but the poem is unwilling to reduce 'tradition' to 'ideology' by expressing it directly.[22] This is why the redemptive voices always speak from outside the immediate context of the poem, and why (in marked contrast to Pound's *Cantos* or Joyce's *Ulysses*) 'order' is not something to be discovered in the world but to be induced from beyond.

Now we can begin to see how Eliot's own 'mythical method' differs from that of Joyce, for in *The Waste Land* the practice of textual imitation always uses the cultural echo to reveal a vacancy within the modern event to which it is ironically applied. For this reason, now that the poem's allusions have been run to ground, the principal difficulty of the text lies in its play of tones. Take, for example, the passage from 'The Fire Sermon' in which we see the typist alone in her room after the departure of her lover. Their encounter has been neither passionate nor pleasant, merely one routine moment in a life which can never rise above the mechanical. Eliot's characteristically contemptuous view of love among the lower classes would be of little interest if it were not for the deliberately awkward weighting of tones. The woman herself is made to seem thoroughly inconsequential, and the reference to Goldsmith's lines ('When lovely woman stoops to folly') hammers the point home by equating eighteenth-century melancholy (which 'sooths the heart instead of corroding it') with the contemporary world's more blatant reduction of passion to mechanism.[23] Such moments of compound irony show how the 'timelessness' of the poem is complicit with an absoluteness of moral perspective: even though Eliot does not describe her, we know that the typist cannot be 'lovely' and that she has no moral fineness to compromise; more important, we 'know' this because it is strongly implied that no typist would have these qualities in the first place. Eliot's own version of the 'mythic method' thus tends to produce a high degree of local specificity at the level of tone and idiom, while securing a parallel abstractness in its referents.

The quotations and allusions from which *The Waste Land* is quarried may remind us of the ghost-like presences of Pound's Noh plays, but here the trope of a return does not allow the past to be rewritten and transformed, gesturing instead to a sort of inner vacancy within the forms of modern experience. If myth offers a way out of romantic solipsism, then, it is only by illuminating a public sphere whose narrative forms are aborted and broken, no longer able to meet the challenge of 'working up' brutalised emotions into art or, indeed, of 'working through' the trauma by which they are immobilised. In contrast to *Ulysses*, then, *The Waste Land* ultimately stresses the impossibility of articulating together moments from past and present. This might seem to run against the grain of the poem, for have we not heard many times of the ways in which *The Waste Land* integrates past and present, the line from

Dante suddenly crystallising the crowd that *now* files over London Bridge? But there is an important difference between Eliot's allusion here and, say, Apollinaire's use of myth in 'Zone', or Pound's in the early Cantos; for while the latter employ myth to create fluid and synthetic poetic contexts, Eliot's practice of allusion works to hollow and repudiate the mundanely modern. Nothing can redeem the blight of sexuality which afflicts the poem, and the equation of modernity with figures of an unregenerate femininity chokes any kind of narrative or dialectical movement. The present is paralysed, left desolate and unredeemable by the contagion of the past.

Now we are close to the source of the poem's ambivalence, for Eliot seems in one way to celebrate the past's potential to negate the present, even as the tropes of emptiness and vacuity recall us to a truly 'Jacobean' terror of cultural and personal breakdown. This is his way of turning against romantic individualism, announcing a form of heroism that, as one critic puts it, 'would end the human world, not give new life to it'.[24] It is, finally, less in any systematic mythology that a countervailing hope seems to reside than in a lyric intensity which produces a 'sudden lifting of the burden of anxiety and fear which presses upon our daily life so steadily that we are unaware of it'.[25] This lifting of repression, with its 'breaking down of strong habitual barriers', points towards a momentary sense of social connectedness but one which is achieved only through an intensity of art. *The Waste Land* must await that ideal language which, like Dante's in *Paradise*, can achieve the supreme goal of making the lyric, conventionally the medium of purely personal expression, the vehicle of a society's ideal of its own stable process (Dante's line, 'His will is our peace' thus encodes for Eliot 'the mystery of the inequality, and of the indifference of that inequality, in blessedness, of the blessed'[26]).

* * *

By 1917, Pound was investigating similar problems. Poems like 'Near Perigord' explore different ways in which the writer may reconstruct the past, experimenting first with 'fact' and then with 'fiction'. But to some extent Pound's career had stalled, partly because of the fundamental split in his poetics between temporal and spatial modes. Once freed from the purely elegiac conventions used in the early poems, Pound's experiments (as in the Noh plays) had yielded a highly flexible, 'belated' play with time, but this was counterbalanced by his evolving interest in static structures and 'spatial' modes of juxtaposition. The first drafts of the early Cantos highlight this tension, their moments of self-interrogation betraying not only lack of clear purpose but also Pound's growing awareness of the inadequacy of dramatic monologue as a vehicle for historical materials. In the draft of Canto I, for example, he addresses Robert Browning, whose epic *Sordello* provides his model for a 'poem including history':[27]

And half your dates are out, you mix your eras;
For that great font Sordello sat beside –
'Tis an immortal passage, but the font? –
Is some two centuries outside the picture.
Does it matter?
                  Not in the least. Ghosts move about me
Patched with histories.[28]

Very soon, though, it *would* matter, and by the time *A Draft of XVI Cantos* appeared in 1925 Pound's original conception of the poem as 'a rag-bag for the modern world to dump all its thought in'[29] had given way to a stronger sense of narrative purpose. The elements brought into the poem were now selected for their effectiveness as 'luminous details' which 'govern knowledge as the switchboard governs an electric circuit',[30] and this first suite of Cantos was concerned to trace the history of 'usury' which had culminated in the war and to celebrate forms of constructive activity which might prevent another from taking place.

If Eliot was concerned, as Hugh Kenner says, with effects rather than ideas,[31] for Pound that emphasis was reversed: the 'ideogrammic method' which he had learned from Fenollosa provided not simply a mode of composition but a methodology, a way of managing knowledge.[32] Many of Pound's later political confusions and misjudgements may be traced to his belief in this 'method', with its distrust of abstraction and its often naive commitment to 'the facts'. Yet in the earlier stages of the poem, the practice of cutting between 'luminous details', splicing anecdote with direct quotation, historical narrative with mythological vision, gives the reader an active if exacting role. Here citation and allusion work not to hollow out the present, but to excavate its foundations; and where the fragmentary propositions of *The Waste Land* seem to float in timeless suspension, in *The Cantos* Pound stresses the interaction of past and present by focusing our attention on the process by which history is re-written rather than simply remembered.

In the group of Cantos which presents Sigismundo Malatesta's construction of the Tempio in Rimini (VIII–XI), for example, the memorialising function of the building is given a strongly purposive role, suggesting that it motivates an entire social order. The thrust of these Cantos is to emphasise the foreignness and materiality of Italian history, as something to be interrogated and worked upon. The tangled chronologies in this section, along with Pound's occasional use of anachronism and his way of foregrounding the act of fragmented narration, constantly imply something in excess of a conventional narrative of history. Malatesta's Tempio still stands in Rimini, and the stubborn actuality of its continued existence allows Pound to save it from both the dullness of 'official' history and the unbridgeable remoteness of the imaginary. The 'form' in the past is thus reconstituted in the present, and that labour of reconstruction is at once a memorialising of something lost and the creation of a substitute for it. Renaissance Italy is now both ideal and 'real', not merely the figure for some original loss, but the actual space in which traces of a recoverable history are pursued. It is the tension between those times and spaces which provides the dynamic for the first fifty-one Cantos, allowing a praxis of creation and discovery which sustains the intellectual openness and methodological self-consciousness underlying Pound's earliest plans for the poem.

'There is no mystery about the Cantos,' Pound would declare one year after the Fifth Decad appeared in book-form, 'they are the tale of the tribe.'[33] In this first major section of the poem the narration of that 'tale' uses the discipline of the particular to avoid the closure implicit in a conventional, linear history. The emphasis is on the multiplicity of voices ('ply over ply', as Pound describes his elaborate layering of elements) and in this way authorial presence is dissolved into its many incarnations. The method is a radical one, for it is not simply that the lyric coherence of 'mood' is broken, but that our most fundamental expectations of poetry have to be revised as we are called upon to test and evaluate the extremely varied materials Pound weaves together. The poem is drawn irresistibly towards its moments of hymnic celebration, but Pound seeks to embed these highly stylised passages, with their often rather Pre-Raphaelite decor, in the chaotic processes of history from which, like the Tempio, they are won. And if the lyric moment is envisaged (as Pound explained to his father) as a 'bust thru from quotidian',[34] this too has its own complex temporality. In the opening lines of Canto XX, for example:

> Sound slender, quasi tinnula,
> Ligur' aoide: Si no'us vei, Domna don plus mi cal,
> Negus vezer mon bel pensar no val.'
> Between the two almond trees flowering,
> The viel held close to his side;
> And another: s'adora'.
> 'Possum ego naturae
> non meminisse tuae!' Qui son Properzio ed Ovidio.

The sound is 'slender', like the bride perhaps (*tinnula*, 'ringing', is remembered from Catullus's great marriage-hymn[35]), but it also applies to the 'viel' (an instrument like a lute) and the two almond trees. More important, this 'slender' sound is without undue mass, clearly articulated, a sequence of musical notes perfectly conjoined with the words it articulates.

Characteristically, Pound's allusions perform what they refer to, offering, in Greek, Provençal, Italian and Latin, epitomes of lyric precision and passionate celebration. The passage might be read as the invocation of some perennial tradition, the same conjunction of passion and exactitude appearing in periods far removed in time, yet our work of reading is made more complex than that, for Pound compels an awareness of the historical tension between the various languages. If the voice in *The Waste Land* is finally unable to connect one thing with another, in these early Cantos the web is constantly growing more complex – not because some overall design suddenly becomes clear, but rather because local connections proliferate. In this first phase of *The Cantos*, Pound develops the implications of Imagism, using allusion and citation to create a collision of time-schemes which yields (to borrow Derrida's formulation) 'a series of temporal differences without any central present, without a present of which the past and the future would be but modifications'.[36]

Yet *The Cantos* was not to be a Mallarméan epic, and Pound's direct engagement with the pressing political and economic questions of his day could not long postpone the emergence of a polemical axis to the poem. Once the diagnostic tendency had been fully established it was only a matter of time before 'history' would mutate into a more programmatic narrative of right or wrong choices. By the time Canto XLVI is reached, the reader is therefore not especially surprised to hear Pound announce that he has spent 'nineteen / Years on this case, CRIME / Ov two CENturies, 5 millions bein' killed off / to 1919'. The usurers stand accused, and with history now clearly illuminated as an epic struggle between exploiters and exploited, Pound is in a position to master the past through interpretation. In the next phase of the poem (Cantos LII–LXXI), he accordingly adopts hugely extended Enlightenment narratives which are structured by the demands of repetition, continuity, and identity. Increasingly the poem will concern itself with definitions of just authority, even as the writing begins to close down questions about its own judgemental legitimacy. Where the early Cantos had invited the reader's scepticism, now the poem begins to demand a certain faith; and as Pound begins to discover in Mussolini a stronger, more authoritative self-image, so the poem acquires an intransigent, often hectoring tone.[37]

* * *

Lewis, of course, predicts the problem in advance, seeing in Pound's preoccupation with the past a still romantic need to colonise history. *The Cantos* is, for him, the reflex of a society which is motivated by the search for models to copy and by a desire to feel at home everywhere. That need to live in a world purged of otherness is the principal motive behind what Lewis dismisses as the various romantic fashions of the time (the child-cult, artistic amateurism, homosexuality, and the time-cult[38]). To be 'in love with the past', for example, as Lewis claimed Pound was, is to want to *inhabit* the past, to deny its strangeness in an act of imaginative colonisation. Such projections are, Lewis tells us repeatedly, grounded in the fantasies of the nursery, a site which has an important part to play in the too-cultural world of *The Apes of God*. 'Whenever we get a good thing, the shadow comes with it, its *ape* and familiar', claims Lewis,[39] his choice of words reminding us once more of primary narcissism and the play of imitation which constitutes familiar and familial bonds.

Lewis would also classify Joyce as a member of the 'time-cult', but *Ulysses* offers some instructive contrasts to Poundian 'history'. For where *The Cantos* reveres the past as a purveyor of truth and regards style as an infallible index of ethical integrity, the apparent humanism of Joyce's inclusiveness and attention to detail actually conceals a calculated indifference. Eliot seems to have grasped this aspect of *Ulysses* in his observation that the novel 'showed up the futility of all the English styles',[40] a comment which suggests that (in contrast to Pound's emphasis on satire) Joyce's synoptic history of literary styles was designed to prove them equal in their uselessness as interpreters of reality.[41] *Ulysses* would offer no one style equivalent to that of the lines in which Pound tells of the 'crime' which is his main theme (for Joyce, the transparent and demotic style was but one among many, certainly not the voice of 'ego scriptor'). And while, in *The Cantos*, the precision of a passage from Propertius or Ovid should lead us to understand how language is the sensitive register of a social order, in *Ulysses* we are constantly led to think that we can make anything of any event, that literary expression returns us not to some original event but simply to more writing.

This sense of style as arbitrary may help us to understand Virginia Woolf's perplexity as she read Joyce's work, for, assured by Eliot that *Ulysses* 'has destroyed the whole of the 19th Century', she cannot help feeling that the novel is a 'mis-fire':

> Genius it has, I think; but of the inferior water. The book is diffuse. It is brackish. It is pretentious. It is underbred, not only in the obvious sense, but in the literary sense. A first rate writer, I mean, respects writing too much to be tricky; startling; doing stunts.[42]

Woolf's uneasiness about the book was due in part to a feeling that Joyce's 'trickiness' undermined the authenticity of the interior monologues of which he was so evidently a pioneer. Certainly, her own writing would exhibit an interest in the contents and structures of consciousness which, in its rapt attention to the inner movements of sensibility, had more in common with Proust than with Joyce and the 'Men of 1914'. For although *Remembrance of Things Past* (1913–27) is overwhelmingly concerned with the interaction of different temporalities, these acquire value in so far as they embody infinitely complex strata of the inner self. So, in the final pages of the novel, Marcel recalls the sounding of a bell:

> When the bell of the garden gate had pealed, I already existed and from that moment onwards, for me still to be able to hear that peal, there must have been no break in continuity, no single second at which I had ceased or rested from existing, from thinking, from being conscious of myself, since that moment from long ago still adhered to me and I could still find it again, could retrace my steps to it merely by descending to a greater depth within myself.[43]

Marcel's 'descent' into the self might provide a helpful figure for Woolf's novels, where time is not the time of some objective 'history', but the rhythm of feeling as it is scrutinised and over-looked by the perceiving mind. 'Our self-consciousness is becoming far more alert and better trained', she observes in a later essay, 'We are aware of relations and subtleties which have not yet been explored. Of this school Proust is the pioneer.'[44]

In her attempt to break with the 'materialism' of realists like Arnold Bennett and H. G. Wells, Woolf accordingly situates herself in relation to 'impressionists' like Conrad. This famous passage in 'Modern Fiction' outlines an aesthetic which is therefore quite different from that of Poundian modernism:

> The mind receives a myriad impressions – trivial, fantastic, evanescent, or engraved with the sharpness of steel. From all sides they come, an incessant shower of innumerable atoms.[45]

Life, Woolf continues, is 'a luminous halo, a semi-transparent envelope surrounding us from the beginning of consciousness to the end'. Where Pound had emphasised the need for clarity and 'objectivity', Woolf's sense of interaction with the world is designedly tenuous, a matter of intermittent intensities which seem to befall the perceiver. But the implied passivity is not the only difference, for this 'halo' is also a liminal space in which the self may experience an openness to others, and a temporary relaxing of those psychic defences which had seemed essential to one type of modernist aesthetic. So, Woolf says, it is 'the task of the novelist to convey this varying, *this unknown and uncircumscribed spirit*, whatever aberration or complexity it may display, with as little mixture of the alien and external as possible'. Her inward turn is to 'the dark places of psychology' – to precisely those 'half-lighted places of the mind' which, according to Lewis, prove so refractory to the authentically modernist intelligence.[46] Access to such places is given by 'this secret deposit of exquisite moments', as Woolf puts it in *Mrs Dalloway* (1925), when 'things come together'.[47] The conception, like the vocabulary, calls Pater to mind, and not fortuitously, since, unless referred to the level of aesthetic emotion, Woolf's desire for some sort of collective 'geniality' runs up against her troubled sense of entrenched class divisions.[48]

The resulting tension in her work can be damaging, leading, on the one hand, to brittle and patronising social judgements, and, on the other, to a certain preciosity in the writing when the everyday is self-consciously elevated to the 'poetic'. Both aspects represent the 'Bloomsbury' Woolf derided by Lewis. But there is a complexity in the best of her work which Lewis misses, mainly because it runs so much against the grain of his own brand of modernism. For the dominant temporal structures of Woolf's fiction are ones which produce a sort of loosening of the self's boundaries. Interior monologue and exterior description flow into one another, just as different times merge together ('she was a child throwing bread to the ducks ... and at the same time a grown woman'[49]). Here it is not the striking *juxtaposition* of chronologies which counts, a re-writing of the past which, as we saw, tended to produce an illusion of mastery, but rather a certain permeability of self and other which is felt as an effortless (though temporary) union.

'[T]he rhythm is the main thing in writing', observes Bernard in *The Waves* (1931),[50] and in Woolf's mature prose it certainly functions to transport the self into those larger spaces which the imagination seeks. One famous example:

> Quiet descended on her, calm, content, as her needle, drawing the silk smoothly to its gentle pause, collected the green folds together and attached them, very lightly, to the belt. So on a summer's day waves collect, overbalance, and fall; collect and fall; and the whole world seems to be saying 'that is all' more and more ponderously, until even the heart in the body which lies in the sun on the beach says too, that is all. Fear no more, says the heart, committing its burden to some sea, which sighs collectively for all sorrows, and renews, begins, collects, lets fall.[51]

It is a curiously mixed style, the adventurously 'poetic' rhythm almost concealing the highly conventional use of extended simile nd the contrived allegory of the speaking heart. The rise and fall of the needle as it assembles the green folds carries us towards the vision of some collective peace, but it does so rhythmically, rather than in any direct description of Clarissa's thoughts as she sews. The passage may exemplify 'that woman's gift, of making a world of her own wherever she happened to be' (68), but its larger rhythmic purpose is to achieve that almost trance-like condition in which life and death are inextricably entwined.

'[T]hat is all': the slight but pregnant ambiguity runs through most of Woolf's major fiction, suggesting that the peace which comes from a sense of community with the world is also a kind of finality, an end to struggles which tie us to individual suffering. Yet the 'all' is highly abstract, almost extinguished in the act of thinking it – a necessary condition, we realise, if it is not to incur the same problems as Conrad's rhetoric of collectivity (the impression there connoting 'hands busy about the work of the earth' and 'unavoidable solidarity'[52]). Woolf depends upon certain heightened rhythms to postpone such grand but empty perspectives, and it is here, perhaps, that she has her strongest debt to literary Symbolism. As she remarks in a discussion of De Quincey, for example, 'The rise and fall of the sentence immediately soothes us to a mood and removes us to a distance in which the near fades and detail is extinguished.'[53] This Yeatsian conception of rhythm works to displace direct statement: 'The emotion is never stated; it is suggested and brought slowly by repeated images before us until it stays, in all its complexity, complete.'

Yet the strain of trying to express what is ultimately supposed to be an ineffable sense of community can also produce an awkward solemnity (in *To the Lighthouse*, for example, 'it was impossible to resist the strange intimation which every gull, flower, tree, man and woman, and the white earth itself seemed to declare ... that good triumphs, happiness prevails, order rules'[54]). The lapses into a rhetoric of 'penitence', 'toil' and so on (146) point to concerns which are more serious as they are more difficult to voice. As is especially clear in *The Waves*, the utopian sense of connectedness recalls an original relation to the mother, a tie now broken by the trauma of loss. In *Mrs Dalloway*, the 'figure of the mother whose sons have been killed in the battles of the world' (53) presides over the narrative, as Woolf weaves together the separate stories of Septimus and Clarissa (the two characters 'should be entirely dependent upon each other', she observes in a letter[55]). Utopian figures of community call us back to a maternal origin to which access is, of course, now barred. As a result, Woolf's lyricism seems to carry the trace of failure and mortality, probing depths which reveal ends rather than beginnings.

In *The Waves*, the rhythm of moving waters is also that of a subterranean psychic life, 'a rushing stream of broken dreams, nursery rhymes, street cries, half-finished sentences and sights' (196), and it is here that identity is constantly made and re-made. '[W]e only wish to rejoin the body of our mother from whom we have been severed', complains Neville (179), and the six monologues are spoken with the knowledge of an irreparable loss which is the condition of time itself: 'We suffered terribly as we became separate bodies', recalls Bernard (186). Differentiation here is equivalent to a kind of death, and the ebb and flow of waves complements the shifting rhythms of the self in time – 'I am not one person: I am many people', Bernard concludes (212); as the wave rises to its peak, so one moment of time creates a unity which a second later will be toppled into atoms: 'The moment was all; the moment was enough. And then Neville, Jinny, Susan and I, as a wave breaks, burst asunder, surrendered' (214).

Like much of Woolf's work, this figure of movement encapsulates a sense of mortality which is grasped in each passing moment; as Bernard notes of his friends, 'All had their rapture; their common feeling with death; something that stood them in stead' (205). Yet there is no way that the structures of narrative can encapsulate this flowing away ('Life is not susceptible perhaps to the treatment we give it when we try to tell it' [205]), and seeking some ground of identification beyond the divisive realm of actual social relationships, Woolf is left with either truths of an ineffable order, truths which cannot be spoken, or with the possibility that only with death can there be a return to an ideal unity: 'all deaths are one death', thinks Louis, recalling Mrs Dalloway's vision of oceanic mortality.

* * *

Woolf's modernism seems quite at odds with that of Pound, Eliot and Joyce, though Lewis (whose work we may take to represent a third kind) saw all of them as representatives of a common romanticism. At first sight this is strange, since Woolf's concern with the rhythms of the inner life is very different from the avowedly 'public' interests of the 'Men of 1914'. Again mimesis is the key to Lewis's critique, for he regards all modernism (apart from his own) as in one way or another a variant on the Bergsonian theme of flux, 'identifying yourself with the fluid and the natural'.[56] The 'plunge into the stream of life' (present or past, it makes no difference) erodes the contours of the self and prevents the intelligence from engaging with 'a concrete world'. Instead of thought we find emotional identification, and if Lewis seems rash in bracketing together such diverse writers as subscribers to the Bergsonian 'time-cult' it is because their preoccupation with the past is founded on a will to reanimate and humanise that which, properly, is dead (a form of imaginative 'sympathy' re-opens the self to the kind of 'invasion' of which Eliot spoke). Lewis's own approach to the past is deliberately different:

> The Past as *myth* – as history, that is, in the classical sense – a Past in which events and people stand in an imaginative perspective, a *dead* people we do not interfere with, but whose integrity we respect – that is a Past that any person who has a care for the principle of individual life will prefer to 'history-as-evolution' or 'history-as-communism.'[57]

Lewis's 'classical' version of history thus flatly opposes a romantic 'past' conjured up by a parasitical modernism which, as he observes of Pound's, is always trying to 'get into the skin of somebody else'.[58] Such parasitism makes art merely the reflex of a democratic *zeitgeist*; as Lewis would later remark in *Rude Assignment* (1950), 'There is, indeed, no "other fellow" any longer: *otherness*, like *opposition*, is reactionary. We are all One Fellow.'[59]

It is the function of art, then, to restore that lost 'otherness' and thereby to inhibit the sort of compound identification which makes us 'all One Fellow'. The argument for the 'deadness' of art which Lewis gives to Tarr draws on the nineteenth-century preference for artifice over nature, but does so in such a way as to block any appeal to erotic 'sentiment'. Here we approach Tarr's alternative to the 'time-bound' forms of intertextual mimesis:

> '*deadness* is the first condition of art. A hippopotamus' armoured hide, a turtle's shell, feathers or machinery on the one hand; *that*

opposed to naked pulsing and moving of the soft inside of life, along with infinite elasticity and consciousness of movement, on the other. – Deadness, then,' Tarr went on, 'in the limited sense in which we use that word, is the first condition of art. The second is absence of *soul* in the sentimental human sense. The lines and masses of the statue are its soul. No restless, quick flame-like ego is imagined for the *inside* of it. It has no inside. This is another condition of art; *to have no inside*, nothing you cannot *see*. Instead, then, of being something impelled like an independent machine by a little egoistic fire inside, it lives soullessly and deadly by its frontal lines and masses. (299–300; Lewis's emphases)

Thus conceived, the art-work has no 'flame-like ego' to warm our own, and its pure exteriority signals the death of any compensatory metaphysics. It is easy to underestimate the severity of Lewis's aesthetics, especially as his rejection of naturalism seems to have something in common with Pound's. But Tarr's theory of art has no place for the concept of transcendent 'form' which underpins much of Pound's early thought about representation. For Lewis, the work of art exists as a trace or memory, as part of a temporal continuum which we cannot re-live. Once the habits of identification and assimilation are checked, the way is open to conceive the work as the production of an aesthetic otherness which opens a gap or breach within the rhythmic flow of social life, fracturing the 'everyday drunkenness of the normal real'[60] and confronting the complacent smile of the happy inebriate with the savage 'grimace' of the artist. As Lewis puts it in *Men Without Art*, 'the non-human outlook must be there (beneath the fluff and pulp which is all that is seen by the majority) to correct our soft conceit'.[61]

That desire for the 'non-human' underwrites Tarr's own aesthetic, leading him to conclude that '*Death* is the thing that differentiates art and life. Art is identical with the idea of permanence. It is a continuity and not an individual spasm. Life is the idea of the person' (299). Tarr's position rests, then, on a distinction between death ('the one attribute that is peculiar to life' [298]) and that deadness which is 'the first condition of art' because 'disentangled from death and accident' (299). Art thus allows us passage from a pure present into a kind of history, opening a perspective in which a violent comedy might compensate for the passivity of a generalised social mimetism:

Violence is of the essence of *laughter* … it is merely the inversion or failure of *force*. To put it another way, it is the *grin* upon the Deathshead. It must be extremely primitive in origin, though of course its function in civilized life is to keep the primitive at bay. But it hoists the primitive with its own explosive.[62]

The gap between copy and original is now prised open to become the space of *satire*, a space in which people are seen from the absolutely material perspective of the deathshead as 'necessarily comic: for they are all *things*, and physical bodies, behaving as *persons*'.[63] The perpetual present of mimetic desire is torn apart as it is exposed to the 'intense and even painful sense of the absurd' which characterises satire.[64]

Lewis's conception of satire thus requires a 'petrification' of the human into the thing-like, an ensemble of grotesque surfaces rather than 'classical proportion' ('art consists … in a *mechanising* of the natural'[65]). Hence the distinction he draws between the 'external method' of satire (a product of his 'philosophy of the EYE'[66]) and the 'internal method', which he associates with 'the subterranean stream of the "dark" Unconscious' and with behavioural imitation: 'In dealing with (1) the extremely aged; (2) young children; (3) half-wits; and (4) animals, the *internal* method can be extremely effective. In my opinion it should be entirely confined to those classes of characters.'[67]

The 'external method' will function accordingly as a calculated disruption of mimesis: for satire in Lewis's sense entails at once dispassionate observation and a withering of its objects into art. Satire, then, supplements its object not by breathing new life into it but by 'murdering' it as surely as, in Lacan's words, 'the symbol manifests itself as the murder of the thing'.[68] If Lewis's work seeks to break the hold of social imitation by recasting mimesis as a work of supplementation, it therefore does so in an almost literal sense, by making the lack in its object the condition for a satirical excess in its representation. *The Apes of God* (1930) is in every sense the monumental expression of that process. There Lewis depicts a world of wealth and affectation in which the '*societification* of art'[69] has produced a pervasive amateurism. At the centre of this world is the nursery and its games of narcissistic identification; as Horace Zagreus observes, 'The universal return to the mentality of childhood and of savagery – Nursery after Army, and dugout-canoe after dugouts in trenches – that seems to ensue' (411).

Only the shadowy Pierpoint seems uncontaminated by the mimicry and mockery which are the standard currency of this world; a kind of absent original (or Enemy) who often functions as Lewis's mouthpiece; Pierpoint, in his 'encyclical' to Zagreus, grounds the whole novel in a powerfully stated theory of imitative desire:

> It is to what I have called the Apes of God that I am drawing your attention – *those prosperous mountebanks who alternately imitate and mock at and traduce those figures they at once admire and hate*. And bringing against such individuals and their productions all the artillery of the female, or bi-sexual tongue, will abuse the object of their envy one day, and imitate him the next: will attempt to identify themselves with him in people's minds, but in the same breath to belittle him – to lessen if possible the disadvantage for them that this neighbourhood will reveal.
>
> (123; Lewis's emphases)

In a 'super-democratic' society (118), 'aping' and the 'propagation of the second-rate' (121) are the norm, with 'lifelike imitation' (351) concealing the real absence of both art and 'life'. It is a world seeking stability in familiar self-regarding fantasies – 'the love of babyhood, the return to the womb, the corruption of the cradle' (204) – and Lewis's exuberantly minute dissection of its lore and social mechanisms hollows it from within, exposing its inner fragility by cataloguing the enormity of its pretensions. Here modernist writing performs what Lewis would regard as its most vital role, showing the disastrous aestheticisation of the real while in the same movement making of an 'excessive' satirical style the instrument by which to drive a wedge between art and life. As Zagreus puts it, '*the real* should not compete with creations of Fiction. There should be two worlds, not one' (258).

This radical separation forms the basis of Lewis's art and politics, as he shifts between a strategy of withdrawal (the posture of 'The Enemy') and a humorously aggressive participation in social ritual at the level of *surface* only. As he puts it in *The Art of Being Ruled*, 'it is the spirit of the artist that maintains this superficiality, differentiation of existence, for us: our personal, our detached life, in short, in distinction to our crowd-life'.[70] It is this division between surface and depth, public and private, which Lewis explores in the early sketch called 'Some Innkeepers and Bestre'. Here he celebrates the 'characterless, subtle, protean social self of the modern man' which is made possible by the 'conventional, civilised abstraction of social life':

> And such a result can only be achieved by this modern ideal of abstracting energy from a purely personal and coercive form, and making it a fluid, unaccented medium – the civilised man, in short. This is the modern man's ideal of realising himself in others; that is, the *degree* of himself, and not the specific character, which is inalienable.[71]

While Lewis's fondness for nihilistic laughter may recall Dada negation, it is also characteristic of him to specify a dimension of the 'very self' which must remain disengaged from the agonistics of social life. The distinction is crucial to his thought, since it allows mimetism to be grasped (and controlled) as self-conscious play rather than misconstruing it as self-expression (hence Tarr can allow himself to act the naif, just as the young Lewis could visit a dance-hall in Paris as a character out of Tolstoy[72]).

The problems attaching to Lewis's politics come into focus here, since the polemical role of the Enemy is to restore a certain *distance* to social relations which modern democracies have rendered too proximate. Lewis accordingly found it increasingly difficult to attach his political theory to any political party. The infamous *Hitler* (1931) notwithstanding, the whole thrust of his thought was against identification and he therefore could not share the later enthusiasm of Pound and Eliot for 'strong' figures like Mussolini and Maurras.[73] The concept of the 'Enemy' entails a refusal of *any* identification, a refusal which is in line with Lewis's observation in *The Lion and the Fox* that 'The feudal european [sic] king was essentially not a patriarch, but a stranger and an *enemy*.'[74]

* * *

I have discussed Lewis's work at some length partly because he is the most neglected of the canonical writers, but also because his particular version of modernism falls outside the main lines of development in Britain and America. In marked distinction to the different modernisms of, say, Pound and Woolf, Lewis's writing is animated by a scepticism about metaphysical truths, whether those are to be ascribed to inner experience, the flux of 'life', or to transcendent structures like 'tradition' or the state. In each case, Lewis argues, the Absolute is collapsed into time, whether it be psychological time and sensation, or a metaphysics of modernity or tradition. So in his fiction, the forms of comedy and satire work to reinforce the view that 'Truth has no place in action',[75] and that the dominant versions of modernism are disabled by their attempt to find a home for the metaphysical in the 'fluid' immediacy of existence. Lewis thus eschews fantasies of an 'organic' social order, just as he derides Pound's sense of 'history' as the vehicle of 'truth'. As he puts it in *The Art of Being Ruled*, 'it is the end of history, and the beginning of historical pageant and play. But we are compelled, to some extent, to enter into the spirit of the comedy'[76] – here 'truth' becomes 'value', authority reveals itself as power, and metaphysics is dissolved in fiction.

If Virginia Woolf's fiction has something in common with Proust's conception of the novel, it is to writers like Franz Kafka, Robert Musil and Hermann Broch that we must look for forms of negativity, satire and pastiche which bear comparison with Lewis's. Certainly, Broch's view that 'Satire is ethical art par excellence' seems out of joint with the main lines of Anglo-American modernism, as does his talk of 'the new absolute satire that may have been predestined to become the central art of the twentieth century'.[77] Like Lewis, Broch regards satire not just as a means to attack a particular object, but as a sceptical anti-romanticism which defines art's prime function in modernity. 'Absolute' satire, then, issues in 'a radical attack on everything untruthful ... in contrast to which all the political satire that ever existed with its mockery-with-a-purpose tied to determined empirical standpoints is nothing but a craft'. Broch's novel *The Sleepwalkers* (1931–32) explores the implications of such a view, using stylistic parody to frame its interrogation of 'truth'. Each part of the trilogy pastiches a particular literary convention – *Pasenow the Romantic* indicating a debt to the tradition of Theodor Fontane's *Effi Briest* (1895), *Esch the Anarchist* drawing on the more brutal tropes of naturalism, while the clearer modernism of *Huguenau the Realist* brings to mind Joyce, Gide, and John Dos Passos.

This succession of styles reveals what Broch calls in the essayistic chapters of the final volume 'the disintegration of values', as the romantic 'cult of the [military] uniform' yields to the 'coarse appetites' of Esch and finally to the 'realism' of Huguenau.[78] Lacking any coherent style of its own, modernity degenerates into an age of pastiche. This loss of style, which Broch conceives of as 'something which uniformly permeates all the living expressions of an epoch' (397), is the product of a functionalism which has fragmented culture into separate spheres:

> an economic value-system of 'good business' next to an aesthetic one of *l'art pour l'art*, a military code of values side by side with a technical or an athletic, each autonomous, each 'in and for itself', each 'unfettered' in its autonomy, each resolved to push home with radical thoroughness the final conclusions of its logic and to break its own record.   (448)

Broch thus laments the 'resolution and disintegration of all system into its individual elements' (628–9), and while the novel gestures towards a compensatory Platonism, *The Sleepwalkers* is arguably most powerful in its satirical presentation of 'the Philistinism of a value-system whose field is restricted to the individual and his irrational impulses' (645).

If Broch still sought some kind of metaphysical anchorage in the groundless play of autonomous styles which seemed to characterise the ethical relativity of modern life, for another Austrian novelist, Robert Musil, the sceptical temper was more thoroughgoing. In his massive and unfinished novel-sequence *The Man without Qualities* (1930–43), Musil explored a principle of relativity which he drew from the philosopher and physicist Ernst Mach. Musil had already written a thesis on Mach's empiricism, commending his 'skeptical interpretation' that 'there is no real truth in a genuine sense, but only a practical, conservation-furthering convention'.[79] This emphasis on interpretation rather than on settled belief coloured the whole of *The Man without Qualities*, producing a novel which, like Broch's, also had a strong essayistic element.[80] Musil's critique of modernity was conducted, like Lewis's, in the name of the values of the intellect as opposed to those of 'romanticism'. So, for example, Ulrich's 'musical' friend Walter, who holds 'these billowing surges and emotional strivings of the soul ... to be the simple language of the eternal, uniting all human beings' (I, 167), is horrified by a 'view of art as a negation of life, as something in antagonism to life' (II, 78). Yet Musil, like Lewis, is at pains to emphasise precisely this antagonism and to refuse modern fantasies of 'cosmic man' (II, 119) by driving a wedge between art and action.

If one thing is held by both men to characterise the modern age it is its hostility to intellect,[81] and Musil's cutting assaults on sport and fashion as embodiments of a degraded 'mass-soul' (I, 339) share Lewis's contempt for the new religion of the 'Here and Now' (I, 343). 'Our age drips with practical energy anyway', concludes Ulrich, 'It's stopped caring for ideas, it only wants action' (III, 87). In part Musil has Expressionism in his sights, though the latter's 'abstract outlook, focused on universal and eternal values' (II, 310) also reflects larger tendencies within European thought which are now shaken by the recognition that 'moral values were not absolutes, they were functional concepts' (III, 96). With this Machian view, ethics is drawn into the orbit of fiction, for 'it is difficult to avoid the impression that the concepts and rules of moral life are merely metaphors' (II, 362).

Musil may appear less concerned than Broch about the transition from truths to values, but his presentation of Ulrich's incestuous affair with Agathe gives the later sections of the novel an unexpectedly mythic and utopian dimension. So it is to Kafka's earlier work that we must turn for a more consistently anti-metaphysical view of the incompatibility of truth and experience. In *The Trial* (1914/15, first published 1925), Joseph K.'s principal 'error' is in fact his attempt to grasp his alleged guilt in terms of his past actions.[82] Kafka's point, here as elsewhere, seems to be that the power of the Law is absolute because it is an absent cause – we cannot break our relation to it, but neither can we succeed in making it present, in expressing the metaphysical as a function of 'life'. This is the burden of that intricate parable called 'Before the Law' which first made up part of the ninth chapter of *The Trial*. Here Joseph K. is told the story of the Man from the Country who begs the doorkeeper for admittance to the Law. This is but the first of many such doors and many such doorkeepers, but the man is refused entry. For many years he sits before the door, sometimes conversing with the doorkeeper, sometimes attempting to bribe him to open. All such manoeuvres fail, however, and finally, grown old before the door, the man begs for the answer to one question:

'What do you want to know now?' asks the door-keeper, 'you are insatiable.' 'Everyone strives to attain the Law,' answers the man, 'how does it come about, then, that in all these years no one has come seeking admittance but me?' The door-keeper perceives that the man is nearing his end and his hearing is failing, so he bellows in his ear: 'No one but you could gain admittance through this door, since this door was intended only for you. I am now going to shut it.'[83]

If this conclusion strikes a note of terror it is because of the disjunction it reveals between the sense of some external recognition – the door 'intended only for you' – and the brutal withholding of precisely what is promised.

When the priest tells him this story, Joseph K.'s first reaction is 'So the door-keeper deluded the man.' But as the priest provides further exegetical comment such certainties seem quickly to evaporate. It may be that the door-keeper is subordinate to the man and is in fact incapable of closing the door; or perhaps the door-keeper should be viewed as an expression of the Law, in which case 'to doubt his integrity is to doubt the Law itself'. Either way, the *truth* of the door-keeper's actions cannot be gauged, and as the priest points out, ' "it is not necessary to accept everything as true, one must only accept it as necessary." "A melancholy conclusion," said K. "It turns lying into a universal principle" ' (243). Lying – or fiction – is here a process of constant deferral; the man seeks to establish a relation between his life and the Law, but this is shown to be impossible (as Derrida notes in his discussion of the parable, 'One must *enter into relation* only with the Law's representatives, its examples, its guardians'[84]). For Kafka 'power is evasive, it *withdraws*':[85] so the Law, we might say, is there, concealed behind many doors and emitting a certain 'radiance' (236), but is made manifest only in the desire which marks our lack of it (hence the man's 'insatiability' on which the door-keeper comments, and the refusal of the Law to recognise man's guilt elsewhere in Kafka's fiction).[86]

For Kafka, then, in contrast to Lewis, there is no position of solitariness outside this negative relation from which an 'Enemy' might consolidate power. Kafka, concludes one critic, has a 'horror of all forms of mastery',[87] which helps to explain his own particular way of associating writing with death. Like the Law, of which it may be one incarnation, writing is a process of deferral which endlessly postpones the emergence of 'truth' until it may coincide with the extinction of the real. This may be the lesson of that doorway to the Law: for when the man first sees it he has to bend down 'to peer through the entrance' (235); in his old age, however, he becomes 'childish' and diminishes in size so that '[t]he door-keeper has to bend far down to hear him' (236). Only at the end, when death and the Law are the same thing, will door and man coincide.

But we miss Kafka's point if we read this persistent reference to death as a form of pessimistic existentialism. For, as Blanchot has argued, Kafka's art is motivated by the 'possibility' of death, by the inescapable horizon which makes writing an attempt 'to withdraw language from the world'.[88] Like Lewis's satire which 'murders' its object, Kafka's language constantly struggles against its dependence on the real,[89] though any transcendent ground it might then occupy is gained at the painfully acknowledged cost of the lived experience of the writer. Hence Kafka's aphorism: 'He has found the Archimedean point, but has used it against himself; evidently this is the condition that has enabled him to find it.'[90] With this turn against the self, Kafka displaces Lewis's lingering fetish of authorial power, but in doing so he does not extinguish all hope of an absolute, retaining 'rather a possibility of saying that would say without saying being and without denying it either'.[91] Indeed this sceptical modernism stops short of the free, ungrounded play of a later postmodernism by the particular investment it makes in the aesthetic: here art is neither the privileged bearer of metaphysical truths nor simply a substitute for them – rather, it expresses what Blanchot describes as 'the effort to make manifest, through the image, the error of the imaginary, and eventually the ungraspable, forgotten truth which hides behind this error'.[92]

This is the 'deathly' side of art, which spurns revelation and presence even as it refuses to countenance their impossibility. Hence the endless deferrals of Kafka's texts, which always position writing *below* the Castle and *before* the Law. Perhaps, too, it is what Lewis has in mind when he calls art 'a half-way house, the speech, life, and adornment of a half-way house. Or it is a coin that is used on a frontier, but in neither of the adjoining countries, perhaps.'[93] But it is Kafka's particular grasp of the individual's indissoluble bond with the apparatus which terrorises and oppresses which allows him to decipher art's yearning for the absolute as somehow complicit with a totalitarianism which seems its constant shadow.[94] Only the 'deathly' aspect of art, its never-ending failure to pass through the doorway and to enter the Law, will illuminate the pretensions to 'truth' of the absolute or total forms of this political order. It is not without cost, though, for Kafka allows neither the pathos of negativity nor an illusion of power through criticism;

instead, we find a scepticism which, as Blanchot defines it, 'does not destroy the system; it destroys nothing; it is a sort of gaiety without laughter, in any case without mockery, which suddenly makes us uninterested in affirmation, in negation: thus it is neutral like all language'.[95] As we look back, Kafka's 'neutrality' may stand as a sort of advance warning of the dangerous political errors which less completely sceptical modernisms were soon to make. It remained to Surrealism to take the last avant-garde gamble before Hitler came to power.

12

Death and Desire: The Surrealist Adventure

It is a sunny Spring day in 1934; André Breton is strolling through the Paris flea market with Alberto Giacometti. Like many such occasions valued by the Surrealists, this is a planned adventure, with both men on the lookout for objects which will strike the desired note of the uncanny, something at once unexpected and oddly familiar. Giacometti picks up a rather ominous metal mask which, after seeming to 'entertain some fear about its next destination', he buys; for his part Breton

> made just as elective a choice with a large wooden spoon, of peasant fabrication but quite beautiful, it seemed to me, and rather daring in its form, whose handle, when it rested on its convex part, rose from a little shoe that was part of it. I carried it off immediately.[1]

Breton's find will produce complex reverberations to which we shall return later in this chapter, but we may note here that certain aspects of such an encounter clearly derive from the Dada moment which preceded Surrealism proper. In the first place, such an 'adventure' occurs by chance, and the meanings it generates are ones which are significant precisely because they cannot be known in advance. Furthermore, while Breton's account of this incident occurs in a work of considerable textual sophistication, the encounter itself stages a sort of transposition of aesthetic categories into actual experience. It is in the domain of the 'real' that Breton goes in pursuit of imaginary meanings, and his search for the moment when distinctions between categories break down can only remind us of the Dada rejection of aesthetic autonomy. A certain negativity haunts such experiences, and while Surrealism is commonly presented as the affirmative face of Dada, the intersection of desire and sign is frequently coloured by a violence which still recalls the earlier nihilism of Tzara (a letter from Breton's friend Joë Bousquet will later reveal the 'evil role of this mask' and the deathly associations it carries).[2]

Surrealism had been born nonetheless from a growing wave of disillusionment with Dada. Between 1920, when Tzara arrived in Paris, and 1922, when Breton announced the death of Dada, an increasingly serious commitment had been needed to sustain the sequence of events and performances. As one critic puts it, 'Tzara wanted to prolong artificially, on the ideological level, the anarchic state of the armistice',[3] but, for initially sympathetic writers like Breton, Aragon and Soupault, something more was needed than disintegration for its own sake.[4] Negation itself was also becoming fashionable and Parisian audiences had begun to enjoy the repeated Dada scandals. It was vital, then, as Georges Ribemont-Dessaignes recalls, to avoid 'the acceptance of scandal as a work of art'.[5]

As relations between the Dadaists became more strained and the need for new ideas more pressing, so a sequence of events led inexorably to Dada's dissolution. Indicative of the shift in direction was the staging of a mock 'trial' of the nationalist and anti-semitic author Maurice Barrès, an event which Breton organised with his usual seriousness, but which Tzara in particular burlesqued as much as he could. Others, like Picabia, were not slow to point up the irony of Dada representing the 'law', and it was generally agreed that the event was not a success. But already Breton was trying to expose the 'vicious circle' in which Dada had become trapped – as he recalled much later, the 1918 manifesto had seemed to open many doors, but these had ultimately led to 'a corridor that goes nowhere'.[6] Dada recognised only instinct and had no time for any kind of interpretation, which it simply derided as bourgeois intellectualism;[7] Breton's aim would now be to retain aspects of Dada's negativity – its anti-culturalism, its profound disrespect for family, religion, nation – but to redefine these as a critique capable of opening the way to more constructive enterprises. So in 1922 he attempted to convene a 'Congress of the Modern Spirit', which would consider ways forward, and while this attempt was fatally sabotaged by the refusal of Tzara to participate, its very failure marked a decisive parting of the ways: Surrealism was about to be born.

As usual, though, the critical account risks making the divergence appear too clear-cut, and Breton in much later interviews emphasised that at the beginning of the twenties Dada and Surrealism were like 'overlapping waves'.[8] That intersection is of particular importance when we consider that the discovery of automatic writing, which first differentiated Surrealism from Dada, was announced by the publication of Breton and Soupault's *The Magnetic Fields* in 1920, four years before the appearance of the first Surrealist manifesto. Furthermore, when these pieces first appeared in *Literature* the year before, Breton had not yet declared allegiance to Dada.[9] The interest in automatism, then, precedes both Dada and Surrealism as formal tendencies in France, and perhaps the best way to disentangle their 'overlapping waves' is to compare their respective views of the unconscious.

While Tzara was dismissive of psychoanalysis, Breton had worked as a medical assistant during the war and had supplemented his investigation of Freud's ideas with experiments in recording the dreams of the traumatised soldiers who passed through his hands.[10] The foundations of Surrealism were laid in these years, as Breton familiarised himself with Freudian concepts of the unconscious, repression, complexes and sexuality, and, above all, with the analytic technique of free association. Surrealism would be the only modernist avant-garde to welcome Freud's ideas, though Breton often managed to inflect those ideas in a direction of his own.

In the first place, the Surrealists ignored the therapeutic aims of psychoanalysis (Breton dismisses 'the futile task of curing patients' at the end of the 1924 manifesto [*MS*, 47]) and thereby inverted Freud's hierarchy of consciousness/unconsciousness. For Breton, the unconscious clearly took precedence, and his formulation of the aims of psychoanalysis as 'nothing less than the expulsion of man from himself'[11] was quite at odds with Freud's thought. The Surrealists also passed over the emphasis attaching to guilt and shame in Freud's understanding of the dream-work, and when it came to explicating particular dreams, as in *Communicating Vessels* (1932), Breton tended to focus his attention on recent events as stimuli rather than on the articulation of these with an infantile scene, which underlay Freud's account of dreams.[12] Whereas psychoanalysis was centrally concerned with the function of memory as both malady and therapy, for the Surrealists the voice of the unconscious was above all prophetic, pointing not to some psychic dislocation but rather to a promise of the self's eventual unity.[13] These differences in focus may account in part for the failure of

Breton's meeting with Freud in 1921. Not surprisingly, Freud could not grasp the objectives of Surrealism then or later (in an exchange of letters with Breton in 1932 he confesses that 'I am unable to clarify for myself what Surrealism is and what it wants'[14]).

Similarly, the interest of automatic writing was thus quite removed from Freud's sense of analysis as 'working through', as the 'weav[ing] around a rememorated element an entire network of meaningful relations',[15] since the value of an 'unconscious' language lay in its power to negate from within the thought-forms of 'logic' and 'reason' (the *bêtes noires* of Surrealism, as of Dada). But where Tzara's experiments had produced a language of flux and incoherence, in which sound constantly threatened to destroy meaning altogether, for the Surrealists, automatic writing disclosed the double articulation of the unconscious with the conscious, of desire with reality. So we read in the first manifesto of 'the future resolution of these two states, dream and reality, which are seemingly so contradictory, into a kind of absolute reality, a *surreality*, if one may so speak' (*MS*, 14).

Surrealism was not, then, conceived as a sanctification of the irrational, but rather as an attempt to *integrate* the opposing terms of the Cartesian dualism it regarded as the curse of Western thought. So the title of Breton and Soupault's first experiment with automatism is helpfully precise, proposing 'magnetic fields' (spaces of tension and interaction) rather than bodily flows as the model of psychic activity. If we move to the 1924 manifesto, we can see why this should be so important. There, Breton defines Surrealism in these words:

> SURREALISM, *n*. Psychic automatism in its pure state, by which one proposes to express – verbally, by means of the written word, or in any other manner – the actual functioning of thought. Dictated by thought, in the absence of any control exercised by reason, exempt from any aesthetic or moral concern.   (*MS*, 26)

The 'actual functioning of thought', we soon learn, is associated with 'the omnipotence of dream' and 'the disinterested play of thought'. This last phrase points up the link Breton adduces between 'reason' and forms of thought which are possessive, seeking their own advantage. Automatism releases thought from private goals and objectives and in doing so offers the possibility of a collectivist art. It is something open to all, Breton contends, and he goes on to offer directions which readers might follow to produce their own texts.

Not, of course, that such writing is a pure product of the unconscious: Breton would later stress that '*automatism* alone is the dispenser of the elements on which the secondary work of emotional amalgamation and passage from the unconscious to the preconscious can operate effectively' (*MS*, 230). And although a certain passivity is required of the subject, this may be supplemented by the choice of particular methods, such as varying the speed at which writing takes place.[16] The result, we may assume, is rather like Reverdy's 'subliminal syntax', generated by the mind's refusal or inability to naturalise its contents by adducing connections and context; Surrealism, declares Breton, 'has suppressed the word "like"'.[17] In the first manifesto, he quotes Reverdy's 'extremely revealing' account of the image (*MS*, 20), though a few pages later he disputes the notion that this type of juxtaposition can be produced deliberately ('it is erroneous to claim that "the mind has grasped the relationship" of two realities in the presence of each other' [*MS*, 36]). Yet, in contrast to the lacunary structure of Reverdy's poems, the best-known examples of Surrealist automatism are remarkable for their syntactical regularity. Indeed, Breton is struck by this himself, noting that phrases which come to mind on the verge of sleep do so in a 'perfectly correct syntax'.[18] Surrealism strives as usual to be dialectical, the persistence of grammatical structure pointing up the way in which 'consciousness and reason collaborate with chance and the unconscious'.[19]

Take the following passage from *The Magnetic Fields*:

The corridors of the grand hotels are unfrequented and cigar-smoke keeps itself dark. A man descends the stairs of sleep and notices that it is raining: the window-panes are white. A dog is known to be resting near him. All obstacles are present. There is a pink cup, an order given and the men-servants turn round without haste. A buzzing denotes this hurried departure. Who can be running in so leisurely a way? Names lose their faces. The street is no more than an abandoned track.[20]

The passage reads rather as if it were a parody of the descriptive novel, presenting characters and objects for our consideration but refusing to provide them with any purposive context. This gives us one clue to Breton's adaptation of Apollinaire's coinage

'Surrealism', suggesting that it is a calculated subversion of literary realism. Hence Breton's contempt for those 'empiricists of the novel' who deluge us with circumstantial detail.[21] In the first manifesto, Breton quotes a passage from Dostoyevsky's *Crime and Punishment* ('The small room into which the young man was shown was covered with yellow wallpaper ...'), only to conclude that the author 'is wasting his time, for I refuse to go into his room' (*MS*, 7–8). But this is not the end of the matter since, for the Surrealists, the novel as a form is not flawed by description alone, but by a sense of determinism and fatality, by a species of logic which leaves us subservient to reality as it is.[22]

The passage from *The Magnetic Fields* thus sets out to undermine our power to recognise the world in language, for here even the definite article – 'the grand hotels': *which* hotels? – situates objects in the realm of the uncanny, and the present tense of the text implies both a sense of simultaneous events and of their indefinite prolongation. Harder to describe is the way in which the literal and figurative are interwoven: the man descends the stairs, which then by metaphorical transfer are caught up within his dream (they are 'the stairs of sleep'); yet with the next phrase the metaphor is apparently unravelled, for the narrator's voice assures us that, even while asleep, the man 'notices that it is raining'. Is it raining, then, or not? The fact that the window-panes are white hardly answers the question, and the next sentence, which helpfully reports that 'A dog is known to be resting near him' is, of course, no help at all. The 'correctness' of the syntax constantly leads us to anticipate an order and causality which are not there: 'There is a pink cup, an order given and the men-servants turn round without haste.'

Automatic writing is meant to exhibit thinking rather than a finished thought – Breton calls it 'spoken thought' in the first manifesto (*MS*, 22) – and where conventional narration always deals in actions which are already over, automatism 'in depriving us of any system of reference disorientates us in relation to our own memories'.[23] The words are not meant to refer us to another time or, indeed, to actual things which pre-exist them; as Maurice Blanchot observes, with automatic writing 'language is not discourse, but reality itself'.[24] Here, then, we discover another apparent weakness of conventional narration, for unlike the Freudian unconscious, which is timeless and contradictory, the novel reproduces the discontinuous fabric of mere existence.[25] Surrealism, however, understands experience as essentially *continuous*, and its delight in unbroken contiguity thus distinguishes it not only from fictional realism but also from forms of modernist montage and juxtaposition which, like Imagism, seek to make the space between elements a key to some mysterious plenitude.

But what is the origin of Surrealism's images and events, of phrases like that first one which Breton recalls 'knocking at the window'? (*MS*, 21). For this is no Yeatsian dictation from the spirit-world, as he emphasises in the later *Communicating Vessels*: 'No mystery in the final analysis, nothing that could provoke any belief in some transcendent intervention occurring in human thought during the night.' And he adds: 'I see nothing in the whole working of the oneiric function that does not borrow clearly from the elements of lived life, provided one takes the trouble to examine it.'[26] The crucial thing about automatic writing is, from this point of view, that it shares the immediacy of the dream, making the process of writing continuous with the experience itself and thereby preventing any gap from opening up between sign and event (the space of representation). The Surrealist objective is always to be present at the moment of creation, when thought takes shape, and it is in that sense haunted by the fear that writing will reveal itself as the mimesis of an unconscious which has *already* presented itself in figurative form.[27]

Here the most interesting paradox of Breton's theory begins to emerge, for on the one hand automatic writing purports to provide an *unmediated* experience not of the body (that was Dada's aspiration) but of the unified self, the self in its waking *and* dreaming life. Only in restoring the integral connection of consciousness to the unconscious can experience become whole again. Yet at the same time, the medium of this connection is language, a system of signs whose very mode of operation entails a certain *negation* and separation. Here one may detect the legacy of Hegel's notion that 'all *conceptual*-comprehension (*Begreifen*) is the equivalent of a murder',[28] a notion which has its later echo in the work of Jacques Lacan: 'the symbol manifests itself first of all as the murder of the thing, and this death constitutes in the subject the eternalization of his desire'.[29] The word gives us, then, the meaning of the thing, but in doing so replaces what it names, thus condemning the thing to a kind of non-being. This understanding of the negating power of language, its way of obtaining meaning at the expense of the things it names, might easily produce an elegiac poetics of distance and loss; indeed, we have already examined something rather similar in

Pound's early work. For Breton and the Surrealists, however, not only is this negativity indispensable to language's operation, it is also a condition of the self's freedom. But what kind of freedom can this be, if, as Maurice Blanchot puts it, 'when we speak, we are leaning on a tomb'?[30] Breton's answer would be that it is the freedom to grasp language as the very medium of a desire which (according to Hegel) expresses itself as a force of negation.[31]

This proposition may be understood on several related levels, which together connect Surrealism with the negativist strand of modernism we have traced elsewhere. First, this view of language provides the basis for the Surrealists' elaboration of a political aesthetic, for language's negation of the real, the absence which always echoes within it, is potentially a rejection of reality-as-it-is, that world which, codified by law and logic, exists by exiling what-it-is-not to the fantastic realms of art and the imaginary. This conception of language lies at the heart of Surrealism's politics and is ultimately of more importance to it than its long and awkward relationship with the French Communist Party.[32] As Breton puts it in his 'Introduction to the Discourse on the Paucity of Reality': 'Does not the mediocrity of our universe depend essentially on our power of enunciation? ... Things said over and over again today meet a solid barrier. They have riveted us to this vulgar universe.'[33] Unlike Reverdy's 'barrier', this one may be overcome by developing what Breton defines as a particular 'materialism', a word which in this context is meant to suggest that the worlds of the conscious and unconscious are *of the same order of reality*; hence the argument, in *Communicating Vessels*, that 'Time and space in the dream are the real time and space.'[34]

Secondly, this conception of language as potentially destructive, as a medium with which the writer may 'attack murderously this obvious aspect of things',[35] infects art itself, which can no longer exist without the possibility of death as its absolute horizon (Blanchot remarks in similar vein that 'the only way we can comprehend is by denying ourselves existence, by making death *possible*, by contaminating what we comprehend with the nothingness of death'[36]). Now we can see how Surrealism offers itself as the summation of one major strand of avant-garde activity, as it strives at once to cancel and to preserve the Dada moment of pure negation, its lyric pursuit of the marvellous always shadowed by the death which makes it possible. Here we pass beyond the absolute contradiction of Dada, encapsulated in Tzara's immobile sign of equivalence ('ego = non-ego'), through Hegel's negation of the negation, a dialectical movement which will finally produce an affirmative vision but one which still bears the trace of the negation by which it is gained. Surrealism thus moves from the nihilistic fantasy of Dada, through the Cubist sense of structure, to a third stage in which fantasy and structure are inextricably linked and where 'structure' is shaped not by the conscious mind but by desire and the unconscious. In this way, as Pontalis has shown, Surrealism destroys the limits of a merely 'useful' reality, regarding it as no more than a simulacrum which thwarts the power of the imaginary, and puts in its place not a separate world of 'art', but a world which is (like the dream) made up of elements of reality that have been exposed to the force of desire.[37]

And what of this desire? To negate a reality that is bound by rules and codes which *exclude* what for Surrealism is a full continuum of experience, acknowledging no boundary between the concrete and the imagined, is to assert that an authentic reality comes into being only with a recognition of 'the omnipotence of desire'.[38] As Breton puts it in *Communicating Vessels*:

> Desire abounds, cutting right into the very fabric too slow to change, then letting its thread run between the parts. It would not yield to any objective regulator of human conduct.... And yet the materials it uses here are real, things taken from life itself![39]

Desire, he continues, 'refuses itself nothing', moving 'from one object to another, never valorizing among the objects any but the last one'.[40] Yet this formulation leads not to nostalgia for a primordial lost object but rather to an unending search for connections.[41] Desire, in this sense, can never lose its 'lethal shadow',[42] since the vision of totality which the Surrealists seek will occupy 'a certain point of the mind at which life and death, the real and the imagined, past and future, the communicable and the incommunicable, cease to be perceived as contradictions' (*MS*, 123).

This preoccupation with death, which runs deep in the theoretical speculations of Breton, may suggest a certain decadence. Indeed, a fascination with suicide permeates Surrealism, which reverently memorialises Breton's early friend Jacques Vaché, whose death was one link in a chain that would later connect Jacques Rigaut and René Crevel. There is, too, the overtly Gothic vein of Surrealism and its admiration for the defiant amoralism of Sade.

Yet, beneath these more sensational interests, the death of the real and its endless memorialisation in the fact of the art-work's fundamental *surreality* serves to ensure that a residual opacity clings to the object, preventing its complete assimilation to discourse. The 'lethal shadow' which haunts the word leads not to a mourning of the real (or to a related sense of the work's separation and autonomy), but to an incessant work of *interpretation* in which desire proves legible in its objects.[43]

This aspect of Surrealism deserves emphasis since it is so frequently missed: in contrast to the metaphysical preoccupations of so many of the avant-gardes we have examined, whether those be grounded in fantasies of modernity or tradition, of a disembodied or strongly centred self, Surrealism locates its version of the unconscious firmly within the domain of the sign. For Breton, in fact, desire cannot exist apart from interpretation, since it always expresses 'the need to transform the world radically and to interpret it as completely as possible'.[44] So when Breton gives an account of one of his own dreams, he adds that 'I insist emphatically on the fact that for me it *exhausts* the dream's content and contradicts the diverse allegations that have been made about the "unknowable" character of the dream, or its incoherence.'[45] The apparent contradiction here between, on the one hand, the claim to 'exhaust' the content of the dream, and, on the other, the lingering opacity of the object has to be understood in terms of Breton's notion of interpretation as the very medium of the self's engagement with the world, as a form of praxis which discovers the real in the same movement that it articulates the self. There is, as Breton puts it,'[n]o mystery in the final analysis', because this 'exhaustion' of experience through insistent interpretation submits any fantasy of unmediated revelation to the negating powers of language. This also suggests one reason for Breton's valuation of the then nearly forgotten Lautréamont (Isidore Ducasse) above his other hero Rimbaud, for with the exception of Sade perhaps, no other writer had brought the 'scalpel of analysis' so violently to bear upon human nature and its 'need for the infinite'.[46]

Surrealism's hope, then, is that our interaction with the world may bring us back to a full sense of ourselves by disclosing the ways in which reality is shaped by and responds to our desires (we find ourselves as we find the force of our own desire, out there, at work in the world). For Surrealism always sees itself in 'open conflict with the immediate world' (*MS*, 216), pushing up against 'the thickness of things immediately obvious when I open my eyes'.[47] Poetry disputes this apparently 'immutable' reality, and 'cannot rest until it has placed its negativist hand on the entire universe'.[48] That touch, like the catalysing moment of the image, strips objects of their mask of functionality to reveal the human investment within. Here the theories of Marx and Freud momentarily intersect, as congealed and fetishised forms yield up their repressed elements. For Breton, however, it is less a matter of the effacement of labour as such, than of a subtle convergence in which interpretation reveals desire as the will to social transformation; not work as such, then, but the work of the mind is the crucial index of value. Here, as Fredric Jameson observes, the Surrealists seek 'the release of the subjectivity from the single limited desire', discovering objects which, because they have no clear use, offer a lifted horizon where we may read the promise of a shared will to change.[49]

In the Surrealism of the twenties, that sense of a new 'collective myth' (*MS*, 210) is inextricably linked to the role of chance. As one commentator puts it, the dialectical resolution of objective and subjective 'is made possible only through the interpenetration of the two in their *accidental* forms, i.e., in an interaction of the "disorder" of the spirit and a contradictory, unpredictable and ungovernable Real'.[50] The Surrealist version of narrative is therefore meant to be open and expectant, a waiting upon signs rather than an ordered deployment of them to produce an end known in advance. Apocalyptic as its gestures may be, Surrealism at this moment parts company with most of the other modernist avant-gardes, its ideal of 'lyric behaviour' (*Mad Love*, 53) refusing the ubiquitous trope of mastery. 'Poetic objectivity', remarks the poet Paul Éluard, 'is to be found only in succession, in the interlacing of all the subjective elements of which the poet is … not the master but the slave.'[51]

* * *

Now it is Louis Aragon who strolls through the streets of Paris, deciphering as he goes the coded signs of 'a mythology of the modern'.[52] But the miraculous world of the arcades, with their curious shop-displays and hidden meeting-places, lives on borrowed time, shortly to be razed to the ground to allow the progress of the mighty Boulevard Haussmann. The Passage de l'Opéra, says Aragon, is actually like 'a big glass coffin', the light there 'ranging from the brightness of the tomb to the shadow of sensual pleasure' (47). The conjunction of elements epitomises what Aragon calls 'the vertigo of the modern' (129): at the very junction between 'the reality of the outside world and the subjectivism of the passage' we are caught in a moment of vertigo – 'let us pause in this strange zone,' suggests Aragon, 'where all is distraction, distraction of attention as well as of inattention, so as to experience this vertigo'. Here everything is illusion and chance, full of erotic promise; and the encounters for which Aragon hopes are ones which break the 'interior boundaries of myself', giving 'access to a hitherto forbidden realm that lies beyond my human energies' (101).

The Passage de l'Opéra now becomes the Passage de l'Opéra *onirique*, the passage of dreams, where the 'simulacra on display in the shop window' (54) suddenly become 'real', the stuff of pure fantasy rather than the objects of a narrowly focused consumer desire: 'The canes floated gently like seaweed. I had still not recovered from my enchantment when I noticed that a human form was swimming among the various levels of the window display' (36). This submarine vision of a banal collection of walking-sticks amusingly catches the commodity's pretence of drifting in an immaterial world, and submits it to a play of fantasy which has absolutely no connection with the object's function. If, as Marx had explained, the fetishistic nature of the commodity obscures the traces of the human labour which produced it, here Aragon turns this spectacle against itself, rediscovering that investment as a kind of libidinal energy, as he spots Lisel (an old flame) swimming mermaid-like in the depths of the window (37).[53]

The image is ridiculous, though it may be 'capable of annihilating the entire Universe' (79), reminding us that even here Surrealism walks a tightrope, seeking to promote its sense of the marvellous without capitulating to any desire for the infinite or metaphysical. Against any religion of the modern, Aragon therefore invokes a mythology which, like that of the ancients, is mired in death. Hence this particular kind of celebration: 'I attain myself, I attain the concrete feeling of existence, which is wholly enveloped by death' (156). For if Surrealism is to break through the fetishistic carapace of the real, it will be through the agency of a desire rooted in the real, 'an emanation of the world's very essence' (162), rather than through fantasies of the beyond ('it is only within metaphysics that logic exerts itself and develops its laws' [207]). Humour here becomes an anti-metaphysical principle linking the pleasure principle with the death drive – elsewhere Aragon calls it 'the sine qua non of poetry'[54] – partly because, as Freud had said, humour 'refuses to admit that the traumatisms of the external world could touch it, and even manages to consider them as possible sources of pleasure'.[55] This is perhaps the main aim of Aragon's 'mythology of the modern', which allows him to detect in petrol pumps 'the appearance of the divinities of Egypt or of those cannibal tribes which worship war and war alone' (132).

It is vital to Aragon that such a mythology, comic as it may be, should have the power to express a shared desire which transcends any single object and may thus become, in Breton's words, a 'collective myth' (*MS*, 210). Yet even in *Paris Peasant* events take him in another direction, as an amorous encounter recorded in the final section of the novel leads to the equation of Woman and myth. Suddenly 'It is time to proclaim the religion of love' (191), and Aragon surprises us by invoking 'Woman, the eternal female' (184). The text continues to produce its display of stylistic fireworks, but Aragon's tonal versatility cannot prevent this vision of Woman from admitting a damaging fetishism back into the work. Here the sensual encounters of the first section yield to the purely conventional idiom of romantic love ('She did this extraordinary thing of calling me to her: and I came' [211]). A woman becomes Woman, reality subsumed to symbol – 'For me,' avows Aragon, 'the metaphysical spirit was reborn from love. Love was its source, and I hope never to leave this enchanted forest' (212).

This 'religion of love' would come to occupy an increasingly central place in Surrealism, gaining prominence as the hope of political engagement receded across the thirties. In Breton's *Nadja*, published two years after *Paris Peasant*, an enigmatic young woman provides the central focus of a text which strives to tell a story without falling into the vulgar 'empiricism' of the novel. The result is a work which crosses several genres – autobiographical journal, anecdote, even a quasi-medical record – so as to emphasise the verisimilitude of the events it narrates. Breton's fascination with 'Nadja' was certainly real enough, and the text stresses this by including reproductions of her drawings, along with photographs of places where they encountered each other (he also uses photographs to avoid the necessity of novelistic description). The narrative is one of deliberate surrender to chance and accident, its shape determined less by Breton than by the enigmatic woman on whose presence or absence his own moods and actions come to depend.[56] Mundane locations become charged with an aura of expectancy, as Breton ponders those 'facts which may belong to the order of pure observation, but which on each occasion present all the appearances of a signal, without our being able to say precisely which signal'.[57] Like Philippe Soupault's *Last Nights of Paris* (1928), *Nadja* may be read as a sort of parody of the detective thriller in which an excess of 'clues' leaves the central mystery intact (Breton claims that he is 'interested only in books left ajar, like doors; I will not go looking for keys' [18]).

In Breton's narrative, Nadja becomes the centre of a magnetic field of association and premonition:

> Suddenly, while I am paying no attention whatever to the people on the street, some sudden vividness on the left-hand sidewalk … makes me almost mechanically knock on the window. It is as if Nadja had just passed by. I run, completely at random, in one of the three directions she might have taken. And as a matter of fact it is Nadja. …   (91)

Such moments proliferate as the narrative continues, but so do questions. 'Can it be that this desperate pursuit comes to an end here?' asks Breton at one point (108), but this 'intellectual seduction' continues, even as he worries that 'It is unforgivable of me to go on seeing her if I do not love her' (90). Nadja comes to represent freedom itself, the incarnation of desire, 'like one of those spirits of the air which certain magical practices momentarily permit us to entertain but which we can never overcome' (111). Yet there is a kind of black magic here as well: 'I was told, several months ago, that Nadja was mad' (136), and the story of this woman who takes her name, 'because in Russian it's the beginning of the word hope' (66), ends with her confinement in the Vaucluse sanitarium.

Contradictions now press in at every point: what, for example, is the real import of 'the well-known lack of frontiers between *non-madness* and madness' (144)? And how do we weigh the tragedy of Nadja's confinement against the questions which frame the narrative: 'Who am I?' (1); 'Who goes there? Is it you, Nadja? … Is it only me? Is it myself?' (144)? This narrative will remain unfinished, trailing guilt and perplexity. A door ajar, then, but one through which, suprisingly, another now walks; for in the epilogue to *Nadja* Breton finds the woman he *can* love, and with her 'this succession of terrible or charming enigmas was to come to an end' (158). It is a curious moment, for this 'end' (like that of *Paris Peasant*) seems almost to banish both desire and the work of interpretation it sustains. Yet even in these final pages of the text which bear her name, something of Nadja's presence persists – *her* enigmatic trace cannot (yet) be translated in myth, and will retain all the troubling ambiguity of writing itself.[58]

* * *

Here we can begin to discern two lines of development within Surrealism: one, represented by Breton's work of the thirties, constantly engages this double condition of writing, confronting the operation of the sign as, simultaneously, it seems to 'murder' and to preserve its object; the other, epitomised in Antonin Artaud's Theatre of Cruelty, seeks to negate representation and to escape the condition of language altogether. In the second case, we are dealing not just with the death of the object in the word, but with the destruction of the whole signifying system.[59] Artaud's work would thus take to its limits that struggle against textual authority and the Oedipal plot which had already characterised the development of avant-garde drama.

Surprisingly, though, theatre tended to be generally undervalued by the Surrealists: *If You Please* (1920) was Breton's last play, and after 1925 the group mounted a noisy opposition to productions of work by Aragon and Roger Vitrac. The Théâtre Alfred-Jarry, set up by Vitrac and Artaud in 1927, was actually the direct result of their expulsion from the Movement. Breton's increasingly negative view of the professional theatre ('I have never been able to tolerate the theatre', he remarked in *Nadja* [40]) grew partly from a distrust of 'commercialism' but coincided with that deep antipathy to realism and narrative which led to denunciations of the novel in his various manifestos.

It was in the work of Vitrac and Artaud, however, that the anti-Oedipal thrust of avant-garde theatre received its most powerful and extreme expression. Here the polemic against the family was directly connected with a rejection of the stage as (in Derrida's words) 'a locality always inhabited or haunted by the father'.[60] In Artaud's work this was linked with an ideal of a theatre freed from its dependence upon spoken language: 'the stage', he argued, 'is a physical and concrete place which demands to be filled and which must be made to speak its own concrete language' (*AA*, 231). This 'material and substantial language', of gesture, intonation, and *mise en scène*, would address itself to the senses and be 'truly theatrical only insofar as the thoughts it expresses transcend spoken language'. In putting an end to 'the subjugation of the theater to the text' (*AA*, 242), the new drama would move towards myth and magic, rediscovering human nature in the deepest impulses towards cruelty and sexual violence:

> Without an element of cruelty at the foundation of every spectacle, the theater is not possible. In the state of degeneracy, in which we live, it is through the skin that metaphysics will be made to reenter our minds.   (*AA*, 251)

More is involved here than mere sensation: in an earlier piece, Artaud had spoken of death as 'a shattering and marvellous sensation unlike anything else in the realm of the mind' (*AA*, 121), suggesting that art must strive – again and again – to bring us into the realm of primal terror. Writing must now be redefined as a 'writing of the body', an ideal 'language without trace', as Derrida puts it.[61] Where for Breton, the negativity of language and its association with death are linked to the moment of non-presence in language, for Artaud the Theatre of Cruelty is based on an impossible 'desire for full presence, for nondifference: simultaneously life and death'. We might say that in Artaud's terms, Breton's form of negativity is fatal (the dead hand of the text prevents art from incarnating the 'real'), whereas the idea of 'full presence' is somehow linked to 'this feeling of desperate veracity in which it seems that you are going to die again, that you are going to die *for the second time*' (*AA*, 122; my emphases). This second death is absolute, beyond repetition and symbolisation, a destruction of the very frame of language. To establish this as the horizon of his theatre, Artaud forces the Oedipal narrative to implode at its origin, arresting its trajectory towards the symbolic by making its founding moment one of incestuous passion.

The brief and enigmatic *The Spurt of Blood* (1925) opens with this parodically idyllic exchange between two lovers:

YOUNG MAN: I love you and everything is beautiful.
YOUNG GIRL (*with a strong tremolo in her voice*):
   you love me, and everything is beautiful.   MFT, 223)

This 'shrill' and lyrical dialogue is suddenly disrupted by a cosmic hurricane which rains 'live pieces of human bodies', scorpions, a frog and a beetle upon the lovers. Artaud is burlesquing the more mannered (and 'existential') Surrealism of Armand Salacrou's *The Glass Ball* (1924), but he has added to Salacrou's fantasy one scandalous ingredient: incest. In Artaud's play, The Nurse appeals to the Knight to separate the lovers:

THE NURSE: Look! Our daughter – there – with him!
THE KNIGHT: Bah! There's no girl there!
THE NURSE: I tell you, they're screwing each other.
THE KNIGHT: What the hell do I care if they're screwing each other?
THE NURSE: Incest.   (*MFT*, 223–4)

In the pandemonium that follows (earthquake, thunder and lightning), 'A Priest, a Shoemaker, a Sexton, a Whore, a Judge, and a Street Peddler enter like shadows'. The Priest, representing religious law, seems, like the Knight, to sanction the act of incest, while the Whore embodies a force of corruption associated with sexual desire.

These characters to some extent prefigure those of Artaud's *The Cenci* (1935) who are 'incestuous and sacrilegious, they are adulterers, insurgents and blasphemers' and 'dwell in the realm of cruelty and must be judged *outside of good and evil*'.[62] The plague of the opening scene is a product of sexuality and, more specifically, of the 'lure' of feminine sexuality. At the close of the play, the Nurse lifts her dress, and as the Young Man and the Knight are frozen in horror, scorpions teem from her sex. This lurid finale hints, though, at something beyond sexual morality (and misogyny), for Artaud seeks to register 'cruelty' as fatality, as the 'great metaphysical fear' (*AA*, 236) of sheer Necessity which lies at the core of life and which resists linguistic representation. This is the import of that blasphemous (and virtually unrealisable) moment in *The Spurt of Blood* when the whore 'bites God's wrist' and 'An immense jet of blood shoots across the stage' (*MFT*, 225). Artaud had used the same image three years before, arguing then that 'We must cleanse ourselves of literature. We want to be men above everything, to be human. There are no forms or form. There is only the spouting of life. Life like a spurt of blood, to follow Claudel's felicitous formulation about Rimbaud.'[63]

A chain of connections emerges, then, between a theatre of cruelty (rather than 'literature'), a wounded God/Father, a spurt of blood, and an act of incest which seems to constitute an origin of sexuality. One clue to this aspect of Artaud's thought lies in the section of *The Theatre and Its Double* (1938) which is titled 'Mise en scène and Metaphysics'. The opening of the essay focuses on *Lot and His Daughters*, a painting by the sixteenth-century Dutch artist Lucas van Leyden. Artaud gives a vivid (if sometimes inaccurate) description of this work, which, he says, 'announces a kind of drama of nature' (*AA*, 228). While Lot fondles his daughter in the foreground, 'a shaft of … ominous light' tears the sky, irradiating a landscape in which buildings disintegrate and 'an unprecedented maritime disaster seems to have occurred' (*AA*, 229). Lot is 'seemingly placed there to live off his daughters, like a pimp' (*AA*, 230), an observation which reminds us that the Nurse in *A Spurt of Blood* curses the Knight for being a 'pimp' to his daughter. For Artaud, this powerful image (a 'silent pantomime' [*AA*, 233]) interweaves ideas of Becoming, Fatality, Chaos, the Miraculous, and Equilibrium; 'there are', he adds, 'even one or two ideas about the impotences of Speech, whose uselessness seems to be demonstrated by this supremely physical and anarchic painting' (*AA*, 230). Additionally, 'There is also an idea about sexuality and reproduction *at the origins*, with Lot placed there' (*AA*, 285).

Why does Artaud then conclude that 'this painting is what the theater should be'? Here, I think, we find the most complex statement of that interwoven set of ideas which we have traced through avant-garde drama. For Artaud, it is not just the iconic power of van Leyden's painting which makes it the model for a new theatre, but the subject-matter itself, an 'original' act of incest which somehow generates the conditions for a non-verbal art. The Father's prohibition of incest has been turned back on itself, foreclosed in a terrible parody of domesticity which produces cosmic disorder and seems to signal the ruin of representation. Not only is the paternal law blocked by this 'originary' violation, but the initial threat of castration, which brings representation into play, cannot now be uttered. Such, at any rate, seem to be the implications of the fantastic scene which Artaud places at the centre of his poetics of a non-verbal theatre. Later he will write that 'what men today call *human* is the castration of the superhuman part of man' (*AA*, 404), and, as we already know from *The Theatre and Its Double*, any theatre which seeks to restore the 'superhuman' must evoke a gestural and plastic 'Speech anterior to words' (*AA*, 220).

Artaud's fascination with the story of the Cenci, which he took from Stendhal and Shelley, confirms this suggestion, that the pre-discursive space which is, for him, the domain of authentic theatre is tied, emblematically, to a founding moment in which the Father performs a spectacular disavowal of the paternal function. Commenting on his own version of the story (an attack on 'the social superstition of the family' [*AA*, 341]), Artaud explains that

> In *The Cenci*, the father is a destroyer. And it is there that the subject is reunited with the Great Myths. *The Cenci*, a tragedy, is a Myth, which speaks clearly several truths.... I say rightly a tragedy, and not a drama; for here men are more than men, if they are not yet gods.[64]

The Cenci may be a failure ('still not the Theatre of Cruelty', Artaud admitted[65]) but it provides a climactic expression of the developments we have traced in avant-garde drama: for just as Artaud's 'absolute' theatre is finally impossible, so the anti-Oedipal project of avant-garde theatre remains (obliquely or directly) tied to the parricidal desire which that story narrates. Cenci's crime of incest generates the condition of a Theatre of Cruelty but the necessity of his destruction returns us to 'history' and to representation. *The Cenci*, in that sense, remains in dialectical tension with classical theatre, its forms bound by the very law of repetition which it seeks to escape.[66]

* * *

To return now to the surreal world of Breton's Paris entails an abrupt changing of gears, as we relinquish the titanic emotions of

Artaud's myth for the more nuanced intimations of the everyday. Here the cruel force of Necessity is replaced by what Breton comes to call 'objective chance': 'the encounter of an external causality and an internal finality',[67] or, we might say, the momentary intersection of human desire with an order of events in the external world. And in contrast to Artaud, Breton is at pains to *read* the signs of this encounter, to grasp premonitions as a kind of language:

> A person will know how to proceed when ... he consents to reproduce, without any change, what an appropriate grid [*écran*] tells him in advance of his own acts. This grid exists. Every life contains these homogenous patterns of facts, whose surface is cracked or cloudy. Each person has only to stare at them fixedly in order to read his own future. ... Everything humans might want to know is written upon this grid in phosphorescent letters, in letters of *desire*. (86–7)

A found object, like Breton's peasant spoon, has a 'catalyzing role' (32), offering a complex of signs to the unfocused desire of the stroller. At the same time, such an object brings to the surface a whole sequence of prior events whose significance until now has remained only latent. In this case, the handle of the spoon rests on what looks to Breton like a small shoe, and this then reminds him that some time earlier he had asked Giacometti to sculpt him a glass slipper to use as an ash-tray. The request had been triggered by one of those fragmentary sentences Breton heard while half-asleep: 'the Cinderella ash-tray', *le cendrier de Cendrillon*. The spoon now seems the fulfilment of this earlier desire, and Breton's interpretation of it renders it gradually less 'opaque': 'The wood, which had seemed intractable, took on the transparency of glass' (34). Here, then, is a perfect example of 'objective chance', for 'the object that I had so much wanted to contemplate before, had been constructed outside of me, very different, *very far beyond* what I could have imagined, and regardless of many immediately deceptive elements'.

Yet that is not the end of the matter, and another series of associations produces 'the perfect equation: slipper = spoon = penis = the perfect mold of this penis' (36), and these fetishistic implications are then linked to 'the meaning of the *lost object*' (36), condensing Breton's desire for a woman 'unique and unknown' (37). Other lines of interpretation now begin to emerge as signs proliferate in the text: the 'mysterious exchanges between the material and mental worlds'

(40) seem to constitute a 'chain of glass', 'the beginning of a contact, unimaginably dazzling, between man and the world of things' (40). This 'chain' of images runs through *Mad Love*, connecting glass with crystal, fire, the 'incandescent stone of the sexual unconscious' (67), phosphorous, sperm, lava and snow. But this glass slipper is also an ash-tray (and in the Alaskan craters, snow too seems buried under ash [8]), reminding us that the 'phosphorescent letters of desire' can fall prey at any time to the 'wind of ashes' (99), and that 'It is at the price of a wound required by the adversary powers who control man that living love triumphs' (99). The wound is manifold, prefigured in Breton's mandrake root which bleeds 'at the slightest scratch with an unstoppable dark sap' (16). The mandrake is traditionally held to spring from the ground where the ejaculation of the hanged man falls, and later the evocation of Tenerife contains a cactus which 'hit by a stone, bleeds abundantly white and stains. ... Impossible not to associate with it the idea of mother's milk and also that of ejaculation' (70). The intricate chain of images constantly displaces a point of origin which is somehow double, containing both life and death, desire and its end:

> the incandescent stone of the sexual unconscious, as unparticularized as possible, apart from any idea of immediate possession, forms again at this depth as at no other, all being lost in the first modulations, which are also the last, of the unheard phoenix.   (69)

The phoenix, promise of renewal, is born again and dies (unheard) in the very same moment, providing yet another image of an origin which is both divided and non-existent. All of which may remind us of an earlier passage in *Mad Love* where Breton begins with a quotation from Freud: '"Of Eros and the struggle against Eros!" In its enigmatic form, this exclamation by Freud happens to obsess me on certain days as only some poetry can' (37). In Strachey's translation, the passage from *The Ego and the Id* (1923) from which Breton quotes reads as follows:

> we are driven to conclude that the death instincts are by their nature mute and that the clamour of life proceeds for the most part from Eros. And from the struggle against Eros![68]

Breton uses Freud's discussion of the opposition of the death drive to Eros as a way of interpreting the objects he and Giacometti found (the mask is clearly associated with death, while the discovery of the spoon is linked to the satisfaction of the 'sexual instinct' and will culminate in the fitting of the slipper to an ideal woman's foot, with Cinders released from the hearth). But this convenient categorisation will not survive in a text which, as we have seen, constantly shows one trope to be inhabited by its opposite. Even in the exotic 'dream country' of Tenerife, where it seems that 'We will never again be done with this foliage of the Golden Age' (75), the 'Delirium of absolute presence' (76) bears a 'lethal shadow', since Eros is always intertwined with its other, Thanatos.[69]

The great dream, then, of 'reciprocal love' (93) can never detach itself from the language whose 'phosphorescent letters' are at once ashes and embers. The cinder from which the enigmatic beauty takes her name is both dead and alive, caught between being and non-being, a condition which epitomises Breton's conception of desire and the sign. It is a powerful image which Breton uses to convey the heat of vision even as he situates its object elsewhere. In this respect, *Mad Love* is perhaps the classic Surrealist text, supplying virtually all the movement's principal tropes and preoccupations at the same time as it defines their limits. It is difficult not to see this figure of the burning coal as in some way comparable to Kafka's sense of the doubleness of the Law, for in each case writing expresses a desire for presence even as it calls into question literature's truth-telling capacity. Surrealism's own sense of itself as the ultimate avant-garde thus contained a certain ambiguity, for if it was indeed the end or summation of modernism it was also conceived as an end without finality or closure. Such an 'end' might seem to recapitulate the larger tensions of modernism as we have variously construed them here, the flamboyant gestures of an 'heroic' avant-garde framed by the intermittent but insistent suspicion that art's real value lay precisely in the *failure* of its metaphysical ambitions.

CODA

That way of situating the aesthetic as neither the privileged bearer of metaphysical truths nor as merely some substitute for them might now seem to characterise the strand of modernism which speaks most directly to our own cultural moment. Ten years after *Mad Love*, however, when Europe lay in ruins after another, more terrible 'wind of ashes' had blown through the continent, the difference between a cruel aesthetic and a negative one was harder to discern. In the face of total cultural collapse, Thomas Mann's *Doctor Faustus* (1947) weighed the consequences of the modernist project and in doing so effectively extinguished the dialectical spark of hope in Breton's narrative.

Mann's narrator, the humanist Serenus Zeitblom, tells the story of composer Adrian Leverkühn, whose life and work are intertwined with the rise of Nazism, the terrible last days of which Zeitblom is witnessing as he writes (Leverkühn dies in 1940). Mann makes sure that the reader will not miss the intricacy of this montage of time frames by having Zeitblom point out that

> This is a quite extraordinary interweaving of time-units, destined, moreover to include even a third; namely, the time which one day the courteous reader will take for the reading of what has been written; at which point he will be dealing with a threefold ordering of time: his own, that of the chronicler, and historic time.[70]

This deliberately intrusive comment contains several layers of implication. First, it reminds us of Mann's avowedly 'constructivist' conception of the novel – a combination of parodic use of other textual materials along with a high degree of reflexive self-consciousness which registers the impossibility of a 'spontaneous' romantic aesthetic. Secondly, Mann's crosscutting of time-frames is the structural analogue to the novel's deeply sceptical treatment of that nostalgia for origin and presence which had led some modernists to the threshold of Nazism.

Leverkühn's works prior to the final *Lamentation* are, like Mann's own later novels, heavily dependent on parody, conceived as the only valid response to a cultural crisis in which pure 'invention' seems no longer possible. Yet at the same time Leverkühn is increasingly occupied with fantasies of the primitive and archaic, with Expressionist desires for some uncontaminated origin. The paradox of his art, then, is that his invention of the Shönbergian twelve-tone scale is a form of neo-classicism which also subserves a romantic fetish of 'arrogant personal uniqueness' (as the impressario Fitelberg remarks [389]). Parody and formalism are not, finally, enough for Leverkühn, who is drawn to the demonic pact through which, in the Devil's words, the artist 'will break through time itself, by which I mean the cultural epoch and its cult, and dare to be barbaric' (236). The political implications of this fantasy of the modern as 'primaeval' are clear and disastrous enough, but underpinning Mann's acount of them is an ironic recognition of the way in which the anti-mimetic thrust of a fundamentally 'romantic' modernism obliterates 'socio-political' values[71] in what turns out to be a hopelessly mimetic gesture of 'return'. There is something ornately repellent about Leverkühn's finding in the farm at Pfeiffering a perfect simulation of his childhood home at Buchel. Everything is duplicated from one scene to the other, right down to the dog, the old tree and the pond, and the effect is to produce a kind of structural aporia within the shifting time-frames of the novel – a moment of frozen identity in which modernity is revealed as pure regression.

It is a final irony, perhaps, that a modernist tradition which began with a dissociation of authentic art from bourgeois political culture should, in *Doctor Faustus*, end with a certain nostalgia for the 'living values' (358) of Serenus Zeitblom. The history of the various modernisms may provide ample demonstration of the unwisdom of Leverkühn's metaphysical art; the choice between a negative aesthetic and the now tarnished humanism of Zeitblom is, however, harder to resolve. It is, in fact, far from certain that our own *post*modernism has made that dilemma any less pressing.

Notes

A List of Abbreviations used in the text and notes is given at the beginning of the book. Unless otherwise indicated, all translations are my own.

Note to the Preface

1. Marjorie Perloff, *Radical Artifice*, pp. 202, 243.

Notes to the Introduction

1. See Valéry Larbaud, 'Trois Belles Mendiantes', in *Oeuvres complètes*, vol. 8, pp. 323–40.
2. See, for example, Charles Dédéyan, *Le Nouveau mal de siècle*, p. 117.
3. My translation draws on those of Francis Scarfe, in *Baudelaire*, vol. 1, *The Complete Verse*, pp. 171–4, and Richard Howard, in *Les Fleurs du mal*, pp. 88–90.
4. Jean Baudrillard (*Seduction*, p. 99) has detected precisely this logic in another text of the period, Søren Kierkegaard's *Diary of a Seducer* (1843), where, he says, 'The seducer by himself is nothing; the seduction originates entirely with the girl. This is why Johannes can claim to have learned everything from Cordelia. He is not being hypocritical. The calculated seduction mirrors the natural seduction, drawing from the latter as its source, all the better to eliminate it.'
5. See Jessica Benjamin, *The Bonds of Love*, p. 164.

Notes to Chapter 1

1. Ralph Waldo Emerson, 'Circles', *Collected Writings*, vol. II, p. 180.
2. Ibid., p. 179.
3. See Karl Marx and Friedrich Engels, *Selected Works*, pp. 31–63. See also Marshall Berman, *All That is Solid Melts into Air*, pp. 87–129, and Jeffrey Mehlman, *Revolution and Repetition*, pp. 5–41.
4. Karl Marx, *The Eighteenth Brumaire*, p. 170.
5. The distinction is helpfully elaborated in Matei Calinescu, *The Faces of Modernity*.
6. Walter Benjamin, 'Central Park', p. 46.
7. Charles Baudelaire, 'Spleen', *The Complete Verse*, p. 156.
8. Théophile Gautier, 'Charles Baudelaire' (1868), *Complete Works*, vol. XII, p. 59. Baudelaire finds the 'monster' present in the work of Poe and distinguishes it from the 'well-bred melancholy' of Tennyson (*BSW*, 207).
9. Quoted in Guy Michaud, *Le Message poétique du symbolisme*, p. 107. The period sees the emergent study of such disorders – see, for example,

on the 'discovery' of manic-depression in the 1850s, Theodore Zeldin, *France, 1848–1945*, vol. 2, p. 781.

10. Fyodor Dostoyevsky, *Notes from Underground*, p. 31.
11. See Terry Eagleton, *The Ideology of the Aesthetic*.
12. Théophile Gautier, *Mademoiselle de Maupin*, p. 30.
13. See Arno Mayer, *The Persistence of the Old Regime*, p. 198.
14. Charles Baudelaire, *My Heart Laid Bare*, p. 172.
15. T. J. Clark, *The Absolute Bourgeois*, p. 171.
16. Jean-Paul Sartre, *Critique of Dialectical Reason*, vol. 1, p. 756.
17. Neil Larsen, *Modernism and Hegemony*, p. xxiv.
18. See, for example, Michael Gilmore, *American Romanticism and the Marketplace*, p. 46.
19. See John Lough, *Writer and Public in France*, p. 303.
20. Charles Baudelaire, *Oeuvres complètes*, vol. II, p. 17.
21. Ibid., vol. II, p. 155.
22. Quoted in J. Mouquet and W. T. Bandy, *Baudelaire en 1848*, p. 45.
23. Gérard de Nerval, *Selected Writings*, p. 54.
24. Gustave Flaubert, *Letters*, vol. II, p. 200.
25. Réne Girard, *Deceit, Desire, and the Novel*, p. 9. Further references will be given in the text.
26. Renato Poggioli, *The Theory of the Avant-Garde*, p. 120.
27. Paul Valéry, 'The Place of Baudelaire' (1924), in *Leonardo Poe Mallarmé*, p. 198.
28. Baudelaire, *My Heart Laid Bare*, pp. 184–5 (his emphasis).
29. Baudelaire, *The Poems in Prose*, p. 197.
30. Baudelaire, *My Heart Laid Bare*, p. 193.
31. Ibid., p. 197.
32. Baudelaire, *Oeuvres complètes*, vol. II, p. 87. The italicised phrase is in English in the original.
33. Baudelaire, *My Heart Laid Bare*, p. 175.
34. See, for example, Charles Dickens, *Little Dorritt* (1857), Friedrich Engels, *The Condition of the Working Class in England* (1845), Fyodor Dostoyevsky, *Winter Notes* (1863), Herman Melville, *Israel Potter* (1855).
35. Engels, *The Condition of the Working Class in England*, p. 60.
36. John Ruskin, 'The Study of Architecture in Our Schools' (1865), in John D. Rosenberg (ed.), *The Genius of John Ruskin*, p. 138.
37. Flaubert, *Letters*, vol. I, p. 212.
38. Baudelaire, *My Heart Laid Bare*, pp. 133–4.
39. Ibid., p. 175
40. Charles Baudelaire, quoted in Guy Michaud, *Le Message poétique du symbolisme*, p. 47; Flaubert, *Letters*, vol. I, p. 56; Dostoyevsky, *Notes from Underground*, pp. 48–9.
41. Baudelaire, *Oeuvres complètes*, vol. I, p. 554, and Jean-Paul Sartre, *Baudelaire*, p. 22. Sartre adds the necessary qualification (p. 156) that 'what he looked for in the glass was himself as he had *composed* himself.'
42. Dostoyevsky, *Notes from Underground*, p. 36. For Dostoyevsky's knowledge of Poe, see Donald Fanger, *Dostoevsky and Romantic Realism*, p. 256.

43. See, for example, John Carroll, *Break-Out from the Crystal Palace.*
44. Quoted in Albert Cassagne, *La Théorie de l'art pour l'art*, pp. 410–11.
45. Baudelaire, *Oeuvres complètes*, vol. II, p. 18.
46. Flaubert, *Letters*, vol. I, pp. 65, 179 (emphasis in original).
47. Ibid., vol. I, p. 154.
48. Ibid.
49. Ibid., vol. I, p. 132.
50. Ibid., vol. I, pp. 171–2; Matthew Arnold, 'Count Leo Tolstoi' (1887), in *Essays in Criticism; Second Series*, p. 362.
51. Charles Baudelaire, *The Poems in Prose*, pp. 36–9.
52. Walter Benjamin, *Charles Baudelaire*, p. 141.
53. Baudelaire, *Complete Verse*, p. 176.
54. Herman Melville, *Moby-Dick*, p. 296.
55. For a discussion of political readings of *Moby-Dick*, see especially Michael Paul Rogin, *Subversive Genealogy.*

Notes to Chapter 2

1. Karl Marx, *Early Writings*, p. 234 (emphases in original). See also Catherine Porter, *Seeing and Being*, chapter 1.
2. Jean Moréas, 'A Literary Manifesto', in Eugen Weber, *Paths to the Present*, p. 206.
3. Charles Baudelaire, *Complete Verse*, p. 61.
4. W. B. Yeats, 'The Symbolism of Poetry' (1900), in *Essays and Introductions*, pp. 153–64.
5. Jean-Paul Sartre, *Saint Genet*, pp. 463–4.
6. See R. Étiemble, *Le Mythe de Rimbaud.*
7. Quoted in Georges Poulet, *Exploding Poetry*, p. 113.
8. These qualities found even more extreme representation in the work of the Comte de Lautréamont whose *Maldoror* (1868) and *Poems* (1870) would become favourite texts of the Surrealists.
9. Ezra Pound, *Translations*, p. 434.
10. Translated in Samuel Beckett, *Collected Poems in English and French*, p. 93 (further quotations are from this version).
11. Cf. Georges Poulet, *Exploding Poetry*, pp. 101–2.
12. Kristin Ross, *The Emergence of Social Space*, p. 113.
13. See Paul Lidsky, *Les Écrivains contre la Commune*. Ross, *The Emergence of Social Space*, p. 149, concludes that anti-Communard rhetoric 'aimed at establishing a massive racially constituted category that would include in one breath animals, workers (particularly working-class women), barbarians, savages, and thieves'. Rimbaud's call for an end to the 'servitude' of women in the letter to Demeny (*RP*, 13) strikes a most unusual note in the development of modernism.
14. Walter Benjamin, 'Conversations with Brecht' (1934), in Ernst Bloch et al., *Aesthetics and Politics*, p. 87.
15. Ross, *The Emergence of Social Space*, p. 124.
16. See Mallarmé's late 'portrait' of Rimbaud (1896) in *Oeuvres complètes*, pp. 512–9.

17. See Maurice Blanchot, *La Part du feu*, pp. 37–8.
18. For Mallarmé's debt to Hegelian idealism, see Janine D. Langan, *Hegel and Mallarmé*.
19. Moréas, 'A Literary Manifesto', p. 206.
20. Walter Benjamin, *Charles Baudelaire*, p. 100.
21. The phrase is used by Mallarmé and was popular in the period – for an historical account see D. J. Mossop, *Pure Poetry*.
22. See Gérard Genette, *Mimologiques*, p. 274.
23. V. N. Vološinov, *Marxism and the Philosophy of Language* (1929), p. 41.
24. M. M. Bakhtin, 'Discourse in the Novel' (1934–5), in *The Dialogic Imagination*, p. 293.
25. Ferdinand de Saussure, *Course in General Linguistics*, p. 120.
26. Ibid.
27. Vološinov's *Marxism and the Philosophy of Language* provides an early critique of the 'abstract objectivism' of Saussurean linguistics (see pp. 58–61).
28. Stéphane Mallarmé, *The Poems*, pp. 166–9.
29. Ibid., p. 297. A helpful account of the poem is given in John Porter Houston, *French Symbolism and the Modernist Movement*, pp. 143ff.
30. Stéphane Mallarmé, 'Préface' to *Un Coup de dés*, in *Oeuvres complètes*, p. 455.
31. Maurice Blanchot, *The Space of Literature*, p. 39.

Notes to Chapter 3

1. Leconte de Lisle, 'Midi', trans. in Anthony Hartley (ed.), *The Penguin Book of French Verse: 3*, pp. 139–41.
2. Paul Verlaine, *Selected Poems*, p. 53. All translations are from this volume.
3. John Porter Houston, *French Symbolism and the Modernist Movement*, p. 182.
4. See P. Mathieu, 'Essai sur la métrique de Verlaine I', p. 583.
5. See, for example, A. E. Carter, *The Idea of Decadence in French Literature*, p. 131.
6. Théophile Gautier, 'Charles Baudelaire', *Complete Works*, vol. XII, p. 39. Further references will be given in the text.
7. See Elisabeth Bronfen, *Over Her Dead Body*, pp. 68–9: 'By virtue of her second nature, her alterity, Woman is conceived as ornament, artifice or decoration, so that death as corruption, division or duplication presides in two opposed realms which are both associated with the feminine: firstly in the weakness, vulnerability and corruptibility of the flesh, and secondly in the artificial clothes and signs that supplement the naked body of nature.'
8. See, for example, K. W. Swart, *The Sense of Decadence in Nineteenth-Century France*, pp. 138ff.
9. Quoted in Jacques Lethève, 'Le Thème de la décadence dans les Lettres Françaises à la fin du XIXme siècle', pp. 49, 50.
10. Charles Baudelaire, *Oeuvres complètes* vol. II, p. 603.

11. Gustave Flaubert, *Bouvard and Pécuchet*, p. 286.
12. See Lethève, 'Le Thème de la décadence', p. 54.
13. Rpt. in Bonner Mitchell (ed.), *Les Manifestes littéraires de la belle époque*, p. 19.
14. Ibid, p. 16.
15. Arthur Schopenhauer, *Parerga and Parilipomena*, pp. 249–50.
16. Arthur Schopenhauer, *The World as Will and Idea*, vol. I, p. 3. Further references will be given in the text.
17. Ralph Waldo Emerson, 'Nature', *Collected Works*, vol. I, p. 10.
18. A. G. Lehmann, *The Symbolist Aesthetic in France*, p. 204.
19. See Isabella Wyzewska, *La Revue wagnérienne*, p. 82.
20. Walter Pater, *The Renaissance*, p. 106.
21. See, for example, Suzanne Bernard, *Mallarmé et la musique*, pp. 74, 83.
22. Richard Wagner, 'Beethoven', in *Prose Works*, vol. V, p. 104.
23. Teodor de Wyzewa, quoted in Raymond Furness, *Wagner and Literature*, p. 8.
24. Wagner, 'Beethoven', p. 106.
25. See, for example, P-A Villiers de l'Isle-Adam, 'The Two Augurs', in *Cruel Tales*, pp. 27–40.
26. Quoted in G. D. Turbow, 'Wagnerism in France', in D. C. Large and W. Weber (eds), *Wagnerism in European Culture and Politics*, p. 152.
27. Quoted in M. Gaddis Rose, 'Foreword' to Villiers de l'Isle-Adam, *Axël*, p. ix.
28. See Léon Guichard, *La Musique et les lettres en France au temps du wagnérisme*, p. 172, and A. W. Raitt, *Villiers de l'Isle-Adam et le mouvement symboliste*, pp. 133ff.
29. W. B. Yeats, 'Preface', in Gaddis Rose (trans.), Villiers de l'Isle-Adam, *Axël*, p. xiii.
30. Compare Walter Benjamin's discussion of baroque allegory in *The Origin of German Tragic Drama*.
31. Joris-Karl Huysmans, *Against Nature*, p. 98. Further references will be given in the text.
32. See, for example, the opening scene of Octave Mirbeau's *The Torture Garden*, where the male assembly ponders the proposition that 'As soon as man awakens to consciousness, we instill the spirit of murder in his mind. Murder, expanded to the status of a duty, and popularized to the point of heroism, accompanies him through all the stages of his existence' (p. 13).
33. Gabriele D'Annunzio, *The Triumph of Death*, pp. 253–4. Further references will be given in the text.
34. See especially Rosalind H. Williams, *Dream Worlds*.
35. Quoted in Mario Praz, *The Romantic Agony*, p. 291.
36. Cf. Walter Benjamin, *One-Way Street and Other Writings*, pp. 48–9: 'The bourgeois interior of the 1860s to the 1890s, with its gigantic sideboards distended with carvings, the sunless corners where palms stand, the balcony embattled behind its balustrade, and the long corridors with their singing gas flames, fittingly houses the corpse.'
37. Compare my discussion of Baudelaire's 'To a Red-haired Beggar Girl', pp. 2–3, above.

38. See J. Laplanche and J.-B. Pontalis, *The Language of Psychoanalysis*, p. 473, on the 'process whereby the instinct replaces an independent object by the subject's own self'.
39. Quoted in Guy Michaud, *Le Message poétique du symbolisme*, p. 87.
40. Sigmund Freud, 'Instincts and Their Vicissitudes' (1915), *Pelican Freud Library*, vol. 11, p. 126. See also the discussion in Leo Bersani and Ulysse Dutoit, *The Forms of Violence*, pp. 24–39.
41. See Sigmund Freud, *Beyond the Pleasure Principle* (1920), *Pelican Freud Library*, vol. 11, p. 310.
42. Oscar Wilde, *Plays, Prose Writings and Poems*, p. 173.
43. Gautier, 'Charles Baudelaire', p. 40.
44. See Enid L. Duthie, *L'Influence du symbolisme français dans le renouveau poétique de l'Allemagne*, pp. 169–71.
45. Nietzsche draws on Paul Bourget's two-volume *Essai de psychologie contemporaine* (1883–5) in *The Case of Wagner* (1888). References to Bourget's *Essai* will be given in the text.
46. Roland Barthes, *Writing Degree Zero*, pp. 49, 44.
47. My phrasing adapts Jacques Lacan, *Écrits*, p. 104: 'The symbol manifests itself as the murder of the thing'.
48. Stéphane Mallarmé, *The Poems*, p. 113.
49. A. C. Swinburne, 'Anactoria', in *Collected Poetical Works*, vol. I, p. 60.
50. T. S. Eliot, *Selected Essays*, p. 327.
51. Remy de Gourmont, *Decadence and Other Essays on the Culture of Ideas*, p. 124.

Notes to Chapter 4

1. Tristan Corbière, *The Centenary Corbière*, p. 3.
2. Jules Laforgue, *Mélanges posthumes*, p. 121.
3. Ibid., pp. 19, 142.
4. Ibid., p. 10.
5. James Gibbons Huneker, *Ivory, Apes, and Peacocks* (1915), p. 30.
6. See, for example, Jules Laforgue, 'Complaint of the Barrel-Organ', in *PL*, 56–9.
7. Jean Moréas, 'A Literary Manifesto', p. 209.
8. For Joyce's view of Dujardin, see Frank Budgen, *James Joyce and the Making of 'Ulysses'*, p. 94.
9. Laforgue's irony also connects him to this tradition of 'plastic' values – Pound observes in 'Irony, Laforgue, and Some Satire' (1917) that 'he marks the next phase after Gautier' (*Literary Essays*, p. 282).
10. Stefan George, 'Parting', in *The Works of Stefan George*, p. 16.
11. See below, Chapter 7. The combination of Symbolist and Parnassian elements also characterises the early work of Rubén Darío – see especially the collections *Azul* (1888) and *Prosas profanas* (1896), in *Rubén Darío: Páginas escogidas*.
12. Hugo von Hofmannsthal, *Selected Prose*, pp. 134–5.
13. Ibid., p. 140.
14. Hugo von Hofmannsthal, *Poems and Verse Plays*, p. 103.

15. Quoted by Michael Hamburger, 'Introduction' to Hofmannsthal, *Poems and Verse Plays*, p. xxxviii. Cf. Hofmannsthal's remark that 'Plasticity develops not through observation, but through identification' (quoted in Hermann Broch, *Hugo von Hofmannsthal and His Time*, p. 118).
16. Walter Pater, *The Renaissance*, p. 168. Further references will be given in the text.
17. Pater, *Imaginary Portraits*, p. 47 (my emphases).
18. For France, see especially, Gabriel Sarrazin, *Poètes modernes de L'Angleterre*. Translations of Swinburne's work appeared in Stefan George's *Blätter für die Kunst* (see Enid Duthie, *L'Influence du symbolisme français*, p. 507) and Hofmannsthal published a study of him in the *Deutsche Zeitung* in 1893.
19. See, for example, Ruth Z. Temple, *The Critic's Alchemy* and Cyrena N. Pondrom, *The Road from Paris*.
20. See, for example, Edgar Saltus, *The Philosophy of Disenchantment* (1885), where Schopenhauer is presented as 'this Emerson in black' (p. 61). The Symbolist drama became a nineties vogue mainly through the enormously popular work of Maeterlinck – see, for example, Arnold T. Schwab, *James Gibbons Huneker*, p. 73.
21. See, for example, René Wellek, *Discriminations*, p. 103.
22. Much information on Symbolism as an international phenomenon is given in Anna Balakian (ed.), *The Symbolist Movement in the Literature of European Languages*.
23. Jean Moréas, in Bonner Mitchell (ed.), *Les Manifestes littéraires*, p. 47.
24. Quoted in Marcel Raymond, *De Baudelaire au Surréalisme*, p. 64.
25. Tolstoy, *What is Art?*, excerpted in R. N. Stromberg, *Realism, Naturalism, and Symbolism*, pp. 210, 211, 217–18.
26. André Gide, *Journals*, p. 129.
27. Quoted in Henri Peyre, *What is Symbolism?*, p. 136.
28. Marcel Proust, 'Contre l'obscurité (1896), in *Chroniques*, pp. 137–44; Apollinaire, *Oeuvres complètes*, vol. II, pp. 286–9.
29. André Gide, *Fruits of the Earth*, p. 9. Further references will be given in the text.
30. Gide, *Journals*, p. 174. Gide, however, is still ambivalent about the effects of *vagabondance*, noting that it is 'one of the chief causes of the deteriorating of the personality'.
31. See Betsy Erkkila, *Walt Whitman among the French*, p. 62.
32. Whitman, 'Preface', *Leaves of Grass*, p. 714.
33. Guy Michaud, *Le Message poétique du symbolisme*, p. 464. See also Eugenia W. Herbert, *The Artist and Social Reform*.
34. Quoted in Michel Décaudin, *La Crise des valeurs symbolistes*, p. 106.
35. Émile Verhaeren, *Les Campagnes hallucinées*, p. 156.
36. Horace B. Samuel, *Modernities*, p. 196.
37. Henri Meschonnic, *Modernité, Modernité*, p. 196.
38. Quoted in René Taupin, *L'Influence du symbolisme français sur la poésie américaine*, p. 104.
39. Mitchell (ed.), *Les Manifestes littéraires*, p. 57. Further references will be given in the text.

40. Émile Zola, *The Kill*, p. 109.
41. Charles Maurras, *L'Avenir de l'intelligence* (1905), p. 212 (emphasis in original).
42. Ibid., p. 214.
43. Nordau, excerpted in Stromberg, *Realism, Naturalism, and Symbolism* pp. 265, 269.
44. Friedrich Nietzsche, *The Gay Science* (1882), p. 338.
45. Noted in John H. White, *Literary Futurism*, p. 8.
46. One of the few critics to note the implications of the early downgrading of prose is Henri Meschonnic, *Critique du rythme*, p. 396. See also Michel Raimond, *La Crise du roman*.
47. Antonio Gramsci, *Selections from the Prison Notebooks*, p. 260.
48. Rudolf Hilferding, *Finance Capital*, p. 235.
49. On 'capital fetishism', see, for example, G. A. Cohen, *Karl Marx's Theory of History*, pp. 115–24.
50. Valéry Larbaud, 'Ode', trans. in Paul Auster (ed.), *The Random House Book of Twentieth Century French Poetry*, p. 85.
51. Valéry Larbaud, *Les Poésies de A. O. Barnabooth*, p. 55. Further references will be given in the text.
52. Valéry Larbaud, 'Music after Reading', in Auster (ed.), *The Random House Book*, p. 91.
53. Jules Romains, *La Vie unanime*, p. 132. Further references will be given in the text.
54. Translated in Marianne W. Martin, 'Futurism, Unanimism and Apollinaire', p. 261. On the influence of Romains, see also Daniel Robbins, 'From Symbolism to Cubism: The Abbaye of Créteil'.
55. Mitchell (ed.), *Les Manifestes littéraires*, pp. 82–3.
56. Quoted in Ezra Pound, 'Unanimism' (1918), p. 30.

Notes to Chapter 5

1. See the discussion of 'the self as origin' in Rosalind E. Krauss, *The Originality of the Avant-Garde and other Modernist Myths*, p. 157. See also F. T. Marinetti, *Let's Murder the Moonshine* (1909), *F*, 47–8: 'Enrico Cavacchioli was dozing and dreaming out loud: "I feel my twenty-year-old body growing young again! ....With an ever-younger step, I return to my cradle. ...Soon I'll reenter my mother's womb! ...For me, then, everything is lawful!" ' Futurism is thus a perfect expression of what Jacques Derrida describes as 'the complicity of Western metaphysics with a notion of male firstness' – see Peggy Kamuf (ed.), *A Derrida Reader*, p. 445.
2. Quoted in Caroline Tisdall and Angelo Bozzolla, *Futurism* , p. 130.
3. Marinetti also predicted another modernist habit by identifying the crowd or mass audience as 'feminine' – see, for example, *F*, 143: 'I have had enough experience of the femininity of crowds and the weakness of their collective virginity in the course of forcing Futurist free verse upon them.' See the discussion of this theme in Andreas Huyssen, *After the Great Divide*, chapter 3.

4. Cf. *F*, 73: 'In this campaign of ours for liberation, our best allies are the suffragettes, because the more rights and powers they win for woman, the more she will be deprived of *Amore*, and by so much will she cease to be a magnet for sentimental passion or lust.'
5. Quoted in Claudia Salaris, *Le futuriste*, p. 23. This anthology is the principal source for information on women and Futurism, though Salaris's *Storia del futurismo* is also helpful.
6. Salaris's anthology indicates two main centres of activity for these women writers: the Florentine review *L'Italia futurista* (1916–18) and *Roma futurista* (1918–20). Contributions to the former include a number of interesting responses to Marinetti's *Come si seducono le donne* (1917) – see particularly those of Enif Robert, Rosa Rosà, and Shara Marini. Interventions in *Roma futurista* indicate feminist initiatives within the Futurist Political Party (1918–20).
7. Cf. Marinetti's description of D'Annunzio's poems as 'chiseled and polished like jewels, that false decorative verdure, those ideas sick and plaintive beneath the weight of useless riches', in *Les Dieux s'en vont, D'Annunzio reste* (1908), *Scritti francesi*, p. 436.
8. Joris-Karl Huysmans, *Against Nature*, pp. 196–7.
9. Marinetti, *Scritti francesi*, p. 424.
10. Friedrich Nietzsche, *On the Genealogy of Morals*, p. 184. Emphases in original.
11. See, for example, *F*, 89: 'we must renounce being understood. It is not necessary to be understood.'
12. Cangiullo, *Lights!*, in Michael Kirby and Victoria Nes Kirby, *Futurist Performance*, p. 254.
13. Ibid., p. 275.
14. Prampolini, *Futurist Scenic Atmosphere* (1924), in Kirby, *Futurist Performance*, p. 230.
15. Trans. in Felix Stefanile, *The Blue Moustache*, p. 29. The best anthology is *Poeti futuristi*, ed. Guido Ravegnani.
16. Stefanile, *The Blue Moustache*, p. 34.
17. The term 'crepuscular' was applied to turn of the century Italian poetry by the critic Giuseppe Antonio Borgese in an article of 1911, 'Poesia crepuscolare'. It implies a poetry of lowered sights, tending toward a sense of ending, sentimental and keenly aware of the past.
18. Pier Vincenzo Mengaldo (ed.), *Poeti Italiani del Novecento*, p. 338.
19. Stefanile, *The Blue Moustache*, p. 55.
20. Marinetti, *Destruction*, in *Scritti francesi*, pp. 147–269.
21. F. T. Marinetti, excerpt trans. in Richard J. Pioli, *Stung by Salt and War*, p. 71. For the full text, see *TIF*, 563–699.
22. See *F*, 84–5: 'Every noun should have its double; that is, the noun should be followed, with no conjunction, by the noun to which it is related by analogy. Example: man–torpedo-boat, woman–gulf, crowd–surf, piazza–funnel, door–faucet.'
23. Marjorie Perloff, *The Futurist Moment*, p. 60.
24. The main idea which the Futurists drew from Bergson was that of the indivisibility of movement, as noted in Umberto Boccioni, *The Plastic Foundations of Futurist Sculpture and Painting* (1913), *FM*, 89. The

Futurists ignored the role of memory in Bergson's theory of perception, just as they passed over his rejection of instantaneity.

25. Gilles Deleuze and Félix Guattari, *Anti-Oedipus*, p. 26.
26. See Marinetti, *F*, 73: 'The carnal life will be reduced to the conservation of the species', *F*, 69: 'To possess a woman is not to rub against her but to penetrate her.'
27. Umberto Eco, *Reflections on The Name of the Rose*, p. 57.
28. Perry Anderson , 'Modernity and Revolution', p. 105, thus misses the mark somewhat when he claims that 'In no case was capitalism as such ever exalted by any brand of "modernism".'
29. Walter Benjamin, *Illuminations*, p. 244.
30. Jessica Benjamin, *The Bonds of Love* , p. 33.
31. Ibid., p. 78 (my emphases). It is, arguably, a limitation of Benjamin's argument (though not one which bears directly on the present discussion) that she restricts her presentation of Hegel's concept of 'recognition' to the Master/Slave dialectic. For a fuller account of modalities of love, friendship and forgiveness in the *Phenomenology*, see Robert R. Williams, *Recognition*.
32. Mario Isnenghi, *Il Mito della Grande Guerra da Marinetti a Malaparte*, p. 170. Cf. Eduardo Sanguinetti, 'La Guerre Futuriste', in Giovanni Lista (ed.), *Marinetti et le Futurisme*, pp. 107–11.
33. *F*, 67. Marinetti deliberately modifies Baudelaire's account of 'the transient, the fleeting, the contingent' as *'one half* of art' (see Chapter 1, above).
34. Germano Celant, 'Futurism as Mass Avant-garde', in Anne D'Harnoncourt (ed.), *Futurism and the International Avant-garde*, p. 39.
35. Fillia (Luigi Colombo), *La morte della donna* (1925), quoted in Roberto Tessari, *Il mito della macchina*, p. 258.
36. Georges Bataille, *Visions of Excess*, pp. 116–29.
37. Noted in G. B. Nazzaro, 'La poetica della macchina', in Isabella Gheraducci (ed.), *Il futurismo italiano*, p. 246.
38. Caroline Tisdall and Angelo Bozzolla, *Futurism*, p. 179.
39. Of the three poets, Ungaretti had the closest connection: having made contact with Soffici, Palazzeschi and Pappini at the 1912 Futurist exhibition in Paris, he began a brief collaboration with *Lacerba* (see Frederic J. Jones, *Giuseppe Ungaretti*).
40. Eugenio Montale, *Selected Essays*, p. 114.
41. Ibid., pp. 133–4.
42. Giuseppe Ungaretti, *Vita d'un uomo: Saggi e interventi*, pp. 171–2 (hereafter cited as *Saggi*). See also ibid., p. 361, where Ungaretti characterises Surrealism as 'blind subjectivism' and Futurism as 'blind objectivism'. Like most modernist critics of Marinetti's movement, Ungaretti regards the dependence on onomatopoeia as a serious limitation (see ibid., p. 357).
43. Ungaretti, *Saggi*, p. 357.
44. The word originated with Francisco Flora's *La poesia ermetica* (1936), which blamed Ungaretti's lack of clarity on his subservience to the French tradition.
45. Giuseppe Ungaretti, *Vita d'un uomo: Tutte le poesie*, p. 77 (hereafter cited as *Poesie*). See also Jones, *Giuseppe Ungaretti*, pp. 35–6.

46. Giuseppe Ungaretti, 'Interview with Denis Roche' (1965), p. 108.
47. Ungaretti, *Poesie*, p. 5. The lines were originally part of a five-line poem called 'Eternity', first published in 1915. There 'nothingness' was 'vanity'. See Joseph Cary, *Three Modern Italian Poets*, pp. 148–50.
48. Ungaretti, 'Interview with Denis Roche', p. 108.
49. Quoted in Cary, *Three Modern Italian Poets*, p. 151.
50. Giuseppe Ungaretti, 'Vanità', trans. Andrew Wylie, *Agenda*, 8.2 (Spring 1970) p. 25.
51. Mengaldo (ed.), *Poeti Italiani del Novecento*, p. 385. Ungaretti often uses the traditional eleven-syllable line in highly fragmented combinations.
52. Quoted in Cary, *Three Modern Italian Poets*, p. 154.
53. Giuseppe Ungaretti, 'Mattina', trans. John F. Nims, in Stanley Burnshaw (ed.), *The Poem Itself*, p. 311.
54. Giuseppe Ungaretti, 'Veglia', trans. Andrew Wylie, *Agenda*, 8.2 (Spring 1970) p. 12. See also, 'Fratelli', *Poesie*, p. 39.
55. Ungaretti, *Saggi*, p. 652.
56. Ungaretti, *Poesie*, p. 539.
57. Ungaretti, 'Ragioni d'una poesia', *Poesie*, p. xcvii; trans. Cary, *Three Modern Italian Poets*, p. 169.
58. 'And so it was that I felt my poetry had increasingly to infuse itself [*compenetrarsi*] with memory as its substantial theme' (trans. Cary, *Three Modern Italian Poets*, p. 175).
59. Ungaretti, *Poesie*, p. 537; trans. Jones, *Giuseppe Ungaretti*, p. 30.
60. See Peter Bürger, *Theory of the Avant-Garde*.
61. Henri Meschonnic, *Modernité, Modernité*, p. 95.
62. Ungaretti, 'Ragioni d'una poesia', *Poesie*, p. xcvi.
63. Eugenio Montale, *The Bones of Cuttlefish*, p. 30.
64. Eugenio Montale, *Selected Essays*, p. 207. See also the discussion of this passage in relation to the idea of 'a complicated experience of *blockade*' in Montale's verse, in Cary, *Three Modern Italian Poets*, pp. 239–41. The concept of the 'barrier' in the work of Pierre Reverdy is also relevant – see below, Chapter 10.
65. Montale, *The Bones of Cuttlefish*, p. 29.

Notes to Chapter 6

1. For the impact of this essay, see Marianne Martin, *Futurist Art and Theory*, pp. 104ff.
2. See *FM*, 90, for Boccioni's critique of Cubism's static quality. Where the aim of Futurism is 'to show the living object in its dynamic growth', the Cubist 'spectacle itself did not change'. Boccioni concludes: 'We reject any *a priori* reality; this is what divides us from the Cubists and places us Futurists on the extreme fringe of the painting world.' Cf. Apollinaire, *AOA*, 334: 'Forms and matter – these are the objects and the subjects of today's best painters, who are not at all concerned with movement, becoming, and other fluid qualities that properly belong only to music.'
3. Edward Fry (ed.), *Cubism*, p. 95.
4. Ibid., p. 108.

5. The manifesto provided a model for Wyndham Lewis's *Blast*, published the next year. For a detailed discussion of relations to Futurist manifestos, see Pasquale Jannini, *La fortuna del futurismo in Francia*.
6. Walter Pater, *The Renaissance*, p. 107.
7. See also Timothy Mathews, *Reading Apollinaire*, p. 21.
8. Charles Baudelaire, *Complete Verse*, p. 91.
9. Rainer Maria Rilke, *Selected Letters*, p. 156.
10. Cf. Ezra Pound, *Literary Essays*, p. 45: 'The cult of ugliness, Villon, Baudelaire, Corbière, Beardsley are diagnosis. Flaubert is diagnosis. Satire, if we are to ride this metaphor to staggers, satire is surgery, insertions and amputations.'
11. Hence Apollinaire's limiting judgement that 'Greek art had a purely human conception of beauty' (*AOA*, 223).
12. Guillaume Apollinaire, 'Zone', in *Selected Writings*, p. 117 (all further references will be made to this translation).
13. This aspect of 'Zone' is almost certainly indebted to Blaise Cendrars's 'Easter in New York' (1912); see Marie-Jeanne Durry, *Guillaume Apollinaire: Alcools*, vol. I, pp. 234ff.
14. Mathews, *Reading Apollinaire*, p. 68.
15. Guillaume Apollinaire, 'The Betrothal', *Selected Writings*, p. 71.
16. Guillaume Apollinaire, *L'Enchanteur pourrissant*, p. 94.
17. See Umberto Eco, *Le forme del contenuto*, pp. 73–5.
18. Quoted in John White, *Literary Futurism*, p. 305.
19. Blaise Cendrars, *Complete Poems*, p. 87.
20. For a strong critique of various forms of dialectical 'assimilation', see Hal Foster, *Recodings*, p. 191.
21. Shklovsky, *Mayakovsky and His Circle*, p. 114.
22. See André Malraux, *Picasso's Mask*, p. 11; Blaise Cendrars, in 'Picasso' (1919), *Oeuvres complètes*, vol. IV, p. 189, describes Picasso's painting as 'exorcism of a religious kind'.
23. See, for example, Max Kozloff, *Cubism/Futurism*, p. 83.
24. Noted in Pierre Daix and Joan Rosselet, *Picasso: The Cubist Years*, p. 24.
25. Ibid., p. 63: the motif 'no longer structured the painting. It was the composition, by its contrasting rhythms, which revealed the structural element in the motif – always supposing that this is legible.'
26. D.H. Kahnweiler, 'Negro Art and Cubism', pp. 418–19. For a critical view of Kahnweiler's reading, see Robert Goldwater, *Primitivism in Modern Art*, p. 160. Picasso's metal *Guitar* (1912) provides a well-known example of such formal inversion – see Daix and Rosselet, *Picasso*, p. 118.
27. Daix and Rosselet, *Picasso*, p. 39.
28. *Passage* may be defined as 'the setting up of visual communication between the solid bulk of an object and the space external to and surrounding this bulk' (Daix and Rosselet, *Picasso*, p. 52).
29. See Mathews, *Reading Apollinaire*, pp. 38–9, for a comparison of the 'seamless interchange of memory and the present' in Cubist painting and Apollinaire's verse.
30. See, for example, Rosalind Krauss, *The Originality of the Avant-Garde*, p. 38, on the function of the ground in collage: 'It enters our experi-

ence not as an object of perception, but as an object of discourse, of *re*presentation.' Cf. Norman Bryson, Michael Ann Holly, and Keith Moxey (eds), *Visual Theory*, p. 66, on the view of painting as 'an art of the sign, which is to say an art of discourse'.

31. Yves-Alain Bois, 'Kahnweiler's Lesson', p. 53.
32. Blaise Cendrars, 'Why is the "Cube" Disintegrating?', in Edward Fry (ed.), *Cubism*, pp. 155–6.
33. See L.C. Breunig, 'Apollinaire et le Cubisme', p. 23.
34. Blaise Cendrars, 'Braque', *Oeuvres complètes*, vol. IV, p. 190.
35. Guillaume Apollinaire, *The Cubist Painters* (1913), excerpted in Herschel B. Chipp (ed.), *Theories of Modern Art*, pp. 227–8.
36. Ibid., p. 228.
37. Robert Delaunay, *Du Cubisme à l'art abstrait*, p. 110.
38. Ibid., p. 64.
39. See Mathews, *Reading Apollinaire*, p. 118. The theory derives in part from Michel-Eugène Chevreul.
40. Delaunay, *Du Cubisme*, pp. 63–4.
41. Lynn Gamwell, *Cubist Criticism*, p. 50.
42. Guillaume Apollinaire, *Calligrammes*, p. 53. 'Windows' has clear references to Delaunay – see the translator's commentary, pp. 349–55.
43. Ibid., p. 5.
44. Apollinaire, *Selected Writings*, p. 228. One of his models is the 'encyclopedic' daily newspaper (ibid., p. 229).
45. Shattuck (trans), 'Apollinaire, Hero-Poet', in Apollinaire, *Selected Writings*, p. 46.
46. See Apollinaire, *Selected Writings*, pp. 227–37.
47. Delaunay, *Du Cubisme*, p. 114.
48. The translation (slightly modified) is from the anonymous version published as 'Profound Today', in *Broom*, 1.3 (1922) pp. 265–7.
49. Cendrars, *Complete Poems*, p. 77.
50. Maurice Merleau-Ponty, *The Primacy of Perception*, p. 180.
51. Cendrars, 'Why is the "Cube" Disintegrating?', p. 156.
52. Blaise Cendrars, 'L'ABC du Cinéma', *Oeuvres complètes*, vol. IV, p. 162. In 'The Principle of Utility' (*Oeuvres complètes*, vol. IV, p. 135), this taking on of 'body' is directly linked to the language of international trade, to 'the language – of words and things, of discs and runes, Portuguese and Chinese, numbers and trade marks, industrial patents, postage stamps, passenger tickets, bills of lading, signal codes, wireless radio. …'
53. Virginia Spate, *Orphism*, p. 343.
54. André Green, 'The Unbinding Process', p. 31.
55. See Vladimir Markov, *Russian Futurism*, p. 135.
56. See the account in G. Donchin, *The Influence of French Symbolism on Russian Poetry*, pp. 151–61.
57. Even Vadim Shershenevich, translator of Marinetti's manifestos, argued that Russian Futurism 'is ahead of Italian Futurism, because the latter is only an *ars vivendi*, while Russian Futurism deals exclusively with art' (*RFM*, 153).
58. Benedikt Livshits, *The One-And-a-Half-Eyed Archer*, p. 182.

59. See Markov, *Russian Futurism*, pp. 147–61.
60. Livshits, *The One-And-a-Half-Eyed Archer*, p. 197.
61. Ibid., p. 191.
62. Edward J. Brown, *Mayakovsky*, p. 69.
63. See Anne d'Harnoncourt (ed.), *Futurism and the International Avant-Garde*, p. 18.
64. Kasimir Malevich, 'From Cubism to Futurism to Suprematism' (1915), in J. E. Bowlt, (ed. and trans.), *Russian Art of the Avant-Garde*, p. 132. See also, for the general relevance of Cubism, Krystyna Pomorska, *Russian Formalist Theory and Its Poetic Ambiance*.
65. Roman Jakobson, 'Modern Russian Poetry' (1919), in Edward J. Brown (ed.), *Major Soviet Writers*, p. 72.
66. Yury Tynyanov, 'On Khlebnikov', in Edward J. Brown (ed.), *Major Soviet Writers*, p. 95. He continues (p. 96): 'If you should write a line absolutely devoid of any meaning but in an impeccable iambic meter, it will turn out to be almost comprehensible.'
67. Tzvetan Todorov, *The Poetics of Prose*, p. 200.
68. Vladimir Markov and Merrill Sparks, *Modern Russian Poetry*, p. 327.
69. See ibid., p. 833.
70. See the discussion of Saussure in Chapter 2, above.
71. See Yury Tynyanov, 'Interval' (1924), in Chris Pike (ed.), *The Futurists, the Formalists, and the Marxist Critique*: 'he introduced the word into relationships with words which were strange to it. He achieved this by consciously recognising that verse was a *structure*. If different but like-sounding words are placed in a *series* or structure, they become relatives of each other.'
72. See Vahan D. Barooshian, *Russian Cubo-Futurism*, p. 81.
73. As transliterated in Brown, *Mayakovsky*, p. 58.
74. See Susan Compton, *The World Backwards,* and Marjorie Perloff, *The Futurist Moment*, pp. 116–61.
75. Vladimir Markov, *Russian Futurism*, p. 342.
76. See Agnès Sola, 'Cubisme et futurisme russe', p. 148. Victor Erlich, 'The Place of Russian Futurism within the Russian Poetic Avantgarde', p. 7, associates Kruchenykh's experiments with Dada. Interestingly, Mayakovsky, in *How Are Verses Made?* (1926), warns against the use of such 'shifts'.
77. Leon Trotsky, *Literature and Revolution*, p. 130. Trotsky concludes that although Futurism cannot be considered the 'art of the proletariat', 'this does not signify a contemptuous attitude towards the work of the Futurists. In our opinion they are the necessary links in the forming of a new and great literature' (p. 159).
78. Vladimir Mayakovsky, *Selected Works*, vol. 1, p. 46.
79. Ibid., vol. I, p. 48.
80. Quoted in Brown, *Mayakovsky*, p. 79; trans. in Mayakovsky, *Selected Works*, vol. I, p. 47: 'Street- / spaces. / The faces / of days, / great danes, / grow tougher.'
81. Vladimir Mayakovsky, 'A Cloud in Trousers', trans. Bob Perelman and Kathy Lewis, in John Glad and Daniel Weissbort (eds), *Russian Poetry*, p. 8 (all references are to this translation).

82. See 'An Amazing Adventure of Vladimir Mayakovsky', *Selected Works*, vol. I, pp. 79–82.
83. Trotsky, *Literature and Revolution*, p. 149.
84. See Chapter 2, above.
85. Vladimir Mayakovsky, *How Are Verses Made?*, p. 84.

Notes to Chapter 7

1. Rainer Maria Rilke, *The Notebook of Malte Laurids Brigge*, p. 3 Further references will be given in the text.
2. Thomas Mann, *Buddenbrooks*, p. 574. In 'Thomas Mann's "Buddenbrooks" ' (1901), Rilke remarked that 'even a few years ago a modern writer would have found it sufficient to portray the last stages of this decline, the last scion, who dies of his own and his forefathers' illness' (quoted in Judith Ryan, *The Vanishing Subject*, p. 58).
3. The emotional and temporal complexity of this moment is registered. similarly in Arthur Schnitzler's *The Road into the Open* (1908), p. 215: 'And it seemed to him like a vague and sweet dream, as if he lay as a boy at the feet of his mother, and this moment was already a memory, remote and painful, as he was experiencing it.'
4. Rainer Maria Rilke, *Rodin and Other Prose Pieces*, p. 15.
5. Ibid., p. 17.
6. Ibid., p. 46.
7. Ibid., p. 112.
8. Rainer Maria Rilke, *Letters on Cézanne*, pp. 32–3.
9. See also Rainer Maria Rilke, *Selected Letters*, p. 123: 'Looking is such a marvellous thing, of which we know but little; through it, we are turned absolutely towards the Outside, but when we are most of all so, things happen in us that have waited longingly to be observed, and while they reach completion in us, intact and curiously anonymous, *without our aid*, – their significance grows up in the object outside.'
10. 'Der Dichter', quoted in Patricia Pollock Brodsky, *Rainer Maria Rilke*, p. 103.
11. Rainer Maria Rilke, *Selected Poetry*, p. 135.
12. Ibid., p. 199.
13. Rilke, *Selected Letters*, p. 394.
14. Martin Heidegger, *Poetry, Language, Thought*, p. 113.
15. Wassily Kandinsky, *Concerning the Spiritual in Art*, p. 26.
16. Ulrich Weisstein, 'Introduction' to *Expressionism as an International Phenomenon*, p. 23.
17. Hermann Bahr, *Expressionism* (1916), p. 83.
18. Ibid., p. 85.
19. Kasimir Edschmid, 'Concerning Poetic Experience' (1917), quoted in Mardi Valgemae, *Accelerated Grimace*, p. 4.
20. Arnold Schönberg, 'The Relationship of the Text', in Wassily Kandinsky and Franz Marc (eds), *The Blaue Reiter Almanac*, p. 102.
21. See Ulrich Weisstein, 'Futurism in Germany and England: Two Flashes in the Pan?', p. 471; Lionel Richard, 'Futurisme et

Expressionisme en Allemagne', pp. 193–8; Hanne Bergius, 'Contribution à la réception du futurisme en Allemagne', in Giovanni Lista (ed.), *Marinetti et le futurisme*, pp. 171–4.

22. Herman George Scheffauer, *The New Vision in the German Arts* (1924), pp. 26–7.
23. August Stramm, 'Melancholy', trans. in Michael Hamburger (ed.), *German Poetry 1910–1975*, p. 9.
24. Ibid., p. 83.
25. Ibid., p. xxv.
26. See Michael Hamburger, *The Truth of Poetry*, pp. 176–80.
27. Karl Pinthus (ed.), *Menschheitsdämmerung*.
28. Georg Trakl, *Georg Trakl: A Profile*, ed. Frank Graziano, p. 59.
29. Quoted in Herbert Lindenberger, *Georg Trakl*, p. 42.
30. Georg Trakl, *Autumn Sonata: Selected Poems of Georg Trakl*, p. 57. See also the commentary in Francis Michael Sharp, *The Poet's Madness*, pp. 106–9.
31. *Georg Trakl: A Profile*, p. 31.
32. Quoted from 'Year', in Martin Heidegger, *On the Way to Language*, p. 176.
33. 'Dream and Derangement', *Georg Trakl: A Profile*, p. 80.
34. Heidegger, *On the Way to Language*, p. 177.
35. *Georg Trakl: A Profile*, p. 77.
36. Ibid., p. 52.
37. Noted in Jacques Derrida, 'Geschlecht: Sexual Difference, Ontological Difference', *A Derrida Reader*, p. 385.
38. Heidegger, *On the Way to Language*, pp. 195, 185. See also, Sharp, *The Poet's Madness*, p. 159, on 'Dream and Degeneration': 'The guiltless recognition of the tie between siblings undermines the incest taboo and anticipates the destruction of the family.'
39. For German texts of the play, see Oskar Kokoschka, *Dichtungen und Dramen*, pp. 33–51. The translation quoted is by Michael Hamburger, from Walter H. Sokel (ed.), *Anthology of German Expressionist Drama*, pp. 17–21. There are four versions of the play (hereafter referred to as *Murderer*); an account of textual variations is given in Horst Denkler, 'Die Druckfassungen der Dramen Oskar Kokoschkas', pp. 90–108. Carol Diethe, *Aspects of Distorted Sexual Attitudes in German Expressionist Drama*, pp. 130–5, divides the main variants to produce an 'A text' and a 'B text'. Sokel translates the 'A text', while the other available English version, in *Seven Expressionist Plays*, trans. J. M. Ritchie and H. F. Garten, pp. 25–32, uses the later 'B text'. Confusingly, neither Ritchie nor Sokel indicates which version is the one translated.
40. See Michael Patterson, *The Revolution in German Theatre*, pp. 194, 196.
41. Roger Cardinal, *Expressionism*, p. 96.
42. *Murderer*, in Sokel, *Anthology*, p. 20.
43. T. S. Eliot, *Selected Essays*, p. 145.
44. See Jacqueline Rose, *Sexuality in the Field of Vision*, pp. 123–40.
45. See Andrew Ross, *The Failure of Modernism*, p. 22.
46. Frank Whitford, *Oskar Kokoschka: A Life*, p. 37.
47. Peter Vergo and Yvonne Modlin, '*Murderer Hope of Women*', p. 31.

48. Quoted in ibid., p. 29.
49. Quoted in ibid., p. 31, n.61.
50. Oskar Kokoschka, *My Life*, p. 26.
51. Ibid., pp. 26, 27.
52. Nietzsche's description of the theme of Strindberg's *The Father*, quoted in Raymond Williams, *The Politics of Modernism*, p. 50.
53. J. M. Ritchie, *German Expressionist Drama*, p. 45.
54. Otto Weininger, *Sex and Character*, p. 92; further references will be given in the text. This idea is a recurrent one in the obsessive preoccupation with prostitution in German literature; in Wedekind's *Pandora's Box* (1904), for example, it is said of Lulu that 'she can't make a living out of love because love is her life'.
55. See Jacques Le Rider, *Le Cas Otto Weininger*, p. 221.
56. See Jacques Le Rider, 'Modernisme-Féminisme/Modernité-Virilité', pp. 5–20.
57. Oskar Kokoschka, 'On the Nature of Visions', in V. H. Miesel (ed.), *Voices of German Expressionism*, p. 98. Further references will be given in the text.
58. Christine Buci-Glucksman, *La Raison baroque*, p. 214. See also, the discussion of woman as commodity in Wedekind's drama in Gail Finney, *Women in Modern Drama*, pp. 79–101.
59. Paul Klee, *On Modern Art*, p. 45.
60. Strindberg's *Stationen* are 'stages in the central character's journey toward spiritual renewal' (Henry L. Schvey, *Oskar Kokoschka*, p. 24).
61. August Strindberg, *The Plays*, vol. 2, p. 555. Further references will be given in the text.
62. See Sigmund Freud, 'The Unconscious' (1915), *Pelican Freud Library*, vol. 11, pp. 190–1.
63. Noted by Vergo and Modlin, and by Donald E. Gordon, 'Oskar Kokoschka and the Visionary Tradition', in Gerald Chappel and Hans H. Schulte (eds), *The Turn of the Century*, pp. 23–52.
64. See, for example, Le Rider, *Le Cas Otto Weininger*, p. 127, and the discussion of the Cosmic Circle in Martin Green, *The Von Richthofen Sisters*.
65. J. J. Bachofen, *Myth, Religion, and Mother Right*, p. 93.
66. Ibid., p. 109.
67. Sokel, *Anthology*, p. 21. In the 'B text' the references to vampirism disappear and the Woman claims to be the Man's wife.
68. Jacques Derrida, *Writing and Difference*, p. 239. Further references will be given in the text.
69. On Kandinsky's other related experiments, see Peg Weiss, *Kandinsky and Munich*, p. 92. The translation of *The Yellow Sound* used here is from the *Blaue Reiter Almanac*, pp. 207–25.
70. *Blaue Reiter Almanac*, p. 147.
71. Ibid., p. 194, n. 4.
72. Ibid., p. 205.
73. Ibid., p. 206.
74. Paul Vogt, *The Blue Rider*, p. 81. Peg Weiss, *Kandinsky and Munich*, p. 99, notes the importance of the Shadow-play theatre (founded in

1907) in suggesting 'mystical or psychic spaces beyond the limits of conventional perspective'. The idea of an alternative spatial dimension might be compared with Robert Delaunay's concept of 'depth', an important reference point for early Expressionist art.

75. See André Green, *The Tragic Effect*, p. 16.
76. Sokel, *Anthology*, p. xvi, remarks that 'Expressionist drama is theme-centered rather than plot- or conflict-centered', and Carl E. Schorske, 'Generational Conflict and Social Change', in Gerald Chapple and Hans H. Schulte (eds), *The Turn of the Century*, p. 428, concludes that 'Musil and the Expressionist generation totally dismissed the Oedipal problem by subsuming it under a historical reality proclaimed dead.'
77. Quoted in Peter Szondi, *Theory of the Modern Drama*, p. 65.
78. Richard Sheppard, 'Unholy Families', p. 363. Further references will be given in the text.
79. Quoted in Ritchie, *German Expressionist Drama*, p. 70.
80. On dramatic technique, see, for example, Mel Gordon, 'German Expressionist Acting', pp. 34–50.
81. Georg Kaiser, *Five Plays*, pp. 168–9.
82. Peter Gay, *Weimar Culture*, pp. 102–18.
83. Ernst Toller, *Seven Plays*, p. 102.
84. Ernst Toller, 'My Works', p. 222; *Masses and Man* (1920), in *Seven Plays*, p. 150.
85. Georg Lukács, 'Expressionism: Its Significance and Decline' (1934), in *Essays on Realism*, p. 110.
86. For an account of the *Neue Sachlichkeit*, see John Willett, *The New Sobriety*.
87. Brecht, *Baal*, in *Collected Plays*, vol. 1, 6.
88. Ronald Speirs, *Brecht's Early Plays*, p. 20.
89. Bertolt Brecht, *Collected Plays*, vol. 1, p. 406.
90. Ibid., vol. 1, p. 118.
91. Ibid., vol. 1, p. 178.
92. Quoted in Ronald Speirs, *Brecht's Early Plays*, p. 131. As Peter Brooker notes in *Bertolt Brecht*, p. 110, Brecht's poetry during the twenties is also much concerned with 'the theme of the loss of self'.
93. Bertolt Brecht, *A Man's a Man*, in *Seven Plays*, p. 103.
94. Quoted in Willett, *The New Sobriety*, p. 153.

Notes to Chapter 8

1. Henry James, *The Ambassadors*, pp. 136–7. Further references will be given in the text.
2. Ezra Pound, *Collected Shorter Poems*, p. 205.
3. The phrase 'Men of 1914' is from Wyndham Lewis, *Blasting and Bombadiering* (1937), p. 252.
4. W. B. Yeats, *Essays and Introductions*, p. 243.
5. Ezra Pound, *Collected Early Poems*, p. 115.
6. Ezra Pound, 'Anima Sola', *Collected Early Poems*, p. 19.
7. Ezra Pound, 'Piere Vidal Old', ibid., p. 109.

8. Ezra Pound, 'Und Drang', ibid., p. 169.
9. Ezra Pound, 'Histrion', ibid., p. 71.
10. Peter Sacks, *The English Elegy*, p. 6.
11. The classic account is Sigmund Freud's 'Mourning and Melancholia' (1917), *Pelican Freud Library*, vol. 11, pp. 245–68. See also, my 'Lost Object(s): Ezra Pound and the Idea of Italy'.
12. Walter Pater, *The Renaissance*, p. 118.
13. Ezra Pound, *Literary Essays*, p. 4.
14. F. S. Flint, 'Imagisme' (1913), p. 129.
15. Ezra Pound, *Selected Letters*, p. 158.
16. Pound, *Collected Shorter Poems*, p. 118.
17. Ezra Pound, 'Vorticism' (1914), in *Gaudier-Brzeska*, p. 92.
18. Ibid., p. 89.
19. Joseph Conrad, *The Nigger of the 'Narcissus'*, pp. xlix–l.
20. Ford Madox Ford, *Critical Writings*, p. 40. Ford goes on to say that impressionism allows for 'superimposed emotions', but it is clear from the thrust of his argument that he is concerned primarily with 'the record of the impression of a moment', 'the impression, not the corrected chronicle' (p. 41).
21. Ibid., p. 73.
22. Pound, 'Vorticism', p. 82.
23. See Giovanni Cianci, 'Futurism and the English Avant-Garde', and Marjorie Perloff, *The Futurist Moment*, pp. 170–7.
24. Paul de Man, *Blindness and Insight*, p. 162.
25. Wyndham Lewis, 'Essay on the Objective of Plastic Art in Our Time' (1922), *Wyndham Lewis on Art*, p. 213.
26. Ibid., p. 212.
27. See Perloff, *The Futurist Moment*, p. 175, and Richard Cork, *Vorticism and Abstract Art in the First Machine Age*, vol. I, p. 255.
28. Hugh Kenner, *The Pound Era*, p. 239.
29. Ezra Pound, 'Vortex. Pound', *Blast*, I (1914) p. 153.
30. Pound, 'Vorticism', p. 92.
31. Ibid.
32. Wyndham Lewis, 'Manifesto', *Blast*, I (1914) p. 33.
33. Wyndham Lewis, 'The Melodrama of Modernity', *Blast*, I (1914), p. 143. For Lewis on Picasso's 'little *natures-mortes*', see 'Relativism and Picasso's Latest Work', *Blast*, I (1914) pp. 139–40.
34. Pound, 'Vorticism', p. 92.
35. Wyndham Lewis, *Letters*, p. 491.
36. Pound, 'Vorticism', p. 94.
37. Noted in Ronald Bush, *The Genesis of Ezra Pound's Cantos*, p. 104.
38. Pound, 'Vorticism', p. 85.
39. See Ezra Pound, *ABC of Reading* (1934), p. 52.
40. Kunio Komparu, *The Noh Theater*, p. 41. Further references will be given in the text.
41. Nobuko Tsukui, *Ezra Pound and Noh Plays*, p. 3.
42. For a discussion of Pound's own attempt at writing plays modelled on Noh, see my 'An Experiment with Time: Ezra Pound and the Example of Japanese Noh'.

43. The concept of the 'supplement' is used in Derrida's sense of a 'necessary surplus'; see Jacques Derrida, *Writing and Difference*, pp. 211–2.

44. John Forrester, *The Seductions of Psychoanalysis*, p. 206.

45. Jacques Derrida, *Memoires for Paul de Man*, p. 58.

46. Wyndham Lewis, *Tarr: The 1918 Version*, p. 29. Further references will be given in the text.

47. 'Modern Art' (1914), in T. E. Hulme, *Speculations*, p. 96.

48. Pound, *Selected Letters*, p. 40 (his emphasis).

49. Arthur Symons, *The Symbolist Movement in Literature*, p. 56.

50. Ezra Pound, 'Irony, Laforgue, and Some Satire' (1917), *Literary Essays*, p. 282.

51. Pound, *Collected Shorter Poems*, p. 74; T. S. Eliot, *Complete Poems and Plays*, pp. 18–21.

52. T. S. Eliot, *Selected Essays*, pp. 19–20. Further references will be given in the text.

53. T. S. Eliot, 'Introduction: 1928', *Ezra Pound: Selected Poems*, p. 10. Eliot observes that 'Pound is often most "original" in the right sense, when he is most "archaeological" in the ordinary sense.'

54. Noted in Hugh Kenner, *The Invisible Poet*, p. 21.

55. Eliot, *Selected Essays*, p. 26.

56. See the editorial note on p. 5 of this edition for Lewis's odd use of the double hyphen as a punctuation device. The novel was revised for a new edition in 1928.

57. Wyndham Lewis, *Men Without Art* (1934), p. 108.

58. Ibid., p. 62 (his emphases).

59. Wyndham Lewis, *The Art of Being Ruled* (1926), p. 25.

60. Ibid., p. 148.

61. Wyndham Lewis, *The Caliph's Design* (1919), p. 30.

62. Wyndham Lewis, *Time and Western Man* (1927), p. 132.

63. Ford Madox Ford, *The Good Soldier*, p. 37; further references will be given in the text. Dowell also likens himself to a child and patient (p. 50), a 'male sick nurse' (p. 68), and 'a woman or a solicitor' (p. 224).

64. Lewis, *The Art of Being Ruled*, p. 250. Fredric Jameson, *Fables of Aggression*, p. 97, observes that, for Lewis, 'The positive term which logically corresponds to the negative one of the female principle is not the male ... but rather art, which is not the place of a subject, masculine or otherwise, but rather impersonal and inhuman ...'.

65. Lewis, *The Art of Being Ruled*, p. 29 (Lewis's emphasis).

66. James Joyce, *The Essential James Joyce*, pp. 99, 110, 131, 133. Further references will be given in the text.

67. See also, Suzette Henke, 'Stephen Dedalus and Women', p. 83, and Jean Kimball, 'Freud, Leonardo, and Joyce', pp. 165–82.

68. Ezra Pound, *Hugh Selwyn Mauberley (Life and Contacts)*, in *Collected Shorter Poems*, pp. 203–22.

69. Tristan Corbière, *The Centenary Corbière*, p. 6.

70. The second is now the more common view; see, for example, Ronald Bush, 'It Draws One to Consider Time Wasted: *Hugh Selwyn Mauberley*', pp. 56–78. I have discussed the problem in more detail in

'"A Consciousness Disjunct": Sex and the Writer in Ezra Pound's *Hugh Selwyn Mauberley*'.

71. Ezra Pound, 'Music. By William Atheling' (1920), in Murray Schafer (ed.), *Ezra Pound and Music*, p. 225.

Notes to Chapter 9

1. Wyndham Lewis, *Rude Assignment* (1950), p. 180.
2. James Joyce, for example, seems to have regarded psychoanalysis as damagingly mechanical – see Richard Ellman, *James Joyce*, p. 382. D. H. Lawrence, in *Fantasia of the Unconscious* (1923) p. 166, also complains that Freud's 'dream-images…are mechanical phenomena like mirages'.
3. See Mikkel Borch-Jacobsen, 'The Freudian Subject, from Politics to Ethics', in Eduardo Cadava et al. (eds), *Who Comes After the Subject?*, pp. 65–6.
4. Wyndham Lewis, *The Complete Wild Body*, p. 18.
5. W. B. Yeats, *The Letters*, p. 434.
6. Cf. Jessica Benjamin, *The Bonds of Love*, p. 164.
7. T. S. Eliot, *The Use of Poetry*, pp. 33–4. Cf. *Selected Prose*, p. 108, where Eliot speaks similarly of 'an invasion of the adolescent self by Shelley'. See also Cassandra Laity, 'H.D. and A. C. Swinburne: Decadence and Modernist Women's Writing', pp. 467–70.
8. See, for example, Roger Kojecky, *T. S. Eliot's Social Criticism*, pp. 59–69.
9. T. S. Eliot, *Selected Essays*, p. 145. Further references will be given in the text.
10. Eliot, *Selected Prose*, pp. 267–8.
11. Ibid., p. 121. See also the discussion of these aspects of Eliot's poetics in Andrew Ross, *The Failure of Modernism*.
12. T. S. Eliot, 'London Letter' (1921), pp. 216–7.
13. T. S. Eliot, 'Observations' (1918), p. 70.
14. See Cantos LXXX and XLV, for example, in *The Cantos of Ezra Pound*, pp. 511, 229.
15. Wyndham Lewis, *Time and Western Man*, pp. 59, 89.
16. Ibid., p. 352.
17. Ezra Pound, 'Vorticism' (1914), in *Gaudier-Brzeska*, p. 92. Further references will be given in the text.
18. Ezra Pound, 'Affirmations' (1915), in *Gaudier-Brzeska*, p. 121.
19. Ezra Pound, 'Translator's Postscript' (1922) to Remy de Gourmont, *The Natural Philosophy of Love*, p. 150.
20. Eliot, *Selected Essays*, p. 327.
21. See Pound, *Gaudier-Brzeska*, p. 97: 'We all of us like the caressable, but most of us in the long run prefer the woman to the statue.' The 'caressable' in art is always mimetic and hence 'always a substitute'.
22. H.D., *Collected Poems*, p. 18. Further references will be given in the text.
23. See Cyrena Pondrom, 'H.D. and the Origins of Imagism', pp. 73–97.
24. Ezra Pound, *Selected Letters*, p. 11.

25. See Brendan Jackson, 'The Fulsomeness of Her Prolixity', pp. 91–102, and Shari Benstock, *Women of the Left Bank*, pp. 321ff.
26. H. R. Fairclough, *The Classics and Our Twentieth-Century Poets* (1927), p. 297.
27. H.D., *Notes on Thought and Vision and The Wise Sappho* (1919), p. 67.
28. H.D., *Her*, p. 187. Further references will be given in the text. See also Claire Buck, 'Freud and H.D. – Bisexuality and Feminine Discourse', pp. 53–66.
29. See Diane Chisholm, *H.D.'s Freudian Poetics*, p. 19.
30. See H.D., *Her*, pp. 77, 98, 105, 106. Chisholm, *H.D.'s Freudian Poetics*, p. 55, sees the 'whirling' as 'signifying the absence of a subjective point of reference from which self can be distinguished from world'.
31. Significantly, it is George, the character representing Pound, who criticises Her for being 'Narcissus in the reeds. Narcissa' (p. 170).
32. As Laity notes in 'H.D. and A. C. Swinburne', the key poems to which *Her* alludes include 'Itylus' ('Sister, my sister') and 'Before the Mirror' ('Art thou the ghost, my sister, / White sister there, / Am I the ghost, who knows?').
33. H.D., *Tribute to Freud* (1956), p. 40.
34. Quoted in Jayne L. Walker, *The Making of a Modernist*, p. 13.
35. Quoted in Stephen Fredman, *Poet's Prose*, p. 19.
36. Samuel Beckett, et al. (eds), *Our Exagmination Round His Factification for Incamination of Work in Progress* (1929), p. 14.
37. Harriet Scott Chessman, *The Public is Invited to Dance*, p. 87.
38. Dorothy Richardson, 'Foreword' (1938) to *Pilgrimage*, vol. I (1915–17), p. 12.
39. Dorothy Richardson, *Honeycomb* (1917), in *Pilgrimage*, vol. I, p. 354.
40. Gertrude Stein, *Three Lives*, p. 182.
41. Walker, *The Making of a Modernist*, p. 51.
42. Gertrude Stein, *The Making of Americans*, p. 227.
43. See, for example, Randa Dubnick, *The Structure of Obscurity*, p. 33.
44. Gertrude Stein, *Picasso* (1938), p. 35.
45. T. S. Eliot, *Knowledge and Experience in the Philosophy of F. H. Bradley*, p. 134.
46. Sigmund Freud, *Jokes and Their Relation to the Unconscious* (1905), *Pelican Freud Library*, vol. 6, pp. 167–8.
47. Gertrude Stein, *The Yale Gertrude Stein*, pp. 124, 115.
48. Jacques Derrida, 'Choreographies', *A Derrida Reader*, p. 445.
49. Ezra Pound, *Patria Mia and the Treatise on Harmony* (1912), p. 26.
50. First American exhibitions were held at the gallery by Matisse (1908), Picasso (1911), Picabia (1913) and Brancusi (1914). The gallery also held the first American exhibition of African sculpture in 1914.
51. For accounts of New York Dada, see Ileana B. Leavens, *From '291' to Zurich*; Dickran Tashjian, *Skyscraper Primitives*; Bram Dijkstra, *Cubism, Stieglitz, and the Early Poetry of William Carlos Williams*.
52. See, for example, Frederic Hoffman, *The Twenties*.
53. Noted in Carolyn Burke, 'The New Poetry and the New Woman: Mina Loy', pp. 45–6.
54. Williams Carlos Williams, *The Collected Poems 1909–1939*, p. 473.

55. Ibid., p. 85.
56. See *I*, pp. 100–1, on the 'use of the word "like" or that "evocation" of the "image" which served us for a time'. Cf. ibid., p. 299, on his own work: 'There is no symbolism, no evocation of an image.'
57. Williams Carlos Williams, *Selected Essays*, p. 177.
58. Williams Carlos Williams, *I Wanted to Write a Poem*, p. 27.
59. Fredman, *Poet's Prose*, p. 52.
60. Williams, *Collected Poems 1909–1939*, p. 502.
61. The phrase, which Williams originally applied to Whitman, is quoted in Sherman Paul, 'A Sketchbook of the Artist in his Thirty-Fourth Year', p. 28.
62. See also Fredman, *Poet's Prose*, pp. 41–2.
63. Wallace Stevens, *The Necessary Angel*, p. 171.
64. Wallace Stevens, *Collected Poems*, p. 59.
65. Stevens, *The Necessary Angel*, p. 144.
66. Stevens, *Collected Poems*, p. 291.
67. Ibid., p. 16.
68. Kenneth Rexroth, *American Poetry in the Twentieth Century*, p. 68.
69. Stevens, *The Necessary Angel*, p. 25.
70. Ibid., p. 36.
71. Ibid., p. 33. Cf. *The Letters of Wallace Stevens*, p. 316, on 'the relation or balance between imagined things and real things which…is a constant source of trouble to me'.
72. Stevens, *The Necessary Angel*, p. 71.
73. Paul Ricoeur, 'The Metaphorical Process and Cognition, Imagination, and Feeling', p. 152.
74. Ezra Pound,'Irony, Laforgue, and Some Satire' (1917), *Literary Essays*, p. 283.
75. Ezra Pound, 'Others' (1917), *Selected Prose*, p. 394.
76. Marianne Moore, 'The Buffalo', in *Complete Poems*, p. 27.
77. Rexroth, *American Poetry in the Twentieth Century*, pp. 69–70.
78. Mina Loy, *The Last Lunar Baedeker*, p. 91. Further references will be given in the text. The lines have been corrected following Virginia Kouidis, *Mina Loy*, p. 64.
79. Some of Laura (Riding) Jackson's early poems provide a suggestive point of comparison – see, for example, 'The Mask', from *The Close Chaplet* (1926), in *The Poems of Laura Riding*, p. 27.

Notes to Chapter 10

1. Mina Loy, *The Last Lunar Baedeker*, p. 269.
2. Hans Richter, *Dada*, p. 80.
3. André Breton, *Les Pas perdus*, p. 64.
4. Hans Arp, *On My Way*, p. 39.
5. Hugo Ball, 'Dada Fragments, 1916–1917', in Robert Motherwell (ed.), *The Dada Painters and Poets*, p. 51 (hereafter cited as Motherwell).
6. Ibid., p. 54.
7. Richard Huelsenbeck, *En Avant Dada*, in Motherwell, p. 24.

8. In his *Zurich Chronicle (1915–1919)*, Tzara observed of Kokoschka's work: 'This performance decided the role of our theatre...' (Motherwell, p. 238).
9. Hugo Ball, 'Cabaret Voltaire' (1916), quoted in Richter, *Dada*, p. 14.
10. Ball, 'Dada Fragments, 1916–1917', Motherwell, p. 52.
11. See Raoul Hausmann, 'The Optophonetic Dawn', pp. 19ff.
12. Quoted in Richter, *Dada*, p. 121.
13. Ibid., p. 30.
14. Hugo Ball, *Flight out of Time*, pp. 71, 68.
15. Ibid., p. 70.
16. Quoted above, p. 209.
17. Wassily Kandinsky, *Concerning the Spiritual in Art*, p. 34.
18. Tristan Tzara, *Zurich Chronicle (1915–1919)*, Motherwell, p. 236.
19. Jürgen Habermas, *Legitimation Crisis*, p. 85.
20. Walter Benjamin, *Illuminations*, p. 239.
21. Georges Ribemont-Dessaignes, *Déjà jadis*, p. 154.
22. Ball, *Flight out of Time*, p. 67.
23. Richter, *Dada*, p. 65.
24. Peter Sloterdijk, *Critique of Cynical Reason*, pp. 397–8. Sloterdijk's initial disagreement is with the influential account of Dada in Peter Bürger, *Theory of the Avant-Garde*.
25. Richard Huelsenbeck, *Memoirs of a Dada Drummer*, p. 70.
26. Louis Aragon, *Treatise on Style* (1928), p. 90.
27. Huelsenbeck, *En Avant Dada*, Motherwell, p. 44.
28. Quoted in Motherwell, p. xxv.
29. Richard Huelsenbeck, 'Dada Lives', pp. 77–8. Hans Arp, 'Declaration', in Lucy R. Lippard (ed.), *Dadas on Art*, p. 22, credits Tzara with its discovery, while Breton attributes it to Walter Serner (*Les Pas perdus*, p. 104). Disregarding the various rivalries involved here, it is usually thought that Tzara was responsible for the discovery.
30. Michel Sanouillet, 'Dada: A Definition', in Stephen C. Foster and Rudolf E. Kuenzli (eds), *Dada Spectrum*, p. 21.
31. Ball, 'Dada Fragments, 1916–1917', Motherwell, p. 52.
32. Breton, *Les Pas perdus*, p. 65.
33. See Jean-Claude Blachère, *Le Modèle nègre*, pp. 126, 137.
34. Ibid., pp. 163, 168.
35. See, for example, Ribemont-Dessaignes, *Déjà jadis*, p. 21: 'one is at the same time happy and cruel, because the characteristic of life and happiness is being cruel'.
36. Arp quotes from his 1915 catalogue in 'Dadaland', *On My Way*, p. 40 (my emphases).
37. Ball, 'Dada Fragments, 1916–1917', Motherwell, p. 53.
38. Cf. Richard Boothby, *Death and Desire*, p. 11. I am indebted to Boothby's reading of Lacan for this part of my argument.
39. Cf. Boothby, *Death and Desire*, p. 87: 'The activity of the death drive involves a profound sense of pleasure, if we understand by the 'death drive' not the self-destructiveness of organic material but rather the struggle toward discharge of vital energies against the constraints of the ego.' Boothby also observes (p. 85) that 'The death drive is the force of the instinctual as such.'

40. Sloterdijk, *Critique of Cynical Reason*, p. 398.
41. Arp, 'Dadaland', *On My Way*, p. 48.
42. See Marc Le Bot, *Francis Picabia et la crise des valeurs figuratives 1900–1925*, p. 123.
43. Octavio Paz, *Marcel Duchamp*, p. 22.
44. See Michel Carrouges, *Les Machines célibataires*, p. 60.
45. See Harriet and Sidney Janis, 'Marcel Duchamp: Anti-Artist' (1945), Motherwell, p. 311, for Duchamp's view that 'Irony is a playful way of accepting something. Mine is the irony of indifference.'
46. Paz, *Marcel Duchamp*, p. 6; Cf. Haim N. Finkelstein, *Surrealism and the Crisis of the Object*, p. 80: 'Irony of indifference results in the ability to accept at one time both a thing and its negation.'
47. Huelsenbeck, *En Avant Dada*, Motherwell, p. 41.
48. Ibid., p. 39.
49. Richter, *Dada*, p. 80.
50. Robert Short, 'Paris Dada and Surrealism', in Richard Sheppard (ed.), *Dada: Studies of a Movement*, p. 78.
51. Tzara's sense of the unconscious as instinctual and eluding representation is clearly pre-Freudian. Compare Sigmund Freud, 'The Unconscious', *Pelican Freud Library*, vol. 11, p. 179: 'An instinct can never become an object of consciousness – only the idea that represents the instinct can. Even in the unconscious, moreover, an instinct cannot be represented otherwise than by an idea. If the instinct did not attach itself to an idea or manifest itself as an affective state, we could know nothing about it.' Tzara's sense of the unconscious is curiously close to that of Deleuze and Guattari – see my 'Anti-Oedipus? Dada and Surrealist Theatre, 1916–35', p. 336.
52. See Lionel Richard, 'Sur l'expressionisme allemand et sa réception critique en France de 1910 à 1925', pp. 266–89.
53. Louis Aragon, 'A Man', (1923/24), pp. 20–1.
54. Jonathan Culler, *The Pursuit of Signs*, p. 174.
55. Fernand Léger, 'The Spectacle' (1924), in *Functions of Painting*, p. 40.
56. Quoted in Peter Jelavich, *Munich and Theatrical Modernism*, p. 224.
57. See Jarry's famous 'Letter to Lugné-Poë', in Alfred Jarry, *Selected Works*, pp. 67–8, and especially his view that 'a descriptive placard has far more "suggestive" power than any stage scenery'.
58. Jarry, *Selected Works*, p. 83.
59. See, for example, ibid., p. 79.
60. On surrealism, see Guillaume Apollinaire, 'Préface', in *L'Enchanteur pourrissant*, p. 94.
61. Michel Sanouillet, *Dada à Paris*, p. 167.
62. Tristan Tzara, 'Memoirs of Dadaism', in Edmund Wilson, *Axel's Castle*, p. 242. The text of the play is given in Michel Corvin, 'Le théâtre Dada existe-t-il?', pp. 288–93. Further references will be given in the text.
63. Sanouillet, *Dada à Paris*, p. 167.
64. His *Poèmes nègres* had appeared in the magazine *Dada* in 1917.
65. See Jean-Claude Blachère, *Le Modèle nègre*, p. 155.
66. Régis Durand, 'The Disposition of the Voice', p. 101. See also, John D. Erickson, *Dada*, pp. 65–7.
67. See, for example, David G. Zinder, *The Surrealist Connection*, p. 8.

68. Erickson, *Dada*, p. 75; Corvin, 'Le théâtre Dada', p. 259.
69. Corvin, 'Le théâtre Dada', p. 282.
70. Quoted in Annabelle Henkin Melzer, *Latest Rage the Big Drum*, p. 183.
71. Quoted in ibid., p. 183.
72. Pierre-F. Quesnoy, *Littérature et Cinéma* (1928), p. 29. For a contemporary and Surrealist view of Chaplin, see Philippe Soupault, *Charlot* (1931).
73. Recalled in Ribemont-Dessaignes, *Déjà jadis*, p. 122.
74. Breton, *Les Pas perdus*, pp. 110, 109.
75. Guillaume Apollinaire, *Selected Writings*, pp. 227–37.
76. See Kenneth E. Silver, *Esprit de Corps*, passim.
77. Christopher Green, *Cubism and its Enemies*, p. 37.
78. Silver, *Esprit de Corps*, p. 427.
79. Paul Dermée, 'Quand le Symbolisme fut mort', p. 3.
80. Silver, *Esprit de Corps*, p. 254.
81. See Étienne-Alain Hubert in *NS*, p. 284.
82. Blaise Cendrars, 'La Prose du Transsibérien et de la Petite Jehanne de France', in Antoine Sidotti (ed.), *La Prose du Transsibérien*, p. 99.
83. Julien Benda, *Belphégor*, p. 8. Further references will be given in the text.
84. See Pär Bergman, *'Modernolatria' et 'Simultaneità'*, p. 273.
85. Frédéric Lefèvre, *La Jeune poésie française* (1917).
86. Jacob defines his own work (and Reverdy's) as Cubist in a letter of 1917; see Étienne-Alain Hubert and Michel Décaudin, 'Petite Histoire d'une appellation', p. 14.
87. Jean Schroeder, *Pierre Reverdy*, p. 41.
88. Pierre Reverdy, *Note éternelle du présent*, pp. 89–90.
89. Max Jacob, *The Dice Cup*, pp. 6–7.
90. Ibid., p. 7.
91. 'Creationism', excerpted in Vicente Huidobro, *Selected Poetry*, pp. 4, 5.
92. One not considered here relates to 'fantaisiste' poetry – see my 'From Fantasy to Structure: Two Moments of Literary Cubism', p. 229.
93. J. Laplanche and J.-B. Pontalis, *The Language of Psychoanalysis*, pp. 314–15.
94. See, for example, the passages quoted in André Ombredane, 'Critique de la méthode d'investigation psychologique de Freud', in *Le Disque vert*, special issue on Freud (1924), pp. 172–3. Freud's *Phantasie* is also translated in this way in E. Régis and A. Hesnard, *La Psychanalyse* (1914) – see, for example, p. 206.
95. A. Hesnard, 'L'Opinion scientifique française et la psychanalyse', in *Le Disque vert*, p. 6. For an account of this opposition, see Elisabeth Roudinesco, *La Bataille de cent ans*, vol. 1.
96. Silver, *Esprit de Corps*, p. 181.
97. Pierre Reverdy, *Le Livre de mon bord*, p. 132.
98. Theo Hermans, *The Structure of Modernist Poetry*, p. 164.
99. Kenneth Rexroth, *American Poetry in the Twentieth Century*, p. 61. See also Rexroth's introduction to his *Pierre Reverdy: Selected Poems*, pp. v–xiii.
100. Rexroth, *Pierre Reverdy*, p. vii.
101. Max Jacob, *Le Cornet à dés*, p. 69; *The Dice Cup*, p. 41.

102. Pierre Reverdy, *Le Gant de crin*, p. 29.
103. Pierre Reverdy, *Cette émotion appelée poésie*, p. 42.
104. Rexroth, *Pierre Reverdy*, p. 5.

Notes to Chapter 11

1. Wyndham Lewis, *The Caliph's Design* (1919), p. 30.
2. Henry James, *The American Scene*, p. 168.
3. On this aspect of Lewis's early work, see Alan Munton, 'Wyndham Lewis: The Transformations of Carnival', pp. 141–57.
4. Wyndham Lewis, *The Writer and the Absolute*, p. 198.
5. Wyndham Lewis, *The Art of Being Ruled*, p. 69.
6. Ibid., p. 142 (Lewis's emphasis).
7. Wyndham Lewis, *Time and Western Man*, p. 12.
8. Wyndham Lewis, *Men Without Art*, p. 120 (his emphases).
9. Lewis, *The Art of Being Ruled*, p. 362: 'In all this vast smooth-running process you see the image of a political state in which no legislation, police, or any physical compulsion would be required; in which everything would be effected by public opinion, snobbery, and the magic of *fashion*.'
10. On 'belatedness', see above pp. 178–9.
11. Sigmund Freud, 'From the History of an Infantile Neurosis' (1918), *Pelican Freud Library*, vol. 9, p. 284: 'these scenes from infancy are not reproduced during the treatment as recollection, they are the products of construction'.
12. Cf. Jacques Derrida, *Writing and Difference*, p. 212.
13. For another account of 'trauma' in relation to Eliot's work, see David Trotter, *The Making of the Reader*, pp. 36–57.
14. See, for example, Frank Budgen, *James Joyce and the Making of 'Ulysses'*, p. 20.
15. See Ezra Pound, '*Ulysses*' (1922), in *Literary Essays*, pp. 403–9. Cf. Ezra Pound, *Guide to Kulchur* (1938), p. 96: 'The katharsis of 'Ulysses'...was to feel that here was the JOB DONE and finished, the diagnosis and cure was here.'
16. Lewis, *Time and Western Man*, pp. 73, 89.
17. T. S. Eliot, '*Ulysses*, Order and Myth' (1923), in *Selected Prose*, p. 177. Further references will be given in the text.
18. T. S. Eliot, *Selected Essays*, p. 262.
19. Eliot, *Selected Essays*, p. 17.
20. Franco Moretti, *Signs Taken for Wonders*, p. 222.
21. Quoted in Roger Kojecky, *T. S. Eliot's Social Criticism*, p. 100.
22. Terry Eagleton, *Criticism and Ideology*, pp. 149–50.
23. Oliver Goldsmith, *The Vicar of Wakefield*, pp. 148, 147. Permission to quote from *The Waste Land* has been refused by Eliot's publishers.
24. A. D. Moody, *Thomas Stearns Eliot*, p. 111.
25. T. S. Eliot, *The Use of Poetry*, p. 144.
26. Eliot, *Selected Essays*, p. 265.
27. Ezra Pound, *ABC of Reading*, p. 46.

28. Ezra Pound 'Three Cantos: I', *Poetry*, X, 3 (June 1917) p. 114.
29. Ibid., p. 113.
30. Ezra Pound, 'I Gather the Limbs of Osiris' (1911), *Ezra Pound: Selected Prose 1909–1965*, p. 23.
31. Hugh Kenner, *The Invisible Poet*, p. 4.
32. See Ernest Fenollosa, *The Chinese Written Character as a Medium for Poetry*, ed. Ezra Pound (1920).
33. Pound, *Guide to Kulchur*, p. 194.
34. Ezra Pound, *Selected Letters*, p. 210.
35. Gaius Valerius Catullus, LXI, in *Catullus, Tibullus and Pervigilium Veneris*, pp. 69–85.
36. Jacques Derrida, *Dissemination*, p. 210.
37. On this phase of *The Cantos* and subsequent developments in the poem, see my *Ezra Pound*.
38. Lewis's way of connecting homosexuality with social identification has something in common with Freud's later work (Lewis may have known *Totem and Taboo* – see *The Art of Being Ruled*, p. 253, for a reference to the son consuming the father).
39. Lewis, *The Art of Being Ruled*, p. 196.
40. Quoted in Virginia Woolf, *A Writer's Diary*, p. 75.
41. The point is powerfully made by Moretti, *Signs Taken for Wonders*, p. 206. Gerald L. Bruns, *Modern Poetry and the Idea of Language*, p. 153, observes that in *Ulysses* 'finally what is satirized is not this or that category of utterance but human speech itself.'
42. Woolf, *A Writer's Diary*, pp. 74, 73–4.
43. Marcel Proust, *Remembrance of Things Past*, vol. III, pp. 1105–6.
44. Virginia Woolf, 'Phases of Fiction' (1929), *Collected Essays*, vol. II, p. 102.
45. Virginia Woolf, 'Modern Fiction' (1919), *Collected Essays*, vol. II, p. 106.
46. Lewis, *Men Without Art*, p. 139.
47. Virginia Woolf, *Mrs Dalloway*, pp. 28, 135.
48. See, for example, Woolf, *Mrs Dalloway*, p. 122: 'She penetrated a little farther in the direction of St Paul's. She liked the geniality, sisterhood, motherhood, brotherhood of this uproar. It seemed to her good.'
49. Woolf, *Mrs Dalloway*, p. 39.
50. Virginia Woolf, *The Waves*, p. 58.
51. Woolf, *Mrs Dalloway*, pp. 36–7.
52. See above, p. 171.
53. Virginia Woolf, 'De Quincey's Autobiography', *Collected Essays*, vol. IV, p. 2.
54. Virginia Woolf, *To the Lighthouse*, pp. 150–1.
55. *The Letters of Virginia Woolf*, vol. III, p. 189; see also Makiko Minow-Pinkney, *Virginia Woolf and the Problem of the Subject*, p. 79.
56. Lewis, *The Art of Being Ruled*, p. 338.
57. Lewis, *Time and Western Man*, p. 230 (his emphases).
58. Ibid., p. 70.
59. Wyndham Lewis, *Rude Assignment*, p. 73 (his emphases).
60. Wyndham Lewis, *The Complete Wild Body*, p. 149
61. Lewis, *Men Without Art*, p. 99.

62. Lewis, *The Complete Wild Body*, p. 101 (Lewis's emphases). The obvious comparison is with Walter Benjamin's account of the deathshead in *The Origin of German Tragic Drama*, p. 166.
63. Lewis, *The Complete Wild Body*, p. 158 (his emphases).
64. Lewis, *Men Without Art*, p. 232.
65. Ibid., p. 129 (Lewis's emphasis).
66. Ibid., p. 97.
67. Ibid., pp. 99, 98 (Lewis's emphasis).
68. Jacques Lacan, *Écrits: A Selection*, p. 104.
69. Wyndham Lewis, *The Apes of God*, p. 131 (his emphasis). Further references will be given in the text.
70. Lewis, *The Art of Being Ruled*, p. 232.
71. Lewis, *The Complete Wild Body*, p. 224.
72. Lewis, *Rude Assignment*, p. 159.
73. In *The Art of Being Ruled*, p. 54, for example, Lewis comments on 'the senseless bellicosity of the reactionary groups of the *Action Française* type'. His own presentation of Hitler emphasises his subject's typical rather than heroic aspects: 'Adolf Hitler is just a very typical german [*sic*] "man of the people". …As even his appearance suggests, there is nothing whatever eccentric about him. He is not only satisfied with, but enthusiastically embraces, his *typicalness*' (*Hitler* [1931], pp. 31–2). See also Fredric Jameson, *Fables of Aggression*, pp. 179–85.
74. Wyndham Lewis, *The Lion and the Fox*, p. 125 (Lewis's emphasis).
75. Wyndham Lewis, 'Guns' (1919), in *Wyndham Lewis on Art*, p. 105.
76. Lewis, *The Art of Being Ruled*, p. 165.
77. Hermann Broch, *Hugo von Hofmannsthal and His Time*, pp. 179–80.
78. Hermann Broch, *The Sleepwalkers*, pp. 20, 193. Further references will be given in the text.
79. Quoted in Burton Pike, *Robert Musil*, p. 36.
80. See Robert Musil, *The Man Without Qualities*, vol. I, pp. 294–305, on the 'Utopian idea of Essayism'. Further references will be given in the text.
81. See, for example, Lewis, *The Art of Being Ruled*, p. 338, on 'the typical conventional *modernist*, false-revolutionary tendency; and the support for the organized hatred of the intellect'.
82. See, for example, Stanley Corngold, *Franz Kafka*, p. 246.
83. Franz Kafka, *The Trial*, p. 237. Further references will be given in the text.
84. Jacques Derrida, 'Devant la loi', p. 141 (his emphases).
85. Elias Canetti, 'Kafka's Other Trial', p. 66.
86. Cf. Franz Kafka, *The Castle*, p. 200: 'Yet before he could be forgiven he had to prove his guilt, and that was denied in all the bureaux.'
87. Corngold, *Franz Kafka*, p. 156.
88. Maurice Blanchot, *The Space of Literature*, p. 26.
89. See Franz Kafka, *Diaries 1910–23*, p. 398: 'Metaphors are one among many things which make me despair of writing. Writing's lack of independence of the world, its dependence on the maid who tends the fire, on the cat warming itself by the stove; it is even dependent on the poor old human being warming himself by the stove. All these are independent activities ruled by their own laws; only writing is helpless, cannot live in itself, is a joke and a despair.'

90. Quoted and discussed in Anthony Thorlby, 'Kafka and Language', p. 139.
91. Maurice Blanchot, *The Infinite Conversation*, p. 73. The phrase is not originally applied to Kafka.
92. Blanchot, *The Space of Literature*, p. 83.
93. Wyndham Lewis, 'The Credentials of the Painter' (1922), *Creatures of Habit and Creatures of Change*, p. 76.
94. See Gustav Janouch, *Conversations with Kafka*, p. 172: 'Mankind can only become a grey, formless, and therefore nameless mass through a fall from the law which gives it form.'
95. Maurice Blanchot, *The Writing of the Disaster*, p. 76.

Notes to Chapter 12

1. André Breton, *Mad Love* (1937), p. 30. Man Ray's photograph of Breton's object faces p. 30.
2. For Surrealism as affirmation, see, for example, Patrick Waldberg, *Surrealism*, p. 13: 'André Breton and his friends were not deniers, like the systematic Dadaists. Through all those vociferations, refusals and deliberate absurdities, they were seeking a guiding light, a way to make a new truth dawn.'
3. Maurice Nadeau, *The History of Surrealism*, p. 85.
4. Michel Carrouges, *André Breton et les données fondamentales du surréalisme*, p. 103.
5. Georges Ribemont-Dessaignes, *Déjà jadis*, p. 124.
6. André Breton, *Entretiens (1913–1952)*, p. 52.
7. André Breton, *Les Pas perdus*, p. 65.
8. Breton, *Entretiens (1913–1952)*, pp. 56–7.
9. Noel Arnaud, 'Dada et surréalisme', in Ferdinand Alquié (ed.), *Entretiens sur le surréalisme*, p. 357.
10. See especially Marguerite Bonnet, *André Breton: Naissance de l'aventure surréaliste* , pp. 102–7.
11. André Breton, *Nadja* (1928), p. 24.
12. See J.-B. Pontalis, 'Les vases non communicants', p. 38; J-P. Morel, 'Aurélia, Gradiva, X: Psychanalyse et poésie dans *Les Vases Communicants*', p. 73. See also André Breton, *Communicating Vessels*, p. 44, where he decides that the 'reminder' of the infantile scene 'could only present a secondary interest in this case'.
13. Gerald Mead, 'Language and the Unconscious in Surrealism', p. 286.
14. Letter from Freud to Breton, 26 December 1932, in Breton, *Communicating Vessels*, p. 152.
15. Jean Laplanche and Serge Leclaire, 'The Unconscious: A Psychoanalytic Study', p. 128. Freud's main essay on the topic is 'Remembering, Repeating and Working-Through' (1914).
16. Breton, *Les Pas perdus*, p. 124. Cf. Louis Aragon, *Treatise on Style*, p. 94, on Surrealism as 'a conscious form of inspiration'.
17. André Breton, *Point du jour*, p. 60. An example would be Pierre Reverdy's line 'A heart hops in a cage' ('Departure', trans.

Michael Benedikt, *The Poetry of Surrealism: An Anthology*, p. 64).
18. See, for example, Breton, *Les Pas perdus*, p. 124.
19. Ferdinand Alquié, *The Philosophy of Surrealism*, p. 141.
20. André Breton and Philippe Soupault, *The Magnetic Fields*, p. 79.
21. Breton, *Nadja*, p. 17.
22. *MS*, 9. For Surrealism's hostility to the novel, see Jacqueline Chénieux-Gendron, *Le Surréalisme et le roman 1922–1950*.
23. Breton, *Les Pas perdus*, p. 87.
24. Maurice Blanchot, *La Part du feu*, p. 93.
25. The distinction is explored in Fredric Jameson, *Marxism and Form*, pp. 97–8.
26. Breton, *Communicating Vessels*, p. 45.
27. J.-B. Pontalis, 'Les vases non communicants', p. 32.
28. The sentence is from Alexandre Kojève's account of Chapter VIII of *The Phenomenology of Spirit*, quoted in Anthony Wilden, 'Lacan and the Discourse of the Other', in Jacques Lacan, *Speech and Language in Psychoanalysis*, p. 195. Breton attended Kojève's hugely influential seminar on Hegel, as did Lacan.
29. Jacques Lacan, *Écrits*, p. 104. On Lacan's relation to the Surrealists, see David Macey, *Lacan in Contexts* and Elisabeth Roudinesco, *Jacques Lacan & Co.*
30. Maurice Blanchot, *The Gaze of Orpheus*, p. 55.
31. Cf., for example, Judith Butler, *Subjects of Desire*, pp. 29–30: 'In distinguishing something as different from consciousness, consciousness makes a determination of something negative. In *stating* "that it is not me", a positive reality is born.'
32. For a detailed account, see Helena Lewis, *Dada Turns Red*.
33. André Breton, *What is Surrealism?*, p. 25.
34. Breton, *Communicating Vessels*, p. 48.
35. Ibid.
36. Blanchot, *The Gaze of Orpheus*, p. 61.
37. See J.-B. Pontalis, 'Les vases non communicants', pp. 34–5.
38. Breton, *What is Surrealism?*, p. 137.
39. Breton, *Communicating Vessels*, p. 104.
40. Ibid., pp. 109, 130.
41. J.-B. Pontalis, 'Les vases non communicants', p. 40.
42. Breton, *Mad Love*, p. 76.
43. Salvador Dali's 'paranoiac criticism' would give an extreme inflection to this tendency.
44. Breton, *Communicating Vessels*, p. 127.
45. Ibid., p. 45 (his emphasis). Breton's reference is presumably to Freud's idea of 'the dream's navel, the spot where it reaches down into the unknown' – see Sigmund Freud, *Interpretation of Dreams*, Pelican Freud Library, vol. 4, p. 671.
46. Comte de Lautréamont, *Maldoror* (1868), pp. 157, 39. In *Entretiens*, p. 42, Breton recalls that 'Nothing, not even Rimbaud, had up to that time affected me as much.'
47. Breton, *Communicating Vessels*, p. 139.
48. Breton, *What is Surrealism?*, p. 24.

49. Jameson, *Marxism and Form*, p. 102.
50. Haim N. Finkelstein, *Surrealism and the Crisis of the Object*, p. 8.
51. Quoted in René Passeron, *The Concise Encyclopedia of Surrealism*, p. 46.
52. Louis Aragon, *Paris Peasant* (1926), p. 130. Further references will be given in the text.
53. Note the Surrealist contempt for work, as in Breton, *Nadja*, p. 60: 'The event from which each of us is entitled to expect the revelation of his own life's meaning ...*is not earned by work*' (Breton's emphases).
54. Louis Aragon, *Treatise on Style*, p. 69.
55. Quoted in André Breton, 'Préface' to *Anthologie de l'humour noir*, p. 20. On the link between pleasure and death, see Annie Le Brun, 'L'Humour noir', in Ferdinand Alquié (ed.), *Entretiens sur le surréalisme*, p. 103.
56. See Michel Beaujour, 'Qu'est-ce que "Nadja"?', pp. 215–16.
57. Breton, *Nadja*, p. 19. Further references will be given in the text.
58. On the 'failure' of myth here, see ibid., pp. 218–19. Interestingly, though, Breton does associate Nadja with Melusina (129), the child-woman of the Tarot, who will reappear in the more clearly mythic *Arcane 17* (1945). On Nadja's description of herself as a 'trace', see Margaret Cohen, *Profane Illumination*, pp. 71–2.
59. The difference is strangely similar to two phases in Lacan's theory of the death drive – see Slavoj Žižek, *The Sublime Object of Ideology*, pp. 131–2.
60. Jacques Derrida, *Writing and Difference*, p. 249.
61. Ibid., p. 175; see also above, pp. 157–8.
62. Antonin Artaud, 'A Propos de *Cenci*', *Oeuvres complètes*, vol. V, pp. 157–8. (my emphases).
63. Quoted in Jacques Derrida, 'Forcener le subjectile', p. 63.
64. Antonin Artaud, 'Ce que sera la tragédie *Les Cenci* aux Folies-Wagram', *Oeuvres complètes*, vol. V, p. 48.
65. Antonin Artaud, 'Les Cenci', *Oeuvres complètes*, vol. V, p. 45.
66. See Derrida, *Writing and Difference*, p. 249.
67. Breton, *Mad Love*, p. 21. Further references will be given in the text.
68. Sigmund Freud, *The Ego and the Id*, in *On Metapsychology, Pelican Freud Library*, vol. 11, p. 378.
69. As it is in Buñuel and Dali's *L'Age d'or*, which Breton here calls 'the only enterprise of exaltation of total love as I envisage it' – see the 'Manifesto of the Surrealists Concerning *L'Age d'or*', in Paul Hammond (ed.), *The Shadow and Its Shadow*, pp. 195–203.
70 Thomas Mann, *Doctor Faustus*, p. 244. Further references will be given in the text.
71. See 'Germany and the Germans', where Mann writes of 'the musicality of the German soul, that which we call its inwardness, its subjectivity, the divorce of the speculative from the socio-political element of human energy, and the complete predominance of the former over the latter' (quoted in Gunilla Bergsten, *Thomas Mann's Doctor Faustus*, p. 162).

Bibliography

The Bibliography gives details of works referred to in the main text; it is not intended to provide an exhaustive listing of works by and about modernist writers.

PRIMARY TEXTS

Apollinaire, Guillaume, *Apollinaire on Art: Essays and Reviews, 1902–1918*, ed. Leroy C. Breunig, trans. Susan Suleiman (New York: Viking Press, 1972).
——, *Calligrammes*, trans. Anne Hyde Greet (Berkeley, Los Angeles and London: University of California Press, 1991).
——, *L'Enchanteur pourrissant* (Paris: Gallimard, 1972).
——, *Oeuvres complètes*, 4 vols, ed. Michel Décaudin (Paris: Balland, 1966).
——, *Selected Writings*, trans. Roger Shattuck (New York: New Directions, 1971).
Aragon, L., 'A Man', *Little Review*, IX, 4 (Autumn/Winter 1923/24) pp. 18–22.
——, *Paris Peasant*, trans. Simon Watson-Taylor (London: Picador, 1980).
——, *Treatise on Style*, trans. Alyson Waters (Lincoln, NE and London: University of Nebraska Press, 1991).
Arp, Hans, *On My Way: Poetry and Essays 1912–1947* (New York: Wittenborn, Schultz, 1948).
Artaud, Antonin, *Desseins et portraits*, ed. Paule Thévenin and Jacques Derrida (Paris: Gallimard, 1986).
——, *Oeuvres complètes*, vol. V: *Autour du Théâtre et son Double et des Cenci* (Paris: Gallimard, 1964).
——, *Selected Writings*, ed. Susan Sontag (Berkeley and Los Angeles: University of California Press, 1988).
Arnold, Matthew, *Essays in Criticism; Second Series* (London and New York: Dent, 1964).
Bahr, Hermann, *Expressionism*, trans. R. T. Gribble (London: Frank Henderson, 1925).
Ball, Hugo, *Flight Out of Time: A Dada Diary*, ed. John Elderfield (New York: Viking Press, 1974).
Bachofen, J. J., *Myth, Religion, and Mother Right*, trans. Ralph Manheim (London: Routledge & Kegan Paul, 1967).
Baudelaire, Charles, *The Complete Verse*, trans. Francis Scarfe (London: Anvil Press, 1986).
——, *Les Fleurs du mal*, trans. Richard Howard (Brighton: Harvester Press, 1982).
——, *My Heart Laid Bare and Other Prose Writings*, trans. Norman Cameron (London: Soho Book Company, 1986).
——, *Oeuvres complètes*, 2 vols, ed. Claude Pichois (Paris: Pléiade, 1975, 1976).

——, *The Poems in Prose*, trans. Francis Scarfe (London: Anvil Press, 1989).

——, *Selected Writings on Art and Artists*, trans. P. E. Charvet (Harmondsworth: Penguin Books, 1972).

Beckett, Samuel, *Collected Poems in English and French* (London: John Calder, 1977).

Beckett, Samuel et al. (eds.), *Our Exagmination Round His Factification for Incamination of Work in Progress* (London: Faber and Faber, 1972).

Benda, Julien, *Belphégor* (Paris: Émile-Paul Frères, 1947).

Bourget, Paul, *Essais de psychologie contemporaine*, 2 vols (Paris: Plon, 1924).

Brecht, Bertolt, *Collected Plays*, vol. 1, ed. John Willett and Ralph Manheim (London: Methuen, 1970).

——, *Seven Plays*, trans. Eric Bentley (New York: Grove Press, 1961).

Breton, André (ed.), *Anthologie de l'humour noir* (Paris: J. J. Pauvert, 1966).

——, *Communicating Vessels*, trans. Mary Ann Caws and Geoffrey T. Harris (Lincoln, NE and London: University of Nebraska Press, 1990).

——, *Entretiens 1913–1952* (Paris: Gallimard, 1969).

——, *Mad Love*, trans. Mary Ann Caws (Lincoln, NE and London: University of Nebraska Press, 1988).

——, *Manifestoes of Surrealism*, trans. Richard Seaver and Helen R. Lane (Ann Arbor: University of Michigan Press, 1972).

——, *Nadja*, trans. Richard Howard (New York: Grove Press, 1960).

——, *Les Pas perdus* (Paris: Gallimard, 1979).

——, *Point du jour* (Paris: Gallimard, 1970).

——, *What is Surrealism? Selected Writings*, ed. Franklin Rosemont (London: Pluto Press, 1978).

Breton, André and Philippe Soupault, *The Magnetic Fields*, trans. David Gascoyne (London: Atlas Press, 1985).

Broch, Hermann, *Hugo von Hofmannsthal and His Time: The European Imagination, 1860–1920*, trans. Michael P. Steinberg (Chicago and London: University of Chicago Press, 1984).

——, *The Sleepwalkers*, trans. Willa and Edwin Muir (London: Quartet Books, 1986).

Catullus, Gaius Valerius, *Catullus, Tibullus and Pervigilium Veneris*, trans. F. W. Cornish (London: William Heinemann, 1968).

Cendrars, Blaise, *Complete Poems*, trans. Ron Padgett (Berkeley, Los Angeles and Oxford: University of California Press, 1992.

——, *Oeuvres complètes*, 8 vols (Paris: Denoël, 1960–5).

——, 'Profound Today', *Broom*, 1.3 (1922) pp. 265–7.

Conrad, Joseph, *The Nigger of the 'Narcissus'*, ed. Cedric Watts (Harmondsworth: Penguin Books, 1989).

Corbière, Tristan, *The Centenary Corbière*, trans. Val Warner (Cheadle: Carcanet New Press, 1975).

D'Annunzio, Gabriele, *The Triumph of Death*, trans. Georgina Harding (Sawtry: Dedalus, 1990).

Darío, Rubén, *Páginas escogidas*, ed. Ricardo Gullón (Madrid: Ediciones Cátedra, 1986).

Delaunay, Robert, *Du Cubisme à l'art abstrait* (Paris: S.E.V.P.E.N., 1957).

Dermée, Paul, 'Quand le Symbolisme fut mort', *Nord-Sud*, 1.1 (March 1917) pp. 2–4.

D[oolittle], H[ilda], *Collected Poems 1912–1944*, ed. Louis Martz (Manchester: Carcanet Press, 1984).

——, *Her*, introd. Helen McNeill (London: Virago, 1984).

——, *Notes on Thought and Vision and The Wise Sappho* (San Francisco: City Lights, 1982).

——, *Tribute to Freud*, introd. Peter Jones (Oxford: Carcanet Press, 1971).

Dostoyevsky, Fyodor, *Notes from Underground*, trans. Jessie Coulson (Harmondsworth: Penguin Books, 1972).

Eliot, T. S., *Complete Poems and Plays* (London: Faber and Faber, 1970).

——, *Knowledge and Experience in the Philosophy of F. H. Bradley* (London: Faber and Faber, 1964).

——, 'London Letter', *Dial*, 71 (August 1921) pp. 213–17.

——, 'Observations', *Egoist*, V (1918) pp. 69–70.

——, *Selected Essays* (London: Faber and Faber, 1972).

——, *Selected Prose*, ed. Frank Kermode (Harmondsworth: Penguin Books, 1965).

——, *The Use of Poetry and the Use of Criticism* (London: Faber and Faber, 1964).

Emerson, Ralph Waldo, *Collected Works*, vol. I: *Nature, Addresses, and Lectures* (Cambridge, MA: Belknap Press, 1971). *Collected Works*, vol. II: *Essays: First Series* (Cambridge, MA: Belknap Press, 1979).

Fenollosa, Ernest, *The Chinese Written Character as a Medium for Poetry*, trans. Ezra Pound (San Francisco: City Lights, 1969).

Flaubert, Gustave, *Bouvard and Pécuchet*, trans. A. J. Krailsheimer (Harmondsworth: Penguin Books, 1976).

——, *Letters*, ed. Francis Steegmuller, 2 vols (Cambridge, MA: Belknap Press, 1980, 1982).

——, *Madame Bovary: A Story of Provincial Life*, trans. Alan Russell (Harmondsworth: Penguin Books, 1984).

Flint, F. S., 'Imagisme', in Peter Jones (ed.), *Imagist Poetry* (Harmondsworth: Penguin Books, 1972).

Ford, Ford Madox, *Critical Writings*, ed. Frank MacShane (Lincoln, NE: University of Nebraska Press, 1964).

——, *The Good Soldier: A Tale of Passion* (Harmondsworth: Penguin Books, 1988).

Gautier, Théophile, *Mademoiselle de Maupin*, trans. Joanna Richardson (Harmondsworth: Penguin Books, 1981).

——, *The Complete Works*, 12 vols, trans. and ed. S. C. De Sumichrast (London: The Athenaeum Press, n.d).

George, Stefan, *The Works*, trans. Olga Marx and Ernst Morwitz (Chapel Hill, NC: University of North Carolina Press, 1974).

Gide, André, *Fruits of the Earth*, trans. Dorothy Bussy (London: Secker, 1949).

——, *Journals 1889–1949*, trans. Judith O'Brien (Harmondsworth: Penguin Books, 1984).

Goldsmith, Oliver, *The Vicar of Wakefield*, ed. Stephen Coote (Harmondsworth: Penguin Books, 1982).

Gourmont, Remy de, *Decadence and other Essays on the Culture of Ideas*, ed. J. E. Spingarn (New York: Harcourt, Brace & Company, 1921).

——, *The Natural Philosophy of Love*, trans. Ezra Pound (New York: Collier, 1961).

Hausmann, Raoul, 'The Optophonetic Dawn', trans. Frank W. Lindsay, *Studies in Twentieth Century Literature*, 3 (Spring 1969) pp. 51–4.

Hofmannsthal, Hugo von, *Selected Prose*, trans. Mary Hottinger and Tania and James Stern (London: Routledge and Kegan Paul, 1952).

——, *Poems and Verse Plays*, trans. Michael Hamburger (London: Routledge and Kegan Paul, 1961).

Huelsenbeck, Richard, 'Dada Lives', *transition*, 23 (Fall 1936) pp. 77–80.

——, *Memoirs of a Dada Drummer*, ed. H. J. Kleinschmidt (New York: Viking Press, 1974).

Huidobro, Vicente, *Selected Poetry*, ed. David M. Guss (New York: New Directions, 1981).

Hulme, T. E., *Speculations*, ed. Herbert Read (London: Kegan Paul, 1936).

Huneker, James Gibbons, *Ivory, Apes and Peacocks* (New York: Sagamore Press, 1957).

Huysmans, Joris-Karl, *Against Nature*, trans. Robert Baldick (Harmondsworth: Penguin Books, 1959).

Jackson, Laura (Riding), *The Poems of Laura Riding* (Manchester: Carcanet New Press, 1980).

Jacob, Max, *Le Cornet à dés* (Paris: Gallimard, 1967).

——, *The Dice Cup: Selected Prose Poems*, ed. Michael Brownstein (New York: Sun, 1979).

James, Henry, *The Ambassadors*, ed. Harry Levin (Harmondsworth: Penguin Books, 1986).

——, *The American Scene*, ed. W. H. Auden (New York: Scribner's, 1946).

Jarry, Alfred, *Selected Works*, ed. Roger Shattuck and Simon Watson-Taylor (London: Eyre Methuen, 1980).

Joyce, James, *The Essential James Joyce*, ed. Harry Levin (Harmondsworth: Penguin Books, 1965).

——, *Ulysses*, ed. and introd. Jeri Johnson (Oxford: Oxford University Press, 1993).

Kafka, Franz, *The Castle*, trans. Willa and Edwin Muir (London: Minerva, 1992).

——, *Diaries 1910–1923*, ed. Max Brod (Harmondsworth: Penguin Books, 1964).

——*Letters to Felice*, trans. James Stern and Elizabeth Duckworth (Harmondsworth: Penguin Books, 1983).

——*The Trial*, trans. Willa and Edwin Muir (Harmondsworth: Penguin Books, 1953).

Kaiser, Georg, *Five Plays*, trans. J. Kenworthy et al. (London: Calder, 1971).

Kandinsky, Wassily and Franz Marc (eds.), *The Blaue Reiter Almanac*, ed. Klaus Lankheit (New York: Da Capo, 1974).

Kandinsky, Wassily, *Concerning the Spiritual in Art*, trans. M. T. H. Sadler (New York: Dover, 1977).

Khlebnikov, Velimir, *Collected Works*, trans. Paul Schmidt and Charlotte Douglas, vol. I: *Letters and Theoretical Writings* (Cambridge, MA and London: Harvard University Press, 1987).

Kirby, Michael and Victoria Nes Kirby, *Futurist Performance* (New York: PAJ Publications, 1986).

Klee, Paul, *On Modern Art*, trans. Paul Findlay (London: Faber and Faber, 1948).

Kokoschka, Oskar, *Dichtungen und Dramen*, vol. 1 of *Das Schriftliche Werk* (Hamburg: Christians, 1973).

——, *My Life*, trans. David Britt (London: Thames and Hudson, 1974).

Laforgue, Jules, *Mélanges posthumes*, ed. Philippe Bonnefis (Geneva: Slatkine Reprints, 1979).

——, *Moral Tales*, trans. William Jay Smith (London: Pan Books, 1985).

——, *Poems of Jules Laforgue*, trans. Peter Dale (London: Anvil Press, 1986).

Larbaud, Valéry, *Oeuvres complètes* (Paris: Gallimard, 1953).

——, *Les Poésies de A. O. Barnabooth* (Paris: Gallimard, 1966).

Lautréamont, Comte de, *Maldoror and Poems*, trans. Paul Knight (Harmondsworth: Penguin Books, 1978).

Lawrence, D. H., *Fantasia of the Unconscious; Psychoanalysis and the Unconscious* (Harmondsworth: Penguin Books, 1973).

Lefèvre, Frédéric, *La Jeune poésie française, hommes et tendances* (Paris: Rouart, 1917).

Léger, Fernand, *Functions of Painting*, trans. Alexandra Anderson, ed. Edward F. Fry (London: Thames and Hudson, 1973).

Lewis, Wyndham, *The Apes of God*, ed. Paul Edwards (Santa Barbara, CA: Black Sparrow Press, 1981).

——, *The Art of Being Ruled*, ed. Reed Way Dasenbrock (Santa Rosa, CA: Black Sparrow Press, 1989).

——, *Blast*, 1 and 2 (1914–15).

——, *Blasting and Bombadiering: An Autobiography (1914–1926)* (London: Calder and Boyars, 1967).

——, *The Caliph's Design*, ed. Paul Edwards (Santa Barbara, CA: Black Sparrow Press, 1986).

——, *The Complete Wild Bod*, ed. Bernard Lafourcade (Santa Barbara, CA: Black Sparrow Press, 1982).

——, *Creatures of Habit and Creatures of Change: Essays on Art, Literature and Society 1914–1956*, ed. Paul Edwards (Santa Rosa, CA: Black Sparrow Press, 1989).

——, *Hitler* (London: Chatto & Windus, 1931).

——, *The Letters of Wyndham Lewis*, ed. W. K. Rose (London: Methuen, 1963).

——, *The Lion and the Fox: the Role of the Hero in the Plays of Shakespeare* (New York and London: Harper, 1927).

——, *Men Without Art*, ed. Seamus Cooney (Santa Rosa, CA: Black Sparrow Press, 1987).

——, *Rude Assignment: An Intellectual Autobiography*, ed. Toby Foshay (Santa Barbara, CA: Black Sparrow Press, 1984).

——, *Tarr: the 1918 Version*, ed. Paul O'Keefe (Santa Rosa, CA: Black Sparrow Press, 1990).

——, *Time and Western Man*, ed. Paul Edwards (Santa Rosa, CA: Black Sparrow Press, 1993).

——, *The Writer and the Absolute* (London: Methuen, 1952).

——, *Wyndham Lewis on Art: Collected Writings 1913–1956*, ed. Walter Michel and C. J. Fox (London: Thames and Hudson, 1969).

Livshits, Benedikt, *The One-And-a-Half-Eyed Archer*, trans. John E. Bowlt (Newtonsville, MA: Oriental Research Partners, 1977).

Loy, Mina, *The Last Lunar Baedeker*, ed. Roger L. Conover (Highlands, NJ: The Jargon Society, 1982).

Mallarmé, Stéphane, *Oeuvres complètes*, ed. Henri Mondor and G. Jean-Aubry (Paris: Gallimard, 1979).

——, *The Poems*, trans. Keith Bosley (Harmondsworth: Penguin Books, 1977).

——, *Selected Prose Poems, Essays and Letters*, trans. Bradford Cook (Baltimore: Johns Hopkins University Press, 1956).

Mann, Thomas, *Buddenbrooks: The Decline of a Family*, trans. H. T. Lowe-Porter (Harmondsworth: Penguin Books, 1986).

——, *Doctor Faustus: The Life of the German Composer Adrian Leverkühn As Told by a Friend*, trans. H. T. Lowe-Porter (Harmondsworth: Penguin Books, 1968).

Marinetti, F. T., *Marinetti: Selected Writings*, trans. R. W. Flint (London: Secker & Warburg, 1972).

——, *Opere di F. T. Marinetti*, ed. Luciano De Maria, vol. 2: *Teoria e invenzione futurista* (Milan: Mondadori, 1968).

——, *Scritti francesi*, ed. Pasquale A. Jannini, vol. 1 (Milan: Mondadori, 1983).

——, *Stung by Salt and War: Creative Texts of the Italian Avant-Gardist F. T. Marinetti*, trans. Richard J. Pioli (New York and Bern: Peter Lang, 1987).

Maurras, Charles, *L'Avenir de l'intelligence* (Paris: Flammarion, 1927).

Mayakovksy, Vladimir, *How Are Verses Made?*, trans. George Hyde (Bristol: Bristol Classical Press, 1990).

——, *Selected Works*, 3 vols (Moscow: Raduga, 1985).

Melville, Herman, *Moby-Dick; or, The Whale*, ed. Harold Beaver (Harmondsworth: Penguin Books, 1972).

Mirbeau, Octave, *The Torture Garden*, trans. Alvah C. Bessie (San Francisco: Re/Search Publications, 1989).

Montale, Eugenio, *The Bones of Cuttlefish*, trans. Antonio Mazza (Oakville, Ontario: Mosaic Press, 1983).

——, *Selected Essays*, trans. G. Singh (Manchester: Carcanet Press, 1978).

Moore, Marianne, *Complete Poems* (London: Faber and Faber, 1968).

Musil, Robert, *The Man Without Qualities*, ·3 vols, trans. Eithne Wilkins and Ernst Kaiser (London: Picador, 1979).

Nerval, Gérard de, *Selected Writings*, trans. Geoffrey Wagner (London: Panther Books, 1968).

Nietzsche, Friedrich, *The Gay Science*, trans. Walter Kaufmann (New York: Vintage Books, 1974).

——, *On the Genealogy of Morals*, trans. Walter Kaufmann (New York: Vintage Books, 1969).

Pater, Walter, *Imaginary Portraits* (London: Macmillan, 1910).

——, *The Renaissance: Studies in Art and Poetry (The 1893 Text)*, ed. Donald E. Hill (Berkeley and Los Angeles: University of California Press, 1980).

Poe, Edgar Allan, *Selected Writings: Poems, Tales, Essays and Reviews*, ed. David Galloway (Harmondsworth: Penguin Books, 1967).

Pound, Ezra, *ABC of Reading* (London: Faber and Faber, 1961).

——, *The Cantos* (New York: New Directions, 1971).

——, *Collected Early Poems*, ed. Michael John King (London: Faber and Faber, 1977).

——, *Collected Shorter Poems* (London: Faber and Faber, 1968).

——, *Ezra Pound and Music: The Complete Criticism*, ed. R. Murray Schafer (London: Faber and Faber, 1978).

——, *Gaudier-Brzeska: A Memoir* (Hessle: Marvell Press, 1960).

——, *Guide to Kulchur* (London: Peter Owen, 1966).

——, *Literary Essays*, ed. T. S. Eliot (London: Faber and Faber, 1960).

——, *Patria Mia and the Treatise on Harmony* (London: Peter Owen, 1962).

——, *Selected Letters 1907–1941*, ed. D. D. Paige (London: Faber and Faber, 1971).

——, *Selected Poems*, introd. T. S. Eliot (London: Faber and Faber, 1967).

——, *Selected Prose 1909–1965*, ed. William Cookson (London: Faber and Faber, 1973).

——, 'Three Cantos: I', *Poetry*, *x*, 3 (June 1917) pp. 113–21.

——, *The Translations of Ezra Pound*, introd. Hugh Kenner (London: Faber and Faber, 1953).

——, 'Unanimism', *Little Review*, IV, 2 (April 1918) pp. 26–32.

Pound, Ezra and Ernest Fenollosa, *The Classic Noh Theatre of Japan* (New York: New Directions, 1959).

Proust, Marcel, *Chroniques* (Paris: Gallimard, 1949).

——, *Remembrance of Things Past*, 3 vols, trans. C. K. Scott Moncrieff, Terence Kilmartin, Andreas Mayor (London: Chatto & Windus, 1981).

Quesnoy, Pierre-F., *Littérature et Cinéma* (Paris: Le Rouge et le Noir, 1928).

Régis, Emmanuel and Angelo L. M. Hesnard, *La Psychanalyse: des névroses et des psychoses* (Paris: Alcan, 1914).

Reverdy, Pierre, *Cette émotion appelée poésie: Écrits sur la poésie* (Paris: Flammarion, 1974).

——, *Le Gant de crin: notes* (Paris: Flammarion, 1968).

——, *Le Livre de mon bord: notes 1930–1936* (Paris: Mercure de France, 1948).

——, *Nord-Sud, Self-defence et autres écrits sur l'art et la poésie 1917–1926* (Paris, Flammarion, 1975).

——, *Note éternelle du présent: Ecrits sur l'art 1923–1960* (Paris: Flammarion, 1973).

——, *Selected Poems*, trans. Kenneth Rexroth (New York: New Directions, 1969).

Ribemont-Dessaignes, Georges, *The Mute Canary*, trans. Victoria Nes Kirby, *Drama Review*, 16.1 (March 1972) pp. 110–16.

Richardson, Dorothy, *Pilgrimage*, 4 vols (London: Virago, 1979).

Rilke, Rainer Maria, *Letters on Cézanne*, ed. Clara Rilke, trans. Joel Agee (London: Jonathan Cape, 1988).

——, *Notebook of Malte Laurids Brigge*, trans. John Linton (Oxford: Oxford University Press, 1984).

—— *Rodin and Other Prose Pieces*, trans. C. Craig Houston (London: Quartet Books, 1986).

——, *Selected Letters 1902–1926*, trans. R. F. C. Hull (London: Quartet Books, 1988).

——, *Selected Poetry*, trans. Stephen Mitchell (London: Picador, 1987).

Rimbaud, Arthur, *Collected Poems*, trans. Oliver Bernard (Harmondsworth: Penguin Books, 1987).

Romains, Jules, *La Vie unanime* (Paris: Éditions de 'L'Abbaye', 1908).

Saltus, Edgar, *The Philosophy of Disenchantment* (New York: Brentano's, 1925).

Samuel, Horace, B., *Modernities* (London: Kegan Paul, 1913).

Sarrazin, Gabriel, *Poètes modernes de l'Angleterre* (Paris: P. Ollendorf, 1885).

Scheffauer, Herman George, *The New Vision in the German Arts* (New York and London: E. Benn, 1924).

Schnitzler, Arthur, *The Road into the Open*, trans. Roger Byers (Berkeley, Los Angeles, Oxford: University of California Press, 1992).

Schopenhauer, Arthur, *Parerga and Parilipomena: Short Philosophical Essays*, trans. E. F. J. Payne (Oxford: Clarendon Press, 1974).

——, *The World as Will and Idea*, 2 vols, trans. E. F. J. Payne (New York: Dover, 1969).

Soupault, Philippe, *Charlot* (Paris: Plon, 1931).

——, *Last Nights of Paris*, trans. William Carlos Williams (New York: Full Court Press, 1982).

Stein, Gertrude, *Look at Me Now and Here I Am: Writings and Lectures 1909–45*, ed. Patricia Meyerowitz (Harmondsworth: Penguin Books, 1971).

——, *The Making of Americans, being a History of a Family's Progress* (London: Peter Owen, 1968).

——, *Picasso* (New York: Dover, 1984).

——, *Three Lives* (Harmondsworth: Penguin Books, 1979).

——, *The Yale Gertrude Stein*, ed. Richard Kostelanetz (New Haven and London: Yale University Press, 1980).

Stevens, Wallace, *Collected Poems* (London: Faber and Faber, 1971).

——, *Letters*, ed. Holly Stevens (London: Faber and Faber, 1967).

——, *The Necessary Angel: Essays on Reality and the Imagination* (New York: Vintage Books, 1951).

Strindberg, August, *The Plays*, vol. II, trans. Michael Meyer (London: Secker, 1975).

Swinburne, A. C., *Collected Poetical Works*, 2 vols (London: Heinemann, 1924).

Symons, Arthur, *The Symbolist Movement in Literature* (New York: Dutton, 1958).

Toller, Ernst, 'My Works', trans. Marketa Goetz, in Toby Cole (ed.), *Playwrights on Playwriting* (New York: Hill and Wang, 1961).

——, *Seven Plays*, trans. E. Crankshaw et al. (London: Lane, 1935).

Trakl, Georg, *Autumn Sonata: Selected Poems of Georg Trakl*, trans. Daniel Simko (Mt Kisko, NY: Mayer Bell, 1989).

——, *Georg Trakl: A Profile*, ed. Frank Graziano (Manchester: Carcanet Press, 1984).

Tzara, Tristan, *Seven Dada Manifestos and Lampisteries*, trans. Barbara Wright (London: John Calder, 1977).

Ungaretti, Giuseppe, 'Interview with Denis Roche', *Agenda*, 8.2 (Spring 1970) pp. 105–10.

——, *Vita d'un uomo: Saggi e interventi*, ed. Mario Diacono and Luciano Rebay (Milan: Mondadori, 1974).

——, *Vita d'un uomo: Tutte le poesie*, ed. Leone Riccioni (Milan: Mondadori, 1969).

Valéry, Paul, *Leonardo Poe Mallarmé*, trans. Malcolm Lawler, vol. 8 of *The Collected Works of Paul Valéry*, ed. Jackson Mathews (London: Routledge and Kegan Paul, 1972).

Verhaeren, Émile, *Les Campagnes hallucinées; Les Villes Tentaculaires*, ed. Maurice Piron (Paris: Gallimard, 1982).

Verlaine, Paul, *Selected Poems*, trans. Charles MacIntyre (Berkeley and Los Angeles: University of California Press, 1961).

Villiers de l'Isle-Adam, Philippe-Auguste, *Axël*, trans. M. Gaddis Rose (London: Soho Book Company, 1986).

——, *Cruel Tales*, trans. A. W. Raitt (Oxford: Oxford University Press, 1985).

Wagner, Richard, *Richard Wagner's Prose Works*, vol. V, trans. W. A. Ellis (London: Paul, Trench and Trubner, 1896).

Wedekind, Frank, *The Lulu Plays and other Sex Tragedies*, trans. Stephen Spender (London: John Calder, 1977).

Weininger, Otto, *Sex and Character* (New York: AMS Press, 1975).

Whitman, Walt, *Leaves of Grass*, ed. Sculley Bradley and Harold W. Blodgett (New York: Norton, 1973).

Wilde, Oscar, *Plays, Prose Writings and Poems*, introd. Hesketh Pearson (London: J. M. Dent & Sons, 1961).

Williams, William Carlos, *Collected Poems 1909–1939*, ed. A. Walton Litz and Christopher MacGowan (Manchester: Carcanet Press, 1987).

——, *Imaginations*, ed. Webster Schott (New York: New Directions, 1971).

——, *I Wanted to Write a Poem* (London: Jonathan Cape, 1967).

——, *Selected Essays* (New York: New Directions, 1969).

Woolf, Virginia, *Collected Essays*, 4 vols (London: Hogarth Press, 1966–7).

——, *The Letters of Virginia Woolf*, 6 vols, ed. Nigel Nicolson and Joanne Trautmann (London: Hogarth Press, 1975–80).

——, *Mrs Dalloway* (London: Grafton Books, 1987).

——, *To the Lighthouse* (Harmondsworth: Penguin Books, 1974).

——, *The Waves*, ed. Kate Flint (Harmondsworth: Penguin Books, 1992).

——, *A Writer's Diary*, ed. Leonard Woolf (London: Grafton Books, 1978).

Yeats, W. B., *Collected Poems* (London: Macmillan, 1971).

——, *Essays and Introductions* (New York: Macmillan, 1961).

——, *The Letters*, ed. Allen Wade (New York: Macmillan, 1955).

Zola, Émile, *The Kill*, trans. A. Teixeira de Mattos (London: Panther Books, 1985).

ANTHOLOGIES

Apollonio, Umbro (ed.), *Futurist Manifestos* (London: Thames and Hudson, 1973).

Auster, Paul (ed.), *The Random House Book of Twentieth Century French Poetry* (New York: Vintage Books, 1984).

Benedikt, Michael (ed.), *The Poetry of Surrealism: An Anthology* (Boston and Toronto: Little, Brown and Co., 1974).

Bowlt, John E. (ed. and trans.), *Russian Art of the Avant-Garde* (New York: Viking Press, 1976).

Fry, Edward (ed.), *Cubism* (London: Thames and Hudson, 1978).

Glad, John and Daniel Weissbort (eds), *Russian Poetry: The Modern Period* (Iowa City: University of Iowa Press, 1978).

Hamburger, Michael (ed. and trans.), *German Poetry 1910–1975* (Manchester: Carcanet Press, 1977).

Hartley, Anthony (ed.), *The Penguin Book of French Verse 3* (Harmondsworth: Penguin Books, 1967).

Jones, Peter (ed.), *Imagist Poetry* (Harmondsworth: Penguin Books, 1972).

Lawton, Anna and Herbert Eagle (trans.), *Russian Futurism through Its Manifestoes* (Ithaca and London: Cornell University Press, 1988).

Lippard, Lucy R. (ed.), *Dadas on Art* (Englewood Cliffs, NJ: Prentice-Hall, 1971).

Markov, Vladimir and Merrill Sparks, *Modern Russian Poetry* (London: MacGibbon & Kee, 1966).

Mengaldo, Pier Vincenzo (ed.), *Poeti italiani del novecento* (Milan: Mondadori, 1987).

Miesel, V. H. (ed.), *Voices of German Expressionism* (Englewood Cliffs, NJ: Prentice-Hall, 1970).

Mitchell, Bonner (ed.), *Les Manifestes littéraires de la belle époque* (Paris: Seghers, 1966).

Motherwell, Robert (ed.), *The Dada Painters and Poets: An Anthology*, 2nd edn (Cambridge, MA and London: Harvard University Press, 1989).

Pinthus, Karl (ed.), *Menschheitsdämmerung* (1920) (Berlin: Rowohly, 1959).

Ravegnani, Guido (ed.), *Poeti futuristi* (Milan: Nuova Accademia, 1963).

Ritchie, J. M. and H. F. Garten (trans.), *Seven Expressionist Plays* (London: John Calder, 1980).

Sokel, Walter H. (ed.), *Anthology of German Expressionist Drama: A Prelude to the Absurd* (Ithaca and London: Cornell University Press, 1984).

Stefanile, Felix (trans.), *The Blue Moustache: Some Futurist Poets* (Manchester: Carcanet Press, 1981).

Stromberg, Roland N. (ed.), *Realism, Naturalism, and Symbolism: Modes of Thought and Expression in Europe, 1848–1914* (London and Melbourne: Macmillan, 1968).

Weber, Eugen (ed.), *Paths to the Present: Aspects of European Thought from Romanticism to Existentialism* (New York and Toronto: Dodd, Mead & Company, 1960).

Wellwarth, George and Michael Benedikt (trans.), *Modern French Theater – the Avant-Garde, Dada and Surrealism* (New York: Dutton, 1966).

SECONDARY TEXTS

Alquié, Ferdinand (ed.), *Entretiens sur le surréalisme* (Paris and The Hague: Mouton, 1968).

——, *The Philosophy of Surrealism*, trans. Bernard Waldrop (Ann Arbor, MI: University of Michigan Press, 1965).

Anderson, Perry, 'Modernity and Revolution', *New Left Review*, 144 (March/April 1984): pp. 96–113.

Bakhtin, M. M., *The Dialogic Imagination: Four Essays*, trans. Caryl Emerson and Michael Holquist (Austin: University of Texas Press, 1981).

Balakian, Anna (ed.), *The Symbolist Movement in the Literature of European Languages* (Budapest: Akadémiai Kiadó, 1982).

Barooshian,Vahan D., *Russian Cubo-Futurism 1910–1930* (The Hague and Paris: Mouton, 1974).

Barthes, Roland, *Writing Degree Zero*, trans. Annette Lavers and Colin Smith (New York: Hill and Wang, 1968).

Bataille, Georges, *Visions of Excess: Selected Writings*, trans. Alan Stoekl et al. (Manchester: Manchester University Press, 1985).

Baudrillard, Jean, *Seduction*, trans. Brian Singer (Basingstoke: Macmillan, 1990).

Beaujour, Michel, 'Qu'est-ce que "Nadja"?', *Nouvelle Revue Française*, 172 (1 April 1967) pp. 780–99.

Benjamin, Jessica, *The Bonds of Love: Psychoanalysis, Feminism, and the Problem of Domination* (London: Virago Press, 1990).

Benjamin, Walter, 'Central Park', trans. Lloyd Spencer, *New German Critique*, 34 (Winter 1985) pp. 32–58.

——, *Charles Baudelaire: A Lyric Poet in the Era of High Capitalism*, trans. Harry Zohn (London: Verso Editions, 1983).

——, *Illuminations*, trans. Harry Zohn (London: Fontana, 1977).

——, *One-Way Street and Other Writings*, trans. Edmund Jephcott and Kingsley Shorter (London: NLB, 1979).

——, *The Origin of German Tragic Drama*, trans. John Osborne (London: NLB, 1977).

Benstock, Shari, *Women of the Left Bank: Paris, 1900–1940* (London: Virago, 1987).

Bergman, Pär, *'Modernolatria' et 'Simultaneità': Recherches sur deux tendances dans l'avant-garde littéraire en Italie et en France á la veille de la premiére guerre mondiale* (Stockholm: Svenska Bokforlaget, 1962).

Bergsten, Gunilla, *Thomas Mann's Doctor Faustus: The Sources and Structure of the Novel*, trans. Krishna Winston (Chicago and London: University of Chicago Press, 1969).

Berman, Marshall, *All that is Solid Melts into Air: The Experience of Modernity* (London: Verso, 1983)

Bernard, Suzanne, *Mallarmé et la musique* (Paris: Nizet, 1959).

Bersani, Leo, and Ulysse Dutoit, *The Forms of Violence: Narrative in Assyrian Art and Modern Culture* (New York: Schoken Books, 1985).

Blachère, Jean-Claude, *Le Modèle nègre: Aspects littéraires du mythe primitiviste au XXme siècle chez Apollinaire, Cendrars, Tzara* (Dakar: Nouvelles Éditions Africaines, 1981).

Blanchot, Maurice, *The Gaze of Orpheus, and other literary essays*, trans. Lydia Davis (New York: Station Hill, 1981).

——, *The Infinite Conversation*, trans. Susan Hanson (Minneapolis and London: University of Wisconsin, 1993).

——, *La Part du feu* (Paris: Gallimard, 1949).

——, *The Space of Literature*, trans. Ann Smock (Lincoln, NE and London: University of Nebraska Press, 1989).

——, *The Writing of the Disaster*, trans. Ann Smock (Lincoln, NE and London: University of Nebraska Press, 1986).

Bloch, Ernst et al., *Aesthetics and Politics* (London: NLB, 1977).

Bois, Yves-Alain, 'Kahnweiler's Lesson', *Representations*, 18 (Spring 1987) pp. 33–68.

Bonnet, Marguerite, *André Breton: Naissance de l'aventure surréaliste* (Paris: José Corti, 1975).

Boothby, Richard, *Death and Desire: Psychoanalytic Theory in Lacan's Relation to Freud* (New York and London: Routledge, 1991).

Breunig, L-C., 'Apollinaire et le Cubisme', *Revue des lettres modernes*, 69/70 (Spring 1962) pp. 7–24.

Brodsky, Patricia Pollock, *Rainer Maria Rilke* (Boston: Twayne, 1985).

Bronfen, Elisabeth, *Over Her Dead Body: Death, Femininity, and the Aesthetic* (Manchester: Manchester University Press, 1992).

Brooker, Peter, *Bertolt Brecht: Dialectics, Poetry, Politics* (London: Croom Helm, 1988).

Brown, Edward J. (ed.), *Major Soviet Writers: Essays in Criticism* (Oxford: Oxford University Press, 1973).

——, *Mayakovsky: A Poet in the Revolution* (Princeton, NJ; Princeton University Press, 1973).

Bruns, Gerald L., *Modern Poetry and the Idea of Language* (New Haven, CT and London: Yale University Press, 1974).

Bryson, Norman, Michael Ann Holly and Keith Moxey (eds), *Visual Theory: Painting and Interpretation* (Cambridge: Polity Press, 1991).

Buci-Glucksman, Christine, *La Raison baroque: de Baudelaire à Benjamin* (Paris: Éditions Galilée, 1984).

Buck, Claire, 'Freud and H.D. – Bisexuality and Feminine Discourse', *m/f*, 8 (1983) pp. 53–66.

Budgen, Frank, *James Joyce and the Making of 'Ulysses'* (London, Oxford and Melbourne: Oxford University Press, 1972).

Bürger, Peter, *Theory of the Avant-Garde*, trans. Michael Shaw (Manchester: Manchester University Press, 1984).

Burke, Carolyn, 'The New Poetry and the New Woman: Mina Loy', in Diane Wood Middlebrook and Marilyn Yalom (eds), *Coming to Light: American Woman Poets in the Twentieth Century* (Ann Arbor, MI: University of Michigan Press, 1985).

Burnshaw, Stanley (ed.), *The Poem Itself* (New York: Horizon Press, 1981).

Bush, Ronald, *The Genesis of Ezra Pound's Cantos* (Princeton, NJ: Princeton University Press, 1976).

——, 'It Draws One to Consider Time Wasted: *Hugh Selwyn Mauberley*', *American Literary History*, 2.2 (Summer 1990) pp. 56–78.

Butler, Judith, *Subjects of Desire: Hegelian Reflections in Twentieth-Century France* (New York: Columbia University Press, 1987).

Cadava, Eduardo et al. (eds), *Who Comes After the Subject?* (London: Routledge, 1991).

Calinescu, Matei, *The Faces of Modernity: Avant-Garde, Decadence, Kitsch* (Bloomington, IN: Indiana University Press, 1977).

Canetti, Elias, 'Kafka's Other Trial', in Franz Kafka, *Letters to Felice*, trans. James Stern and Elizabeth Duckworth (Harmondsworth: Penguin Books, 1983).

Cardinal, Roger, *Expressionism* (London: Paladin Books, 1984).

Carey, John, *The Intellectuals and the Masses: Pride and Prejudice among the Literary Intelligentsia, 1880–1939* (London: Faber and Faber, 1992).

Carroll, John, *Break-Out from the Crystal Palace: The Anarcho-Psychological Critique. Stirner, Nietzsche, Dostoevsky* (London and Boston: Routledge and Kegan Paul, 1974).

Carrouges, Michel, *André Breton et les données fondamentales du surréalisme* (Paris: Gallimard, 1950).

——, *Les Machines célibataires* (Paris: Éditions du chêne, 1976).

Carter, A. E., *The Idea of Decadence in French Literature 1830–1900* (Toronto: Toronto University Press, 1958).

Cary, Joseph, *Three Modern Italian Poets: Saba, Ungaretti, Montale* (New York: New York University Press, 1969).

Cassagne, Albert, *La Théorie de l'art pour l'art en France chez les derniers romantiques et les premiers réalistes* (Paris: Dorbon, 1906).

Chapple, Gerald and Hans H. Schulte (eds), *The Turn of the Century: German Literature and Art 1890–1915* (Bonn: Bouvier Verlag, 1983).

Chénieux-Gendron, Jacqueline, *Le Surréalisme et le roman 1922–1950* (Lausanne: L'Age d'homme, 1983).

Chessman, Harriet Scott, *The Public is Invited to Dance: Representation, the Body, and Dialogue in Gertrude Stein* (Stanford, CA: Stanford University Press, 1989).

Chipp, Herschel B. (ed.), *Theories of Modern Art* (Berkeley, Los Angeles and London: University of California Press, 1968).

Chisholm, Diane, *H.D.'s Freudian Poetics: Psychoanalysis in Translation* (Ithaca and London: Cornell University Press, 1992).

Clark, T. J., *The Absolute Bourgeois: Artists and Politics in France 1848–1851* (London: Thames and Hudson, 1973).

Cianci, Giovanni, 'Futurism and the English Avant-Garde: the Early Pound between Imagism and Vorticism', *Arbeiten aus Anglistik und Amerikanistik*, 1 (1981) pp. 3–39.

Cohen, G. A., *Karl Marx's Theory of History* (Oxford: Oxford University Press, 1982).

Cohen, Margaret, *Profane Illumination: Walter Benjamin and the Paris of Surrealist Revolution* (Berkeley, Los Angeles and London: University of California Press, 1993)

Compton, Susan, *The World Backwards: Russian Futurist Books 1912–16* (London: The British Library, 1978).

Cork, Richard, *Vorticism and Abstract Art in the First Machine Age*, 2 vols. (London: Fraser, 1976).

Corngold, Stanley, *Franz Kafka: the Necessity of Form* (Ithaca and London: Cornell University Press, 1988).

Corvin, Michel, 'Le théâtre Dada existe-t-il?', *Revue d'Histoire du Théâtre*, 23 (1971) pp. 219–310.

Culler, Jonathan, *The Pursuit of Signs: Semiotics, Literature, Deconstruction* (London: Routledge and Kegan Paul, 1981).

Daix, Pierre and Joan Rosselet, *Picasso: the Cubist Years 1907–1916* (London: Thames and Hudson, 1979).

Décaudin, Michel, *La Crise des valeurs symbolistes: Vingt ans de poésie française, 1895–1914* (Toulouse: Privat, 1960).

Dédéyan, Charles, *Le Nouveau mal de siècle* (Paris: Société d'Enseignement supérieur, 1968).

Deleuze, Gilles and Félix Guattari, *Anti-Oedipus: Capitalism and Schizophrenia*, trans. Robert Hurley, et al. (London: Athlone Press, 1984).

Denkler, Horst, 'Die Druckfassungen der Dramen Oskar Kokoschkas', *Deutsche Vierteljahrsschrift für Literaturwissenchaft und Geistegeschichte*, 40 (1966) pp. 90–108.

Derrida, Jacques, *A Derrida Reader: Between the Blinds*, ed. Peggy Kamuf (Hemel Hempstead: Harvester Wheatsheaf, 1991).

——, 'Devant la loi', trans. Avital Ronnell, in Alan Udoff (ed.), *Kafka and the Contemporary Critical Performance: Centenary Readings* (Bloomington and Indianapolis: Indiana University Press, 1987).

——, *Dissemination*, trans. Barbara Johnson (Chicago: University of Chicago Press, 1981).

——, 'Forcener le subjectile', in Jacques Derrida and Paule Thévenin (eds), *Antonin Artaud; dessins et portraits* (Paris: Gallimard, 1986).

——, *Memoires for Paul de Man*, rev. edn, trans. Cecile Lindsay et al. (New York: Columbia University Press, 1989).

——, *Writing and Difference*, trans. Alan Bass (London: Routledge and Kegan Paul, 1978).

Diethe, Carol, *Aspects of Distorted Sexual Attitudes in German Expressionist Drama* (New York: Peter Lang, 1988).

D'Harnoncourt, Anne (ed.), *Futurism and the International Avant-Garde* (New Haven, CT: Philadelphia Museum of Art, 1980).

Dijkstra, Bram, *Cubism, Stieglitz, and the Early Poetry of William Carlos Williams* (Princeton, NJ: Princeton University Press, 1969).

Donchin, G., *The Influence of French Symbolism on Russian Poetry* (The Hague: Mouton, 1958).

Dubnick, Randa, *The Structure of Obscurity: Gertrude Stein, Language, and Cubism* (Urbana and Chicago: University of Illinois Press, 1984).

Durand, Régis, 'The Disposition of the Voice', in Michel Benamou and Charles Caramello (eds), *Performance in Postmodern Culture* (Milwaukee WI: Center for Twentieth Century Studies, 1977) pp. 99–110.

Durry, Marie-Jeanne, *Guillaume Apollinaire: Alcools*, 3 vols (Paris; Société d'Édition d'Enseignement Supérieur, 1956–64).

Duthie, Enid L., *L'Influence du symbolisme français dans le renouveau poétique de l'Allemagne. Les Blätter für die Kunst de 1892 à 1900* (Paris: Bibliothèque de la Revue de littérature comparée, 1933).

Eagleton, Terry, *Criticism and Ideology* (London: Verso, 1978).

——, *The Ideology of the Aesthetic* (Oxford: Basil Blackwell, 1990).

Eco, Umberto, *Le forme del contenuto* (Milan: Bompiani, 1971).

——, *Reflections on The Name of the Rose* (London: Secker & Warburg, 1985).

Ellman, Richard, *James Joyce*, rev. edn. (Oxford: Oxford University Press, 1983).

Engels, Friedrich, *The Condition of the Working Class in England* (London: Lawrence & Wishart, 1973).

Erickson, John D., *Dada: Performance, Poetry, and Art* (Boston: Twayne, 1984).

Erkkila, Betsy, *Walt Whitman among the French* (Princeton, NJ: Princeton University Press, 1980).

Erlich, Victor, 'The Place of Russian Futurism within the Russian Poetic Avantgarde: A Reconsideration', *Russian Literature*, 13 (1983) pp. 1–18.

Étiemble, R., *Le Mythe de Rimbaud*, 2 vols (Paris: Gallimard, 1954, 1961).

Fairclough, H. R., *The Classics and Our Twentieth-Century Poets* (Stanford, CA: Stanford University Press, 1927).

Fanger, Donald, *Dostoevsky and Romantic Realism* (Cambridge, MA: Harvard University Press, 1965).

Finkelstein, Haim N., *Surrealism and the Crisis of the Object* (Ann Arbor, MI: UMI Press, 1979).

Finney, Gail, *Women in Modern Drama: Freud, Feminism, and European Theatre at the Turn of the Century* (Ithaca and London: Cornell University Press, 1989).

Forrester, John, *The Seductions of Psychoanalysis: Freud, Lacan, and Derrida* (Cambridge: Cambridge University Press, 1990).

Foster, Hal, *Recodings: Art, Spectacle, Cultural Politics* (Seattle, WA: Bay Press, 1985).

Foster, Stephen C. and Rudolf E. Kuenzli (eds), *Dada Spectrum; the Dialectics of Revolt* (Iowa City, IA: University of Iowa Press, 1979).

Fredman, Stephen, *Poet's Prose: the Crisis in American Verse*, 2nd edn (Cambridge: Cambridge University Press, 1990).

Freud, Sigmund, *The Interpretation of Dreams*, Pelican Freud Library, vol. 4, trans. James Strachey (Harmondsworth: Penguin Books, 1983).

——, *Jokes and Their Relation to the Unconscious*, Pelican Freud Library, vol. 6, trans. James Strachey (Harmondsworth: Penguin Books, 1983).

——, *Case Histories, II, Pelican Freud Library*, vol. 9, trans. James Strachey (Harmondsworth: Penguin Books, 1979).

——, *On Metapsychology, Pelican Freud Library*, vol. 11, trans. James Strachey (Harmondsworth: Penguin Books, 1984).

——, 'Remembering, Repeating and Working-Through', *Standard Edition*, vol. 12, trans. James E. Strachey (London: Hogarth Press, 1958) pp. 147–56.

Furness, Raymond, *Wagner and Literature* (Manchester: Manchester University Press, 1982).

Gamwell, Lynn, *Cubist Criticism* (Ann Arbor: UMI Press, 1980).

Gay, Peter, *Weimar Culture: The Outsider as Insider* (London: Secker & Warburg, 1968).

Genette, Gérard, *Mimologiques: Voyage en Cratylie* (Paris: Seuil, 1976).

Gheraducci, Isabella (ed.), *Il futurismo italiano* (Rome: Editi Riuniti, 1976).

Gilmore, Michael T., *American Romanticism and the Marketplace* (Chicago: University of Chicago Press, 1985).

Girard, René, *Deceit, Desire, and the Novel: Self and Other in Literary Structure*, trans. Yvonne Freccero (Baltimore and London: Johns Hopkins University Press, 1988).

Goldwater, Robert, *Primitivism in Modern Art*, rev. edn (Cambridge, MA: Harvard University Press, 1987).

Gordon, Mel, 'German Expressionist Acting', *Drama Review*, 19.3 (1975) pp. 34–50.

Gramsci, Antonio, *Selections from the Prison Notebooks*, ed. and trans. Quintin Hoare and Geoffrey Nowell Smith (London: Lawrence and Wishart, 1971).

Green, André, *The Tragic Effect: The Oedipus Complex in Tragedy*, trans. Alan Sheridan (Cambridge: Cambridge University Press, 1979).

——, 'The Unbinding Process', trans. Lionel Duisit, *New Literary History*, xii, I (1980) pp. 11–39.

Green, Christopher, *Cubism and its Enemies: Modern Movements and Reaction in French Art 1916–1928* (New Haven, CT and London: Yale University Press, 1987).

Green, Martin, *The Von Richthofen Sisters: The Triumphant and the Tragic Modes of Love* (New York: Basic Books, 1974).

Guichard, Léon, *La Musique et les lettres en France au temps du wagnérisme* (Paris: PUF, 1963).

Habermas, Jürgen, *Legitimation Crisis*, trans. Thomas McCarthy (London: Heinemann, 1976).

Hamburger, Michael, *The Truth of Poetry: Tensions in Modern Poetry from Baudelaire to the 1960s* (Harmondsworth: Penguin Books, 1969).

Hammond, Paul (ed.), *The Shadow and Its Shadow: Surrealist Writings on Cinema*, 2nd edn (Edinburgh: Polygon, 1991).

Heidegger, Martin, *On the Way to Language*, trans. Peter D. Hertz (New York: Harper & Row, 1971).

——, *Poetry, Language, Thought*, trans. Albert Hofstadter (New York: Harper & Row, 1975).

Henke, Suzette, 'Stephen Dedalus and Women: A Portrait of the Artist as a Young Misogynist', in Henke and Elaine Unkeless (eds), *Women and Joyce* (Brighton: Harvester Press, 1982).

Herbert, Eugenia W., *The Artist and Social Reform: France and Belgium, 1885–1898* (New Haven CT: Yale University Press, 1961).

Hermans, Theo, *The Structure of Modernist Poetry* (London: Croom Helm, 1982).

Hilferding, Rudolf, *Finance Capital: A Study of the Latest Phase of Capitalist Development*, ed. Tom Bottomore, trans. Morris Watnick and Sam Gordon (London: Routledge, 1981).

Hoffman, Frederic, J., *The Twenties: American Writing in the Postwar Decade*, rev. edn (New York: Free Press, 1965).

Houston, John Porter, *French Symbolism and the Modernist Movement: A Study of Poetic Structures* (Baton Rouge and London: Louisiana State University Press, 1980).

Hubert, Étienne-Alain and Michel Décaudin, 'Petite Histoire d'une appellation', *Europe*, 638/9 (June/July) pp. 7–25.

Huyssen, Andreas, *After the Great Divide: Modernism, Mass Culture, Postmodernism* (Bloomington and Indianapolis: Indiana University Press, 1986).

Isnenghi, Mario, *Il Mito della Grande Guerra da Marinetti a Malaparte* (Bari: Laterza, 1970).

Jackson, Brendan, 'The Fulsomeness of Her Prolixity', *South Atlantic Quarterly*, 83 (1984) pp. 91–102.

Jameson, Fredric, *Fables of Aggression: Wyndham Lewis, the Modernist as Fascist* (Berkeley, Los Angeles and London: University of California Press, 1979).
——, *Marxism and Form: Twentieth-Century Dialectical Theories of Literature* (Princeton, NJ: Princeton University Press, 1971).
Jannini, Pasquale A., *La fortuna del futurismo in Francia* (Rome: Bulzoni, 1979).
Janouch, Gustav, *Conversations with Kafka*, trans. Goronwy Rees (London: Quartet Books, 1985).
Jelavich, Peter, *Munich and Theatrical Modernism: Politics, Playwriting, and Performance 1890–1914* (Cambridge, MA and London: Harvard University Press, 1985).
Jones, Frederic J., *Giuseppe Ungaretti: Poet and Critic* (Edinburgh: Edinburgh University Press, 1977)
Kahnweiler, D-H., 'Negro Art and Cubism', *Horizon* (December 1948) pp. 412–20.
Kamuf, Peggy (ed.), *A Derrida Reader: Between the Blinds* (Hemmel Hempstead: Harvester Wheatsheaf, 1991).
Kenner, Hugh, *The Invisible Poet: T. S. Eliot* (London: Methuen, 1979).
——, *The Pound Era* (Berkeley and Los Angeles: University of California, 1971).
Kimball, Jean, 'Freud, Leonardo, and Joyce: the Dimensions of a Childhood Memory', *James Joyce Quarterly*, 17 (Winter 1980) pp. 165–82.
Kojecky, Roger, *T. S. Eliot's Social Criticism* (London: Faber and Faber, 1971).
Komparu, Kunio, *The Noh Theater: Principles and Perspectives* (New York, Tokyo, Kyoto: Weatherhill/Tankosha, 1983).
Kouidis, Virginia, *Mina Loy: American Modernist Poet* (Baton Rouge: Louisiana State University Press, 1980).
Kozloff, Max, *Cubism/Futurism* (New York: Charterhouse, 1973).
Krauss, Rosalind E., *The Originality of the Avant-Garde and other Modernist Myths* (Cambridge, MA and London: MIT Press, 1987).
Lacan, Jacques, *Écrits: A Selection*, trans. Alan Sheridan (London: Tavistock, 1980).
——, *Speech and Language in Psychoanalysis*, trans. Anthony Wilden (Baltimore, MD and London: Johns Hopkins University Press, 1984).
Laity, Cassandra, 'H.D. and A. C. Swinburne: Decadence and Modernist Women's Writing', *Feminist Studies*, 15.3 (Fall 1989) pp. 461–84.
Langan, Janine D., *Hegel and Mallarmé* (Lanham, MD. and London: University Press of America, 1986)
Laplanche, J. and J.-B. Pontalis, *The Language of Psychoanalysis*, trans. Donald Nicholson-Smith (London: Karnac Books, 1988).
——, and Serge Leclaire, 'The Unconscious: A Psychoanalytic Study', *Yale French Studies*, 48 (1972) pp. 118–78.
Large, D. C. and W. Weber (eds), *Wagnerism in European Culture and Politics* (London and Ithaca: Cornell University Press, 1984).
Larsen, Neil, *Modernism and Hegemony; A Materialist Critique of Aesthetic Agencies* (Minneapolis: University of Minnesota Press, 1990).
Leavens, Ileanna B., *From '291' to Zurich: the Birth of Dada* (Ann Arbor, MI: UMI Press, 1983).

Le Bot, Marc, *Francis Picabia et la crise des valeurs figuratives 1900–1925* (Paris: Klincksieck, 1968).

Lehmann, A. G., *The Symbolist Aesthetic in France 1885–1895*, 2nd edn (Oxford: Blackwell, 1968).

Le Rider, Jacques, *Le Cas Otto Weininger: Racines de l'antiféminisme et de l'antisémitisme* (Paris: PUF, 1982).

——, 'Modernisme–Féminisme/Modernité–Virilité', *L'Infini*, 4 (1983) pp. 5–20.

Lethève, Jacques, 'Le Théme de la décadence dans les lettres françaises à la fin du XIXme siècle', *Revue d'histoire littéraire de la France*, 63.1 (Jan/March 1963) pp. 46–61.

Lewis, Helena, *Dada Turns Red: The Politics of Surrealism* (Edinburgh: Edinburgh University Press, 1990).

Lidsky, Paul, *Les Écrivains contre la Commune* (Paris: Maspero, 1970).

Lindenberger, Herbert, *Georg Trakl* (New York: Twayne, 1971).

Lista, Giovanni (ed.), *Marinetti et le futurisme: études, documents, iconographie* (Lausanne: L'Age d'Homme, 1973).

Lough, John, *Writer and Public in France from the Middle Ages to the Present Day* (Oxford: Clarendon Press, 1978).

Lukács, Georg, *Essays on Realism*, ed. Rodney Livingstone, trans. David Fernbach (London: Lawrence and Wishart, 1980).

Macey, David, *Lacan in Contexts* (London and New York: Verso Books, 1988).

Malraux, André, *Picasso's Mask*, trans. June Guicharnaud (London: Macdonald and Jane's, 1976).

Man, Paul de, *Blindness and Insight: Essays in the Rhetoric of Contemporary Criticism* (New York: Oxford University Press, 1971).

Markov, Vladimir, *Russian Futurism: A History* (London: MacGibbon & Kee, 1969).

Martin, Marianne W., 'Futurism, Unanimism and Apollinaire', *Art Journal*, 28.3 (Spring 1969) pp. 258–68.

——, *Futurist Art and Theory 1909–1915* (Oxford: Clarendon Press, 1968).

Marx, Karl, *Early Writings*, trans. Rodney Livingstone (Harmondsworth: Penguin Books, 1975).

——, *The Eighteenth Brumaire of Louis Bonaparte*, trans. Ben Fowkes, in *Surveys from Exile*, ed. David Fernbach (Harmondsworth: Penguin Books, 1973).

——, and Friedrich Engels, *Manifesto of the Communist Party*, in *Selected Works* (London: Lawrence and Wishart, 1977).

Mathews, Timothy, *Reading Apollinaire* (Manchester: Manchester University Press, 1987).

Mathieu, P., 'Essai sur la métrique de Verlaine I', *Revue d'histoire littéraire de la France*, 38 (October/December 1931) pp. 561–92.

Mayer, Arno, *The Persistence of the Old Regime: Europe to the Great War* (London: Croom Helm, 1981).

Mead, Gerald, 'Language and the Unconscious in Surrealism', *Centennial Review*, 20 (1976) pp. 278–89.

Mehlman, Jeffrey, *Revolution and Repetition: Marx/Hugo/Balzac* (Berkeley, CA: University of California Press, 1977).

Melzer, Annabelle Henkin, *Latest Rage the Big Drum: Dada and Surrealist Performance* (Ann Arbor, MI: UMI Press, 1980).

Merleau-Ponty, Maurice, *The Primacy of Perception*, ed. James Edie (Evanston: Northwestern University Press, 1971).

Meschonnic, Henri, *Critique du rythme: anthropologie historique du langage* (Paris: Verdier, 1982).

——, *Modernité, Modernité* (Paris: Verdier, 1988).

Michaud, Guy, *Message poétique du symbolisme* (Paris: Nizet, 1961).

Minow-Pinkney, Makiko, *Virginia Woolf and the Problem of the Subject* (Brighton: Harvester Press, 1987).

Moody, A. D., *Thomas Stearns Eliot: Poet* (Cambridge: Cambridge University Press, 1979).

Morel, J-P., 'Aurélia, Gradiva, X: Psychanalyse et poésie dans *Les Vases Communicants'*, *Revue de littérature comparée*, 46.1 (1972) pp. 68–89.

Moretti, Franco, *Signs Taken for Wonders: Essays in the Sociology of Literary Forms* (London: Verso, 1983).

Mossop, D. J., *Pure Poetry: Studies in French Poetic Theory and Practice, 1746 to 1945* (Oxford: Clarendon Press, 1971).

Mouquet, J. and W. T. Bandy, *Baudelaire en 1848: la Tribune nationale* (Paris: Émile-Paul, 1946).

Munton, Alan, 'Wyndham Lewis: the Transformations of Carnival', in Giovanni Cianci (ed.), *Wyndham Lewis: Letteratura/Pintura* (Palermo: Sellerio, 1982) pp. 141–57.

Nadeau, Maurice, *The History of Surrealism*, trans. Richard Howard (Harmondsworth: Penguin Books, 1978).

Nicholls, Peter, ' "A Consciousness Disjunct": Sex and the Writer in Ezra Pound's *Hugh Selwyn Mauberley'*, *Journal of American Studies*, 28 (April 1994) pp. 61–75.

——, 'Anti-Oedipus? Dada and Surrealist Theatre, 1916–35', *New Theatre Quarterly*, VII.28 (1991) pp. 331–47.

——, 'An Experiment with Time: Ezra Pound and the Example of Japanese Noh', *Modern Language Review*, forthcoming.

——, *Ezra Pound: Politics, Economics and Writing* (London: Macmillan, 1984).

——, 'From Fantasy to Structure: Two Moments of Literary Cubism', *Forum for Modern Language Studies*, 28.3 (Summer 1992) pp. 223–34.

——, 'Lost Object(s): Ezra Pound and the Idea of Italy', in Richard Taylor and Claus Melchior (eds), *Ezra Pound and Europe* (Amsterdam and Atlanta, GA: Rodopi, 1993).

Ombredane, André, 'Critique de la méthode d'investigation psychologique de Freud', *Le Disque Vert*, 2.3 (1924) pp. 165–77.

Passeron, René, *The Concise Encyclopedia of Surrealism* (London: Omega Books, 1984).

Patterson, Michael, *The Revolution in German Theatre 1900–1933* (London: Routledge and Kegan Paul, 1981).

Paul, Sherman, 'A Sketchbook of the Artist in his Thirty-Fourth Year: William Carlos Williams's *Kora in Hell: Improvisations'*, in *The Shaken Realist*, ed. M. J. Friedman and J. B. Vickery (Baton Rouge, LA: Louisiana State University Press, 1970).

Paz, Octavio, *Marcel Duchamp: Appearance Stripped Bare*, trans. Rachel Phillips and Donald Gardner (New York: Seaver Books, 1978).

354   *Bibliography*

Perloff, Marjorie, *The Futurist Moment: Avant-Garde, Avant-Guerre, and the Language of Rupture* (Chicago and London: University of Chicago Press, 1986).
——, *Radical Artifice: Writing in the Age of Media* (Chicago and London: University of Chicago Press, 1991).
Peyre, Henri, *What is Symbolism?* (Alabama: University of Alabama Press, 1980).
Pike, Burton, *Robert Musil: An Introduction to his Work* (Ithaca, NY: Cornell University Press, 1961).
Pike, Chris (ed.), *The Futurists, the Formalists, and the Marxist Critique* (London: Ink Links, 1979).
Poggioli, Renato, *The Theory of the Avant-Garde* (Cambridge, MA: Belknap Press, 1968).
Pomorska, Krystyna, *Russian Formalist Theory and its Poetic Ambiance* (The Hague and Paris: Mouton, 1968).
Pondrom, Cyrena, 'H.D. and the Origins of Imagism', *Sagetrieb*, IV.I (1985) pp. 73–97.
——, *The Road from Paris: French Influence on English Poetry, 1900–1920* (Cambridge: Cambridge University Press, 1974).
Porter, Catherine, *Seeing and Being: The Plight of the Participant Observer in Emerson, James, Adams, and Faulkner* (Middletown, CT: Wesleyan University Press, 1981).
Pontalis, J.-B., 'Les vases non communicants', *Nouvelle Revue Française*, 302 (1 March 1978) pp. 26–45.
Poulet, Georges, *Exploding Poetry: Baudelaire/Rimbaud* (Chicago: University of Chicago Press, 1984).
Praz, Mario, *The Romantic Agony*, trans. Angus Davidson (London: Oxford University Press, 1933).
Raimond, Michel, *La Crise du roman: des lendemains du naturalisme aux années vingt* (Paris: Corti, 1966).
Raitt, A. W., *Villiers de l'Isle-Adam et le mouvement symboliste* (Paris: Corti, 1965).
Raymond, Marcel, *De Baudelaire au Surréalisme*, rev. edn (Paris: Corti, 1940).
Rexroth, Kenneth, *American Poetry in the Twentieth Century* (New York: Herder and Herder, 1971).
Ribemont-Dessaignes, Georges, *Déjá jadis, ou Du movement Dada à l'espace abstrait* (Paris: René Juillard, 1958).
Richard, Lionel, 'Futurisme et Expressionisme en Allemagne', *Europe*, 552 (April 1975) pp. 193–8.
——, 'Sur l'expressionisme allemand et sa réception critique en France de 1910 à 1925', *Arcadia*, x.3 (1974) pp. 266–89.
Richter, Hans, *Dada: Art and Anti-Art*, trans. David Britt (London: Thames and Hudson, 1978).
Ricoeur, Paul, 'The Metaphorical Process and Cognition, Imagination, and Feeling', in Sheldon Sacks (ed.), *On Metaphor* (Chicago and London: University of Chicago Press, 1979).
Ritchie, J. M., *German Expressionist Drama* (Boston: Twayne, 1976).
Robbins, Daniel, 'From Symbolism to Cubism: The Abbaye of Créteil', *Art Journal*, 23.2 (Winter 1963/64) pp. 111–16.

Rogin, Michael Paul, *Subversive Genealogy: The Politics and Art of Herman Melville* (New York: Knopf, 1983).

Rose, Jacqueline, *Sexuality in the Field of Vision* (London: Verso, 1986).

Rosenberg, John D. (ed.), *The Genius of John Ruskin* (New York: Brazilier, 1963).

Ross, Andrew, *The Failure of Modernism: Symptoms of American Poetry* (New York: Columbia University Press, 1986).

Ross, Kristin, *The Emergence of Social Space: Rimbaud and the Paris Commune* (London: Macmillan, 1988).

Roudinesco, Elisabeth, *La Bataille de cent ans: histoire de la psychanalyse en France* (Paris: Seuil, 1986).

——, *Jacques Lacan & Co. A History of Psychoanalysis in France 1925–1985*, trans. Jeffrey Mehlman (London: Free Association Books, 1990).

Ryan, Judith, *The Vanishing Subject: Early Psychology and Literary Modernism* (Chicago and London: University of Chicago Press, 1991).

Sacks, Peter, *The English Elegy: Studies in the Genre from Spenser to Yeats* (Baltimore and London: Johns Hopkins University Press, 1985).

Salaris, Claudia, *Le futuriste: donne e letterature d'avanguardia in Italia (1909/1944)* (Milan: Edizioni delle donne, 1982).

——, *Storia del futurismo* (Rome: Editori Riuniti, 1985).

Sanouillet, Michel, *Dada à Paris* (Paris: J-J. Pauvert, 1965).

Sartre, Jean-Paul, *Baudelaire*, trans. Martin Turnell (New York: New Directions, 1967).

——, *Critique of Dialectical Reason*, vol. 1, trans. Alan Sheridan-Smith (London: NLB, 1976).

——, *Saint Genet: Actor and Martyr*, trans. Bernard Frechtman (New York: Pantheon Books, 1963).

Saussure, Ferdinand de, *Course in General Linguistics*, rev. edn trans. Wade Buskin (London: Fontana/Collins, 1974).

Schvey, Henry L., *Oskar Kokoschka: The Painter as Playwright* (Detroit: Wayne State University Press, 1982).

Schroeder, Jean, *Pierre Reverdy* (Boston: Twayne, 1981).

Schwab, Arnold T., *James Gibbons Huneker: Critic of the Seven Arts* (Stanford, CA: Stanford University Press, 1963).

Sharp, Francis Michael, *The Poet's Madness: A Reading of George Trakl* (Ithaca and London: Cornell University Press, 1981).

Sheppard, Richard, 'Unholy Families: The Oedipal Psychopathology of Four Expressionist *Ich- Dramen'*, *Orbis Litterarum*, 41 (1986) pp. 355–83.

Shklovsky, Victor, *Mayakovsky and His Circle*, trans. Lily Feiler (New York: Dodd, Mead and Co., 1972).

Short, Robert, 'Paris Dada and Surrealism', in Richard Sheppard (ed.), *Dada: Studies of a Movement* (Chalfont St Giles: Alpha Academic, 1979).

Sidotti, Antoine (ed.), *La Prose du Transsibérien et de la Petite Jehanne de France* (Paris: Lettres Modernes, 1987).

Silver, Kenneth E., *Esprit de Corps: the Art of the Parisian Avant-Garde and the First World War, 1914–1925* (London: Thames and Hudson, 1989).

Sloterdijk, Peter, *Critique of Cynical Reason*, trans. Michael Eldred (London: Verso, 1988).

Sola, Agnès, 'Cubisme et futurisme russe', *Europe*, 638–9 (June–July 1982) pp. 144–50.

Spate, Virginia, *Orphism: The Evolution of Non-figurative Painting in Paris 1910–1914* (Oxford: Clarendon Press, 1979).

Speirs, Ronald, *Brecht's Early Plays* (London: Macmillan, 1982).

Swart, K. W., *The Sense of Decadence in Nineteenth-Century France* (The Hague: Nijhoff, 1964).

Szondi, Peter, *Theory of the Modern Drama*, trans. Michael Hays (Cambridge: Polity Press, 1987).

Tashjian, Dickran, *Skyscraper Primitives: Dada and the American Avant-Garde 1910–1925* (Middletown, CT: Wesleyan University Press, 1975).

Taupin, René, *L'Influence du symbolisme français sur la poésie américaine* (Geneva: Slatkine, 1975).

Temple, Ruth Z., *The Critic's Alchemy: A Study of the Introduction of French Symbolism into England* (New York: Twayne, 1953).

Tessari, Roberto, *Il Mito della macchina: letteratura e industria nel primo novecento* (Milan: Mursia, 1973).

Thorlby, Anthony, 'Kafka and Language', in J. P. Stern (ed.), *The World of Franz Kafka* (London: Weidenfeld and Nicolson, 1980).

Tisdall, Caroline and Angelo Bozzolla, *Futurism* (London: Thames and Hudson, 1985).

Todorov, Tzvetan, *The Poetics of Prose*, trans. Richard Howard (Oxford: Basil Blackwell, 1977).

Trotsky, Leon, *Literature and Revolution*, trans. Rose Seransky (Ann Arbor: University of Michigan Press, 1975).

Trotter, David, *The Making of the Reader: Language and Subjectivity in Modern American, English, and Irish Poetry* (London: Macmillan, 1984).

Tsukui, Nobuko, *Ezra Pound and Noh Plays* (Washington, DC: University Press of America, 1983).

Valgemae, Mardi, *Accelerated Grimace: Expressionism in American Drama of the 1920s* (Carbondale: Southern Illinois University Press, 1972).

Vergo, Peter and Yvonne Modlin, '*Murderer Hope of Women: Expressionist Drama and Myth*', in *Oskar Kokoschka 1886–1980* (London: Tate Gallery, 1986).

Vogt, Paul, *The Blue Rider*, trans. Joachim Neugroschel (London: Barron's, 1980).

Vološinov, V. N., *Marxism and the Philosophy of Language*, trans. Ladislav Matejka and I. R. Titunik (Cambridge, MA. and London: Harvard University Press, 1973).

Waldberg, Patrick, *Surrealism* (London: Thames and Hudson, 1965)

Walker, Jayne L., *The Making of a Modernist: Gertrude Stein from Three Lives to Tender Buttons* (Amherst, MA: University of Massachusetts Press, 1984).

Weiss, Peg, *Kandinsky and Munich: The Formative Jugendstil Years* (Princeton, NJ: Princeton University Press, 1979).

Weisstein, Ulrich (ed.), *Expressionism as an International Phenomenon* (Paris and Budapest: Didier and Akadémiai Kiadó, 1973).

——, 'Futurism in Germany and England: Two Flashes in the Pan?', *Revue des langues vivantes*, XLIV.6 (1978) pp. 467–97.

Wellek, René, *Discriminations: Further Concepts of Criticism* (New Haven, CT and London: Yale University Press, 1970).

White, John H., *Literary Futurism: Aspects of the First Avant-Garde* (Oxford: Clarendon Press, 1990).

Whitford, Frank, *Oskar Kokoschka: A Life* (London: Weidenfeld & Nicolson, 1986).

Willett, John, *The New Sobriety: Art and Politics in the Weimar Period 1917–33* (London: Thames and Hudson, 1978).

Williams, Raymond, *The Politics of Modernism: Against the New Conformists*, ed. Tony Pinkney (London: Verso, 1989).

Williams, Robert R., *Recognition: Fichte and Hegel on the Other* (Albany, NY: SUNY, 1992).

Williams, Rosalind H., *Dream Worlds: Mass Consumption in Late Nineteenth-Century France* (Berkeley and Los Angeles: University of California Press, 1982).

Wilson, Edmund, *Axel's Castle: A Study in the Imaginative Literature of 1870–1930* (London: Fontana, 1979).

Wyzewska, Isabella, *La Revue wagnérienne, Essai sur l'interprétation esthétique de Wagner en France* (Paris: Perrin, 1934).

Zeldin, Theodore, *France, 1848–1945*, vol. 2: *Intellect, Taste and Anxiety* (Oxford: Clarendon Press, 1977).

Zinder, David G., *The Surrealist Connection: An Approach to a Surrealist Aesthetic of Theater* (Ann Arbor, MI: UMI Press, 1980).

Žižek, Slavoj, *The Sublime Object of Ideology* (London and New York: Verso Books, 1989).

Index